ZAGAT®

London
Restaurants
2012

LOCAL EDITORS
Sholto Douglas-Home and Susan Kessler
with Claire Coleman
STAFF EDITOR
Bill Corsello

Published and distributed by
Zagat Survey, LLC
4 Columbus Circle
New York, NY 10019
T: 212.977.6000
E: london@zagat.com
www.zagat.com

ACKNOWLEDGMENTS

We thank Deborah Bennett, Karen Bonham, Ricki Conway, Alex, Louis and Tallula Douglas-Home, Rosanne Johnston, Larry Kessler, Pamela and Michael Lester, Margaret Levin, Ian Turner, Mary Jane Weedman and Susan Wilen, as well as the following members of our staff: Danielle Borovoy (assistant editor), Aynsley Karps (editorial assistant), Brian Albert, Sean Beachell, Maryanne Bertollo, Reni Chin, Larry Cohn, Nicole Diaz, Kelly Dobkin, Alison Flick, Jeff Freier, Matthew Hamm, Justin Hartung, Marc Henson, Natalie Lebert, Mike Liao, James Mulcahy, Polina Paley, Chris Walsh, Jacqueline Wasilczyk, Art Yaghci, Sharon Yates, Anna Zappia and Kyle Zolner.

The reviews in this guide are based on public opinion surveys. The ratings reflect the average scores given by the survey participants who voted on each establishment. The text is based on quotes from, or paraphrasings of, the surveyors' comments. Phone numbers, addresses and other factual data were correct to the best of our knowledge when published in this guide.

Our guides are printed using environmentally preferable inks containing 20%, by weight, renewable resources on papers sourced from well-managed forests. Deluxe editions are covered with Skivertex Recover® Double containing a minimum of 30% post-consumer waste fiber.

SUSTAINABLE FORESTRY INITIATIVE	Certified Sourcing
	www.sfiprogram.org
	SFI-00993

ENVIROINK

The inks used to print the body of this publication contain a minimum of 20%, by weight, renewable resources.

Maps © Antenna International™, except for front panel of foldout map, © Transport for London

Contents

Ratings & Symbols

Zagat Top Spot	Name	Symbols	Cuisine	Zagat Ratings			
				FOOD	DECOR	SERVICE	COST

Area, Address & Contact*

🅉 Tim & Nina's ◗ *British*

▽ 23 | 5 | 9 | £15

Covent Garden | West St., WC2 (Leicester Sq.) | 020-7123-4567 | www.zagat.com

Review, surveyor comments in quotes

"How do they do it?" wonder groupies of the eponymous "international bons vivants", who offer "delectable", "dazzlingly devised" Modern British dishes for "a mind-boggling discount" at this Covent Garden "foodie find"; perhaps the answer is in the "destitute digs" ("there's no such thing as 'bivouac chic!'") and "daft staff."

Ratings

Food, Decor & **Service** are rated on a 30-point scale.

0	–	9	poor to fair
10	–	15	fair to good
16	–	19	good to very good
20	–	25	very good to excellent
26	–	30	extraordinary to perfection

▽ low response | less reliable

Cost

The price of dinner with a drink and service; lunch is usually 25% less. For unrated **newcomers** or **write-ins,** the price range is as follows:

I	£20 and below	E	£41 to £60
M	£21 to £40	VE	£61 or above

Symbols

🅉	highest ratings, popularity and importance
◗	serves after 11 PM
🅈 🄼	closed on Sunday or Monday
⊄	no credit cards accepted

Maps

Index maps show restaurants with the highest Food ratings in those areas.

---

* **Phone:** From outside the U.K., dial international code (e.g. 011 from the U.S.) +44, then omit the first zero of the listed number.

Vote at ZAGAT.com

About This Survey

Here are the results of our **2012 London Restaurants Survey,** covering 1,187 eateries in the city as well as favourites outside the M25. Like all our guides, this one is based on input from avid local consumers – 5,497 all told. Our editors have synopsised this feedback, highlighting representative comments (in quotation marks within each review). To read full surveyor comments – and share your own opinions – visit **ZAGAT.com,** where you will also find the latest restaurant news, special events, deals, reservations, menus, photos and lots more, all for free.

ABOUT ZAGAT: In 1979, we started asking friends to rate and review restaurants purely for fun. The term "user-generated content" had not yet been coined. That hobby grew into Zagat Survey; 32 years later, we have over 375,000 surveyors and cover airlines, bars, dining, fast food, entertaining, golf, hotels, movies, music, resorts, shopping, spas, theatre and tourist attractions in over 100 countries. Along the way, we evolved from being a print publisher to a digital content provider, e.g. **ZAGAT.com** and Zagat mobile apps (for iPad, iPhone, Android, BlackBerry, Windows Phone 7 and Palm webOS). We also produce marketing tools for a wide range of blue-chip corporate clients. And you can find us on Twitter (twitter.com/zagat), Facebook, Foursquare and just about any other social media network.

THREE SIMPLE PREMISES underlie our ratings and reviews. First, we believe that the collective opinions of large numbers of consumers are more accurate than those of any single person. (Consider that our surveyors bring some 684,000 annual meals' worth of experience to this survey, visiting London-area restaurants year-round, anonymously – and paying their own way.) Second, food quality is only part of the equation when choosing a restaurant, thus we ask our surveyors to separately rate food, decor and service and report on cost. Third, since people need reliable information in a fast, easy-to-digest format, we strive to be concise and we offer our content on every platform – print, online and mobile. Our Top Ratings lists (pages 10–19) and indexes (starting on page 184) are also designed to help you quickly choose the best place for any occasion, be it business or pleasure.

THANKS: We're grateful to our local editors, Sholto Douglas-Home, a London restaurant critic for the past two decades, Susan Kessler, cookbook author and consultant for numerous lifestyle publications in the U.K. and U.S., and Claire Coleman, lifestyle journalist and all-round epicurean enthusiast. Thank you, guys. We also sincerely thank the thousands of surveyors who participated – this guide is really "theirs."

JOIN IN: To improve our guides, we solicit your comments; it's vital that we hear your opinions. Just contact us at **nina-tim@zagat.com.** We also invite you to join our surveys at **ZAGAT.com.** Do so and you'll receive a choice of rewards in exchange.

New York, NY
September 14, 2011

Nina and Tim Zagat

What's New

Whilst many businesses continue to cut costs amidst lingering fears about the economy, London's restaurateurs are premiering exciting debuts in all four corners of town, for example Camden's **Shaka Zulu** in the North, Pimlico's **Tinello** in the South, Jamie Oliver's City behemoth **Barbecoa** in the East End and Knightsbridge's **Cassis Bistro** in the West End. What's more, the September 2011 launch of West-field Stratford City, the new shopping centre across from the Olympic Park, brings with it a host of arrivals (see Olympic Tips on page 7).

UP AND UP: Recessionary mind-sets seem to be on the wane. Surveyors are eating out more frequently – 2.4 times per week, up from 2.2 last year – despite spending significantly more, with the average price of a meal having risen to £43.40, a 6.3% jump from £40.84. If service isn't included in the bill, they're leaving an average tip that's ticked up from 11.8% to 12% – this in spite of the fact that 73% name poor service as their No. 1 dining-out irritant (cost is a distant second, cited by 10%). Furthermore, fewer diners are being enticed by set-price menus (48% this year vs. 65% last) and food discounts (51% vs. 62%).

GRAND HOTELS: Big names and big budgets are behind some ambitious unveilings at plush capital hotels, including this Survey's No. 1 and No. 2 Rated Newcomers: **Dinner by Heston Blumenthal** (in the Mandarin Oriental Hyde Park), starring the eponymous chef's in-spired cuisine, and **Koffmann's** (The Berkeley), marking the return of the esteemed Pierre Koffmann to the scene. Also making London come-backs are Jean-Georges Vongerichten, at **Spice Market** (W Leicester Square), and Joël Antunes, at **Brasserie Joël** (Park Plaza Westminster Bridge). Two grand West End premieres feature menus by two re-spected chefs from Rome: Massimo Riccioli at **Massimo** (Corinthia) and Adriano Cavagnini at **Amaranto** (Four Seasons at Park Lane). Fergus Henderson adds **St. John Hotel** to his empire, and father-son team Albert and Michel Jr bring **Roux at the Landau** (The Langham) into their stable. Last but not least, Marcus Wareing, of his namesake Belgravia eatery, moonlights at **Gilbert Scott** (St. Pancras Renaissance).

WELL GROUNDED: Confirming the enduring appeal of simplicity, many midpriced newcomers are proving to be major draws. Of particular note are **Bar Battu, Brawn, Chabrot, Dishoom, Henry Root, Opera Tavern, Polpetto, Spuntino** and **28-50 Wine Workshop & Kitchen.** Of course, this focus on informality doesn't mean expensive 'event dining' is a thing of the past, as evidenced by this Survey's No. 1 Food winner, **The Ledbury,** the No. 1 Service winner, **Waterside Inn,** and to a lesser extent, London's Most Popular restaurant, **The Wolseley.**

DINING OUT IN THE DIGITAL AGE: Although only 37% of respondents book via the Internet (up just two percentage points from last year), 78% check out a restaurant's website before visiting . . . 53% think it's rude or inappropriate to talk on the phone or text at the table, whilst only 23% feel the same about taking pictures during a meal (59% say it's acceptable in moderation).

London
September 14, 2011

Sholto Douglas-Home

Vote at ZAGAT.com

Olympic Tips

If you're one of the millions who will be descending on London for the 2012 Olympics, July 27–August 12, here are some tips on where to go, how to get around and where to dine. (For more information, visit the games' official site, **www.london2012.com.**)

THE BASICS: Whilst some events – such as football, sailing and canoeing – are being held in other areas of the country, most are taking place in London and many at the newly built Olympic Park, a 2.5-sq.-km. site in Stratford, East London (not to be confused with Stratford-upon-Avon). The park will be home to nine sporting venues, including the 80,000-seat Olympic Stadium and the impressive Aquatics Centre, designed by renowned architect Zaha Hadid and featuring a 160-m.-long, wavelike roof.

NEAR THE PARK: With McDonald's as a sponsor, no other branded catering will be permitted at the Olympic Park. Previously, Stratford was a gastronomic desert, but that's changing thanks to the advent of Westfield Stratford City, across from the Olympic Park and slated to open September 2011. The shopping centre's roster of eateries is set to include branches of **Balans, Bumpkin, Comptoir Libanais, Franco Manca, Jamie's Italian, Wahaca** and **Yo! Sushi,** amongst others.

FURTHER AFIELD: Beyond the Olympic Park, some of the most iconic venues in and around the capital are hosting tournaments. In Central London, beach volleyball and athletics will take place at the Horse Guards Parade and The Mall, around St. James's Park; and the triathlon and marathon swimming will be in Hyde Park. For a taste of the myriad culinary options nearest these venues, see our Location Indexes (beginning on page 195) for St. James's and Westminster; and Knightsbridge and Mayfair (of particular note in the latter is the Survey's No. 1 Decor winner, **Sketch – The Lecture Room & Library**). Tennis is being played at Wimbledon's All England Club, situated near eateries such as **San Lorenzo Fuoriporta,** a well-regarded Italian; **Fox & Grapes,** a new gastropub from celebrated chef Claude Bosi; and **Light House,** an Eclectic alternative. In St. John's Wood, archery is taking over Lord's Cricket Ground, which is close to highly rated restaurants **L'Aventure** and **Oslo Court,** both serving French classics, and **Red Pepper,** offering casual Italian fare. Also near the sporting action are **The Troubadour,** a 1960s holdover in Earl's Court (volleyball); and **Old Brewery,** a beer-lover's paradise in Greenwich (equestrian events).

TRANSPORT HINTS: If you purchase a ticket for an event, you'll automatically get a Games Travelcard for that day, allowing access to the entire London public transport network. The closest stations to the Olympic Park are Stratford (served by the Central and Jubilee tube lines, National Rail, Docklands Light Railway and London Overground) and West Ham (District, Jubilee and Hammersmith & City tube lines, National Rail, DLR). The fastest option from Central London is the Javelin, a new high-speed train linking St. Pancras International (at King's Cross) to Stratford International in just seven minutes.

London
September 14, 2011

Claire Coleman

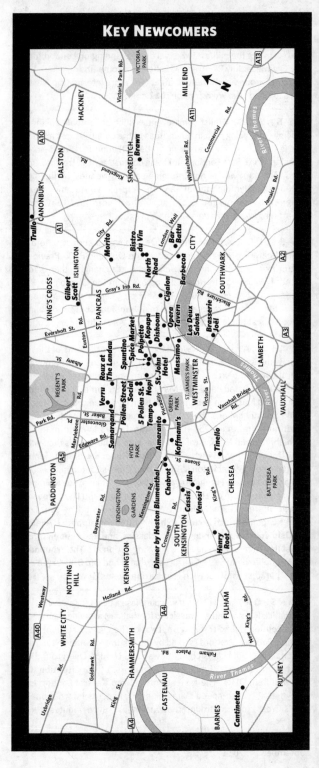

KEY NEWCOMERS

Vote at ZAGAT.com

Key Newcomers

Our editors' picks amongst this year's arrivals. See full list at p. 231.

Amaranto | *Italian* | Opulence in the revamped Four Seasons

Bar Battu | *Euro.* | Art deco–influenced City wine bar

Barbecoa | *BBQ* | Jamie Oliver's City foray into American meats

Bistro du Vin | *Euro.* | Wines and grilled fare in Clerkenwell

Brasserie Joël | *French* | Joël Antunes surfaces in Waterloo

Brawn | *British/French* | Cool Shoreditch addition

Cantinetta | *Italian* | Upscale eats in an easy-going Putney setting

Cassis | *French* | South Ken nook for Provençal provender

Chabrot | *French* | Southern French Knightsbridge bistro

Cigalon | *French* | Holborn haunt serving Southern French fare

Dinner by Heston Blumenthal | *British* | Latest from famed chef

Dishoom | *Indian* | Atypical grazing plates in Covent Garden

5 Pollen St. | *Italian* | Sophistication in intriguing Mayfair digs

Gilbert Scott | *British* | Marcus Wareing moonlights in King's Cross

Henry Root | *British/Euro.* | Unpretentious Chelsea bistro

Ilia | *Italian* | Regionally diverse tucker in Chelsea

Koffmann's | *French* | Rustic dishes by Pierre Koffmann in Belgravia

Kopapa | *Eclectic* | All-day dining option for Covent Garden

Les Deux Salons | *French* | Beautiful Trafalgar Square neophyte

Massimo | *Med.* | Formality in an imposing new Westminster hotel

Morito | *African/Spanish* | Next-door sibling to Clerkenwell's Moro

Nopi | *Asian/Mideastern* | Exotic Soho brasserie

North Road | *Euro.* | Scandinavian-centric cooking in Clerkenwell

Opera Tavern | *Italian/Spanish* | Revamp of a Covent Garden boozer

Pollen St. Social | *British* | Jason Atherton's Mayfair premiere

Polpetto | *Italian* | Polpo offshoot serving Venetian tapas to Soho

Roux at The Landau | *Euro.* | Reimagining of Langham Hotel eatery

Samarqand | *Central Asian* | Unusual cuisines come to Marylebone

Spice Market | *Asian* | Chinatown meets Jean-Georges Vongerichten

Spuntino | *American/Italian* | Soho small-platery from the Polpo folks

St. John Hotel | *British* | Fergus Henderson's latest, in Soho

Tempo | *Italian* | Modern-leaning, small-plates-heavy Mayfair haunt

Tinello | *Italian* | Tuscan hit in Pimlico

Trullo | *Italian* | Casual Islington pleaser

Venosi | *Italian* | Long-time restaurateurs set down roots in Chelsea

Verru | *E Euro./Scandinavian* | Tiny, plush Marylebone debut

Most Popular

Plotted on the map at the back of this book.

❶	Wolseley	*European*	
❷	Gordon Ramsay/68 Royal	*Fr.*	
❸	J. Sheekey	*Seafood*	
❹	Nobu London	*Japanese*	
❺	Ivy	*British/European*	
❻	Gordon Ramsay/Clar.	*Euro.*	
❼	Hakkasan	*Chinese*	
❽	Wagamama	*Japanese*	
❾	Le Gavroche	*French*	
❿	Ledbury	*French*	

❶ Wolseley | *European*
❷ Gordon Ramsay/68 Royal | *Fr.*
❸ J. Sheekey | *Seafood*
❹ Nobu London | *Japanese*
❺ Ivy | *British/European*
❻ Gordon Ramsay/Clar. | *Euro.*
❼ Hakkasan | *Chinese*
❽ Wagamama | *Japanese*
❾ Le Gavroche | *French*
❿ Ledbury | *French*
⓫ River Café | *Italian*
⓬ Square | *French*
⓭ Zuma | *Japanese*
⓮ L'Atelier/Joël Robuchon | *Fr.*
⓯ Scott's | *Seafood*
⓰ Alain Ducasse/Dorchester | *Fr.*
⓱ Amaya | *Indian*
⓲ Zafferano | *Italian*
⓳ Chez Bruce | *British*
⓴ Bar Boulud | *French*
㉑ Rules | *Chophouse*
㉒ St. John | *British*
㉓ Gaucho | *Argent./Chophouse*
㉔ Fat Duck | *European*
㉕ Bibendum | *French*
㉖ Le Caprice | *British/European*

㉗ Marcus Wareing | *French*
㉘ Tamarind | *Indian*
㉙ Wilton's | *British/Seafood*
㉚ Arbutus | *European*
㉛ Yauatcha* | *Chinese*
㉜ Pied à Terre | *French*
㉝ Roka | *Japanese*
㉞ Locanda Locatelli | *Italian*
㉟ Murano* | *European*
㊱ Bentley's | *British/Seafood*
㊲ Simpson's/Strand* | *British*
㊳ Clos Maggiore | *French*
㊴ Cinnamon Club | *Indian*
㊵ Busaba Eathai | *Thai*
㊶ Asia de Cuba | *Asian/Cuban*
㊷ La Petite Maison* | *Med.*
㊸ Pizza Express | *Pizza*
㊹ Galvin Bistrot | *French*
㊺ Le Manoir/Quat'Saisons | *Fr.*
㊻ Nobu Berkeley St | *Japanese*
㊼ Wild Honey* | *British*
㊽ Bocca di Lupo/Gelupo | *Italian*
㊾ Belgo | *Belgian*
㊿ Goodman | *Chophouse*
51 La Trompette* | *Euro./Fr.*
52 Ottolenghi | *Bakery/Med.*

Many of the above restaurants are amongst the London area's most expensive, but if popularity were calibrated to price, a number of other restaurants would surely join their ranks. To illustrate this, we have added lists of Best Buys on pages 17–19.

* Indicates a tie with restaurant above

Vote at ZAGAT.com

Top Food

29 Ledbury | *French*

28 Pied à Terre | *French*
Dinings | *Japanese*
Le Manoir/Quat'Saisons | *Fr.*
Le Gavroche | *French*
Waterside Inn | *French*
Hunan | *Chinese*
Gordon Ramsay/68 Royal | *Fr.*

27 Square | *French*
Dinner/Heston | *British*
Chez Bruce | *British*
Marcus Wareing | *French*
Café Japan | *Japanese*
L'Oranger* | *French*
Nobu London | *Japanese*
Fat Duck | *European*
River Café | *Italian*
Scott's | *Seafood*
Murano | *European*
Alain Ducasse/Dorchester | *Fr.*
L'Atelier/Joël Robuchon | *Fr.*
Wilton's | *British/Seafood*
Harwood Arms | *British*
La Petite Maison | *Med.*
Kiku | *Japanese*

26 Umu | *Japanese*
Zuma | *Japanese*
Roussillon | *French*
Tayyabs | *Pakistani*
Club Gascon | *French*
Oslo Court | *French*
Koffmann's | *French*
Capital | *French*
La Trompette | *Euro./Fr.*
Gate | *Vegetarian*
Defune | *Japanese*
Miyama | *Japanese*
Zafferano | *Italian*
Goodman | *Chophouse*
Clarke's | *British*
Glasshouse* | *European*
Assaggi | *Italian*
Greenhouse* | *French*
Jin Kichi | *Japanese*
Roka | *Japanese*
Hawksmoor | *Chophouse*
Hibiscus | *French*
Barrafina | *Spanish*
Rasoi Vineet Bhatia | *Indian*
Hakkasan | *Chinese*

BY CUISINE

AMERICAN

23 Palm
20 Barbecoa
19 Christopher's
Lucky 7
Bodeans

BRITISH (MODERN)

27 Dinner/Heston
Chez Bruce
Harwood Arms
26 Clarke's
St. John

BRITISH (TRAD.)

27 Wilton's
26 Bentley's
Hinds Head
25 Ritz
24 Goring Dining Rm.

CHINESE

28 Hunan
26 Hakkasan
Kai Mayfair
25 Barshu
Yauatcha

CHOPHOUSES

26 Goodman
Hawksmoor
23 Palm
Rules
Hix Oyster/Chop

ECLECTIC

25 Viajante
Providores
23 Mosimann's (club)
Books for Cooks
22 Modern Pantry

Excludes places with low votes, unless otherwise indicated

EUROPEAN (MODERN)

27 Fat Duck
Murano
26 La Trompette
Glasshouse
25 Kitchen W8

FISH 'N' CHIPS

25 Golden Hind
24 Rock & Sole Plaice
North Sea
23 Sweetings

FRENCH (BISTRO)

25 Bar Boulud
24 Galvin Bistrot
Le Boudin Blanc
Le Café/Marché
Le Colombier

FRENCH (BRASSERIE)

23 Racine
Angelus
22 Le Café Anglais
Brasserie Roux
Pig's Ear

FRENCH (CLASSIC)

28 Le Gavroche
Waterside Inn
27 L'Oranger
26 Oslo Court
Koffmann's

FRENCH (NEW)

29 Ledbury
28 Pied à Terre
Le Manoir/Quat'Saisons
Gordon Ramsay/68 Royal
27 Square

INDIAN

26 Rasoi Vineet Bhatia
Trishna
Quilon
Amaya
25 Cinnamon Club

ITALIAN

27 River Café
26 Zafferano
Assaggi
Mennula
25 Enoteca Turi

JAPANESE

28 Dinings
27 Café Japan

Nobu London
Kiku
26 Umu

LEBANESE

25 Ishbilia
24 Al Waha
23 Al Hamra
Al Sultan
22 Fairuz

MEDITERRANEAN

27 La Petite Maison
25 Ottolenghi
23 Morton's (club)
Terroirs
22 Eagle

MEXICAN

22 Chilango
Mestizo
20 Taqueria
Wahaca

PIZZA

25 Osteria Basilico
24 Franco Manca
Oliveto
21 Delfino
20 Rocket

SEAFOOD

27 Scott's
Wilton's
26 J. Sheekey Oyster
J. Sheekey
Wright Brothers

SPANISH

26 Barrafina
Moro
24 Fino
Dehesa
23 Tendido Cero

THAI

25 Nahm
24 Patara
23 Busaba Eathai
21 Blue Elephant
Mango Tree

VEGETARIAN

26 Roussillon
Gate
Morgan M
24 Rasa
22 Food for Thought

BY SPECIAL FEATURE

BREAKFAST

25 Cinnamon Club
   St. John Bread/Wine
24 Roast
22 Wolseley
   Baker & Spice

BRUNCH

24 Hélène Darroze
23 Cecconi's
   Angelus
22 Tom's Kitchen
   Modern Pantry

BUSINESS LUNCH

27 Square
   Scott's
25 Galvin La Chapelle
   Bar Boulud
23 Savoy Grill

CHEESE BOARDS

29 Ledbury
28 Pied à Terre
   Le Gavroche
27 Marcus Wareing
26 Greenhouse

CHILD-FRIENDLY

27 River Café
26 Zafferano
   Barrafina
25 Yauatcha
22 Tom's Kitchen

COMMUNAL TABLES

25 Providores
   Ottolenghi
23 Dishoom
   Busaba Eathai
22 Tom's Kitchen

EXPERIMENTAL

27 Fat Duck
26 Hibiscus
25 Viajante
   Trinity
24 Sketch/Lecture

GASTROPUBS

27 Harwood Arms
24 Great Queen St.
23 Thomas Cubitt
   Wells
   Anchor & Hope

HOTEL DINING

28 Le Manoir/Quat'Saisons
   Waterside Inn
27 Dinner/Heston
     (Mandarin Oriental)
   Marcus Wareing
     (The Berkeley)
   Nobu London
     (Metropolitan)

LATE NIGHT

26 Tayyabs
   Roka
   Hakkasan
   J. Sheekey
25 Nobu Berkeley St

MEET FOR A DRINK

27 L'Atelier/Joël Robuchon
26 Zuma
   Roka
   Hakkasan
25 Nobu Berkeley St

NEWCOMERS (RATED)

27 Dinner/Heston
26 Koffmann's
24 Tinello
23 Savoy Grill
   Dishoom

OLDE ENGLAND

27 Wilton's (1742)
26 Hinds Head (1690)
23 Sweetings (1889)
   Rules (1798)
22 Simpson's/Strand (1828)

PEOPLE-WATCHING

29 Ledbury
   Nobu London
27 Scott's
   La Petite Maison
26 Hakkasan

PRIVATE CLUBS

24 Mark's Club
23 Harry's Bar
   Morton's
   Mosimann's
22 George

SMALL PLATES

28 Dinings
    Hunan
27 L'Atelier/Joël Robuchon
26 Club Gascon
    Amaya

SUNDAY LUNCH (COUNTRY)

28 Le Manoir/Quat'Saisons
    Waterside Inn
27 Fat Duck
26 Hinds Head
24 Aubergine

SUNDAY LUNCH (TOWN)

27 La Petite Maison
26 Hawksmoor
25 Launceston Pl.
23 Le Caprice
    Bistrot Bruno Loubet

TASTING MENUS

29 Ledbury
28 Hunan
27 Fat Duck
    L'Atelier/Joël Robuchon
26 Umu

TEA SERVICE (OTHER THAN HOTELS)

25 Yauatcha
23 Sketch/Parlour
    Ladurée
    St. James's
    Chor Bizarre

WINNING WINE LISTS

29 Ledbury
28 Pied à Terre
    Gordon Ramsay/68 Royal
27 Square
26 Greenhouse

BY LOCATION

BAYSWATER

25 Mandarin Kitchen
24 Al Waha
23 Leong's Legend
    Angelus
    Royal China

BELGRAVIA

27 Marcus Wareing
26 Koffmann's
    Zafferano
    Amaya
25 Apsleys

BLOOMSBURY

28 Pied à Terre
26 Roka
    Hakkasan
    Mennula
25 Tsunami

BOROUGH

26 Wright Brothers
24 Roast
    Magdalen
23 Brindisa
19 Black & Blue

CANARY WHARF

26 Roka
23 Royal China
22 Gaucho

20 Gun
    Boisdale

CHELSEA

28 Gordon Ramsay/68 Royal
26 Rasoi Vineet Bhatia
25 Le Cercle
    Tom Aikens
24 Ziani

CHISWICK

26 La Trompette
24 Franco Manca
23 Le Vacherin
21 Annie's
19 Singapore Garden

CITY

26 Miyama
    Goodman
25 Café Spice Namasté
    Galvin La Chapelle
    L'Anima

CLERKENWELL/ FARRINGDON

26 Club Gascon
    St. John
    Moro
24 Le Café/Marché
    Cellar Gascon

COVENT GARDEN

- 27 L'Atelier/Joël Robuchon
- 26 Hawksmoor
- J. Sheekey Oyster
- J. Sheekey
- 25 Moti Mahal

HAMPSTEAD

- 26 Jin Kichi
- 23 Wells
- 22 Gaucho
- 21 Artigiano
- 20 Xo

ISLINGTON

- 26 Morgan M
- 25 Ottolenghi
- 24 Santa Maria/Garufa
- Rasa
- 22 La Fromagerie

KENSINGTON

- 26 Clarke's
- 25 Kitchen W8
- Launceston Pl.
- Koi
- Zaika

KNIGHTSBRIDGE

- 27 Dinner/Heston
- 26 Zuma
- Capital
- 25 Bar Boulud
- Ishbilia

MARYLEBONE

- 28 Dinings
- 26 Defune
- Trishna
- 25 Texture
- Phoenix Palace

MAYFAIR

- 28 Le Gavroche
- 27 Square
- Nobu London
- Scott's
- Murano

NOTTING HILL

- 29 Ledbury
- 26 Assaggi
- 25 Hereford Road
- Osteria Basilico
- Ottolenghi

PICCADILLY

- 26 Bentley's
- 23 Ladurée
- 22 Gaucho
- Wolseley
- Yoshino

PIMLICO

- 28 Hunan
- 26 Roussillon
- 25 About Thyme
- 24 Tinello
- 22 Orange

SHOREDITCH/HOXTON

- 26 Hawksmoor
- 25 St. John Bread/Wine
- 23 Song Que Café
- Busaba Eathai
- 22 Cây Tre

SOHO

- 26 Barrafina
- Wright Brothers
- 25 Barshu
- Yauatcha
- Arbutus

SOUTH KENSINGTON

- 25 Star of India
- 24 L'Etranger
- Patara
- Bibendum Oyster
- 23 Tendido Cero

ST. JAMES'S

- 27 L'Oranger
- Wilton's
- 25 Ritz
- 24 Matsuri
- 23 Le Caprice

VICTORIA

- 26 Quilon
- 24 Goring Dining Rm.
- 23 Olivo
- 21 Noura
- Mango Tree

IN THE COUNTRY

- 28 Le Manoir/Quat'Saisons
- Waterside Inn
- 27 Fat Duck
- 26 Hinds Head
- 24 Aubergine
- 23 Cliveden House
- – Gravetye Manor

Top Decor

28	Sketch/Lecture		Dinner/Heston
	Le Manoir/Quat'Saisons	25	L'Oranger
	Mark's Club (club)		Rules
	Ritz		Gilgamesh
	Sketch/Parlour		Pearl
27	Waterside Inn		Clos Maggiore
	Sketch/Gallery		Gordon Ramsay/68 Royal
	Bob Bob Ricard		Goring Dining Rm.
	Espelette*		Hakkasan
	Mosimann's* (club)		Babylon
26	Wolseley		Momo*
	Cliveden House		Savoy Grill*
	Umu*		Galvin at Windows
	Criterion		Ledbury
	Les Trois Garçons		Apsleys
	Alain Ducasse/Dorchester		Crazy Bear
	Galvin La Chapelle	24	Scott's
	Marcus Wareing		Square
	Hélène Darroze		Le Gavroche
	Gordon Ramsay/Clar.		L'Escargot

OUTDOORS

Boundary	Le Pont/Tour
Coq d'Argent	L'Oranger
La Famiglia	Modern Pantry
La Poule au Pot	Ritz
Ledbury	River Café

PRIVATE ROOMS

Alain Ducasse/Dorchester	Min Jiang
Amaya	Nobu London
China Tang	Spice Market
Dinner/Heston	Square
L'Anima	Zafferano
Marcus Wareing	Zuma

ROMANCE

Clos Maggiore	Le Gavroche
Crazy Bear	Le Manoir/Quat'Saisons
Galvin at Windows	Le Pont/Tour
Gilbert Scott	Les Trois Garçons
Gordon Ramsay/68 Royal	Marcus Wareing
La Poule au Pot	Sketch/Lecture

VIEWS

Aqua Kyoto	Oxo Tower
Boundary	Paramount
Galvin at Windows	Rhodes 24
Le Pont/Tour	Smiths/Top Fl.
Min Jiang	Waterside Inn

Vote at ZAGAT.com

Top Service

28
- Waterside Inn
- Ledbury
- Mark's Club (club)
- Le Manoir/Quat'Saisons
- Gordon Ramsay/68 Royal

27
- Square
- L'Oranger
- Fat Duck
- Pied à Terre
- Le Gavroche
- Wilton's

26
- Alain Ducasse/Dorchester
- Enoteca Turi
- Ritz
- Chez Bruce
- Texture
- Oslo Court
- Marcus Wareing
- Goring Dining Rm.
- Murano

- Lucio
- Petrus*
- Capital
- Mosimann's (club)
- Hélène Darroze
- Dorchester/Grill

25
- Rasoi Vineet Bhatia
- Gordon Ramsay/Clar.
- Dinner/Heston
- River Café
- Koffmann's
- Glasshouse
- Roussillon
- Umu
- Clarke's
- Greenhouse
- 28-50 Wine Workshop
- Orrery
- Morgan M
- Scott's

Best Buys

1. Chilango
2. Franco Manca
3. Golden Hind
4. Benito's Hat
5. Princi London
6. Food for Thought
7. Books for Cooks
8. Churchill Arms
9. Leon
10. Ed's Easy Diner
11. Rock & Sole Plaice
12. Gallipoli
13. Pho
14. Tayyabs
15. Song Que Café
16. Little Bay
17. North Sea
18. Wagamama
19. La Porchetta
20. Byron
21. Dishoom
22. Two Brothers Fish
23. Nando's
24. Koya
25. Whole Foods
26. Busaba Eathai
27. Ask Pizza
28. Comptoir Libanais
29. Vapiano
30. Le Pain Quotidien
31. Haché
32. Pizza Express
33. Yalla Yalla
34. Gourmet Burger
35. Masala Zone
36. Leong's Legend
37. Tas
38. Cha Cha Moon
39. Caravan
40. Original Lahore
41. Lucky 7
42. La Fromagerie
43. Baker & Spice
44. Gate
45. Wahaca
46. Bodeans
47. Patisserie Valerie
48. Ishtar
49. Kulu Kulu
50. Ye Olde Cheshire

OTHER GOOD VALUES

ALL YOU CAN EAT

23 Bombay Brasserie
Bengal Clipper▽
22 Brasserie Roux
La Porte des Indes
21 222 Veggie Vegan▽
Blue Elephant
18 Khan's
15 Rodizio Rico

BAKERIES

25 Ottolenghi
23 Ladurée
22 Princi London
Baker & Spice
17 Le Pain Quotidien

CHAINS

22 Gaucho
21 Noura
Tas
20 Wahaca
19 Byron
Masala Zone
Wagamama
17 Côte
Feng Sushi
Leon

CHILD-FRIENDLY

26 Barrafina
24 Oliveto
22 Tom's Kitchen
Le Café Anglais
La Famiglia
20 Chuen Cheng Ku
Wahaca
19 Byron
Masala Zone
Bodeans

COMMUNAL TABLES

25 Ottolenghi
23 Busaba Eathai
22 Princi London
La Fromagerie
Chilango
Tom's Kitchen
20 Pizza East
19 Jenny Lo's Tea▽
Wagamama
17 Aubaine

EARLY BIRD

26 Roussillon
25 Kitchen W8
Locanda Ottoemezzo
24 L'Etranger
Maze
23 Theo Randall
22 Maze Grill
21 Narrow
Daphne's
20 Rocket

PIZZA

25 Osteria Basilico
24 Franco Manca
Oliveto
23 Red Pepper▽
Delfino
20 Pizza East
Made in Italy
19 Rocket
La Porchetta
16 Pizza Express

PRE-THEATRE MENUS

27 L'Atelier/Joël Robuchon
26 Mennula
25 Cinnamon Club
Arbutus
Tamarind
Le Cercle
Ritz
Bar Boulud
Moti Mahal
24 L'Autre Pied

TAKEAWAY

27 Kiku
26 Defune
Jin Kichi
25 Koi
Original Lahore
Tamarind
Café Spice Namasté
Star of India
Ottolenghi
Ishbilia

SET-PRICE BARGAINS

DINNER: £40 & UNDER

Al Duca	£23	Le Caprice	20
Alloro	34	Le Relais/l'Entrecôte	21
Almeida	29	Le Vacherin	35
Artigiano	17	Memories of China	32
Blue Elephant	30	Miyama	38
Café Spice Namasté	16	Mr. Chow	39
Cambio de Tercio	37	1901 Restaurant	29
Caravaggio	17	Noura	38
Criterion	18	Painted Heron	35
Efes 2 Turkish Restaurant	19	Pasha	13
Enoteca Turi	27	Patara	38
Gallipoli	15	Pearl Liang	25
Galvin at Windows	39	Phoenix Palace	28
Gauthier Soho	35	Plateau	28
Gilgamesh	38	Plum Valley	38
Glasshouse	40	Princess Garden	30
Good Earth	39	Rasa	16
Haz	11	Rhodes W1	40
Hinds Head	30	Royal China	30
Il Convivio	24	R.S.J.	17
Ishtar	28	Sartoria	20
Joe Allen	20	Singapore Garden	22
Kensington Place	16	Sofra	16
Koi	34	Tas	9
La Porte des Indes	37	Vivat Bacchus	15
Latium	30	Wahaca	10
La Trompette	40	Wheeler's	22
Le Café/Marché	29	Zilli Fish	20

LUNCH: £25 & UNDER

About Thyme	£18	Le Cercle	15
Amaya	16	Mandarin Kitchen	13
Arbutus	17	Mennula	18
Bar Boulud	20	Miyama	11
Cinnamon Club	19	Morgan M	24
Club Gascon	22	Moti Mahal	19
Defune	23	Nahm	20
Galvin La Chapelle	25	Pied à Terre	24
Greenhouse	25	Quilon	21
Haozhan	8	Rasoi Vineet Bhatia	21
Hereford Road	13	Tamarind	18
Kiku	16	Texture	20
Kitchen W8	18	Trinity	20
Koffmann's	22	Trishna	15
L'Anima	25	Tsunami	15
L'Atelier/Joël Robuchon	22	Umu	25
Launceston Pl	22	Zaika	21

RESTAURANT
DIRECTORY

	FOOD	DECOR	SERVICE	COST

Abbeville, The *British/European* — ▽ 17 | 19 | 15 | £26

Clapham | 67-69 Abbeville Rd., SW4 (Clapham S.) | 020-8675-2201 | www.theabbeville.com

A "charming" "village atmosphere" pervades this "convivial" Clapham gastropub, a "steadfast local" for "meeting neighbours" amongst cosy crannies and people-watching from pavement tables; though often "good", the Modern European menu sometimes "overreaches" say critics who've noticed that "service is short" when it's "busy."

Abeno *Japanese* — 22 | 13 | 17 | £27

Bloomsbury | 47 Museum St., WC1 (Holborn) | 020-7405-3211

Abeno Too *Japanese*

Covent Garden | 17-18 Great Newport St., WC2 (Leicester Sq.) | 020-7379-1160
www.abeno.co.uk

"Superb" okonomiyaki (savory pancakes with "yummy" toppings), prepared right "in front of you", satisfy "a yen for Japanese" at these "busy", "economical" siblings in Covent Garden and "around the corner from the British Museum" in Bloomsbury; just "don't wear your Sunday best", because "your clothes will smell of it by the end."

Abingdon, The *European* — 20 | 17 | 20 | £38

Kensington | 54 Abingdon Rd., W8 (Earl's Ct./High St. Kensington) | 020-7937-3339 | www.theabingdonrestaurant.com

"Well-heeled locals" pay "sensible prices" for "consistent", "delicious" Modern European dishes at this "relaxed" Kensington gastropub where "unflappable" staffers serve "with a smile"; the decor may look "a little old fashioned", but it's "relatively easy to get a table" or a space at the "big, welcoming" bar, so it's usually "a safe bet."

About Thyme *European* — 25 | 18 | 22 | £38

Pimlico | 82 Wilton Rd., SW1 (Victoria) | 020-7821-7504 | www.aboutthyme.co.uk

The purple facade hints at the "atmospheric" vibe inside this place in Pimlico, where "friendly" staff who are "always on top of things" convey "innovative" Modern Euro fare; it's as "great for business" as it is "casual dining" and, best of all, "inexpensive by London standards."

A Cena *Italian* — 23 | 19 | 22 | £40

Richmond | 418 Richmond Rd., TW1 (Richmond) | 020-8288-0108 | www.acena.co.uk

"Unprepossessing from the outside, brilliant inside" say devotees of this "intimate, relaxed" Italian near Richmond Bridge, citing its "impeccable" fare and "great wine list"; everything's overseen by an owner-host who also "looks after his guests" while ensuring staff stay "friendly and efficient."

Acorn House *British* — 21 | 17 | 16 | £42

King's Cross | 69 Swinton St., WC1 (King's Cross St. Pancras) | 020-7812-1842 | www.acornhouserestaurant.com

"Sustainably sensitive decor" and "sustainably sourced food" signify the "noble aims" of this "unassuming" Modern British spot around the corner from King's Cross Station, whose "adventure-some" dishes "pack a punch", and for "democratic prices" too; staff are often "knowledgeable" and "friendly", but they can also be "dilatory", which is why some respondents feel "let down."

Admiral Codrington *British/European*   19 | 18 | 19 | £34

Chelsea | 17 Mossop St., SW3 (South Kensington) | 020-7581-0005 | www.theadmiralcodrington.co.uk

"Popular, and for good reason", this "down-to-earth" Chelsea gastropub offers a "cosy" bar and "smart" dining room (with a glass roof that retracts in summer) serving "good-value" Modern British-Euro cuisine; though there are a few rumblings about "haughty" servers, most are "friendly", and not just to "celebs"; P.S. it underwent a refurbishment post-Survey, possibly outdating the Decor score.

Aglio e Olio ● *Italian*   21 | 14 | 18 | £32

Chelsea | 194 Fulham Rd., SW10 (Chelsea) | 020-7351-0070

"Generous portions" of "delicious, varied" Italian fare are sold for "reasonable prices" at this "high-energy" Fulham Road trattoria; it's "not a romantic spot", as it's "cramped", "crowded" and "the acoustics are appalling", but it's "well worth going" if you have your "business associates or your kids" in tow.

☒ Alain Ducasse at   27 | 26 | 26 | £111
The Dorchester ☒ Ⓜ *French*

Mayfair | The Dorchester | 53 Park Ln., W1 (Hyde Park Corner/ Marble Arch) | 020-7629-8866 | www.alainducasse-dorchester.com

"The room sparkles but the food and service are the stars" of "genius" chef Alain Ducasse's "spectacular, beautifully lit" "nirvana" in The Dorchester, where "impeccable" staff "guide diners" through the "intricacies" of the "sublime" New French menu; the set-price lunch is "fantastic value", and while everything else (especially the "fabu-lous wine" list) is "very expensive", "you only live once!"

Albannach *Scottish*   16 | 17 | 16 | £40

Soho | 66 Trafalgar Sq., WC2 (Charing Cross/Leicester Sq.) | 020-7930-0066 | www.albannach.co.uk

Surveyors say this contemporary-looking Scottish spot on Trafalgar Square does "an ok job", citing "decent" "traditional" fare, "medio-cre" service and a "pleasant" vibe; things are more "lively and buzzy" in the basement bar, which is "great for malt whisky fans" thanks to over 100 varieties.

Albemarle, The *British*   23 | 22 | 24 | £59

Mayfair | Brown's Hotel | 30-34 Albemarle St., W1 (Green Park) | 020-7518-4060 | www.thealbemarlerestaurant.com

Thanks to "huge tables with good distances between them", "you can talk without being bothered by neighbours" at this "clubby", "classy" dining room in Brown's Hotel employing "exemplary" staff to ferry the "superb", "rich" Traditional British fare; cocktails are "to die for" and tea in the "lovely" adjacent library is "outstanding", which leaves only one thing to grouse about: "mad" prices.

	FOOD	DECOR	SERVICE	COST

Alberico at Aspinall's ⏺ *Italian*   ▽ 24 | 24 | 27 | £66

Mayfair | private club | 27-28 Curzon St., W1 (Green Park) | 020-7499-4599 | www.aspinalls-club.com

The somewhat "gaudy" but "attractive" Aspinall's private gambling club in Mayfair is the setting of this discreet, leather-embellished first-floor Italian dining room, open to nonmembers; here, "excellent" staff ferry dishes that are so "special", they're "well worth" the "incredibly expensive" fees.

Albion, The *British*   19 | 20 | 17 | £36

Islington | 10 Thornhill Rd., N1 (Angel) | 020-7607-7450 | www.the-albion.co.uk

"An awesome Sunday roast" is the highlight of the Traditional British fare at this gastropub in a "lovely", wisteria-clad Georgian building in Islington; "service is slow at times", especially "on a summer day" when the garden is "mobbed", but staff are usually "courteous."

Al Duca ⧄ *Italian*   19 | 18 | 18 | £44

St. James's | 4-5 Duke of York St., SW1 (Green Park/Piccadilly Circus) | 020-7839-3090 | www.alduca-restaurant.co.uk

"Given the pricey neighbourhood", this "fairly slick" Italian in St. James's offers "value" in its customisable, "well-prepared" prix fixes at breakfast, lunch and dinner; some find the tables too "closely spaced", but that's a quibble considering how "reliable" and "efficient" it is, especially for "business" and pre-theatre.

Al Hamra ⏺ *Lebanese*   23 | 16 | 19 | £39

Mayfair | 31-33 Shepherd Mkt., W1 (Green Park) | 020-7493-1954

Brasserie Al Hamra ⧄ *Lebanese*

Mayfair | 52 Shepherd Mkt., W1 (Green Park) | 020-7493-1068 www.alhamrarestaurant.co.uk

Aficionados say you can't get "closer to Beirut" than this "well-located" Shepherd Market stalwart offering "delicious" Lebanese victuals whose "large portions" are "good value for money"; quarters are "close", "crowded" and "slightly dated" inside, but "you can eat outside" in summer here and at the even more affordable brasserie across the street.

Alloro ⧄ *Italian*   21 | 19 | 20 | £56

Mayfair | 19-20 Dover St., W1 (Green Park) | 020-7495-4768 | www.alloro-restaurant.co.uk

"Reliable" cooking, a "superb" wine list and a "buzzing atmosphere" (at lunchtime at least) keep this Mayfair Italian on the radar for "business" people who find it "easier to get a reservation" here than at other "high-end" places nearby; bargain-hunters find "value" in the set menus, and while the "decor is a bit drab", "attentive service" is a bright spot.

All Star Lanes *American*   12 | 17 | 15 | £24

Bloomsbury | Victoria Hse. | Bloomsbury Pl., WC1 (Holborn) | 020-7025-2676

Shoreditch | Old Truman Brewery | 95 Brick Ln., E1 (Liverpool St.) | 020-7426-9200

(continued)

All Star Lanes

Bayswater | Whiteleys Shopping Ctr. | 6 Porchester Gdns., W2 (Bayswater) | 020-7313-8363
www.allstarlanes.co.uk

"American expats enjoy a bit of home" alongside "hooting hen parties" and "big" "corporate groups" at these "cute, kitschy" bowling alley/restaurants; ok, so the diner-style fare is "unexceptional", but for a "novel", "cheap night out", it can be "so much fun"; P.S. the Shoreditch branch offers karaoke too.

Almeida *French*

20 | 18 | 19 | £41

Islington | 30 Almeida St., N1 (Angel/Highbury & Islington) | 020-7354-4777 | www.almeida-restaurant.co.uk

A "convenient" location across the road from the Almeida Theatre plus "value"-priced set menus make this "lovely" New French bistro a "good bet" pre- and post-show; it "might not be the most original restaurant in the world", but it's "dependable", "satisfying" and staff are as "pleasant" as the ambience.

Alounak ● *Persian*

21 | 13 | 15 | £26

Bayswater | 44 Westbourne Grove, W2 (Bayswater/Royal Oak) | 020-7229-4158
Olympia | 10 Russell Gdns., W14 (Olympia) | 020-7603-1130

It's "always busy with long queues at the door" of these "old-school" Persians in Olympia and Westbourne Grove, where "huge portions" of "tasty food" come for "prices that can't be beat"; don't miss the "excellent bread, straight from the oven", and don't forget to "bring your own wine" (no licence).

Al Sultan *Lebanese*

23 | 17 | 21 | £36

Mayfair | 51-52 Hertford St., W1 (Green Park) | 020-7408-1155 | www.alsultan.co.uk

There's "always a warm welcome" at this Mayfair Lebanese whose "excellent quality food", including a "seemingly endless" mezze selection, "draws a lot of Gulf visitors" ("just the place to see bling!"); true, it's "not worth a special trip" if you're looking for more than a "simple" setting, but if you seek "good value", you'll find it here.

Al Waha *Lebanese*

24 | 16 | 22 | £31

Bayswater | 75 Westbourne Grove, W2 (Bayswater/Queensway) | 020-7229-0806 | www.alwaharestaurant.com

"Amazingly good" grills are just some of the "incredible" wares at this "great-value" Westbourne Grove Lebanese that boasts "nice staff"; the "only problems" are the "dated decor" and tables that are "too cramped", so it helps that it's "excellent for delivery."

NEW Amaranto *Italian*

- | - | - | VE

Mayfair | Four Seasons Hotel London at Park Ln. | Hamilton Pl., Park Ln., W1 (Hyde Park Corner) | 020-7319-5206 | www.fourseasons.com

The unashamedly opulent, £125 million refit of Mayfair's Four Seasons Hotel bore this sultry red-hued restaurant and clubby lounge, both offering sophisticated, very pricey all-day Italian fare by respected chef Adriano Cavagnini (Rome's Hotel Eden); the rich ensemble extends to an intriguing Boot-dominated wine list, afternoon tea and a landscaped garden terrace.

☑ Amaya ● *Indian*

26	23	22	£57

Belgravia | 15-19 Halkin Arcade, Motcomb St., SW1 (Knightsbridge) | 020-7823-1166 | www.amaya.biz

The "modern decor" is "chic" and the patrons are "stylish", but the "fragrant", "complex" Indian fare is the most "sophisticated" aspect of this "hip, happening spot" in Belgravia, where mostly "welcoming staff" ferry the fare from the "attractive open kitchen"; the "tapas-style" portions mean the "bill adds up quickly", but it's "worth it for a special dining experience" – just plan ahead, because "getting a reservation is difficult."

Ambassador, The *European*

-	-	-	E

Clerkenwell | 55 Exmouth Mkt., EC1 (Farringdon) | 020-7837-0009 | www.theambassadorcafe.co.uk

So "relaxed", it "feels like you are in someone's dining room", this "unpretentious" Exmouth Market bistro employs "knowledgeable", "personable" staff to serve its "great" all-day Modern European fare; other selling points include a "good" wine list and "nice" lunch prix fixes starting at £10.

Anchor & Hope *British*

23	15	19	£31

Waterloo | 36 The Cut, SE1 (Southwark/Waterloo) | 020-7928-9898

Despite its "no-frills" setting, this "convivial" Waterloo "grande dame" of the gastropub scene is more like a "gastronomic palace", with "hearty yet refined" Modern British fare that's "cooked with passion" and "not expensive" either; it's "a shame about the no-booking policy" (excepting Sunday lunch) – good thing "well-informed" staff are "laid-back" enough to cope.

Andrew Edmunds *European*

23	19	21	£40

Soho | 46 Lexington St., W1 (Oxford Circus/Piccadilly Circus) | 020-7437-5708

"Cosy", "dark" digs and "attentive service with a smile" "put you in the mood" for either a "romantic dinner or a heart-to-heart with a friend" at this "bohemian" Modern European bistro in Soho; though some customers find some of the tables "cramped", that's easily forgiven in light of the "superb value" found in both the "wonderful", "rustic" dishes and "amazing wine list" (featuring many "steals").

Angels & Gypsies *Spanish*

-	-	-	E

Camberwell | Church Street Hotel | 29-33 Camberwell Church St., SE5 | 020-7703-5984 | www.churchstreethotel.com

Attached to a Latin-themed boutique hotel, this trendy, relatively recent "major addition to Camberwell's sparse food scene" serves "tasty", organically biased Spanish tapas amidst exposed-brick-and-tile decor.

| | FOOD | DECOR | SERVICE | COST |

Angelus *French*
23 | 20 | 22 | £49

Bayswater | 4 Bathurst St., W2 (Lancaster Gate) | 020-7402-0083 | www.angelusrestaurant.co.uk

In a "neighbourhood not known for good restaurants", aka Bayswater, this French "gem" with "attentive service" rustles up "splendid interpretations of brasserie classics" in "polished" (though "rather cramped") quarters "not too far from Paddington Station"; while some peg it as a "super local", others save it for "a special occasion" since it's "expensive"; P.S. seating six, the "chef's table is great fun."

Anglesea Arms *British*
18 | 17 | 15 | £30

Shepherd's Bush | 35 Wingate Rd., W6 (Goldhawk Rd./Ravenscourt Park) | 020-8749-1291

With a "cosy pub on one side, family restaurant on the other", this Shepherd's Bush gastropub is always "heaving with people" who are "never disappointed" with the moderately priced Modern British cuisine; service is "iffy", but the outdoor seating is a sure bet when the weather's warm.

Annabel's ◐⊠ *British/French*
21 | 24 | 23 | £87

Mayfair | private club | 44 Berkeley Sq., W1 (Bond St./Green Park) | 020-7629-1096 | www.annabels.co.uk

"Couture cocktail dresses", "fine suits with Hermes ties" and "dancing shoes" are the preferred costumes for this "beautiful Aladdin's cave" below Berkeley Square, a "very selective private club" where "new money" feasts on "sophisticated", "expensive" Classic French–Traditional British cuisine brought by "outstanding" staff; old-timers who've spied too many "C-list celebs" scoff that it's "lost its edge and class", but most say it's still a "'wow' place to be seen."

Annie's *British*
21 | 20 | 21 | £33

Barnes | 36-38 White Hart Ln., SW13 (Barnes Bridge Rail) | 020-8878-2020
Chiswick | 162 Thames Rd., W4 (Kew Bridge Rail) | 020-8994-6848
www.anniesrestaurant.co.uk

"Attractive", "eclectic" rooms that "would not be out of place in a Jane Austen novel" make this "relaxed", "charming" Modern British duo in Chiswick and Barnes "perfect for a girlie lunch"; affordable rates for "enormous portions" of "wholesome" fare mean it's also suitable for a "weekday evening out or brunch on Sunday with the family", and every meal comes with "knowledgeable", "friendly" service.

Anthologist, The ⊠ *European*
17 | 22 | 17 | £31

City | 58 Gresham St., EC2 (Bank/St. Paul's) | 0845-468-0101 | www.theanthologistbar.co.uk

"Real buzz" permeates this "vast", "stylish" City venue whipping up affordable Modern European eats, which pair with "lots of wine choices"; "maybe it's too big" and the "food is an afterthought", but for the "suits massed around the bar", the "feel-good atmosphere" is all that matters.

| | FOOD | DECOR | SERVICE | COST |

NEW Antidote Wine Bar *French* — — — M

Soho | 12A Newburgh St., W1 (Oxford Circus) | 020-7287-8488 |
www.antidotewinebar.com

This casual wine bar in an earthy, bi-level setting on a cobbled Soho
street corner offers gutsy, fairly priced Gallic fare that includes simple grills and platters of cheese and charcuterie; a notable wine list
from the South of France exhibits a passion for biodynamic, organic
and sustainable viticulture.

Antonio's Ristorante *Italian* — — — M

Islington | Rear of 137 Upper St., N1 (Angel) | 020-7226-8994 |
www.antoniosristorante.co.uk

"Worth finding down an alley" in Islington, this "warm", candlelit
ristorante where wine bottles line exposed-brick walls is appreciated as much for its "wonderful", "super-affordable", "rustic" Italian
cuisine as for "friendly, on-the-ball staff"; for Almeida ticket-
holders, it's also "perfect pre-theatre", being just around the corner.

Apsleys *Italian* 25 25 24 £76

Belgravia | The Lanesborough | Hyde Park Corner, SW1
(Hyde Park Corner) | 020-7333-7254 | www.lanesborough.com

"High ceilings", "immense chandeliers" and "well-spaced tables"
set a scene of "pure serenity" at this "spectacular" dining room in
The Lanesborough offering a "fabulous" Italian menu by esteemed
Roman chef Heinz Beck, complemented by an "extensive" wine list;
the "professional" service helps make it "worthy of a special occasion" or "romantic" encounter, but "be prepared to pay for it" (or go
for the "excellent-value" set-price lunch).

Aqua Kyoto ⊠ *Japanese* 20 24 17 £68

Soho | 240 Regent St., W1 (Oxford Circus) | 020-7478-0540 |
www.aqua-london.com

With a "trendy" vibe in the "beautiful" main room, a "lively bar" full of
"fantastic eye candy" and a summer scene on the "amazing terrace
overlooking Regent Street", this "spacious" Soho Japanese venue is
thought of as "more of a nightclub"; that said, most diners deem the
"high-cost" costs "worth it", with the sushi being the "way to go."

Aqua Nueva ⊠ *Spanish* 19 23 20 £53

Soho | 240 Regent St., W1 (Oxford Circus) | 020-7478-0540 |
www.aqua-london.com

Set next to its sibling, Aqua Kyoto, this equally "buzzy" Soho Spaniard
pairs "decent", "expensive" small and large plates with "delicious"
Iberian wines and "great cocktails"; the "stylish interior" is marked by
an illuminated glass walkway and hanging strands of wooden beads,
and "for leperised smokers", there's a "fantastic rooftop patio" bar.

☑ Arbutus *European* 25 19 23 £48

Soho | 63-64 Frith St., W1 (Leicester Sq./Tottenham Court Rd.) |
020-7734-4545 | www.arbutusrestaurant.co.uk

"Unpretentious but special", this "minimalist" Soho sibling of Les
Deux Salons and Wild Honey employs "attentive, knowledgeable

staff" who "never rush" diners when they linger over the "adventuresome", "beautifully prepared" Modern European cuisine, featuring "complex flavours" and "unusual cuts of meat"; like the fare, the "spectacular wine list" offers "amazing value for money", plus the "set lunch is a snip!"

Archipelago ⑤ *Eclectic* ▽ 21 | 22 | 17 | £52

Bloomsbury | 110 Whitfield St., W1 (Goodge St./Warren St.) | 020-7383-3346 | www.archipelago-restaurant.co.uk

"If you're a culinary thrill seeker", hit this "truly different spot" in Fitzrovia, where the Eclectic fare – think "salad with insects, wildebeest, zebra", "alligator" and "probably a slice of Big Foot" – is "not just unusual for the sake of being unusual", it's also "thoroughly delicious"; decor described as a "sensual kaleidoscope" and "themed" cocktails "add to the fun" – too bad staff "seem to be bored with it all."

Ark, The ⑤ *Italian* 21 | 19 | 21 | £38

Kensington | 122 Palace Gardens Terr., W8 (Notting Hill Gate) | 020-7229-4024 | www.ark-restaurant.com

"Intimate", "pretty" and "romantic", this Kensington haunt is a "good local" option for "delicious" Italian fare; "friendly staff" further its appeal, and best of all, "the price is right."

Armani Caffé ⑤ *Italian* 19 | 21 | 19 | £36

Knightsbridge | Emporio Armani | 191 Brompton Rd., SW3 (Knightsbridge) | 020-7584-4549

"Lovely views of Brompton Road" and a "sleek" design define this Italian lunch cafe within Knightsbridge's Emporio Armani; if some feel it's "all about the decor", at least the "simple" fare is of noticeable "quality" and sufficient for a "quick pick-me-up" whilst shopping.

Artigiano *Italian* 21 | 18 | 20 | £41

Hampstead | 12A Belsize Terr., NW3 (Belsize Park/Swiss Cottage) | 020-7794-4288 | www.etruscarestaurants.com

"Sophisticated dining in pretty Belsize Village" comes via this "pleasant" eatery that's "worth the visit" for its "solid" Italian dishes served on two airy floors (insiders suggest you "sit on the upper level by the window"); "charming service" and "reasonable value", especially in the set meals, make it a spot to "keep returning to."

Asadal *Korean* 22 | 17 | 14 | £32

Holborn | 229-231 High Holborn, WC1 (Holborn) | 020-7430-9006 | www.asadal.co.uk

"Not pretty" or "buzzy", this "subterranean surprise" next to Holborn tube is nevertheless a "convenient" go-to for "delicious" Korean cuisine that works for a fast lunch or a "chilled post-work dinner"; prices are always affordable, although "service is hit-or-miss."

Asia de Cuba ◐ *Asian/Cuban* 21 | 23 | 19 | £58

Covent Garden | St. Martins Lane Hotel | 45 St. Martin's Ln., WC2 (Leicester Sq.) | 020-7300-5588

"Fun, sexy" and "high energy", this St. Martins Lane Hotel "hot spot" is for "letting your hair down" amongst "beautiful people" and

| | FOOD | DECOR | SERVICE | COST |

amidst "loud", "constant surround-sound music" whilst sharing "huge servings" of "inventive", "pricey" Asian-Cuban cuisine "executed with finesse"; some surveyors find "nothing special" in the "stark", "modern", "bright-white setting" and "too-cool" service, but for most, it's "always a pleasure."

Ask Pizza *Italian*   15 | 14 | 16 | £19

Bloomsbury | 48 Grafton Way, W1 (Warren St.) | 020-7388-8108 🌙
Bloomsbury | 74 Southampton Row, WC1 (Holborn) | 020-7405-2876
Marylebone | 197 Baker St., NW1 (Baker St.) | 020-7486-6027
Marylebone | 56-60 Wigmore St., W1 (Bond St.) | 020-7224-3484
Mayfair | 121-125 Park St., W1 (Marble Arch) | 020-7495-7760
Victoria | 160-162 Victoria St., SW1 (St. James's Park/Victoria) | 020-7630-8228
Tower Bridge | 34 Shad Thames, Butlers Wharf, SE1 (London Bridge) | 020-7403-4545
Hampstead | 216 Haverstock Hill, NW3 (Belsize Park/Chalk Farm) | 020-7433-3896
South Kensington | 23-24 Gloucester Arcade, SW7 (Gloucester Rd.) | 020-7835-0840
Notting Hill | 145 Notting Hill Gate, W11 (Notting Hill Gate) | 020-7792-9942
www.askcentral.co.uk
Additional locations throughout London

"Solid if not inspired pizza, salads", pastas and the like command "inexpensive" prices at this "convenient, no-hassle" Italian chain that's good for a "quick", "informal" "family meal" or takeaway; if the "overall experience is just too generic" for discerning diners, it's "pleasant enough", and most "never walk out of here harbouring a regret."

Assaggi 🅱 *Italian*   26 | 18 | 24 | £58

Notting Hill | 39 Chepstow Pl., 1st fl., W2 (Notting Hill Gate) | 020-7792-5501

The perennial "struggle to get a table" is "testament to the quality" of this "low-key", "intimate" "destination restaurant" "above a pub" in Notting Hill, serving "beautifully prepared" Sardinian fare with a "contemporary slant"; if some feel the "simple decor" doesn't warrant the "pricey" fees, "expert", "welcoming staff" absolutely do.

Aubaine *French*   17 | 18 | 15 | £33

NEW **Marylebone** | Selfridges | 400 Oxford St., 2nd fl., W1 (Bond St.) | 020-7318-3738
Piccadilly | 4 Heddon St., W1 (Piccadilly Circus) | 020-7440-2510
South Kensington | 260-262 Brompton Rd., SW3 (South Kensington) | 020-7052-0100
NEW **Kensington** | 37-45 Kensington High St., W8 (High St. Kensington) | 020-7368-0950
www.aubaine.co.uk

"Packed from Day One", this "countryside"-style bistro at Brompton Cross has spawned a trio of siblings in Kensington, Piccadilly and

Selfridges, serving its "efficiently executed" French fare all day; now, all are "bustling", despite service that splits between "charming" and "irritating" and the widespread belief that "the same thing in Paris would be half the price."

Auberge du Lac ☒Ⓜ *French*

▽ 24 | 25 | 25 | £71

Welwyn | Brocket Hall | B653 off A1, Hertfordshire | 01707-368888 | www.brocket-hall.co.uk

It's "worth going in the day to appreciate the view" of the "beautiful" parkland surrounding Brocket Hall, the stately lakeside hunting lodge in Hertfordshire (about an hour from Central London) that's home to this Classic French–Modern Euro dining room; "lovely, friendly people" present the "excellent, reliable" menu, which features "good value" in the set lunch and pricier rates in the evening.

Aubergine at
The Compleat Angler Ⓜ *French*

24 | 23 | 24 | £63

Marlow | Macdonald Compleat Angler Hotel | Bisham Rd., Buckinghamshire | 01628-405405 | www.auberginerestaurant.co.uk

With the demise of Aubergine in Chelsea, its "subdued but pleasant" Marlow sibling, "a short drive out of London", is left to fly the flag, with "excellent", "delicious" New French fare and "olde world charm"; it's "expensive", but a "magical" view of a bubbling Thames weir is part of the package.

Aurora *European*

‒ | ‒ | ‒ | E

Soho | 49 Lexington St., W1 (Oxford Circus/Piccadilly Circus) | 020-7494-0514 | www.aurorasoho.co.uk

"Always delightful", this "Soho hideaway" delivers "reliable" Modern European fare in an "intimate, romantic" (and "rather tight") interior and on a "secret summer patio"; it's a bit expensive, but most folks feel it's worth it, judging from how "popular" it is.

Automat ● *American*

18 | 20 | 17 | £36

Mayfair | 33 Dover St., W1 (Green Park) | 020-7499-3033 | www.automat-london.com

"Take a classic American diner, add a touch of Mayfair pretention" and you've got this "laid-back" all-day brasserie doling out "not-too-shabby burgers" and other "typical" U.S. "comfort food"; just know that it's somewhat "expensive for what it is", and "haphazard service" can let the side down; P.S. "the front and back are basically two different restaurants": a "dark" train-carriage facsimile with booths and a "warm" conservatory, respectively.

Avenue ☒ *British*

20 | 20 | 20 | £45

St. James's | 7-9 St. James's St., SW1 (Green Park) | 020-7321-2111 | www.theavenue-restaurant.co.uk

Though its "minimalist", "bright"-white decor with "edgy art–filled walls" says "youthful and trendy", this St. James's Modern British "staple" is still "great for business" thanks to "well-spaced tables" suitable for "private conversation"; the "impressive" fare is "beautifully presented" by "staff that know what they're doing", helping to set a mood that's "unstuffy for the area."

	FOOD	DECOR	SERVICE	COST

Awana *Malaysian*
19 | **18** | **17** | **£41**

Chelsea | 85 Sloane Ave., SW3 (South Kensington) | 020-7584-8880 | www.awana.co.uk

"Fans of Malaysian cuisine" hail the "yummy" signature dishes that are "a trip for your taste buds" – listed on a menu "so vast, it's hard to choose" – at this "contemporary" eatery "in a prime Chelsea location"; staff are often "attentive" and "friendly", however, the owners "need to get back to reality" regarding some "astronomical prices."

Axis ☒ Ⓜ *British*
22 | **21** | **22** | **£47**

Covent Garden | One Aldwych Hotel | 1 Aldwych, WC2 (Charing Cross/ Covent Garden) | 020-7300-0300 | www.onealdwych.com

Guests make grand entrances via a "sweeping staircase" at this subterranean dining room in Covent Garden's One Aldwych Hotel, where the "sophisticated decor" matches the "stylish" Modern British fare; it's "reasonably priced for a 'fancy' restaurant", and "great prix fixes", not to mention "smooth service", make it especially "reliable" for "pre-theatre" and "business."

Babbo ☒ *Italian*
22 | **21** | **22** | **£54**

Mayfair | 39 Albermarle St., W1 (Green Park/Piccadilly Circus) | 020-3205-1099 | www.babborestaurant.co.uk

"Simplicity raised to elegance" is the forte of this "smart" Mayfair venue imbuing "Italian classics" with some "great twists" and backing them with "excellent" wines; although "value for money is not its main feature", the "calm atmosphere" makes it "perfect for business" or with "someone special"; P.S. not affiliated with the same-named NYC eatery.

Babylon *European*
20 | **25** | **21** | **£52**

Kensington | Roof Gdns. | 99 Kensington High St., 7th fl., W8 (High St. Kensington) | 020-7368-3993 | www.roofgardens.com

The Modern European menu is "well constructed" and priced at "the upper end of reasonable", but it's the "great views" and "access to the fabulous roof gardens" that really make Sir Richard Branson's modern, "friendly" Kensington aerie "worthwhile"; what's more, on Fridays and Saturdays, diners can pay to gain access to the private nightclub below, which is prime "first-date territory."

Baker & Spice *Bakery/Mediterranean*
22 | **15** | **13** | **£23**

Belgravia | 54-56 Elizabeth St., SW1 (Sloane Sq./Victoria) | 020-7730-5524

St. John's Wood | 20 Clifton Rd., W9 (Clifton Rd.) | 020-7289-2499

Chelsea | 47 Denyer St., SW3 (Knightsbridge/South Kensington) | 020-7225-3417

www.bakerandspice.uk.com

"Fantastic, mouthwatering bakery items, desserts" and "wonderful", "wholesome" Med savouries draw crowds to this all-day "gourmet deli" trio with "limited communal seating"; however, "grumpy staff" and "extortionate" prices make it a real "pain in the &*%", so most minimise their time there and do takeaway.

	FOOD	DECOR	SERVICE	COST

Balans *British*   17 | 15 | 17 | £25

Soho | 60-62 Old Compton St., W1 (Leicester Sq./Piccadilly Circus) | 020-7439-2183 ●

Earl's Court | 239 Old Brompton Rd., SW5 (Earl's Ct./West Brompton) | 020-7244-8838 ●

Chiswick | 214 Chiswick High Rd., W4 (Turnham Green) | 020-8742-1435 ●

Kensington | 187 Kensington High St., W8 (High St. Kensington) | 020-7376-0115 ●

Shepherd's Bush | Westfield Shopping Ctr. | Ariel Way, lower ground fl., W12 (Shepherd's Bush) | 020-8600-3320

Balans Café ● *British*

Soho | 34 Old Compton St., W1 (Leicester Sq./Piccadilly Circus) | 020-7439-3309
www.balans.co.uk

From Soho roots, where the "entertaining", "much-loved" original is still the "epicenter of Gay London" ("hetero guests feel comfortable" too), this Modern British option now numbers six "buzzy" yet "relaxed" all-day bistros; the fare may be "nothing special", but it's "hearty" and "dependable" – unlike service, which ranges from "sweet to snippy"; P.S. a branch is slated for Westfield Stratford City, the new shopping centre across from the Olympic Park.

Baltic ● *Polish*   23 | 20 | 20 | £38

Southwark | 74 Blackfriars Rd., SE1 (Southwark) | 020-7928-1111 | www.balticrestaurant.co.uk

"The appeal and attraction" of this minimalist, high-ceilinged Southwark spot lies in its "upscale" yet "reasonably priced" Polish-biased Eastern European menu, with fare that's "tasty" and often "lighter than expected"; but the "trendy bar" harbouring a seemingly "infinite number of vodkas" is its own draw, as is "pleasant service."

Bam-Bou 🗷 *Asian*   20 | 21 | 19 | £42

Bloomsbury | 1 Percy St., W1 (Tottenham Court Rd.) | 020-7323-9130 | www.bam-bou.co.uk

"Set in a beautiful old Georgian house" with "cool" decor, this Fitzrovia haunt "caters for expense accounts at lunch and comes alive in the evening" as an "intimate" "first-date place", with a Pan-Asian menu that's speckled with "delicious" "French-Vietnamese accents", "on the pricey side" and proffered by servers who are "generally up to scratch"; "great cocktails" are poured at a "romantic bar" at the top floor, which is reachable by stairs that can be "treacherous" "after one too many."

Bangkok 🗷 *Thai*   ▽ 21 | 16 | 18 | £30

South Kensington | 9 Bute St., SW7 (South Kensington) | 020-7584-8529

"Imaginatively prepared", "reasonably priced" Thai cooking and "warm, courteous service" overshadow the "plain tables and negligible decor" at this "understated", "long-standing" South Kensington stalwart, which dates back to the '60s.

	FOOD	DECOR	SERVICE	COST

Bank Westminster & Zander Bar ⓈEuropean
20 | 21 | 18 | £43

Westminster | 45 Buckingham Gate, SW1 (St. James's Park) | 020-7630-6644 | www.bankrestaurants.com

A "bright, airy" conservatory feel with "large windows", "nice court-yard views" and a "huge bar" are the highlights of this "quiet" Westminster Mod Euro whose "standard brasserie" menu offers "something for everyone"; though area workers deem it "unremarkable", it's "not bad for a business lunch" if you're on "expenses."

NEW Bar Battu ⓈEuropean
- | - | - | M

City | 48 Gresham St., EC2 (Bank) | 020-7036-6100 | www.barbattu.com

At this "refreshing" wine bar, City boys and girls dig into a midpriced Mod European menu, including bar plates and charcuterie, matched by an "exciting, different" wine list that features biodynamic labels; the setting sports a funked-up bistro look laced with art deco influences and cosy red booths set against brick walls.

NEW Barbecoa BBQ
20 | 22 | 18 | £54

City | 20 New Change Passage, EC4 (St. Paul's) | 020-3005-8555 | www.barbecoa.com

"Well done, Jamie" applaud fans of chef Oliver's City venture with NYC-based toque Adam Perry Lang, a "fantastic" newcomer serving "succulent" upscale American BBQ set against "to-die-for" views of St. Paul's Cathedral; there are reports of "birth pangs" – mainly "iffy service" – but all in all, it's "great fun" and "worth every penny" to boot.

🄩 Bar Boulud French
25 | 22 | 23 | £51

Knightsbridge | Mandarin Oriental Hyde Park | 66 Knightsbridge, SW1 (Knightsbridge) | 020-7201-3899 | www.barboulud.com

"Renowned" New York chef Daniel Boulud "pulls out all the stops" at this "upscale", "energetic" (read: "noisy") bistro in the Mandarin Oriental Hyde Park, a "warm, inviting" space where "slick", "friendly" staffers serve "glamourous diners" "sublime" charcuterie and other "refined" French fare, complemented by "well-chosen" wines; it's "a bit expensive", but there are "amazing" prix fixe "deals" to be had at lunch and pre-theatre.

Barrafina Spanish
26 | 16 | 20 | £38

Soho | 54 Frith St., W1 (Leicester Sq./Piccadilly Circus) | 020-7813-8016 | www.barrafina.co.uk

"After waiting in line for what seems an eternity" (no reservations) for one of the 23 "shoulder-to-shoulder" counter seats (no tables), patient punters are treated to "high-quality, seafood-oriented" Spanish tapas at this "cool" Soho sibling of Fino; staff are "helpful" and "chatty" too, which adds to the "informal", "fun" atmosphere.

Barrica ⓈSpanish
- | - | - | M

Bloomsbury | 62 Goodge St., W1 (Goodge St.) | 20-7436-9448 | www.barrica.co.uk

Though they come from a "relatively low-key" player in the Fitzrovian culinary hotbed, the moderately priced tapas "rock" at this unpretentious Spaniard that "isn't afraid to stray from the run-of-the-mill"; "friendly" staff ferry the food "quickly", and they've also got a "great list of sherries."

Barshu *Chinese*   25 | 18 | 16 | £35

Soho | 28 Frith St., W1 (Leicester Sq./Tottenham Court Rd.) | 020-7287-8822 | www.bar-shu.co.uk

"If you like your Chinese spicy", or downright "fiery", hit this "real deal" for Sichuan in Soho, where the decor is "surprisingly elegant" and the ambience is often "chaotic"; service is "so-so" and "prices are higher" than others of its ilk, but it's "still worth it", as "everything is so delicious."

Ba Shan *Chinese*   20 | 18 | 18 | £31

Soho | 24 Romilly St., W1 (Leicester Sq.) | 020-7287-3266

"Gird yourself for a deliciously spicy meal" at this Sichuan sibling of Barshu in Soho, where folks who find the menu "unrecognisable" trust staff for "good recommendations" (plus they'll "reduce the heat if you like"); although there's "little ambience" to speak of, most don't mind because the prices are "quite reasonable."

Bedford & Strand 🅈 *British/French*   ▽ 18 | 16 | 19 | £30

Covent Garden | 1A Bedford St., WC2 (Charing Cross) | 020-7836-3033 | www.bedford-strand.com

"Hidden away" in a basement off The Strand, this vino bar features an "excellent wine list", "notably the by-the-glass or carafe" selection, and "great", "well-priced" Mod British–French snacks and mains; it's an especially "ideal pre-theatre venue", as "attentive" staff "make sure you finish on time for your play."

Belgo *Belgian*   19 | 16 | 17 | £26

Covent Garden | 50 Earlham St., WC2 (Covent Garden) | 020-7813-2233
Covent Garden | 67 Kingsway, WC2 (Covent Garden/Holborn) | 020-7242-7469
Chalk Farm | 72 Chalk Farm Rd., NW1 (Chalk Farm) | 020-7267-0718
Clapham | 44-48 Clapham High St., SW4 (Clapham N.) | 020-7720-1118 ●
www.belgo-restaurants.co.uk

"Imagine 101 ways with mussels and 101 varieties of beer served by Trappist monks" in a "high-energy" atmosphere and you've got this "tried-and-tested" quartet whipping up "satisfactory" Belgian fare; the "canteenlike" settings are "basic" but "plainly enjoyed by everyone packed in" – indeed, it's "not the place for an intimate tête-à-tête"; P.S. the 'beat the clock' deal, in which the time of your order is the price you pay, is "one of London's best."

Bellamy's 🅈 *French*   ▽ 23 | 21 | 21 | £62

Mayfair | 18-18A Bruton Pl., W1 (Bond St./Green Park) | 020-7491-2727 | www.bellamysrestaurant.co.uk

"You don't have to be important, but staff make you feel like you are" at this "clubby", "reliable" Mayfair French eatery with an oyster bar; though it's "expensive", there are "a number who swear by" it, especially "for a quiet date, family dinner" or a "men's lunch."

	FOOD	DECOR	SERVICE	COST

Belvedere, The *British/French* | 22 | 24 | 22 | £46
Holland Park | Holland Park | off Abbotsbury Rd., W8 (Holland Park) |
020-7602-1238 | www.belvedererestaurant.co.uk
As "befits" a venue in the middle of "smart" Holland Park, the
setting is "sumptuous" at this "posh" three-tiered "destination",
plus the Modern British–New French fare is "well prepared" and
service is "attentive"; it's unsurprisingly costly, so either opt for
an "excellent-value" set menu or come with "friends who have
money and are treating."

Benares *Indian* | 23 | 23 | 22 | £60
Mayfair | 12A Berkeley Sq., W1 (Green Park) | 020-7629-8886 |
www.benaresrestaurant.com
Chef Atul Kochhar "continues to push Indian cuisine to new
ground", with "innovative" preparations and "vibrant flavours",
at this "grand", "beautiful", contemporary-exotic eatery in
Berkeley Square, whose staff include "gracious, discreet" servers
and a "knowledgeable sommelier"; just be sure to "bring lots of ru-
pees", especially if you opt for the "excellent" tasting menu
with wine matches.

Bengal Clipper ◑ *Indian* | ▽ 23 | 16 | 17 | £31
Tower Bridge | Cardamom Bldg. | 31 Shad Thames, SE1 (London Bridge/
Tower Hill) | 020-7357-9001 | www.bengalclipper.co.uk
"Interesting" Indian fare is served by mostly "attentive" staff amidst
"well-spaced" tables and live piano music (Tuesday–Saturday evenings) at this low-key venue near Tower Bridge; what's more, it can
be a "great bargain" if you come for the all-you-can-eat lunch or opt
for the two-course prix fixe at dinner.

Benihana *Japanese* | 17 | 16 | 19 | £38
Piccadilly | 37 Sackville St., W1 (Green Park/Piccadilly Circus) |
020-7494-2525
NEW **City** | Grange Hotel St. Paul | 10 Godliman St., EC4 (St. Paul's) |
020-7074-1001
Chelsea | 77 King's Rd., SW3 (Sloane Sq.) | 020-7376-7799
www.benihana.com
"The show's a bit cheesy, but it's all good fun" at these Japanese
"food theatres" where "humorous" chefs prepare "diverse" teppanyaki "right in front of you", making it "great for a party" or to "entertain children", even though it's a little "pricey"; if the Chelsea and
Piccadilly branches are "showing their age", the new City iteration
displays a bit of fresh flash.

Benito's Hat *Mexican* | 19 | 11 | 14 | £13
Bloomsbury | 56 Goodge St., W1 (Goodge St.) | 020-7637-3732 |
www.benitos-hat.com
"London needs more" like this "irreplaceable" Bloomsbury counter
doling out bargain "fast food–style Mexican with real flavour", such
as tacos and burritos that "always hit the spot" and are "actually
spicy when you ask for spicy"; just "be prepared to wait" at lunchtime when the queues stretch "around the block."

	FOOD	DECOR	SERVICE	COST

☑ Bentley's *British/Seafood*   26 | 21 | 23 | £57

Piccadilly | 11-15 Swallow St., W1 (Piccadilly Circus) | 020-7734-4756 |
www.bentleys.org

"Long may it endure!" cheer supporters of Richard Corrigan's
"classy", "elegant" Victorian-era Piccadilly place where "high-quality"
British seafood stars in "imaginative interpretations of classics"
both in the "convivial oyster bar" downstairs and the more "quiet"
dining room upstairs; "you do pay for it", but "smooth", "knowledgeable" service and "little treasures on the wine list" add value.

Bertorelli *Italian*   17 | 16 | 18 | £32

Covent Garden | 37 St. Martin's Ln., WC2 (Covent Garden) |
020-7836-5837
City | Plantation Pl. | 15 Mincing Ln., EC3 (Bank/Monument) |
020-7283-3028 🛇
www.bertorelli.co.uk

"Large, flavourful helpings of varied pasta dishes" are the draws at
this "reliable" Italian chain in the City and Covent Garden;
"colleagues", families and "pre-theatre"-goers particularly appreciate the "reasonable prices" and "efficient service", if not the "humdrum decor" and "cramped" tables.

Bevis Marks 🛇 *British/Jewish*   ▽ 20 | 19 | 19 | £50

City | 4 Heneage Ln., EC3 (Aldgate/Liverpool St.) | 020-7283-2220 |
www.bevismarkstherestaurant.com

"Not your grandma's chopped liver and boiled chicken", but "innovative" kosher Jewish fare is what's served in "mounds" (along with
some Mod British dishes) at this "stylish" eatery next to Britain's
oldest synagogue; a City address means that the atmosphere in the
evenings sometimes "lacks", but it's "always full for lunch" with a
"captive clientele" that have no problem paying high prices.

☑ Bibendum *French*   23 | 24 | 23 | £63

South Kensington | Michelin Hse. | 81 Fulham Rd., SW3
(South Kensington) | 020-7581-5817 | www.bibendum.co.uk

Quipsters "never tyre" of this Brompton Cross New French "class
act" in the "iconic" Michelin building, an "elegant", "airy" space with
stained-glass windows that's quite "relaxed", partly because the
"lovely" servers give "no nonsense about turfing you off the table";
furthermore, the "kitchen astounds with its consistency and skill",
while an "excellent sommelier" impresses with "wonderful" wines, and
if the prices can "astound" too, the experience "doesn't disappoint."

Bibendum Oyster Bar *French/Seafood*   24 | 21 | 21 | £41

South Kensington | Michelin Hse. | 81 Fulham Rd., SW3
(South Kensington) | 020-7589-1480 | www.bibendum.co.uk

Since there's usually "not much waiting, even on weekends", fans often "pop in on impulse" for the "succulent seafood" and "superbly
matched wines" at this French venue in the Brompton Cross Michelin
tyre factory; the "informal" tiled environment (some think it "needs
more warmth") is a "nice change of pace" from Bibendum, its
grander upstairs parent, but some still find it "expensive."

	FOOD	DECOR	SERVICE	COST

Big Easy *American* — 17 | 15 | 15 | £33

Chelsea | 332-334 King's Rd., SW3 (Sloane Sq.) | 020-7352-4071 |
www.bigeasy.uk.com

"Pig out" on Southern U.S.-style "surf 'n' turf classics" at this "busy"
Chelsea outpost with a "fun", "diner"-esque setting; sceptics think
it "falls short" with "basic" fare and "haphazard service", but even
they welcome the "bargain" fees and "nightly live music" that's "a
treat" for "groups or parties."

NEW Bill's Produce Store *British* — ∇ 20 | 16 | 17 | £25

Covent Garden | St. Martin's Courtyard | 13 Slingsby Pl., WC2
(Covent Garden) | 020-7240-8183 | www.billsproducestore.co.uk

An "interesting blend of grocery store" and "fun" Traditional British
restaurant sums up this "exciting addition to Covent Garden", the
first London outpost of the Sussex-based chain; the space with
"walls stacked high with food" is "cosy" and often "packed", but it's
"worth the wait" for the "satisfying", "good-value" victuals.

Bincho Yakitori ☽ *Japanese* — 22 | 17 | 20 | £29

Soho | 16 Old Compton St., W1 (Tottenham Court Rd.) | 020-7287-9111 |
www.bincho.co.uk

"Tasty skewers" of charcoal-grilled meats and veggies can be "great
value" at this "simple" Soho yakitori specialist; however, since
they're pretty much "Japanese-style tapas", larger appetites may
have to "order a lot of dishes to fill up", and it's possible to "overdo
it and spend a fortune."

Bingham, The *British/European* — ∇ 25 | 23 | 23 | £58

Richmond | Bingham Hotel | 61-63 Petersham Rd., TW10 (Richmond) |
020-8940-0902 | www.thebingham.co.uk

"Striking just the right balance between tradition and innovation",
this "delightful" Richmond venue offers "rare quality amongst suburban hotel restaurants" thanks to its "superb" Mod British-Euro
cooking, a "stunning setting" by the Thames and "attentive service";
you can book one of the "brilliant rooms if you are too full to return
home", and maybe even crash a "wedding reception" too.

NEW Bistro du Vin *European* — - | - | - | E

Clerkenwell | 38-42 St. John St., EC1 (Farringdon) | 020-7490-9230 |
www.bistroduvinandbar.com

Unsurprisingly, an oenological theme pervades the national Hotel
du Vin chain's inaugural bistro, a cosy, dark Clerkenwell space with
a comfy, grey-hued lounge, a relaxed dining room with a U-shaped,
pewter-topped bar and an open kitchen doling out pricey, grill-
oriented Modern European fare; highlights of the potables include
16 fine wines by the glass, which flow from a high-tech dispenser.

Bistro K Ⓜ *European* — - | - | - | E

South Kensington | 117-119 Old Brompton Rd., SW7 (Gloucester Rd.) |
020-7373-7774 | www.bistro-k.co.uk

Advocates of this "little known" South Kensington Modern
European cite "exceptional food and superb service" as reasons it's

a "gem"; however, "confused" critics say it's "trying to be something it's not", since the "food aspires to high standards" whilst the "decor resembles a train-station waiting area."

Bistrot Bruno Loubet *French*   23 | 19 | 18 | £46

Clerkenwell | The Zetter | 86-88 Clerkenwell Rd., EC1 (Barbican/ Farringdon) | 020-7324-4455 | www.bistrotbrunoloubet.com

"Hail the return of Bruno Loubet" who, after a stint in Australia, is preparing his "superb" French "comfort food" at this "newish", "energetic" bistro with an "appealing, airy space" in Clerkenwell's "trendy" Zetter Hotel; "service is variable" and the prices are just a tad "expensive", but for the most part, it's "off to a flying start."

Bistrotheque *French*   23 | 22 | 22 | £41

Bethnal Green | 23-27 Wadeson St., E2 (Bethnal Green) | 020-8983-7900 | www.bistrotheque.com

"The main attraction" is the "eccentric, amusing cabaret shows downstairs", but this "unique" Bethnal Green venue with a "funky warehouse aesthetic" "holds its own" in the food department, with "reliable", "reasonably priced" French bistro staples; "easy service" is another reason to come, but it may be best to "take a taxi" to get there, as it's "quite far from a tube."

Black & Blue *Chophouse*   19 | 17 | 18 | £32

NEW **Bloomsbury** | 37 Berners St., W1T (Goodge St.) | 020-7436-0451
Marylebone | 90-92 Wigmore St., W1 (Bond St.) | 020-7486-1912
Borough | Borough Mkt. | 1-2 Rochester Walk, SE1 (London Bridge) | 020-7357-9922
South Kensington | 105 Gloucester Rd., SW7 (Gloucester Rd.) | 020-7244-7666 ●
Kensington | 215-217 Kensington Church St., W8 (Notting Hill Gate) | 020-7727-0004
www.blackandbluerestaurants.com

"Giant portions" of "reliable, well-priced" steaks and a "remarkably juicy and delicious burger" are the "strengths" of this chophouse chain; sure, the "cookie-cutter" settings "lack atmosphere" (though the banquettes are quite "comfortable") and service is only "ok-ish", but it's a "safe choice", especially for a "last-minute" "walk-in."

Blakes *Eclectic*   22 | 23 | 21 | £64

South Kensington | Blakes Hotel | 33 Roland Gdns., SW7 (Gloucester Rd./ South Kensington) | 020-7370-6701 | www.blakeshotels.com

"Still going (fairly) strong" after many years, this "cosy enclave" in a "luxe" South Kensington hotel executes "exotic", "delicious" all-day Eclectic cuisine whose "high prices" most feel are "worth every penny"; though a bit of a "time warp", the "gorgeous", "perfectly lit" black-lacquered setting is the scene of many a "romantic" "seduction", with "charming" service that knows how to be discreet.

Bleeding Heart ⊠ *French*   22 | 20 | 21 | £48

Holborn | 4 Bleeding Heart Yard, off Greville St., EC1 (Farringdon) | 020-7242-8238

(continued)

| | FOOD | DECOR | SERVICE | COST |

(continued)

Bleeding Heart Tavern 🗗 *British*

Holborn | 19 Greville St., EC1 (Farringdon) | 020-7242-2056
www.bleedingheart.co.uk

In an "old and charming" courtyard off "Diamond Row" (aka Hatton Garden) in Holborn, this French venue splits its efforts between an "atmospheric", bi-level restaurant and, across the square, an "informal bistro" with alfresco tables, both offering "well-cooked", "hearty, reasonably priced food", a "winning wine list" and "attentive service"; there's also a "quirky", "old-fashioned tavern" around the corner, where simpler, cheaper British dishes are doled out.

Bluebird *British* `16` `19` `17` `£44`

Chelsea | 350 King's Rd., SW3 (Sloane Sq.) | 020-7559-1000 |
www.bluebird-restaurant.co.uk

A "chic", "buzzy" restaurant serving Modern British dishes is augmented with an "intense bar" fuelled by "awesome cocktails" and a "small cafe" offering "snacks, light meals" and a "summer forecourt" at this "large" King's Road complex in a remodeled 1920s garage, which also houses a gourmet retail section; tough customers cite "mediocre", "too-expensive" food and "iffy service" as a sign it's "past its prime", whilst others are more forgiving, mainly due to the "amusing people-watching."

Blue Elephant *Thai* `21` `24` `21` `£43`

Fulham | 4-6 Fulham Broadway, SW6 (Fulham Broadway) |
020-7385-6595 | www.blueelephant.com

The "over-the-top" "rainforest setting" of this Fulham Thai, decked out with "picturesque" "streams, bridges and plants", "still draws crowds", "many tourists" amongst them; the "wide variety" of "solid" fare may be "expensive" for the type, but most call it "quite a treat", whether for "business, pleasure" or a "special occasion", with mostly "attentive service" thrown into the mix.

Blueprint Café *European* `18` `20` `19` `£41`

Tower Bridge | Design Museum | 28 Shad Thames, SE1 (London Bridge/Tower Hill) | 020-7378-7031 | www.blueprintcafe.co.uk

"Fabulous views of the Thames, City" and Tower Bridge (if you're "lucky" enough to be seated by the "large" windows) form the backdrop for "solid", "well-presented" Modern European fare at this "delightful", "relaxed" cafe in the Design Museum; the menu's "well priced, as is the wine list", and as for service, it's wholly "helpful."

🗷 Bob Bob Ricard 🗗Ⓜ *British* `20` `27` `22` `£47`

Soho | 1 Upper James St., W1 (Piccadilly Circus) | 020-3145-1000 |
www.bobbobricard.com

In a "lavish" if somewhat "kitsch" setting "reminiscent of the Orient Express" (it looks like a turquoise "railway carriage"), this "distinctive" Soho Modern British venue offers "cute touches" in each booth, like "a red panic button for emergency champagne"; surveyors split as to whether the "lovely food" is "affordable" or "overpriced", but most everyone marvels at the "super value in fine wines" on offer.

	FOOD	DECOR	SERVICE	COST

Bocca di Lupo ● *Italian* 24 | 18 | 20 | £43
Soho | 12 Archer St., W1 (Piccadilly Circus) | 020-7734-2223 |
www.boccadilupo.com

Gelupo *Italian*
Soho | 7 Archer St., W1 (Piccadilly Circus) | 020-7287-5555 |
www.gelupo.com

Come "curious to sample food that you've never eaten" at this
Soho Italian where the "robust regional" dishes are available in
"large or small servings" and complemented by "serious wines",
all at costs that "won't break the bank"; the "intimate",
"cramped" premises with a counter overlooking the kitchen
"buzz" with "so much energy", it's lucky most of the staff "cope
well without getting ragged"; P.S. "top off the meal" with "amazing"
gelato at Gelupo across the street.

Bodeans *BBQ* 19 | 13 | 16 | £23
Soho | 10 Poland St., W1 (Oxford Circus) | 020-7287-7575
City | 16 Byward St., EC3 (Tower Hill) | 020-7488-3883
Clapham | 169 Clapham High St., SW4 (Clapham Common) |
020-7622-4248
Fulham | 4 Broadway Chambers, SW6 (Fulham Broadway) |
020-7610-0440
www.bodeansbbq.com

"Best enjoyed when thoroughly hungry", this chain doles out
"feast"-sized portions of "tasty" "American-style" barbecue for
"budget" rates; the setting is "nothing pretty", and service spins
from "cheerful" to "scatterbrained", but for "homesick expats" and
"meat-guzzling sports fans" (U.S. football is broadcast on "big
screens"), "it'll do."

Boisdale ⌧ *British/Scottish* 20 | 20 | 18 | £56
Belgravia | 15 Eccleston St., SW1 (Victoria) | 020-7730-6922
NEW Canary Wharf | Cabot Pl. W., E14 (Canary Wharf) |
020-7715-5818 Ⓜ
City | Swedeland Ct. | 202 Bishopsgate, EC2 (Liverpool St.) |
020-7283-1763
www.boisdale.co.uk

"Reminiscent of a bonnie fishing lodge", this "pricey" Belgravia
venue (with Canary Wharf and City offshoots) is a "boys' club, true
and true", with a "reliable" steak-heavy Traditional British menu
that's laced with "great" Scottish dishes ("love the haggis"); a "relaxed cigar terrace", "incredible single malts" and nightly live jazz si-
multaneously "keep things interesting" and compensate when the
"old-school" service gets "disorganised."

Bombay Bicycle Club *Indian* 18 | 16 | 17 | £28
Clapham | 95 Nightingale Ln., SW12 (Clapham S.) | 020-8673-6217
Holland Park | 128 Holland Park Ave., W11 (Holland Park) |
020-7727-7335
www.thebombaybicycleclub.co.uk

"Big flavours and interesting choices" abound on an Indian menu
that's "more colonial than authentic" at this "kitsch" duo in Clapham

and Holland Park (which maybe "could use a face-lift"); opinions on service swing from "reliable" to "under-trained", just like views on the cost alternate between "nice value" and "rather steep", but in any event, takeaway seems dependably "great."

Bombay Brasserie ● *Indian*   23 | 22 | 21 | £46
South Kensington | Courtfield Rd., SW7 (Gloucester Rd.) | 020-7370-4040 | www.bombaybrasserielondon.com
"Around a long time", this "luxurious" Indian with "plenty of space" in South Ken is "as good as ever", with "refined", sometimes "unusual" "regional" dishes that are "efficiently served" (and "rather expensive"); if some lament that it's not the "grande dame" it once was, it's still "several steps above the usual" and at least worth a visit at the weekend for the all-you-can-eat lunch buffet.

Bombay Palace ● *Indian*   21 | 22 | 21 | £34
Bayswater | 50 Connaught St., W2 (Lancaster Gate/Paddington) | 020-7723-8855 | www.bombay-palace.co.uk
The "bright", "plush" setting "bustles" at this Bayswater branch of a "quality" international chain, where the "pricey" (compared to others of its ilk) but "worth it" "classic" Indian dishes "wake up your taste buds"; "courteous" servers are another reason it's "highly recommended" by supporters.

NEW Bond & Brook Ⓩ *Eclectic*   - | - | - | E
Mayfair | Fenwick | 63 New Bond St., 2nd fl., W1 (Bond St./Oxford Circus) | 020-7629-0273 | www.rhubarb.net
A striking oval pewter bar dominates this glossy, "fun" new fashionista hub on the second floor of Fenwick, a "charming respite" where "ladies who lunch" nosh on pricey tapas-focused Eclectic dishes that ebb and flow according to the season; P.S. the name comes from the store's location, straddling New Bond and Brook Streets in Mayfair.

Bonds *French*   21 | 22 | 19 | £54
City | Threadneedles Hotel | 5 Threadneedle St., EC2 (Bank) | 020-7657-8088 | www.theetoncollection.com
"Well-spaced tables" in an "airy" "converted-banking-hall" setting make this eatery in the City's "trendy boutique Threadneedles Hotel" suitable for "power breakfasts", lunches and "formal dinners" with "clients"; "adventurous" foodies say the New French cuisine "rarely disappoints", and though some suspect that "service is not their strong point", quite a few feel it's "reliable."

Books for Cooks Ⓢ Ⓜ *Eclectic*   23 | 19 | 18 | £21
Notting Hill | 4 Blenheim Cres., W11 (Ladbroke Grove/ Notting Hill Gate) | 020-7221-1992 | www.booksforcooks.com
A "dream for cookbook lovers", this "cute", "cosy" bookstore is "made better by having a few solid lunch items" for sale, listed on "excellent" Eclectic daily "changing menus" and prepared by "eager" staff in the test kitchen/cafe at the back; it could possibly be the "best value in Notting Hill", but be sure to "get there early-ish, because it sometimes runs out of food."

	FOOD	DECOR	SERVICE	COST

Botanist, The ● *British* — **17** | **19** | **17** | **£41**

Chelsea | 7 Sloane Sq., SW1 (Sloane Sq.) | 020-7730-0077 |
www.thebotanistonsloanesquare.com

Many "go for the scene" at this "trendy" Chelsea spot's bar, where
"noisy" "Sloane Rangers and cougars" spill out onto the street in the
evening; and although it's merely "ok", the "uncomplicated" all-day
Modern British fare in the somewhat "quieter" dining room (bedecked
with "botanist drawings") is its own draw, as it's "fairly priced."

Boundary, The *British/French* — **20** | **21** | **21** | **£55**

Shoreditch | 2-4 Boundary St., E2 (Liverpool St./Old St.) |
020-7729-1051 | www.theboundary.co.uk

A bit "off the beaten track" in a former Shoreditch warehouse, this
"cool", "pricey" complex from Sir Terence Conran comprises a basement dining room featuring "well-executed" Classic French–Anglo
fare and a "fabulous wine list", a "quick" cafe called Albion and a
roof terrace with "amazing" views, a fireplace and a "tasty" grill-
oriented menu; meanwhile, "friendly" service reigns throughout.

Bountiful Cow ☒ *Chophouse* — ∇ **19** | **14** | **19** | **£28**

Holborn | 51 Eagle St., WC1 (Holborn) | 020-7404-0200 |
www.thebountifulcow.co.uk

At this chophouse in a hard-to-find Holborn street, the "decent
quality meat" and "great value" make it easy to forgive the
"cramped", "rather shabby surroundings", which are marked by
cowboy movie posters on the walls.

Bradley's *British/French* — ∇ **20** | **15** | **19** | **£43**

Swiss Cottage | 25 Winchester Rd., NW3 (Swiss Cottage) |
020-7722-3457 | www.bradleysnw3.co.uk

Though the "solid", "well-presented" Modern British fare with
"French leanings" is "not cheap", most find the prices "fair" at this
Swiss Cottage spot that boasts "friendly" service; the space may be
a bit "indifferently decorated", but still, locals feel "lucky to have
such a good restaurant so close to home", whilst showgoers appreciate that it's "convenient for Hampstead Theatre."

Brasserie Blanc ☒ *French* — ∇ **20** | **19** | **20** | **£42**

City | 60 Threadneedle St., EC2 (Bank) | 020-7710-9440 |
www.brasserieblanc.com

"As you would expect given the location" in the former London Stock
Exchange, this "bright", "informal" City outpost of respected chef
Raymond Blanc's nationwide Gallic brasserie chain attracts "mostly
business types"; "good everyday French fodder" fills the menu, but
critics say it "should be better" given the slightly "pricey" rates.

NEW Brasserie Joël *French* — **-** | **-** | **-** | **E**

Waterloo | Park Plaza Westminster Bridge Hotel |
Park Plaza Westminster Bridge, SE1 (Lambeth North) |
020-7620-7272 | www.brasseriejoel.co.uk

Perched at the Waterloo end of Westminster Bridge, with the Houses
of Parliament at the other side, this French arrival in the Park Plaza

Hotel is the new home of well-travelled chef Joël Antunes (ex Les Saveurs in Mayfair from a decade ago); the moodily lit, red-hued dining room offers a refined, pricey menu laced with classic bistro fare, and there's also a sushi bar, though it's not under Antunes' tutelage.

Brasserie Roux *French*

22	22	22	£45

St. James's | Sofitel St. James London | 8 Pall Mall, SW1 (Piccadilly Circus) | 020-7968-2900 | www.brasserieroux.com
You can sample consultant chef Albert Roux's "fantastic" French brasserie fare and "not break the bank" at this Sofitel St. James dining room whose "lightly formal" setting feels "welcoming" thanks to the "warm" atmosphere and "friendly staff"; it's a "good place for a power breakfast", whilst early evening, it offers "one of the best prix fixe pre-theatre bargains" around.

Brasserie St. Jacques ⓧ *French*

21	19	20	£48

St. James's | 33 St. James's St., SW1 (Green Park) | 020-7839-1007 | www.brasseriestjacques.co.uk
St. James's diners utilise this "mainstay" for "quick" meals of "reliable" French brasserie fare complemented by "excellent" wines; if its "consistency" comes "at the price of being slightly dull", well then, at least the bill won't be too high.

NEW Brawn *British/French*

▽ 23	19	25	£43

Shoreditch | 49 Columbia Rd., E2 (Hoxton) | 020-7729-5692
Expect "astonishingly big tastes at astonishingly small prices" (comparatively) at this "welcome addition" to Shoreditch, a Terroirs sibling whose "earthy", "hearty" Modern British-French fare (meant for sharing) matches the "stripped-down styling" of the nevertheless "comfortable" setting; a "cool crowd" generates "great buzz", as do staffers who are "clued up" not only about the regular menu but the wine list as well, including "organic and biodynamic offerings."

Brindisa, Tapas *Spanish*

23	17	18	£33

Soho | 46 Broadwick St., W1 (Oxford Circus/Tottenham Court Rd.) | 020-7534-1690 | www.tierrabrindisa.com
Borough | Borough Mkt. | 18-20 Southwark St., SE1 (London Bridge) | 020-7357-8880 | www.tapasbrindisa.com

Brindisa, Casa *Spanish*

South Kensington | 7-9 Exhibition Rd., SW7 (South Kensington) | 020-7590-0008 | www.casabrindisa.com
"Flavoursome tapas with a twist" await at this "buzzy" Spanish trio luring a "hip" crowd for "fab" fare and charcuterie backed by a "terrific wine list"; usually "efficient" staff work the "stylish", "noisy" surroundings, and whilst prices are "decent", overzealous orderers find that the bill "can grow quickly"; P.S. the "bustling" Borough Market original doesn't take reservations, so "be prepared to wait."

Brinkley's *Eclectic*

▽ 17	15	16	£47

Chelsea | 47 Hollywood Rd., SW10 (Earl's Ct./South Kensington) | 020-7351-1683 | www.brinkleys.com
Known "forever" (over three decades) as a "people-watching fest", this venue off Fulham Road "feels more like a club than a restau-

rant", but the "no-pretentions" Eclectic grub is "reliable" and offered along with "great wines at shop prices"; if there's one grievance, it's that service can be "overwhelmed" at weekends when the "place is booming."

NEW Broadway Bar & Grill *British*   - | - | - | M

Fulham | 474-476 Fulham Broadway, SW6 (Fulham Broadway) | 020-7610-3137 | www.broadwaybandg.co.uk

The busy Fulham Broadway junction has been joined by this "casual" arrival with a "mellow vibe" and a British gastropub menu that won't break the bank; the earthy, cavernous ground-floor environs feature a long mahogany bar, Parliament-green banquettes and a liberal sprinkling of giant TV screens, while upstairs resides the quieter Brasa, specialising in charcoal-grilled meats.

Brompton Bar & Grill *British/European*   22 | 20 | 21 | £43

Knightsbridge | 243 Brompton Rd., SW3 (Knightsbridge/
South Kensington) | 020-7589-8005 | www.bromptonbarandgrill.com

"Deliberately simple" Modern British–Euro cooking proves most "agreeable" at this "attractive", "intimate" Knightsbridge bistro with "friendly service" and a "corking wine list at reasonable prices"; the fare is also "great value for money", and the "convivial" atmosphere further makes it "worth trying."

Brompton Quarter Brasserie *Eclectic*   19 | 18 | 16 | £34

Knightsbridge | 223-225 Brompton Rd., SW3 (Knightsbridge/
South Kensington) | 020-7225-2107 | www.bqbrasserie.com

It "always seems busy" at this Brompton Road "bright spot" boasting a "crisp" setting and many "crowd-pleasing offerings" on the affordable all-day Eclectic menu; service can be "utterly charming" and "accommodating", but be warned, it can veer toward "snooty."

Browns *British*   17 | 18 | 18 | £36

Covent Garden | 82-84 St. Martin's Ln., WC2 (Leicester Sq.) |
020-7497-5050

Mayfair | 47 Maddox St., W1 (Bond St./Oxford Circus) | 020-7491-4565

Canary Wharf | Hertsmere Rd., E14 (Canary Wharf/
West India Quay DLR) | 020-7987-9777

City | 8 Old Jewry, EC2 (Bank) | 020-7606-6677 🗷

Tower Bridge | Shad Thames, SE1 (London Bridge) | 020-7378-1700

Islington | 9 Islington Green, N1 (Angel) | 020-7226-2555
www.browns-restaurants.com

An "old reliable", this "ubiquitous" Traditional British chain offers a "good variety" of "predictable" "staples"; the "comfortable, spacious" environs are "not massively exciting", but prices are "reasonable", plus it fits the bill for a "quick bite before the theatre" and there's "never too long to wait for a table."

Brula *French*   - | - | - | E

Twickenham | 43 Crown Rd., St. Margaret's, TW1
(St. Margarets (London) Rail) | 020-8892-0602 | www.brula.co.uk

Dwelling amongst an unassuming parade of shops near Twickenham, this "excellent bistro" "never fails" in terms of its "constantly evolving", "excellent-value and great-tasting" French fare; there's "nothing to complain about" regarding its classic setting either, with old-fashioned chandeliers inside and a handful of pavement tables outside.

Buen Ayre Argentinean ∇ 26 14 21 £41
Hackney | 50 Broadway Mkt., E8 (Bethnal Green) | 020-7275-9900 | www.buenayre.co.uk

"You will easily forgive the decor" (or lack thereof), because the grilled steaks are "amazing" and "value"-priced to boot at this *"muy bien"* Argentinean "meatfest" in a "trendy corner" of Hackney; it's also blessed with "pleasant" staff who are "insightful with the wine selection" whilst remaining strict about the twice-per-night seating policy.

Builders Arms British 17 17 15 £25
Chelsea | 13 Britten St., SW3 (Sloane Sq./South Kensington) | 020-7349-9040 | www.geronimo-inns.co.uk

"Comfy, casual and best with a crowd" sums up this "popular" Chelsea gastropub with "fireplaces, rugged furniture" and Traditional British tucker that, whilst achieving "no peaks", is sufficiently "pleasant"; if the service doesn't rate high, at least it's "great value for money."

Bull & Last British 23 19 20 £35
Kentish Town | 168 Highgate Rd., NW5 (Kentish Town) | 020-7267-3641

"Amazing", "seasonally changing" Traditional British dishes, some for "adventurous eaters", plus a "fun, jovial" atmosphere make it easy to "feel at home" at this "cosy, unpretentious" Kentish Town gastropub (whose building dates back 250 years); though usually "packed" on any given day, the Sunday roast is a particularly "big attraction", for which you should "book far in advance."

Bumpkin British 20 19 20 £36
South Kensington | 102 Old Brompton Rd., SW7 (Gloucester Rd./South Kensington) | 020-7341-0802
Notting Hill | 209 Westbourne Park Rd., W11 (Westbourne Park) | 020-7243-9818
www.bumpkinuk.com

"Trendy, young Notting Hill types" fill up this "homey", "little" "hangout" and its younger South Ken offshoot purveying "straightforward" Modern British "home cooking" with a seasonal bent, plus "artisanal ales" and "eclectic wines"; a few find the fare "disappointing", but a "comfortable" atmosphere redeems, and "friendly" (if sometimes "harried") staff lend a pleasantly "laid-back" vibe; P.S. a branch is slated for Westfield Stratford City, the new shopping centre across from the Olympic Park.

Buona Sera Italian - - - M
Battersea | 22-26 Northcote Rd., SW11 (Clapham Junction Rail) | 020-7228-9925 ●
Chelsea | 289A King's Rd., SW3 (Sloane Sq.) | 020-7352-8827

"Good job" applaud the "big groups" who depend on these "busy" trattorias for "great" pizza and other "reliable" Italian fare, plus "fun" service and reasonable prices; Battersea's midnight closing hour makes it a "late-night dining" destination, whilst the Chelsea branch is notable for tables reached by mini ladders, for those who like to dine "Spider-Man-style."

☑ Busaba Eathai *Thai*   23 | 19 | 17 | £24

Bloomsbury | 22 Store St., WC1 (Goodge St.) | 020-7299-7900
Marylebone | 8-13 Bird St., W1 (Bond St.) | 020-7518-8080
Soho | 106-110 Wardour St., W1 (Piccadilly Circus/
Tottenham Court Rd.) | 020-7255-8686
Soho | 35 Panton St., SW1 (Piccadilly Circus) | 020-7930-0088
Shoreditch | 313-319 Old St., EC1 (Old Street) | 020-7729-0808
NEW Shepherd's Bush | Westfield Shopping Ctr. | Ariel Way, lower ground fl., W12 (Shepherd's Bush) | 020-3249-1919
www.busaba.com
"Be prepared to queue" at this "über-busy" Thai chain laying out "fantastic", "fresh" fare on communal tables in "functional"-"trendy" spaces; "fast" service and "bargain prices" make it a "staple" for "quick fill-ups", although the "boisterous" atmosphere is "the antithesis of Zen."

Butcher & Grill *British*   17 | 19 | 17 | £36

Battersea | 39-41 Parkgate Rd., SW11 (Clapham Junction Rail) | 020-7924-3999
Wimbledon | 33 High St., SW19 (Wimbledon) | 020-8944-8269
www.thebutcherandgrill.com
It's a "great concept" say customers of this Traditional British duo in Battersea and Wimbledon, a "convenient combination of restaurant/deli/butcher" with "family-friendly" atmospherics and "value"; but whilst the "meat is usually very good, the other food can be hit-or-miss", just like the service.

Butlers Wharf Chop House *Chophouse*   22 | 20 | 20 | £44

Tower Bridge | Butlers Wharf Bldg. | 36E Shad Thames, SE1
(London Bridge/Tower Hill) | 020-7403-3403 | www.chophouse.co.uk
With "outrageously good views of Tower Bridge" ("be warned, not all tables have them"), this "dependable" riverside chophouse is "ideal for entertaining guests" or a "relaxed after-work dinner"; the "solid" fare, including a "luxurious breakfast", is ferried by "friendly, attentive" staff, and whilst fees are somewhat high, "value" is found at the bar and in prix fixe lunches.

Byron *Burgers*   19 | 15 | 17 | £20

NEW Covent Garden | 33-35 Wellington St., WC2 (Covent Garden) | 020-7420-9850
NEW Soho | 24-28 Charing Cross Rd., WC2 (Leicester Sq.) | 020-7557-9830
Canary Wharf | Cabot Pl. E., 2nd fl., E14 (Canary Wharf) | 020-7715-9360
Kennington | 93-95 Old Brompton Rd., SW7 (Gloucester Rd./South Kensington) | 020-7590-9040
NEW Islington | 341 Upper St., N1 (Angel) | 020-7704-7620
Chelsea | 300 King's Rd., SW3 (Sloane Sq./South Kensington) | 020-7352-6040

(continued)

(continued)

Byron

NEW **Earl's Court** | 242 Earl's Court Rd., SW5 (Earl's Ct.) | 020-7370-9300

South Kensington | 75 Gloucester Rd., SW7 (Gloucester Rd.) | 020-7244-0700

Kensington | 222 Kensington High St., W8 (High St. Kensington) | 020-7361-1717

Shepherd's Bush | Westfield Shopping Ctr. | Ariel Way, mezzanine, W12 (Shepherd's Bush) | 020-8743-7755

www.byronhamburgers.com

Additional locations throughout London

"Serving its purpose well", this "bustling" American-style burger chain with "funky", somewhat "industrial" decor is a "safe" bet for "tasty" burgers (fans of a "non-fussy experience" appreciate that it's "not trying to win the wacky-toppings competition") and "to-die-for" fries, both potato and courgette; "reasonable prices" yield "kid-tastic weekends", when the normally "happy", "prompt" service can become "maddeningly slow."

Cadogan Arms *British*

| 15 | 14 | 13 | £33 |

Chelsea | 298 King's Rd., SW3 (Sloane Sq./South Kensington) | 020-7352-6500 | www.thecadoganarmschelsea.com

Because it's "relatively low-priced for the neighbourhood", this Modern British gastropub "on a busy/touristy section of the King's Road" is "usually crowded" – but it's "not the best value for money" because the fare is often "disappointing" and the service "erratic"; nevertheless, with TVs airing "the big rugby games" at the bar and "billiards upstairs", it can be "fun."

Café Boheme ● *French*

| 18 | 16 | 18 | £35 |

Soho | 13-17 Old Compton St., W1 (Leicester Sq./Tottenham Court Rd.) | 020-7734-0623 | www.cafeboheme.co.uk

"Always busy but never rushed", this "cheerful" Soho bistro is a "good French option in terms of price, quality and location", be it for breakfast or a "late dinner" (open until 2 AM); the dining room is traditionally "tranquil compared to the bar" and the pavement seating, whilst "chatty" staff prove "skilled" whichever area they're serving.

Café des Amis ●🗷 *French*

| 18 | 17 | 17 | £40 |

Covent Garden | 11-14 Hanover Pl., WC2 (Covent Garden) | 020-7379-3444 | www.cafedesamis.co.uk

Concurrently "relaxing" and "buzzy", this Covent Garden long-timer features a "pleasant" ground-floor cafe and patio serving "reliable", "reasonably priced" French dishes ("the set menu is a bargain") and a "basement bar that's good for pre-theatre wine and cheese"; however, some feel that the name's a "misnomer", as "service is neither friendly nor attentive", and on top of that, the decor is "run-of-the-mill."

🆉 Café Japan 🅼 *Japanese*

| 27 | 10 | 21 | £32 |

Golders Green | 626 Finchley Rd., NW11 (Golders Green) | 020-8455-6854

"Glorious", "luxuriant" sushi and sashimi sold in "large slices" for "cheap" prices makes this Golders Green Japanese "popular", and

| | FOOD | DECOR | SERVICE | COST |

sometimes "chaotic", so "booking is more than advisable"; the "neon-lit" decor in the "noisy", "tiny" room may be "old and tired", but "efficient", "caring service" compensates.

NEW Cafe Luc European
— | — | — | E

Marylebone | 50 Marylebone High St., W1 (Baker St./Regent Park) | 020-7258-9878 | www.cafeluc.com

Green hued, wood floored and laced with design touches emulating the grand cafes of Europe, this "elegant new place" on Marylebone High Street produces Modern Euro fare that's "delicious", although a few early samplers believe it's a bit "overpriced for what it is"; however, the set "lunch is a good deal", and "attentive", "friendly service" also gets the thumbs-up.

Café Med Mediterranean
▽ 17 | 17 | 17 | £31

St. John's Wood | 21 Loudoun Rd., NW8 (St. John's Wood) | 020-7625-1222 | www.cafemed.co.uk

St. John's Wood residents "rely" on this local for "sizable dishes" of "decent, reasonably priced" Med fare; those who think the "interior needs a spruce-up" "try to sit by the fireplace" in winter or only "come in summer when the terrace is absolutely divine."

Cafe Pacifico ❷ Mexican
19 | 16 | 17 | £31

Covent Garden | 5 Langley St., WC2 (Covent Garden) | 020-7379-7728 | www.cafepacifico-laperla.com

"It's been around a long time and never disappoints" aver advocates of this "not fancy" yet nevertheless "popular party destination" in Covent Garden; the Mexican fare is wholly "decent", but it's the "scrummy margaritas" and "interesting selection of tequilas" at the "crowded bar" that really make meals here "fun."

Café Rouge French
15 | 15 | 14 | £26

Covent Garden | 34 Wellington St., WC2 (Covent Garden) | 020-7836-0998

Knightsbridge | 27-31 Basil St., SW3 (Knightsbridge) | 020-7584-2345

Canary Wharf | 10 Cabot Sq., E14 (Canary Wharf) | 020-7537-9696

Hampstead | 38-39 High St., NW3 (Hampstead) | 020-7435-4240

Highgate | 6-7 South Grove, N6 (Highgate) | 020-8342-9797

St. John's Wood | 120 St. John's Wood High St., NW8 (St. John's Wood) | 020-7722-8366

Clapham | 40 Abbeville Rd., SW4 (Clapham S.) | 020-8673-3399

Dulwich | 84 Park Hall Rd., SE21 (West Dulwich Rail) | 020-8766-0070

Chiswick | 227-229 Chiswick High Rd., W4 (Chiswick Park) | 020-8742-7447

Shepherd's Bush | 98-100 Shepherd's Bush Rd., W6 (Shepherd's Bush) | 020-7602-7732

www.caferouge.co.uk

Additional locations throughout London

"You know what you're getting every time you walk into" this bistro chain: "reliable" if "predictable" French "staples" in an "informal", "unpretentious" setting; even if it's ultimately "underwhelming", with "spotty service" too, it remains "popular" because it's open all day and the "prices won't make you see rouge."

	FOOD	DECOR	SERVICE	COST

Café Spice Namasté ☒ Indian
25 | 17 | 22 | £42

City | 16 Prescot St., E1 (Aldgate/Tower Hill) | 020-7488-9242 | www.cafespice.co.uk

"An adventure in eating, even for those who think they know Indian" is what's on offer at chef-owner Cyrus Todiwala's "terrific" eatery in a somewhat "hard-to-find" City location (near-ish Tower Bridge); some surveyers feel the "quirky", "colourful" "decor leaves a lot to be desired", but "high ceilings" that "absorb the noise" and "friendly", "helpful" service help make it "an easy place to like."

Caffe Caldesi ☒ Italian
21 | 16 | 19 | £37

Marylebone | 118 Marylebone Ln., W1 (Bond St.) | 020-7935-1144 | www.caldesi.com

Serving up "hearty", "quality" "Tuscan temptations" for a "fair" price, this "charming" Marylebone trattoria houses a "busy", "casual" downstairs cafe "for people in a hurry" and an upstairs with "pleasant" frescoes for more "special" meals; there's also a small pavement dining area when the weather's warm, whilst "lovely people" service the entire venue.

Cambio de Tercio Spanish
23 | 17 | 20 | £49

South Kensington | 163 Old Brompton Rd., SW5 (Gloucester Rd./South Kensington) | 020-7244-8970 | www.cambiodetercio.co.uk

"High-quality" Spanish cuisine with "a nouvelle twist", including "divine" tapas, is complemented by an "amazing wine list" and "friendly service" at this "hectic" South Ken Iberian; prices can be "on the expensive side", but it's "worth a visit" because it's such "great fun."

Camden Brasserie European
∇ 19 | 15 | 18 | £36

Camden Town | 9-11 Jamestown Rd., NW1 (Camden Town) | 020-7482-2114 | www.camdenbrasserie.co.uk

Nearly 30 years old, this Camden "neighbourhood brasserie" "continues to be enjoyable" thanks to its "reliable", "not overly expensive" Modern European fare; what's more, "cheerful service" proves to be as "welcoming" as the contemporary surroundings, adorned with wallpaper that looks like shelves of books.

Camino Spanish
∇ 19 | 16 | 18 | £33

NEW Canary Wharf | 28 Westferry Circus, E14 (Westferry) | 020-7239-9077

King's Cross | 3 Varnishers Yard, Regents Quarter, N1 (King's Cross) | 020-7841-7331

www.camino.uk.com

"Tempting tapas" and "pleasing" wines are served with "finesse" at this unpretentious King's Cross Spaniard, whose new Canary Wharf offshoot boasts deck seating in summer; some find them "too noisy", whilst others appreciate them as "nice places" for a "quick" nibble or to relax with "friends after work."

Canteen British
16 | 14 | 15 | £29

Marylebone | 55 Baker St., W1 (Dorset St.) | 0845-686-1122

Canary Wharf | Park Pavilion, 40 Canada Sq., E14 (Canary Wharf) | 084-5686-1122

(continued)

Canteen

Shoreditch | 2 Crispin Pl., E1 (Liverpool St.) | 0845-686-1122
South Bank | Royal Festival Hall | Belvedere Rd., SE1 (Waterloo) |
0845-686-1122
www.canteen.co.uk

The "retro" British menu is a "trip down memory lane" at this casual chainlet where both the "simple", "ho-hum" fare and "vast", "sterile" settings with "shared tables" have a "school-meal feel" about them; service can be "haphazard" too, but at least the price is right.

Cantina del Ponte *Italian*

| 20 | 16 | 20 | £37 |

Tower Bridge | Butlers Wharf Bldg. | 36C Shad Thames, SE1 (London Bridge/Tower Hill) | 020-7403-5403 | www.cantinadelponte.co.uk

From alfresco tables "right out on the quay", the view of Tower Bridge is "unbeatable" say supporters of this "popular neighbour-hood place" that offers an "unfussy" Italian menu (with "great set-price" options at lunch) alongside a "reasonable wine list"; "friendly service" adds to its appeal – "as long as you're not in a hurry."

NEW Cantina Laredo ● *Mexican*

| - | - | - | E |

Covent Garden | St. Martin's Courtyard | 10 Upper St. Martin's Ln., WC2 (Covent Garden) | 020-7420-0630 | www.cantinalaredo.co.uk

Located in Covent Garden, this first U.K. outpost of the "successful" U.S. chain offers its pricey menu of "tasty", "higher-end Mexican" fare in attractive digs marked by large windows and orange-and-burgundy walls; takeaway is available, but tipplers have a hard time tearing themselves away from the limestone bar, where bartenders "really know how to make a margarita."

Cantina Vinopolis *Eclectic/Mediterranean*

| ∇ 18 | 19 | 20 | £35 |

South Bank | Vinopolis Museum | 1 Bank End, SE1 (London Bridge) | 020-7940-8333 | www.cantinavinopolis.com

Given its location in a South Bank oenological museum, it's little surprise "the emphasis is on the wines" – and indeed, "the selection is very impressive" – at this airy Eclectic-Med with vaulted ceilings and "minimalistic" decor; the menu is "good if not massively impressive", however it is designed for some "interesting pairings", with which "enthusiastic" staff can assist.

NEW Cantinetta *Italian*

| - | - | - | E |

Putney | 162-164 Lower Richmond Rd., SW15 (Putney Bridge) | 020-8780-3131 | www.cantinetta.co.uk

Rebecca Mascarenhas (Sonny's) has teamed up with a chef protégé of Giorgio Locatelli to create this casual Italian in Putney, which marries a bright, easy-going setting (marked by wood floors and canvas seats) with a polished, pricey menu and 80-strong, Boot-only wine list; cheaper *tiraditi* (finger food) are served at the high-stooled bar, whilst an attractive terrace beckons when the weather allows.

	FOOD	DECOR	SERVICE	COST

☑ Capital Restaurant *French* | 26 | 23 | 26 | £78 |

Knightsbridge | Capital Hotel | 22-24 Basil St., SW3 (Knightsbridge) |
020-7591-1202 | www.capitalhotel.co.uk

"It's like eating in the lord of the manor's dining room" at this "elegant" enclave in the "boutique" Capital Hotel in Knightsbridge, where chef Jerome Ponchelle turns out "impeccable" New French dishes with a few "twists" supported by an "excellent" wine selection (don't miss the "wonderful cheese trolley" either); service is "formal but not stuffy", the atmosphere "quiet" and "charming", and if dinner prices are a "splurge", the set lunch is a relative "bargain."

Caraffini ●☑ *Italian* | 21 | 18 | 23 | £44 |

Chelsea | 61-63 Lower Sloane St., SW1 (Sloane Sq.) | 020-7259-0235 |
www.caraffini.co.uk

"After the Royal Court" or the "Chelsea Flower Show", it's "worth beating a path to the door" of this "traditional" Italian "near Sloane Square", which is "always in full swing" with folks toasting with pours from the "extensive but not expensive wine list"; the somewhat "pricey" cuisine is "solid", whilst service is "even better": "warm, enthusiastic", even "flirty."

Caravaggio ☑ *Italian* | 19 | 18 | 19 | £41 |

City | 107-112 Leadenhall St., EC3 (Bank/Monument) |
020-7626-6206 | www.etruscarestaurants.com

"Conveniently located if you work in the City", this low-profile, high-ceilinged former banking hall "never lets you down" for an "upmarket Italian" meal; whilst a few feel it's "looking rather tired decorwise", the "ambience is fine" due mostly to "helpful" staff; P.S. closed at weekends.

Caravan *European* | 22 | 21 | 21 | £28 |

Clerkenwell | 11-13 Exmouth Mkt., EC1 (Farringdon) |
020-7833-8115 | www.caravanonexmouth.co.uk

"Lively young people" fill this "frivolous, fabulous" newish Exmouth Market cafe/bar whose European offerings star "complexly flavoured" small plates and an "awesome" brunch; what's more, the prices are "reasonable" and staff "friendly", making up for tables that can feel "too close for comfort"; P.S. folks "line up out the door" for the "fantastic" "house-roasted coffee."

Carluccio's Caffè *Italian* | 17 | 15 | 16 | £25 |

Bloomsbury | 8 Market Pl., W1 (Oxford Circus) |
020-7636-2228 ●
Covent Garden | Garrick St., WC2 (Covent Garden) | 020-7836-0990 ●
Marylebone | St. Christopher's Pl., W1 (Bond St.) | 020-7935-5927 ●
Mayfair | Fenwick | 63 New Bond St., downstairs, W1 (Bond St.) |
020-7629-0699
Canary Wharf | Reuters Plaza | 2 Nash Ct., E14 (Canary Wharf) |
020-7719-1749 ●
Farringdon | 12 W. Smithfield, EC1 (Farringdon) | 020-7329-5904
Islington | 305-307 Upper St., N1 (Angel) | 020-7359-8167
Fulham | 236 Fulham Rd., SW10 (Fulham Broadway) | 020-7376-5960
Putney | Putney Wharf, SW15 (Putney Bridge) | 020-8789-0591

(continued)

Carluccio's Caffè

Hammersmith | 5-6 The Green, W5 (Ealing Broadway) | 020-8566-4458
www.carluccios.com
Additional locations throughout London

"The formula is a good one" at this "inexpensive, informal" chain: "dependable plates of Italian food" served "any time of the day" with "little fuss" by "generally courteous, quick" staff; on the down side, the decor is "dull" and the atmosphere is often "loud and chaotic", but nonetheless, it usually "hits the mark", so long as you "don't expect too much"; P.S. "gourmet" ingredients are for sale in attached retail areas.

Carob Tree M *Greek/Mediterranean*   - | - | - | M

Highgate | 15 Highgate Rd., NW5 (Crouch Hill) | 020-7267-9880
The "friendly owner makes patrons feel welcome" at this Highgate venue on a busy roundabout near Hampstead Heath, where the "reasonably priced" Greek-Med menu highlights "superb mezze" and "fresh fish"; too bad then that some folks can't get over the "immense noise" when "busy", not to mention the "spartan" setting.

NEW Casa Batavia ● *Italian*   - | - | - | E

Kensington | 135 Kensington Church St., W8 (Notting Hill Gate) | 020-7221-7348 | www.casabatavia.com
After 15 years running the renowned Ristorante Birichin in Turin, TV chef-patron Nicola Batavia has spread his wings overseas, bringing his unfettered style of upscale Italian cooking to Kensington; the narrow, unassuming space is dominated by a domed glass conservatory and startling black-and-white images on the walls.

NEW Cassis Bistro *French*   ∇ 25 | 22 | 20 | £51

South Kensington | 232 Brompton Rd., SW3 (South Kensington) | 020-7581-1101 | www.cassisbistro.co.uk
Accomplished restaurateur Marlon Abela "turns his considerable talent to a less-grand dining establishment than The Greenhouse and Umu" with this South Ken opening where he oversees a relatively "reasonably priced" Provençal menu, complemented by a 700-bin wine list; a zinc-topped bar, classy artwork and leather banquettes adorn the "smart" mushroom-hued interior, and in warm weather, the front opens onto a handful of alfresco tables on Brompton Road.

Cây Tre *Vietnamese*   22 | 10 | 12 | £22

NEW Soho | 42-43 Dean St., W1 (Leicester Square) | 020-7317-9118 | www.caytresoho.co.uk Ⓢ
Hoxton | 301 Old St., EC1 (Old St.) | 020-7729-8662 | www.vietnamesekitchen.co.uk
"Healthy, hearty bowls of goodness" are sold for "bargain prices" at this Hoxton Vietnamese where there's "never any tables free in the evenings" ("must book"); if you ignore the "harried" service, nonexistent decor and "crowded tables", it "ticks all the right boxes" for an "awesome", "authentic" experience; P.S. the Soho branch opened post-Survey.

Cecconi's ● *Italian*   23 | 22 | 22 | £58

Mayfair | 5A Burlington Gdns., W1 (Green Park/Piccadilly Circus) |
020-7434-1500 | www.cecconis.co.uk

"Packed with beautiful people" from breakfast to "late night", this
"chic", jade-coloured Mayfair hot spot owned by Soho House's Nick
Jones delivers "terrific", "something-for-everyone" Italian cuisine
featuring "inventive takes on standard fare"; "reservations are a
must", but "if you just walk in off the street", "professional" staff
might try to "squeeze you in" at the "hopping bar."

Cellar Gascon ●☒ *French*   24 | 18 | 18 | £39

Farringdon | 59 W. Smithfield, EC1 (Barbican/Farringdon) |
020-7600-7561 | www.comptoirgascon.com

Pascal Aussignac's dark-hued sibling of Club Gascon (a few doors
away in Farringdon) is "more a wine bar with snacks" than a
restaurant – however, there's a real "wow" factor in the "innovative
French tapas", which complement the "wide variety" of "carefully chosen wines"; other boons are "reasonable" prices and mostly "friendly"
service, but the whole experience works best "if you're not hungry."

NEW Chabrot ☒ *French*   - | - | - | M

Knightsbridge | 9 Knightsbridge Green, SW1 (Knightsbridge) |
020-7225-2238 | www.chabrot.co.uk

This somewhat hard-to-find arrival in Knightsbridge Green offers a
keenly priced menu of earthy Southern French faves accompanied
by an accessible, international wine list; the narrow, intimate setting
plays the role of an archetypal bistro with traditional lighting, red-
and-white table linens and evocative photos of rural France.

Cha Cha Moon *Chinese*   16 | 15 | 13 | £19

Soho | 15-21 Ganton St., W1 (Oxford Circus/Piccadilly Circus) |
020-7297-9800 | www.chachamoon.com

"Cheap, authentic noodles" and other Chinese plates "will leave you
satisfied" at this "cheerful" Alan Yau venture whose "groovy" Soho
setting is decked out with communal tables; but with no reservations taken, it's "best for a quick bite" "outside conventional eating
hours"; P.S. "outdoor seating is a plus."

Champor-Champor ☒ *Malaysian*   ∇ 22 | 24 | 20 | £32

Tower Bridge | 62-64 Weston St., SE1 (London Bridge) |
020-7403-4600 | www.champor-champor.com

"A find" in the Tower Bridge area, this "charming" "nirvana" presents
"delectable" Malaysian meals amidst tribal artefacts, Buddha statues
and other "eccentric", "eclectic" Southeast Asian accoutrements;
"reasonable prices" add to its repute as a "must try", especially for
those with an "inclination to try some very unusual cuisine."

Chapters All Day Dining *European*   - | - | - | M

Blackheath | 43-45 Montpelier Vale, SE3 (Blackheath Rail) |
020-8333-2666 | www.chaptersrestaurants.com

"Delicious" meals, "fair prices" and "friendly service" "never fail to
impress" at this all-day Modern European in Blackheath Village; the

| | FOOD | DECOR | SERVICE | COST |

airy premises present the "traditional atmosphere" of an "easy-going" brasserie, with views of the Heath visible through the front windows.

Chelsea Brasserie *European*

| | 18 | 15 | 20 | £39 |

Chelsea | Sloane Square Hotel | 7-12 Sloane Sq., SW1 (Sloane Sq.) | 020-7881-5999 | www.sloanesquarehotel.co.uk

"Great for discreet breakfast meetings" as well as "pre/post-Royal Court dinners", this "lively" spot in Sloane Square supplies "quality", "no-frills" Modern European meals; furthermore, both the "airy", "unpretentious" interior and "few prime outdoor tables" offer similarly "enjoyable people-watching", supported by "attentive", "friendly" service.

Chelsea Kitchen *British*

| | 15 | 12 | 17 | £21 |

Fulham | 451 Fulham Rd., SW10 (Fulham Broadway) | 020-3055-0088 | www.thechelseakitchen.com

"From its early King's Road days" to its current "bright, homey" Fulham Road location, this "London institution" continues to serve "decent", "familiar" Traditional British "basics", including breakfast; ok, so maybe there's "not the same buzz as the old" venue, but for a "quick bite", it remains a "reliable" "value."

NEW Chesterfield, The *Asian*

| | - | - | - | M |

Notting Hill | 39 Chepstow Pl., W2 (Notting Hill Gate) | 020-7229-0323 | www.thechesterfield.co

Newly revamped, this chilled, "fun" gastropub below the acclaimed Assaggi in Notting Hill merges a contemporary, meaty Pan-Asian menu (short on choice, but long on value) with traditional features, such as stained-glass windows, wall clocks and well-worn Chesterfield sofas; for imbibers, there's a wide selection of cocktails and wines from under £15 a bottle.

Cheyne Walk Brasserie *French*

| | 21 | 22 | 19 | £54 |

Chelsea | 50 Cheyne Walk, SW3 (Sloane Sq./South Kensington) | 020-7376-8787 | www.cheynewalkbrasserie.com

The "cosy feeling" and "scent" of "rosemary" from the "open grill" is alone "worth the journey" to this "charming", "lovely" Chelsea brasserie offering "confidently prepared French regional classics" at "upper-scale" prices; bargain-hunters turn up at lunchtime for the "value set menu", whilst "stylish" types come for "romantic" dinners, abetted by "an excellent wine list" and "warm, helpful" service.

Z Chez Bruce *British*

| | 27 | 21 | 26 | £64 |

Wandsworth | 2 Bellevue Rd., SW17 (Balham/ Wandsworth Common Rail) | 020-8672-0114 | www.chezbruce.co.uk

"Understated elegance" still sums up the decor of this "pride of Wandsworth Common", but a recent expansion has imbued it with "new vim and vigour", whilst chef-owner Bruce Poole's "inventive" Modern British menu is as "superb" as ever (and "pricey" too, but ultimately "phenomenal value"); it's a bit "out of town", but with an "adventurous wine list", "not-to-be-missed cheese board" and "attentive", "charming service" as part of the package, it's "well worth the trek."

	FOOD	DECOR	SERVICE	COST

Chez Gérard *French* | 17 | 17 | 16 | £36 |

Bloomsbury | 8 Charlotte St., W1 (Goodge St./Tottenham Court Rd.) | 020-7636-4975
Covent Garden | Covent Garden Piazza | 35 The Market, WC2 (Covent Garden) | 020-7379-0666
Holborn | 119 Chancery Ln., WC2 (Chancery Ln.) | 020-7405-0290 🗷
Mayfair | 31 Dover St., W1 (Green Park) | 020-7499-8171 🗷
City | 1 Watling St., EC4 (Mansion Hse./St. Paul's) | 020-7213-0540 🗷
City | 14 Trinity Sq., EC3 (Tower Hill) | 020-7480-5500 🗷
City | 64 Bishopsgate, EC2 (Bank/Liverpool St.) | 020-7588-1200 🗷
Waterloo | 9 Belvedere Rd., SE1 (Waterloo) | 020-7202-8470
www.chezgerard.co.uk

"No surprises, good or bad" make this chain with many "convenient" locations a "dependable" option for "simple" French brasserie fare; yes, the setting is "uninspiring" and "service could be better", but for a "casual", "good-value" meal, it's quite "useful."

Chicago Rib Shack *BBQ* | 15 | 13 | 15 | £31 |

Knightsbridge | 145 Knightsbridge, SW1 (Knightsbridge) | 020-7591-4664 | www.thechicagoribshack.co.uk

"If you want a rib fix", check out this spacious American BBQ joint in Knightsbridge whose "massive portions" make it "reasonable value", even if the eats are only "ok"; try it for a "quick" meal with the "family" or a "kids birthday", just "don't go for the service."

☑ Chilango *Mexican* | 22 | 14 | 18 | £11 |

NEW **Holborn** | 76 Chancery Ln., WC2 (Chancery Ln.) | 020-7430-1231 🗷
City | 142 Fleet St., EC4 (Blackfriars) | 020-7353-6761 🗷
Islington | 27 Upper St., N1 (Angel) | 020-7704-2123
www.chilango.co.uk

The "queue outside can be discouraging, but it moves at amazing speed" at this "simple" Mexican pair on Fleet and Upper Streets, where "large" "burritos filled to bursting" and such are as "delicious" as they are "hard to beat" for "value" – indeed, it's once again voted London's No. 1 Best Buy; considering the dearth of similar spots, it's a "breath of fresh air", whether you "eat in or (more likely) eat out"; P.S. the Chancery Lane branch premiered post-Survey.

China Tang ● *Chinese* | 21 | 23 | 20 | £61 |

Mayfair | The Dorchester | 53 Park Ln., W1 (Hyde Park Corner/Marble Arch) | 020-7629-9988 | www.dorchesterhotel.com

"Elegant" and "opulent" (think "Shanghai in the 1920s"), this Chinese in The Dorchester majors on "upscale" Cantonese classics that are mostly "fantastic" – and priced for "VIPs"; surveyors split on service ("impeccable" vs. "unacceptable"), but all agree the "swanky" "bar is a fun place to hang out"; P.S. "good dim sum" too.

Chisou 🗷 *Japanese* | 22 | 14 | 19 | £50 |

Mayfair | 4 Princes St., W1 (Oxford Circus) | 020-7629-3931 | www.chisou.co.uk

The "fantastic" sushi is "expensive", but compared to "top-tier places" with higher profiles, the prices seem quite "reasonable" at this

Vote at ZAGAT.com

	FOOD	DECOR	SERVICE	COST

"friendly" Mayfair Japanese; "the decor is a bit bland", but that doesn't stop fans from "finding an excuse to go here wherever possible."

Chor Bizarre ● Indian
23 | 20 | 21 | £42

Mayfair | 16 Albemarle St., W1 (Green Park) | 020-7629-9802 | www.chorbizarre.com

"Chintzy", "funky" and sometimes "hilarious" decorations fill this Mayfair branch of a New Delhi eatery done up to resemble an Indian bazaar, whilst the "varied" "street food"-inspired menu takes a similarly "lighthearted approach" – and the results taste "superb"; "generous portions" make it seeem "lighter on the wallet than others in the area", and "attentive" service adds to the value.

Chowki Bar & Restaurant ● Indian
∇ 20 | 15 | 17 | £24

Piccadilly | 2-3 Denman St., W1 (Piccadilly Circus) | 020-7439-1330 | www.chowki.com

Expect a "comprehensive choice (not just the standards)" on a "bargain" Indian menu of "well-executed", "regionally themed" fare served by "charming" staff at this simple, casual venue behind Piccadilly Circus; "given its location", it's unsurprisingly "great for a pre- or post-theatre meal", especially if you go with the "value" set menu.

Christopher's
19 | 18 | 17 | £44

Covent Garden *American/Chophouse*
Covent Garden | 18 Wellington St., WC2 (Covent Garden) | 020-7240-4222 | www.christophersgrill.com

Steaks "so fresh, they may have flown first class from Omaha" pair with "consistent" seafood preparations at this "airy, bright", "unstuffy" Covent Garden American "institution", which is as "lovely for a decadent dinner" as it is a "real weekend brunch"; "so-so" service can let the side down, but the "excellent" downstairs bar mixing "spectacular cocktails" is a "bonus."

Chuen Cheng Ku ● Chinese
20 | 8 | 13 | £23

Chinatown | 17 Wardour St., W1 (Leicester Sq./Piccadilly Circus) | 020-7437-1398 | www.chuenchengku.co.uk

You "can't beat" the "tried-and-true" trolleys of "fresh, hot" dim sum and other "dependable" Cantonese dishes at this "old standby" in Chinatown; indeed, most respondents pay little mind to the "crowded", "barnlike", ready-for-an-"upgrade" setting and "brusque" service, because the prices are so "cheap."

Churchill Arms *Thai*
21 | 18 | 16 | £19

Kensington | 119 Kensington Church St., W8 (High St. Kensington/ Notting Hill Gate) | 020-7727-4242 | www.fullers.co.uk

A "beautiful old pub" steeped in "genuine [Winston] Churchill history" gives way to a "charming" rear dining room "festooned with flowers" and doling out "generous portions" of "hearty" Thai for "very little expense" at this "unique" Kensington institution; the main "issue is the wait for a table" (it's "always crowded"), not to mention that "once you're finished with your meal, you do get rushed away."

	FOOD	DECOR	SERVICE	COST

Chutney Mary ● _Indian_ | 23 | 22 | 22 | £44

Chelsea | 535 King's Rd., SW10 (Fulham Broadway) | 020-7351-3113 |
www.chutneymary.com

It "looks like a dentist's office from the outside", but you'll feel like
you're in a "beautiful" "palace" inside this "classy" Indian where "ex-
plosions of flavour" are presented by "accommodating servers";
sure, its location at the far end of King's Road is "off the beaten
path", and it helps to be "on expenses" when the bill comes, but it's
"worth the trip" and the "dear" prices for such a "festive" experience.

Cigala _Spanish_ | ∇ 20 | 15 | 17 | £38

Bloomsbury | 54 Lamb's Conduit St., WC1 (Holborn/Russell Sq.) |
020-7405-1717 | www.cigala.co.uk

Belying its "simple", streamlined setting in Bloomsbury, this Spaniard
draws a "noisy" crowd for its "genuine" tapas and entrees, including
"some great seasonal dishes"; also keeping the atmosphere lively
are a "nice selection" of "reasonable wines" and "great sangria."

NEW Cigalon ⌧ _French_ | - | - | - | M

Holborn | 115 Chancery Ln., WC2 (Chancery Ln.) | 020-7242-8373 |
www.cigalon.co.uk

"Character" and "comfort" are the hallmarks of both the "stunning"
setting, dominated by circular mauve banquettes, and the "prettily
presented Southern French favourites" at this "relaxed" new Holborn
endeavour; "warm service" and reasonable prices add to its appeal,
and it's an especially "useful lunch resource" for nearby workers.

⊠ Cinnamon Club ⌧ _Indian_ | 25 | 24 | 23 | £55

Westminster | Old Westminster Library | 30-32 Great Smith St., SW1
(Westminster) | 020-7222-2555 | www.cinnamonclub.com

"New Delhi meets Old Westminster" at this "top-end" "designer
Indian" from Vivek Singh, where "stunning", "beautifully spiced"
subcontinental cuisine "at its most sophisticated" is served all day
in an "elegant" "historic library" sprinkled with "business" and
"political" types; yes, it's "expensive", but given the "remarkable"
service and overall "wow factor", "it's a real treat"; P.S. don't miss
the "great bar downstairs with signature cocktails."

Cinnamon Kitchen ●⌧ _Indian_ | 23 | 20 | 20 | £46

City | 9 Devonshire Sq., EC2 (Liverpool St.) | 020-7626-5000 |
www.cinnamon-kitchen.com

"Imaginative", "modern" Indian cuisine is the thing at this "upmarket"
City sib of Cinnamon Club, where "sure-handed" staff set out "fabulous", "clever" dishes that "really deliver on flavour"; despite the
somewhat "clinical" decor, it's still a "scene" with a "high-decibel"
noise level to boot; P.S. the set menu at lunch is "an absolute steal."

Ciro's Pizza Pomodoro ● _Italian_ | ∇ 13 | 13 | 15 | £26

Knightsbridge | 51 Beauchamp Pl., SW3 (Knightsbridge) |
020-7589-1278 | www.pomodoro.co.uk

"Where would Beauchamp Place be without this old standby?"
muse _amici_ who appreciate that "you can count on" it for a "fun night

out", with "live bands", drinks, pizza and Italian trattoria tucker; just know that "you come here for the atmosphere, not the food" – but at least "you can eat without taking out a mortgage."

Citrus *Italian*

| - | - | - | E |

Piccadilly | Park Lane Hotel | 112 Piccadilly, W1 (Green Park) | 020-7290-7364 | www.citrusrestaurant.co.uk

"A peaceful place to dine and enjoy a glass of wine" inside or "outside on Piccadilly", this bistro in the Park Lane Hotel – quirkily decorated with black-and-white-portraiture wallpaper – offers an Italian menu that "provides little in terms of innovation" but is nonetheless "not bad"; it's "not cheap" either, though there is a bargain weekday lunch prix fixe.

◪ Clarke's *British*

| 26 | 21 | 25 | £61 |

Kensington | 124 Kensington Church St., W8 (High St. Kensington/ Notting Hill Gate) | 020-7221-9225 | www.sallyclarke.com

This "quiet classic" in Kensington features chef Sally Clarke's "sophisticated" seasonal menu of "delicious" Modern British fare that "hits the mark every time"; it's "expensive", but "attentive" servers "take care of everything", so its "posh" clientele find it "worth a visit"; P.S. the attached gourmet shop vends breads, pastries and prepared meals.

Cliveden House *British/French*

| 23 | 26 | 24 | £80 |

Taplow | Cliveden Country Hse. Hotel | off Bourne End Rd., Berkshire | 01628-668561 | www.clivedenhouse.co.uk

"Stunning views of beautifully kept gardens" abound at this "elegant" country-house hotel (once home to the Astor family) in Berkshire, "a special experience" with two dining rooms: the Terrace, serving "well-executed" Traditional British–French cuisine, and the "charming" subterranean Waldo's, specialising in often "superb" New French cooking; whichever venue you choose, expect to "pay a lot", but also to be "treated well."

C London ◐ *Italian*

| 21 | 21 | 22 | £73 |

Mayfair | 25 Davies St., W1 (Bond St.) | 020-7399-0500 | www.cipriani.com

"Wealthy" "celebrities" and "sugar daddies" accompanying "overdressed ladies" pay "largely marked-up prices" at this "loud, bright", "amusing" Mayfair Italian; fittingly "posh" staff are at their beck and call, and while the dishes are roundly considered "delicious", "don't go for the food, go for the theatre."

◪ Clos Maggiore *French*

| 24 | 25 | 23 | £60 |

Covent Garden | 33 King St., WC2 (Covent Garden/Leicester Sq.) | 020-7379-9696 | www.closmaggiore.com

"Wonderful for a quiet dinner *à deux*" – especially if you nab a seat by the fireplace – this "charming", flower-filled Covent Garden "hideaway" features "high-end", "beautifully presented" New French cuisine backed by a "brilliant" *vin* selection; "formal", "old-fashioned" service helps distract from the "pricey" bills, as does a pre-theatre prix fixe that's "an amazing bargain."

	FOOD	DECOR	SERVICE	COST

❷ Club Gascon Ⓩ *French* — 26 | 22 | 23 | £69

Farringdon | 57 W. Smithfield, EC1 (Barbican/Farringdon) |
020-7796-0600 | www.clubgascon.com

Pascal Aussignac's "oft-imitated" "foodie" haunt next to Smithfield
Market is known for its "sublime", "innovative" shared-plates menu
from the Southwest of France, starring "amazing" foie gras "served
a hundred ways", backed by "unusual" regional wines; "knowledgeable" service and a "bright, airy" setting increase the appeal, even if
most find it "rather expensive" for what you get.

Cocoon ●Ⓩ *Asian* — 20 | 23 | 16 | £51

Piccadilly | 65 Regent St., W1 (Piccadilly Circus) | 020-7494-7600 |
www.cocoon-restaurants.com

A "sultry" "club atmosphere" pervades this "exciting" Piccadilly
Pan-Asian with "views of Regent Street", where the "great", "pricey"
fare is "nicely presented" in "swanky" 'cocoons' and a "trendy bar";
at its best, service is "attentive", but at its worst, it's "overbearing."

Colony *Indian* — ▽ 21 | 17 | 19 | £45

Marylebone | 8 Paddington St., W1 (Baker St.) | 020-7935-3353 |
www.colonybarandgrill.com

"If you want something different", this Marylebone Indian is "a good
bet", with "interesting", "delicious" dishes, "well-made" Eastern-
tinged cocktails and nightly live jazz in the "great" lounge; a number of
surveyors find the contemporary setting "nice" enough, but unfortunately, a few feel the whole experience is "overpriced" for what it is.

Como Lario ● *Italian* — 21 | 16 | 19 | £46

Pimlico | 18-22 Holbein Pl., SW1 (Sloane Sq.) | 020-7730-2954 |
www.comolario.co.uk

"Going strong for many years" (over 40, in fact), this "pleasant"
Pimlico Northern Italian trattoria with "tiny tables" is "hectic",
"crowded" and "cramped", yet thankfully, still "conducive to conversation"; the cuisine is somewhat pricey, but it's "reliable", backed by
some "affordable wines" and conveyed by "congenial staff."

Comptoir Gascon ⓏⓂ *French* — 22 | 17 | 18 | £37

Farringdon | 63 Charterhouse St., EC1 (Barbican/Farringdon) |
020-7608-0851 | www.comptoirgascon.com

"Providing the quality of its more illustrious relatives at a fraction of
the price", this "informal" version of chef Pascal Aussignac's Club
Gascon serves up "divine", "rustic French" dishes in "atmospheric"
bistro surroundings in Farringdon; the "decent wine list suits all palates and budgets", and everything comes via "charming staff."

Comptoir Libanais *Lebanese* — 17 | 14 | 13 | £18

Marylebone | 65 Wigmore St., W1 (Bond St.) | 020-7935-1110
Shepherd's Bush | Westfield Shopping Ctr. | Ariel Way, balcony, W12
(Shepherd's Bush) | 020-8811-2222
www.lecomptoir.co.uk

"Amazing deals" are found at these "lively, colourful" Marylebone
and Shepherd's Bush cafeterias doling out a "wide range" of "fairly
good" Lebanese eats that come "quick"; "amateurish service" un-

settles some, which is why they say it's "best enjoyed taken away"; P.S. a branch is slated for Westfield Stratford City, the new shopping centre across from the Olympic Park.

	FOOD	DECOR	SERVICE	COST

Constancia *Argentinean/Chophouse* | - | - | - | E |

Tower Bridge | 52 Tanner St., SE1 (London Bridge) | 020-7234-0676 | www.constancia.co.uk

Arrive with a "huge" "appetite" when you come to this subtly stylish Argentinean chophouse near Tower Bridge, whose "delicious" steaks are served by "friendly, helpful staff" along with "great sides"; as for the cost, it's "a little on the pricey side", but still "less expensive" than some competitors, due in part to the "reasonable wine list."

Coq d'Argent *French* | 20 | 22 | 20 | £57 |

City | 1 Poultry, EC2 (Bank) | 020-7395-5000 | www.coqdargent.co.uk

"Whatever might be wrong with the economy, you wouldn't detect it" amongst the "who's who" of bankers gathered at this French venue high above the City boasting a "lovely" terrace with "stunning views"; despite a "predictable" menu and sometimes "ungracious" service, it's frequently "packed", especially during Sunday's jazz lunch.

Corrigan's *British* | 25 | 22 | 23 | £70 |

Mayfair | Grosvenor Hse. Hotel | 28 Upper Grosvenor St., W1 (Marble Arch) | 020-7499-9943 | www.corrigansmayfair.com

Chef-restaurateur Richard Corrigan "continues to redefine British cuisine" at this "clubby" Mayfair dining room in the Grosvenor House Hotel, attracting "captains of industry and media magnates" with "exquisite", "genuinely surprising" modern fare, including "mind-blowing" game dishes; service is "polished", but some find the "civilised" setting too "subdued", and the cost "beyond the pocket of anything but the most special evening out."

Côte *French* | 17 | 15 | 17 | £29 |

Covent Garden | 17-21 Tavistock St., WC2 (Covent Garden) | 020-7379-9991

Soho | 124-126 Wardour St., W1 (Oxford Circus/Tottenham Court Rd.) | 020-7287-9280

NEW City | 26 Ludgate Hill, EC4 (St. Paul's) | 020-7236-4399

Borough | The Riverside, Hays Galleria | Tooley St., SE1 (London Bridge) | 020-7234-0800

NEW Fulham | 45-47 Parsons Green Ln., SW6 (Parsons Green) | 020-7736-8444

Richmond | 24 Hill St., TW9 (Richmond) | 020-8948-5971

Wimbledon | 8 High St., SW19 (Wimbledon) | 020-8947-7100

NEW Chiswick | 50-54 Turnham Green Terr., W4 (Turnham Green) | 020-8747-6788

Kensington | 47 Kensington Ct., W8 (High St. Kensington) | 020-7938-4147

NEW Notting Hill | 98 Westbourne Grove, W2 (Bayswater/Royal Oak) | 020-7792-3298

www.cote-restaurants.co.uk

Additional locations throughout London

You'll "never feel short-changed" at this "lively" French brasserie chain where there's "tremendous value" in the "no-nonsense", "reliable" "classic dishes"; settings that are "pleasant" but of "little personality" and service that's "well-meaning though haphazard" support its reputation as "somewhere to eat rather than dine", but it's "handy for pre- and post-theatre" or "for an informal meal with friends"; P.S. the "free bottled water is a real plus."

Cottons *Caribbean* — | — | — | M

Camden Town | 55 Chalk Farm Rd., NW1 (Chalk Farm) | 020-7485-8388 | www.cottonscamden.co.uk
Islington | 70 Exmouth Mkt., EC1 (Angel/Farringdon) | 020-7833-3332 | www.cottons-restaurant.co.uk

"Capturing the tastes, sounds and vibes of the West Indies right in Exmouth Market", this "chilled" bar/restaurant with a "cozy" Camden parent prepares Caribbean cuisine that most feel is "solid"; rum-centric "island-oriented" drinks are "lovely", just like the "friendly service", and everything's offered at reasonable prices.

Cow Dining Room *British* 19 | 17 | 17 | £32

Notting Hill | 89 Westbourne Park Rd., W2 (Royal Oak/Westbourne Park) | 020-7221-0021 | www.thecowlondon.co.uk

"Crowded" and "convivial any night of the week", this Notting Hill Modern British "institution" houses an "intimate" (though "rather sterile") upstairs dining room and a ground-floor gastropub, which many feel offers "better atmosphere and value"; as for the "comfy" fare and service, they're "yummy" and "friendly", respectively, though the latter "could be a tad more professional."

Crazy Bear *Thai* 19 | 25 | 18 | £48

Bloomsbury | 26-28 Whitfield St., W1 (Goodge St.) | 020-7631-0088
Covent Garden | 17 Mercer St., W1 (Covent Garden) | 020-7631-0088 ⓢⓜ
www.crazybeargroup.co.uk

The Thai fare is "spicy" but it "won't blow you away" like the "wonderfully eclectic" environment will at this Fitzrovia "hot spot" with a "romantic dining room" upstairs, a "cool" "sexy bar" pouring "great cocktails" downstairs and what may be the "best toilets in London"; no wonder then that a few feel it's "more a club than a restaurant" (and a pricey one at that); P.S. the Covent Garden offshoot is relatively new.

Crazy Homies *Mexican* 18 | 14 | 14 | £27

Notting Hill | 125-127 Westbourne Park Rd., W2 (Royal Oak/Westbourne Park) | 020-7727-6771 | www.crazyhomieslondon.co.uk

A "funky, rowdy atmosphere" permeates this "casual" Notting Hill Mexican where there's "ace value" to be found on the "decent" menu; no reservations are taken and some staffers have "a bit of an attitude", but surveyors are willing to overlook those annoyances for the "great margaritas" and "not-expensive" bills.

Criterion Restaurant ❶ *European* 18 | 26 | 19 | £52

Piccadilly | 224 Piccadilly, W1 (Piccadilly Circus) | 020-7930-0488 | www.criterionrestaurant.com

"A haven amidst the madness" of Piccadilly Circus, this 1873 "landmark" with "efficient" service boasts "spectacular", "glamourous" neo-Byzantine decor featuring "lots of marble, twinkling chandeliers" and gold leaf; the "fancy" Modern European fare may "not be in the Premier League", but it's "competent", plus the prix fixe "deals", especially "pre- and post-theatre", make it "no longer the domain of the rich."

Cross Keys *European*   17 | 18 | 17 | £28

Chelsea | 1 Lawrence St., SW3 (Sloane Sq.) | 020-7349-9111 | www.thexkeys.co.uk

"Lovely" and "full of life", this "casual" gastropub in a "quiet" Chelsea street prepares "pleasant" Modern European fare that's "good value for money"; a seat by the "fireplace is the best winter spot", whilst in summer, "the roof opens for fresh air" in the rear conservatory.

Da Mario ◐ *Italian*   20 | 15 | 19 | £27

South Kensington | 15 Gloucester Rd., SW7 (Gloucester Rd.) | 020-7584-9078 | www.damario.co.uk

Everything is "of the old-fashioned Italian variety" at this South Kensington trattoria, from the "tasty" "mother's-own" dishes to the "homey" decor; so even if they possibly "need to buck up their ideas", it's still a "friendly", "inviting" spot for "a family get-together" or "late-night stop" for disco on the basement dance floor (where children's parties are hosted in the afternoon).

Daphne's ◐ *Italian*   21 | 20 | 20 | £54

Chelsea | 112 Draycott Ave., SW3 (South Kensington) | 020-7589-4257 | www.daphnes-restaurant.co.uk

"Movers and shakers are in abundance" at this "iconic" Chelsea Italian that's "still a favourite with the local gentry" for its "consistent", "classic" fare served by a "gracious" crew in an "elegant contemporary" setting; however, some say the people-watching is "better than the food", and you'll need "lots of money" to settle the bill.

NEW Da Polpo ◐▣ *Italian*   - | - | - | M

Covent Garden | 6 Maiden Ln., WC2 (Embankment/Covent Garden) | 020-7836-8448 | www.dapolpo.co.uk

The similarly outfitted offspring of Polpo, and sibling of Polpetto and Spuntino, this bi-level Covent Garden Italian is flush with reclaimed furniture (old church pews, chemistry lab benches) plus filament light bulbs and antique maps of Venice; but it diverges from its parent in its moderately priced menu, which features an expanded selection heavy on pizzas and meatballs; P.S. no bookings after 5.30 PM.

Daylesford Organic Café *Eclectic*   18 | 18 | 13 | £30

Pimlico | Daylesford Organic Store | 44B Pimlico Rd., SW1 (Sloane Sq.) | 020-7881-8060
Notting Hill | 208-212 Westbourne Grove, W11 (Notting Hill Gate) | 020-7313-8050
www.daylesfordorganic.com

"Cashmere-swaddled" "yummy mummies", "hedge-fund" types and "the occasional celeb" head to these "bustling", "modern" all-day cafes in Notting Hill and Pimlico for "luxury organic" Eclectic fare, with "gorgeous" produce and groceries available from the in-house market; "hit-or-miss" service can make for frequent "queues", and "oh, those prices!"

Dean Street Townhouse ● British — 21 | 24 | 21 | £49

Soho | Dean Street Townhse. | 69-71 Dean St., W1 (Leicester Sq./Tottenham Court Rd.) | 020-7434-1775 | www.deanstreettownhouse.com
This "cosy", "clubby" all-day hotel brasserie from the folks behind Soho House offers an "appealing", "fairly simple" menu of seasonal British fare in a "lovely" room that recalls an updated "English country house"; never mind the "distant" service or "expensive bills" – if you fancy "over-the-top" "people-watching", it's the "place to be."

🅉 Defune Japanese — 26 | 18 | 20 | £70

Marylebone | 34 George St., W1 (Baker St./Bond St.) | 020-7935-8311
It's "expensive" and there's practically "no atmosphere", but that doesn't deter fish-fans from stopping into this "excellent" Marylebone Japanese for "superb little pieces of the highest quality sushi"; it's "always a good bet for a quick bite" since it's almost "never crowded", however, frequent diners wish that the service would "improve."

Dehesa Italian/Spanish — 24 | 16 | 19 | £37

Soho | 25 Ganton St., W1 (Oxford Circus/Piccadilly Circus) | 020-7494-4170 | www.dehesa.co.uk
Charcuterie is the "star" of the "fabulous" Italian-Spanish tapas selection that's paired with "intriguing wines" at this "vibrant", "informal retreat" in Soho; although the "small", "noisy" space with "communal tables" is "not madly comfortable", at least the service is "quick" ("attentive" too).

Del'Aziz African/Mediterranean — 16 | 18 | 15 | £29

Borough | Bermondsey Sq. | 11 Bermondsey Sq., SE1 (London Bridge) | 020-7407-2991
Southwark | Blue Fin Bldg. | 5 Canvey St., SE1 (Southwark) | 020-7633-0033
Camden Town | Swiss Cottage Leisure Ctr. | Adelaide Rd., NW3 (Swiss Cottage) | 020-7586-3338
Fulham | 24-32 Vanston Pl., W6 (Fulham Broadway) | 020-7386-0086
Shepherd's Bush | Westfield Shopping Ctr. | Ariel Way, ground fl., W12 (Shepherd's Bush) | 020-8740-0666 ●
www.delaziz.co.uk
With a "buzzy atmosphere" and "solid" Mediterranean–North African fare, this "informal", "reasonably priced" deli/cafe chainlet is a "welcome refuge" for a "quick" "meal after a hard day" or even a "girlie dinner"; the "only let down" is "patchy" staff, who redeem themselves with their "tolerance of buggies and children running around."

Delfino 🅉 Italian — 21 | 15 | 18 | £28

Mayfair | 121A Mount St., W1 (Bond St.) | 020-7499-1256 | www.finos.co.uk
Considering its upscale Mayfair location, this trattoria charges "blissfully reasonable" prices for its "great" pizzas with "unique topping

combinations" plus other "casual" Italian dishes; despite the "basic", often "crammed" setting, the atmosphere is "charming" and supported by service that's "friendly if brisk."

Z Dinings ⓩ *Japanese* 28 | 15 | 21 | £58

Marylebone | 22 Harcourt St., W1 (Edgware Rd.) | 020-7723-0666 | www.dinings.co.uk

Epicures estimate that "90% of the dishes can't be found anywhere else" than at this "innovative" Marylebone Japanese, serving up "smashing" small plates, "outstanding sushi" and "fantastic" cooked dishes in "spartan" basement digs "no larger than a shoebox" and an equally tiny ground-floor sushi bar; no surprise, it's "expensive", but most are "happy to pay the price" – hence, "getting a table is super hard."

Z NEW Dinner by 27 | 26 | 25 | £95
Heston Blumenthal *British*

Knightsbridge | Mandarin Oriental Hyde Park | 66 Knightsbridge, SW1 (Knightsbridge) | 020-7201-3833 | www.dinnerbyheston.com

Possibly the "hottest restaurant" opening of the past year, this Mandarin Oriental newcomer presents chef Heston Blumenthal's "sublime, unique", "exciting" Modern British menu "inspired by historic recipes" and rife with "baffling juxtapositions", such as the "work-of-art" 'meat fruit' starter (the overall concept is "far different than the Fat Duck", but just as "outstanding"); "attentive" staff and a "stylish, grand" setting with "nice views" of Hyde Park and into the "fish-bowl kitchen" add to its appeal, with "expense-account" prices the "only drawback."

NEW Dishoom *Indian* 23 | 22 | 21 | £26

Covent Garden | St. Martin's Courtyard | 12 Upper St. Martin's Ln., WC2 (Leicester Sq.) | 020-7420-9320 | www.dishoom.com

"Zingy" Indian eats with an "emphasis on grazing" ("not your typical curry-house fare") are sold for "reasonable prices" at this "interesting addition to Covent Garden"; "family photos" grace the walls, and "polite, charming" staff work the floor of the "modern" "brasserie surroundings", which are open from breakfast to dinner.

Dock Kitchen *European* 21 | 21 | 19 | £46

Ladbroke Grove | Wharf Bldg., Portobello Dock | 344 Ladbroke Grove, W10 (Kensal Green) | 020-8962-1610 | www.dockkitchen.co.uk

The promise of "fantastic cooking" draws "foodies" to this Modern European with "quirky, stylish" digs "overlooking the canal" at the top of Ladbroke Grove; though a few folks "don't get what the fuss is about" ("disappointing" dishes and service, "high prices"), most agree it's "worth a schlep out for a visit", especially in summer when the "lovely" terrace is open.

Dolada ⓩ *Italian* - | - | - | E

Mayfair | 13 Albemarle St., W1 (Green Park/Piccadilly Circus) | 020-7409-1011 | www.dolada.co.uk

At this Mayfair outpost of a same-named, family-run venue in Northern Italy's Veneto region, the "innovative", "well-executed" fare "stays true to its roots", though it's "quite expensive"; with a "discreet", marble-floored basement setting and "smooth service", the venue seems "primed for business lunches", so reports that it's "quiet in the evenings" are unsurprising.

Don, The 🗷 *European* | 23 | 21 | 23 | £52 |

City | The Courtyard | 20 St. Swithins Ln., EC4 (Bank/Cannon St.) | 020-7626-2606 | www.thedonrestaurant.co.uk

A "superb City venue" with an "interesting history" as an old Sandeman's port warehouse, this Modern European houses an "excellent restaurant" with "cool art" and a basement bistro offering equally "fantastic" dishes and "exceptional value"; "super-slick" staff include a "sommelier who knows his stuff", which comes in handy on Friday nights when everything over £50 on the "exceptional wine list" is half price.

Ⓩ Dorchester - The Grill *British* | 24 | 23 | 26 | £72 |

Mayfair | The Dorchester | 53 Park Ln., W1 (Hyde Park Corner/Marble Arch) | 020-7629-8888 | www.dorchesterhotel.com

"Bursting with testosterone" and "class", this all-day grill off the lobby of The Dorchester presents "wonderful" Modern British fare amidst "over-the-top decor" whose huge Scottish murals and yards of tartan lend it the feel of a "private club"; "gracious" staff provide "impeccable" service as they proffer the "fascinating menu" and "excellent wine list", and whilst you do need to bring a "barrowful of money", such is the cost of a "special" experience.

Dragon Castle *Chinese* | ▽ 23 | 20 | 22 | £30 |

Kennington | 100 Walworth Rd., SE17 (Elephant & Castle) | 020-7277-3388 | www.dragoncastle.eu

"Yummy", "high-quality" Cantonese fare comes for "a great price" at this low-key spot a "short walk" from Elephant & Castle tube in Kennington, where the "cool" old-style Chinese decor is "definitely a bit different" for the 21st century; still, some feel it's "not worth a trip" if you're not already nearby.

NEW Dragoncello *Italian* | - | - | - | E |

Notting Hill | 104 Chepstow Rd., W2 (Royal Oak/Westbourne Park) | 020-7221-1821 | www.dragoncello.co.uk

This pricey new Notting Hill Italian seats just 21 in its postage stamp-sized dining room, which mixes modern design (think dramatic black chandelier) with homey accoutrements (linen chairs and curtains); the sophisticated menu benefits not only from fresh produce delivered daily, but also from a short-but-sweet wine list.

Duke of Cambridge *British* | - | - | - | M |

Islington | 30 St. Peter's St., N1 (Angel) | 020-7359-3066 | www.sloeberry.co.uk

"Healthy portions of well-prepared, evangelically organic" Modern British cuisine come via "quick" service at this "comfortable", "busy" gastropub in Islington; however, even many who "support the principles of the place" think it's "overpriced" for what it is, so some come just "for a drink" at the bar.

	FOOD	DECOR	SERVICE	COST

Eagle, The *Mediterranean* 22 | 15 | 15 | £26

Clerkenwell | 159 Farringdon Rd., EC1 (Farringdon) | 020-7837-1353

Credited by some as being "the one that started" the gastropub "revolution" in the early '90s, this "scruffy-as-ever", "reasonably priced" Clerkenwell "stalwart" proffers "big portions" of "bang-on", "down-to-earth" Med dishes with "interesting" Iberian leanings; "service can be a little slow", but "the wait is bearable" thanks to the salve of "good atmosphere and beer."

Eagle Bar Diner ⓩ *American* ▽ 18 | 15 | 17 | £22

Bloomsbury | 3-5 Rathbone Pl., W1 (Tottenham Court Rd.) | 020-7637-1418 | www.eaglebardiner.com

"Fun every once in a while", this "friendly-enough" American off Oxford Street does "decent", "diner-esque" dishes that include specialty burgers such as wild boar and bison, plus "great milkshakes" and cocktails; prices are reasonable, but go easy on the ordering, as some "tables don't seem big enough to fit the food."

E&O *Asian* 22 | 20 | 18 | £45

Notting Hill | 14 Blenheim Cres., W11 (Ladbroke Grove) | 020-7229-5454 | www.rickerrestaurants.com

"Dark", "chic" and jammed with a "beautiful Notting Hill crowd" (there's "nearly always a celeb sighting"), this "deservedly popular" Pan-Asian marries "interesting, flavourful" dishes with "funky", "innovative cocktails", the former delivered via "friendly" service, the latter coming from the "lively bar"; somewhat shockingly, it's "not even that pricey for what it is", and unsurprisingly, it's "difficult to book."

Ebury Wine 18 | 18 | 17 | £39
Bar & Restaurant *European/French*

Belgravia | 139 Ebury St., SW1 (Sloane Sq./Victoria) | 020-7730-5447 | www.eburywinebar.co.uk

Around since 1959, this "casual", "cosy", "retro-chic" Belgravia eatery and wine bar "never grows old" thanks to the "enduring quality" of its "reasonably priced" Modern Euro-French bistro menu; as for service, it's "acceptable", with "staff generally quite knowledgeable" about the "brilliant wine list", featuring many by-the-glass selections.

Ed's Easy Diner *American* 15 | 16 | 16 | £17

Piccadilly | London Trocadero Ctr. | 19 Rupert St., W1 (Piccadilly Circus) | 020-7287-1951

Soho | 12 Moor St., W1 (Leicester Sq./Tottenham Court Rd.) | 020-7434-4439 ●

www.edseasydiner.co.uk

"You get plenty for your money" at these '50s-style, chrome-and-neon American diners in Piccadilly and Soho, where the burgers, chili dogs, fries and shakes are served by "friendly enough" staff, and customers sitting on red-vinyl stools ("don't expect to linger") drop coins into the "booming" "jukeboxes"; sure, it's "nothing fancy, but sometimes that's exactly what you fancy."

	FOOD	DECOR	SERVICE	COST

Efes 2 Turkish Restaurant ◐ *Turkish*   20 | 13 | 18 | £28

Bloomsbury | 175-177 Great Portland St., W1 (Great Portland St.) |
020-7436-0600 | www.efes2.co.uk

Efes Restaurant ◐⦸ *Turkish*

Bloomsbury | 80-82 Great Titchfield St., W1 (Oxford Circus) |
020-7636-1953 | www.efesrestaurant.co.uk

They've "perfected the art of fine traditional Turkish kebabs" – or so
say groupies of these "casual", separately owned Bloomsbury
Ottomans, which provide "big servings" of "good-value" "comfort
food"; yes, they look "outdated", but at least the "speedy service"
hits the mark, especially when handling "large groups."

Eight Over Eight *Asian*   21 | 19 | 17 | £48

Chelsea | 392 King's Rd., SW3 (Sloane Sq.) | 020-7349-9934 |
www.rickerrestaurants.com

After undergoing a "super refurbishment" following a fire, this
"much missed" E&O sibling is "back in form" as a "sleek", "buzzy"
haunt proffering a "pricey" Chinese-biased Pan-Asian menu with "a
lot of winners"; though there are reports of "inattentive service" at
the tables, the "cool bar at the front" is always "fun" for drinks with
a "well-heeled" King's Road crowd.

El Camion *Mexican*   - | - | - | I

Soho | 25-27 Brewer St., W1 (Piccadilly Circus) | 020-7734-7711
Notting Hill | 272 Portobello Rd., W10 (Ladbroke Grove) | 020-8960-8556
www.elcamion.co.uk

You go to "have fun" whilst downing "amazing cocktails" at these
funky, colourful cantinas in Portobello Road and Soho, which also
rustle up "reliable" Mexican victuals with "a variety of chili sauces if
you want to ramp up the heat"; prices are "cheap", and the "service
is efficient and friendly", even on "busy weekends."

Electric Brasserie *Eclectic*   17 | 16 | 15 | £41

Notting Hill | 191 Portobello Rd., W11 (Ladbroke Grove/
Notting Hill Gate) | 020-7908-9696 | www.electricbrasserie.com

The atmosphere is indeed "electric" at this Portobello Road brasserie
where "lively" folks "having watched a movie next door" power up on
Eclectic fare that's "solid" though "nothing special", therefore possibly
"overpriced" (and delivered by "spotty" staff too); nevertheless,
with a "see-and-be-seen", "cutting-edge-of-cool" reputation, it remains "crowded", so feel free to "drop in" even without a booking –
but risk get stuck at the usually "quieter" "tables at the back."

Elena's L'Etoile ⦸ *French/Italian*   19 | 17 | 20 | £53

Bloomsbury | 30 Charlotte St., W1 (Goodge St.) | 020-7636-1496 |
www.elenasletoile.co.uk

This Charlotte Street brasserie is an "institution that refuses to
change, and rightly so" say fans of its "reliable", "pricey" menu of
French-Italian classics and "stereotypical" red-tinged interior that
"oozes faded grandeur"; they also appreciate that they're "always
made to feel welcome" – however, critics feel that the whole experience is just too "old fashioned."

	FOOD	DECOR	SERVICE	COST

NEW Eleven Park Walk ● *Italian* — | - | - | - | E

Chelsea | 11 Park Walk, SW10 (Gloucester Rd./South Kensington) |
020-7352-3449 | www.atozrestaurants.com

"Intimate and lively at the same time", this "welcome" arrival to
Chelsea has early samplers recommending its "excellent" Italian
cooking, "friendly service" and comfortable surroundings; what's
more, they suspect it will be a "hit" "once word gets out."

El Gaucho *Argentinean/Chophouse* — 23 | 19 | 19 | £45

Chelsea | Chelsea Farmers Mkt. | 125 Sydney St., SW3 (Sloane Sq./
South Kensington) | 020-7376-8514
South Kensington | 30B Old Brompton Rd., SW7 (South Kensington) |
020-7584-8999 ●
www.elgaucho.co.uk

A "large selection of melt-in-your-mouth meat" is shipped from the
Pampas to this pair of "friendly" Argentinean chophouses in Chelsea
and South Ken; despite "nothing-fancy" cow-themed digs and
"ouch-o prices", they're "fun" for a "no-fuss" meal, plus the "music's
loud enough to stop other conversations from invading your space."

Elistano *Italian* — 17 | 13 | 17 | £36

Chelsea | 25-27 Elystan St., SW3 (South Kensington) | 020-7584-5248 |
www.elistano.com

"Comfy Italian food" priced affordably keeps this "cheerful" Chelsea
trattoria "bustly"; indeed, the "casual setting" is "not a place to linger", but the pavement tables are "great" for relaxing "outside in
spring and summer."

Elk in the Woods *Eclectic* — ∇ 16 | 18 | 14 | £29

Islington | 39 Camden Passage, N1 (Angel) | 020-7226-3535 |
www.the-elk-in-the-woods.co.uk

"Kooky decor" comprising "antlers, dog paintings, raw brick" and a
"big communal table in the back" yields "cool" vibes at this "relaxed" Eclectic pub/cafe in Islington; that it "can fill its few tables
many times over without trying too hard" says volumes about its
prospects – why then have some "staff seem to have given up"?

El Parador *Spanish* — - | - | - | M

Camden Town | 245 Eversholt St., NW1 (Mornington Cres.) |
020-7387-2789 | www.elparadorlondon.com

"Still undiscovered", this "friendly" Camden Spaniard with a traditional taverna-style setting (tiled floor, yellow walls, wooden tables)
serves "gutsy", "brilliant" tapas at "bargain" rates, which extend to
the "inexpensive" wine list; P.S. "in summer, try the garden."

El Pirata ●🖾 *Spanish* — 20 | 15 | 18 | £34

Mayfair | 5-6 Down St., W1 (Green Park/Hyde Park Corner) |
020-7491-3810 | www.elpirata.co.uk
El Pirata Detapas *Spanish*
Notting Hill | 115 Westbourne Grove, W2 (Bayswater) |
020-7727-5000 | www.elpiratadetapas.co.uk

It's "all hustle, bustle" and "cheer" at this "casual", "plain"-looking
duo in Mayfair and Westbourne Grove, "consistent" "standbys" for

	FOOD	DECOR	SERVICE	COST

"flavourful, well-priced" Spanish tapas that offer "something for everyone"; their "many loyal clients" "enjoy the camaraderie" with "enthusiastic staff", and the "wine list is great as well" (so too the "late hours").

Empress of India British

▽ 20 | 18 | 18 | £36

Hackney | 130 Lauriston Rd., E9 (Bethnal Green) | 020-8533-5123 | www.theempressofindia.com

"Loved by trendy East Londoners", this "comfortable gastropub near Victoria Park" with "nostalgic" adornments (e.g. wall art evoking colonial India) prepares "creative", "well-executed, seasonal" Modern British dishes from a "varied menu"; a "good beer and wine selection" adds value for tipplers, but still, some feel it's generally "overpriced for what it offers."

Empress of Sichuan Chinese

- | - | - | E

Chinatown | 6 Lisle St., WC2 (Piccadilly Circus) | 020-7734-8128 | www.restaurantprivilege.com

"When one fancies something a little spicier" and "challenging" than what's offered at the Cantonese places nearby, this "impressive", somewhat pricey Sichuan spot is a "must go" in Chinatown; the environment is pleasantly "spacious and comfortable", but unfortunately, "service is perfunctory" at best.

Engineer, The British

21 | 17 | 20 | £35

Primrose Hill | 65 Gloucester Ave., NW1 (Chalk Farm) | 020-7722-0950 | www.the-engineer.com

With "reliably good" Modern British cooking, "friendly, knowledgeable staff" and a "high number of staggeringly beautiful people" at the tables, this "cosy", "comfy" all-day Primrose Hill venue "ticks all the boxes"; if some criticise prices that seem to be "creeping up" for "too much pub and not enough gastro", all have only accolades for the "lovely" summer garden.

Enoteca Turi ⊠ Italian

25 | 22 | 26 | £54

Putney | 28 Putney High St., SW15 (Putney Bridge) | 020-8785-4449 | www.enotecaturi.com

Regulars say they're "always treated well" at this "well-established" venue near Putney Bridge, a "treasure that bats far above its weight" with "inventive", "fantastic" Italian cooking and a "staggering wine list"; it's "a bit out of the way unless you live/work in the area", but it's "worth the hike to get there" – and "generally quite full", so be sure to book.

Enterprise, The Eclectic

20 | 19 | 21 | £39

Chelsea | 35 Walton St., SW3 (Knightsbridge/South Kensington) | 020-7584-3148 | www.theenterprise.co.uk

"Reliably solid" Eclectic fare is sold at "upscale" prices to an "affable", "three-piece-suit" crowd at this "charming" Chelsea gastropub; "friendly" servers patrol the "cosy" setting, whose "comfy furniture" and drapery makes it feels like a "drawing room" – and for which bookings are only taken for weekday lunch; P.S. "Walton Street is wonderful for wandering before or after."

| | FOOD | DECOR | SERVICE | COST |

Esarn Kheaw *Thai* — | − | − | − | M |

Shepherd's Bush | 314 Uxbridge Rd., W12 (Shepherd's Bush Mkt.) | 020-8743-8930 | www.esarnkheaw.co.uk

Uncommon, "authentic Northeastern Thai" cuisine is the speciality of this "excellent", affordable eatery in Shepherd's Bush; locals utilise it as "a go-to for takeaway", but "cheerful service" makes it not bad for dining in, the "small" setting and "bizarre decor" notwithstanding.

Ⓩ Espelette *French* — | 24 | 27 | 24 | £64 |

Mayfair | Connaught | Carlos Pl., W1 (Bond St.) | 020-3147-7100 | www.the-connaught.co.uk

Residing in a prime corner of Mayfair's Connaught, this "spacious, elegant", conservatorylike dining room with street views from "almost all tables" is a "less expensive way" to sample the "excellent" Classic French bistro fare of chef Hélène Darroze; yes, it's still "pricey by any standard", but "professional service" is part of the package; P.S. afternoon tea is "celestial."

Eyre Brothers 🅢 *Portuguese/Spanish* — ▽ | 24 | 24 | 24 | £46 |

Shoreditch | 70 Leonard St., EC2 (Old St.) | 020-7613-5346 | www.eyrebrothers.co.uk

"Chic decor" and a "fine" Portuguese-Spanish menu ("sets a high standard for pork") are the selling points of this haunt in an "unlikely street" in Shoreditch, a "great neighbourhood restaurant in the evening and a cool place to take clients for lunch"; what's more, it's pretty "good value", plus the bar serves "fabulous cocktails" "until late."

Fairuz ◗ *Lebanese* — | 22 | 15 | 18 | £33 |

Marylebone | 3 Blandford St., W1 (Baker St./Bond St.) | 020-7486-8108 | www.fairuz.uk.com

Addicts "can't get enough" of the "reliable" "Lebanese standards" that are served in "generous" portions and "ridiculously cheap for the quality" at this "friendly", "no-frills" venue in Marylebone; just be forewarned that it "can get loud when it fills up", which is often – after all, it is a "legend."

Fakhreldine ◗ *Lebanese* — | 20 | 19 | 19 | £45 |

Piccadilly | 85 Piccadilly, 1st fl., W1 (Green Park) | 020-7493-3424 | www.fakhreldine.co.uk

"If you're in the Piccadilly area and want to nibble some good mezze", join the "beautiful young people" who frequent this Lebanese whose "atmospheric", elevated setting features "views over Green Park" "from the window tables", plus "fun" belly dancing Thursday–Saturday evenings; if a few feel it's "overpriced" for what it is, at least the eats come in large quantities.

Ⓩ Fat Duck Ⓜ *European* — | 27 | 22 | 27 | £200 |

Bray | High St., Berkshire | 01628-580333 | www.fatduck.co.uk

Chef Heston Blumenthal's "culinary prestidigitation" still "astounds" at this "transcendental" experience in a "low-key" Bray cottage where the "experimental", "ingenious" Modern European

	FOOD	DECOR	SERVICE	COST

dishes are ferried by "impeccable" servers, along with a wine list
that "contains some of the hardest-to-get bottles in the world"; after
you score a reservation ("nearly impossible"), you'll need "a second
mortgage" to pay the bill, but it's "well worth the price" (and the
hour or so "foodie pilgrimage" from London) for "a meal you will talk
about for years to come."

Feng Sushi *Japanese*   17 | 11 | 17 | £26

Borough | 13 Stoney St., SE1 (London Bridge) | 020-7407-8744
South Bank | Royal Festival Hall | Belvedere Rd., Festival Terr., SE1
(Waterloo) | 020-7261-0001
Chalk Farm | 1 Adelaide Rd., NW3 (Chalk Farm) | 020-7483-2929
Fulham | 218 Fulham Rd., SW10 (Fulham Broadway) | 020-7795-1900
Kensington | 24 Kensington Church St., W8 (High St. Kensington) |
020-7937-7927
Notting Hill | 101 Notting Hill Gate, W11 (Notting Hill Gate) |
020-7727-1123
www.fengsushi.co.uk

"Nothing exciting" but "reliable" is the consensus on the "midpriced
sushi" and other Japanese victuals that come via conveyor belt at
this chain whose service is mostly "friendly"; speaking of the basic
setting, many plead "please make it a bit more comfy" and recommend doing takeaway or delivery instead.

Ffiona's ⓜ *British*   24 | 18 | 23 | £40

Kensington | 51 Kensington Church St., W8 (High St. Kensington/
Notting Hill Gate) | 020-7937-4152 | www.ffionas.com
"A very special restaurant run by a very special woman", this
"romantic little bistro" in Kensington is the milieu of the "entertaining" Ffiona Reid-Owen, who's "always there to greet you and offer
advice" on the "fantastic" Traditional British fare and "small, well-
chosen wine list"; some find the environs "dark" and "worn", but
nonetheless, it "gets a lot of repeat business", especially from a
"big American following."

Fifteen *Italian*   21 | 19 | 21 | £48

Hoxton | 15 Westland Pl., N1 (Old St.) | 020-3375-1515 | www.fifteen.net
"Hooray" cheer Jamie Oliver fans who "love the idea" of the chef's
"vibrant", "high-quality" all-day Hoxton haunt that equips under-
privileged youths with restaurant-industry skills; but it's more than
a "good deed", as evidenced by the "creative", "wholesome" Italian
dishes served in both the downstairs dining room and the "more casual", "less expensive" upstairs trattoria, both of which benefit from
"energetic, young service."

Fifth Floor *European*   20 | 19 | 19 | £47

Knightsbridge | Harvey Nichols | 109-125 Knightsbridge, 5th fl., SW1
(Knightsbridge) | 020-7235-5250 | www.harveynichols.com
The "more formal choice at Harvey Nichols", this "chic", "bright"
spot offers "tasteful" Modern European dishes, an "exceptional
wine list", "gracious" service and "good" views (if you get the right
table); however, some think it's "no big deal", opining that the adjacent bar is "where it all happens", i.e. it's a "known pickup joint."

	FOOD	DECOR	SERVICE	COST

Fifth Floor Cafe *British/Mediterranean* ⟨18⟩ ⟨14⟩ ⟨16⟩ ⟨£31⟩

Knightsbridge | Harvey Nichols | 109-125 Knightsbridge, 5th fl., SW1 (Knightsbridge) | 020-7823-1839 | www.harveynichols.com

"Buzzy and busy", this all-day "respite" with a small rooftop terrace at Harvey Nichols is "lots of fun" for a mid-shopping "fuel"-up of "light" Modern British–Med fare "with flair"; there's also "great views" and "interesting" people-watching, whilst bargain-hunters like that it's "much less pricey" than its next-door sibling.

Fig *European* ▽ ⟨24⟩ ⟨20⟩ ⟨22⟩ ⟨£35⟩

Islington | 169 Hemingford Rd., N1 (Caledonian Rd.) | 020-7609-3009 | www.fig-restaurant.co.uk

In an "out-of-the-way" Islington locale, this "enjoyable", "intimate" venue proves a "cosy spot for a romantic tryst or casual evening" dinner (or Sunday brunch) of "quality", "so-delicious" Modern European eats, "limited" though they may be; as for the casual decor, fans assure that it's as "good" as the service.

Fino ⓈＺ *Spanish* ⟨24⟩ ⟨20⟩ ⟨21⟩ ⟨£49⟩

Bloomsbury | 33 Charlotte St., W1 (Goodge St./Tottenham Court Rd.) | 020-7813-8010 | www.finorestaurant.com

Tapas-lovers swear you "can't go wrong" on the "brilliantly executed", "high-end" Spanish menu at this "lively" Barrafina sibling in Fitzrovia, whose "warm", "elegant decor transcends its basement location"; "personable staff" "work hard" as they advise on the "excellent wine list" and "fabulous" sherry selection.

Fish *Seafood* ⟨19⟩ ⟨15⟩ ⟨17⟩ ⟨£33⟩

South Bank | Borough Mkt. | Cathedral St., SE1 (London Bridge) | 020-7407-3803 | www.fishkitchen.com

"Enjoy a just-caught meal whilst Borough Market people-watching" at this "bustling", "modern", "glass-walled" and -ceilinged spot where the seafood is "simply cooked" and "dependable"; those who find the prices "high" and service just "adequate" head instead to the "solid" fish 'n' chips stand outside, "a cheaper option."

FishWorks *Seafood* ⟨18⟩ ⟨13⟩ ⟨16⟩ ⟨£36⟩

Marylebone | 89 Marylebone High St., W1 (Baker St.) | 020-7935-9796
Piccadilly | 7-9 Swallow St., W1 (Piccadilly Circus) | 020-7734-5813
Richmond | 13-19 The Square, TW9 (Richmond) | 020-8948-5965
www.fishworks.co.uk

Make "your seafood selection from the fishmonger in front" and the chefs "will cook it" for you to eat in "the restaurant in the back" – that's the "functional" formula at this trio; unfortunately, some find it "too expensive", because the outcome can either be "brilliant" or a "letdown", plus service is generally "ok, not great", and the settings are "rather austere", though "adequately comfortable."

NEW 5 Pollen St. Ｚ *Italian* ⟨-⟩ ⟨-⟩ ⟨-⟩ ⟨E⟩

Mayfair | 5 Pollen St., W1 (Oxford Circus) | 020-7629-1555 | www.pollenst.com

Esteemed chef Stefano Cavallini heads this pricey Mayfair Italian endeavour offering a sophisticated menu that's attracting a young, trendy crowd; White Cube artist Gary Hume adds to the intrigue with bespoke woven silk panels and playful wallpaper depicting cheerleaders' legs.

Flemings Grill *European* | - | - | - | E |

Mayfair | Flemings Hotel | 7-12 Half Moon St., W1 (Green Park) | 020-7499-0000 | www.flemings-mayfair.co.uk

Housed in a smart Mayfair hotel stretched across six Georgian townhouses, this darkened, "sumptuously appointed" dining room is a "little-known" "romantic hideaway" where "eager" staff ferry "great", upscale Modern European dishes; in general, it's rather pricey, though there's an express-lunch option that's "exceptional value", plus dinner prix fixes as well.

Floridita ● 🛇 Ⓜ *Pan-Latin* | ▽ 13 | 17 | 14 | £44 |

Soho | 100 Wardour St., W1 (Leicester Sq./Tottenham Court Rd.) | 020-7314-4000 | www.floriditalondon.com

With its "fun live music", "tiny dance floor" and "cool, happening bar", the Pan-Latin fare is "clearly not the focus" at this "loud" ("everyone shouts to be heard") Soho nightspot; if "you want to reserve a table", "cheeky" staff "insist you have a main course", but some surveyors feel it's "overpriced", so you may want to stick to "snacks" and cocktails.

NEW Folly, The *European* | - | - | - | M |

City | Monument | 41 Gracechurch St., EC3 (Monument/Bank) | 084-5468-0102 | www.thefollybar.co.uk

A deli, florist, pop-up shop, casual bar, snug library and Modern European restaurant are thrown together at this "quirky" bi-level behemoth, which "the City really needed in its sea of sandwich shops and expense-account" places; the sharing-oriented, accessible, affordable menu is served all day alongside snacks and an eclectic wine list, and the bar scene "heaves at night."

Food for Thought ⊅ *Vegetarian* | 22 | 11 | 16 | £15 |

Covent Garden | 31 Neal St., WC2 (Covent Garden) | 020-7836-9072 | www.foodforthought-london.co.uk

"Get there early", because this "'70s throwback" "hole-in-the-wall" vegetarian in a "cosy" Covent Garden basement is usually "packed", with "queues out the door"; some of the vittles "wander into the 'odd'" category, but for the most part, the "hearty" dishes "taste amazing", plus they're "a bargain" – hence the "fanatical following."

Forge, The ● *European* | 23 | 21 | 22 | £43 |

Covent Garden | 14 Garrick St., WC2 (Covent Garden/Leicester Sq.) | 020-7379-1432 | www.theforgerestaurant.co.uk

"Pretty undiscovered" considering its "convenient" Covent Garden location, this "tasteful", brick-lined venue is "ideal for a girls' night out, business meal or romantic dinner" of "fancy", "fantastic" Modern Euro eats backed by a "diverse wine list" (there's a "good pre-theatre" prix fixe too); "friendly", "relaxed" staff add to the overall "tranquility."

	FOOD	DECOR	SERVICE	COST

Forman's Fish Island ☒ *British*
| | - | - | - | E |

Hackney | Stour Rd., E3 (Hackney Wick) | 020-8525-2390 |
www.formansfishisland.com

To allow construction of the 2012 Olympic Park, H. Forman & Sons,
the U.K.'s oldest producer of smoked salmon, relocated from its
long-established home in Hackney Wick to a flash new building 100
meters away, comprising a conference centre-cum-art gallery and a
modern bistro with views over the River Lea to the stadium; the upscale Modern British menu exhibits the expected salmon bias, and
it's offered along with an all-English wine list.

Fortnum's Fountain *British*
| | 20 | 19 | 20 | £33 |

Piccadilly | Fortnum & Mason | 181 Piccadilly, W1 (Green Park/
Piccadilly Circus) | 020-5602-5694 | www.fortnumandmason.com

For an "elegant, calm" "break from gallivanting" about Piccadilly,
try Fortnum & Mason's "dependable" all-day cafe offering
"great-value" "Traditional British goodies" ("ask for the famous
Welsh rarebit"); even modernists who consider it a "tired" "time
warp" that should "smarten up" its act admit it's "memory-making
for kids" who want to experience" "scrumptious", "so-British"
"sweets and tea."

Four Seasons Chinese ◐ *Chinese*
| | 22 | 10 | 14 | £29 |

Chinatown | 12 Gerrard St., W1 (Leicester Sq./Piccadilly Circus) |
020-7494-0870
Bayswater | 84 Queensway, W2 (Bayswater) | 020-7229-4320

It's all about "duck, duck and more duck" ("crispy", "aromatic",
"heavenly") at this "good-value" pair of, well, "duck specialists" in
Queensway ("cramped tables") and Chinatown ("no atmosphere"),
also preparing a "reliable", "diverse selection" of other Cantonese
dishes; although there's "frequently a queue", it moves "fairly
quickly" – despite the sometimes "awful service."

🆕 Fox & Grapes *British*
| | - | - | - | M |

Wimbledon | 9 Camp Rd., SW19 (Wimbledon) | 020-8619-1300 |
www.foxandgrapeswimbledon.co.uk

This formerly bedraggled boozer on Wimbledon Common has been
given a glossy gentrification by Hibiscus' celebrated chef, Claude
Bosi, and his brother, Cedric; the hearty Modern British gastropub
fare is moderately priced and accompanied by a serious selection of
locally brewed beers and ales; P.S. a trio of upstairs bedrooms
are also available.

Foxtrot Oscar *British*
| | 15 | 13 | 13 | £45 |

Chelsea | 79 Royal Hospital Rd., SW3 (Sloane Sq.) | 020-7352-4448 |
www.gordonramsay.com

After getting off to a "terrible start", some say this "cosy"
"Ramsay empire" Chelsea bistro has "improved", with
Traditional British fare that's "pleasant" if still "unexceptional";
however, the majority lament it's still a "kitchen nightmare", with
other issues such as "lack of buzz", "dull decor", "slow, sloppy service" and "expensive" prices.

	FOOD	DECOR	SERVICE	COST

Franco Manca *Pizza*
24 | 14 | 18 | £17

Brixton | 4 Market Row, SW9 (Brixton) | 020-7738-3021
Chiswick | 144 Chiswick High Rd., W4 (Turnham Green) |
020-8747-4822
www.francomanca.co.uk

"Fabulous, Neapolitan-style" sourdough pizzas with "high-quality toppings" are "dirt cheap" at this "noisy" duo; despite "nonexistent decor" in Brixton and "terrible acoustics" in Chiswick, they're always packed, and whilst the "helpful service" works to get everyone in and out quickly, you should still "be prepared to wait"; P.S. a branch is slated for Westfield Stratford City, the new shopping centre across from the Olympic Park.

Franco's ⊠ *Italian/Mediterranean*
22 | 19 | 21 | £48

St. James's | 61 Jermyn St., SW1 (Green Park) | 020-7499-2211 |
www.francoslondon.com

Visitors are greeted with a "smile" by "wonderful" staff at this "enjoyable" St. James's "smooth operation" producing an "interesting mix" of "excellent", "pricey" Italian-Med dishes; "great breakfast" and dinner are offered, but it's particularly "busy at lunchtime", so "better to book" than to come on a whim.

Frankie's *Italian*
15 | 14 | 18 | £35

Knightsbridge | 3 Yeoman's Row, SW3 (Knightsbridge) | 020-7590-9999
Marylebone | Selfridges | 400 Oxford St., lower ground fl., W1 (Bond St.) |
020-7318-3981
Fulham | Chelsea Football Club Complex | Stamford Bridge,
Fulham Rd., SW6 (Fulham Broadway) | 020-7957-8298
Chiswick | 68 Chiswick High Rd., W4 (Stamford Brook/Turnham Green) |
020-8987-9988
www.marcopierrewhite.org

Looking as "kitsch" as ever (disco balls, bling), this Italian chainlet from Marco Pierre White and top jockey Frankie Dettori comes in a mishmash of shapes, sizes and venues, from Selfridges to the Chelsea Football Club stadium; whilst many say "don't miss it if in the area", they "wouldn't recommend a separate trip" because everything's pretty "mediocre" (though to be fair, "good value").

Frederick's ⊠ *British/European*
20 | 23 | 18 | £49

Islington | 106 Camden Passage, N1 (Angel) | 020-7359-2888 |
www.fredericks.co.uk

A chance to "ogle the Islington glitterati" adds to the "joy" of this "swish" dining room with a "lovely conservatory feel", rear "summer garden" and "great" Modern British–Euro fare; "relaxed" service is another reason the "institution" (now into its fifth decade) is "tough to beat" in the area; P.S. it's "excellent value pre-theatre."

French Horn *British/French*
∇ 25 | 25 | 26 | £55

Sonning | French Horn Hotel | Thames St., Berkshire | 011-8969-2204 |
www.thefrenchhorn.co.uk

In a "charming Thames-side" setting "right out of *The Wind in the Willows*", this historic 17th-century coaching inn in Sonning practices "time-warp" British-French cooking that yields "superb results; "lovely staff" that help "soothe you" make it a "favourite place for older relatives' birthday lunches", featuring "excellent-value" prix fixes (à la carte-only dinners are "expensive").

	FOOD	DECOR	SERVICE	COST

French Table ⓜ *French/Mediterranean* `- | - | - | E`
Surbiton | 85 Maple Rd., KT6 (Surbiton Rail) | 020-8399-2365 | www.thefrenchtable.co.uk

Word is spreading about this unassuming venue in a leafy residential street in Surbiton, where the simply appointed, slate-floored space gives little clue as to the sophisticated level of French-Med cooking coming from the kitchen, which is led by chef-patron Eric Guignard; prices for food and wine (on a globe-trotting list) are kept in check, making bookings hard to come by.

Frontline *British* `20 | 21 | 20 | £34`
Paddington | 13 Norfolk Pl., W2 (Paddington) | 020-7479-8960 | www.frontlineclub.com

"Warzone" correspondents and their colleagues are the majority clientele of this public dining room of the same-named private club for journalists, a "cool", "clubby" first-floor venue near Paddington offering "tasty", "diversified" Traditional British fare from "sustainable sources", alongside "an interesting wine list"; even if you're not in the news business, it's a "useful place in the area", as it's "reasonably priced."

Gaby's ⌖ *Jewish/Mideastern* `∇ 22 | 9 | 15 | £20`
Covent Garden | 30 Charing Cross Rd., WC2 (Leicester Sq.) | 020-7836-4233

"Satisfy the urge for a salt beef on rye", "comforting homemade soups" and other "reliable" Jewish–Middle Eastern staples at this "belly-filling pit stop" in Covent Garden; the "ambience hasn't changed much since the '70s", but you don't come here for the setting – you come for value and "convenience" to Theatreland.

Galicia ◑ⓜ *Spanish* `∇ 20 | 15 | 20 | £27`
Notting Hill | 323 Portobello Rd., W10 (Ladbroke Grove) | 020-8969-3539

"After shopping on Portobello", take a trip to Galicia via this "fantastic" Notting Hill Spaniard whose tapas "hit the mark"; though "retro", the surroundings feel "homey" thanks to "welcoming" staff and fittingly "affordable prices."

Gallipoli *Turkish* `21 | 18 | 19 | £21`
Islington | 102 Upper St., N1 (Angel) | 020-7359-0630
Islington | 107 Upper St., N1 (Angel) | 020-7226-5333
Islington | 120 Upper St., N1 (Angel) | 020-7359-1578
www.cafegallipoli.com

Peppered along a single Islington street, these "loud", "hectic" places proffer an "extensive menu" of "consistent", "inexpensive" Turkish fare in "bustling, hectic rooms crammed with interesting ornaments" and some "shared tables"; service can be "hit-and-miss depending on how busy it gets", but it's mostly "friendly", and as accommodating for "quick bites" as "big groups and parties."

	FOOD	DECOR	SERVICE	COST

Galvin at Windows
Restaurant & Bar *French*
| 24 | 25 | 24 | £66 |

Mayfair | London Hilton on Park Ln. | 22 Park Ln., 28th fl., W1 (Green Park/ Hyde Park Corner) | 020-7208-4021 | www.galvinatwindows.com

The "stunning" views "alone would be worth the trip" to chef-patron Chris Galvin's "formal", "romantic location" atop the Hilton Park Lane, but "equivalent quality" is evident in the "fine", "fancy" New French cuisine that's served with "pride" by an "observant" crew; "as expected", it's "expensive", but when factoring in the fact that you "feel special the moment you walk in", most calculate that it's "reasonably priced."

Galvin Bistrot de Luxe *French*
| 24 | 20 | 21 | £49 |

Marylebone | 66 Baker St., W1 (Baker St.) | 020-7935-4007 | www.galvinrestaurants.com

"Luxe by name, luxe by nature", this "fab" Baker Street spot from brothers Chris and Jeff Galvin presents "high-end" French bistro "classics" that "hit the spot", along with a "good-value wine list" in digs that feel "more like a brasserie"; adding to the "lively atmosphere" are "eager-to-please staff" who remain "convivial" even when the place gets "busy" ("always").

Galvin La Chapelle *French*
| 25 | 26 | 24 | £65 |

City | St. Botolph's Hall | 35 Spital Sq., E1 (Liverpool St.) | 020-7299-0400 | www.galvinrestaurants.com

"Striking", "stunning", "spectacular" are some of the accolades bestowed upon the "cavernous" Victorian school-gymnasium setting of this "brilliant" Spital Square member of Chris and Jeff Galvin's stable, where the "artistically presented" New French fare exhibits "technical excellence and sensual flavours"; "warm, attentive service" and a "fantastic" wine list are part of the package – for which "you do pay" ("to save a bit of money, go for the prix fixe lunch"); P.S. there's also an all-day cafe with outdoor seating and a bar.

Z Gate, The 🗷 *Vegetarian*
| 26 | 21 | 24 | £33 |

Hammersmith | 51 Queen Caroline St., W6 (Hammersmith) | 020-8748-6932 | www.thegate.tv

"Hidden" "up a flight of stairs" in an "atmospheric" former "artist's studio" near Hammersmith tube, this "long-standing" vegetarian restaurant enjoys "Rolls-Royce" status with "superior" dishes featuring "unexpected combinations", all brought by "friendly", "knowledgeable staff"; a few folks find it "pricey" for the type, but most are happy to pay for the "amazing adventure."

Z Gaucho *Argentinean/Chophouse*
| 22 | 19 | 20 | £49 |

Holborn | 125-126 Chancery Ln., WC2 (Chancery Ln.) | 020-7242-7727 🗷
Piccadilly | 25 Swallow St., W1 (Piccadilly Circus) | 020-7734-4040 ●
Canary Wharf | 29 Westferry Circus, E14 (Canary Wharf) | 020-7987-9494
City | 1 Bell Inn Yard, EC3 (Bank/Monument) | 020-7626-5180 🗷
City | 5 Finsbury Ave., EC2 (Liverpool St.) | 020-7256-6877 🗷

(continued)

Gaucho

Farringdon | 93A Charterhouse St., EC1 (Barbican/Farringdon) | 020-7490-1676 🛂
Tower Bridge | 2 More London Riverside, SE1 (London Bridge) | 020-7407-5222
Hampstead | 64 Heath St., NW3 (Hampstead) | 020-7431-8222
Chelsea | 89 Sloane Ave., SW3 (South Kensington) | 020-7584-9901
Richmond | The Towpath, TW10 (Richmond) | 020-8948-4030
www.gauchorestaurants.com
Additional locations throughout London

"Masculine and glitzy" all at once, these "dark", "cowhide"-festooned Argentinean chophouses "impeccably cook" "melt-in-the-mouth meats", which are backed by "great" sides and a "superb wine list" (mostly South American); sure, it's "pricey on the whole, but not outrageous", and there's value in staff who "happily explain the different cuts" and "recommend sauces."

Gauthier Soho 🛂 *French*   24 | 19 | 21 | £64

Soho | 21 Romilly St., W1 (Piccadilly Circus) | 020-7494-3111 | www.gauthiersoho.co.uk

Chef Alexis Gauthier's "terrific" New French cuisine is "cooked with skill and imagination" at this "charming" Soho townhouse whose "hushed", "small rooms" are spread out over three storeys and where the "efficient" crew includes a sommelier who "works magic" with the "outstanding wine list"; as for the prices, all things considered, they're "reasonable", especially if you go for the lunch or pre-theatre prix fixes or the tasting menu, boasting "immense value."

Gay Hussar 🛂 *Hungarian*   21 | 20 | 21 | £40

Soho | 2 Greek St., W1 (Tottenham Court Rd.) | 020-7437-0973 | www.gayhussar.co.uk

"In the mood for goulash washed down with bull's blood" wine? – then settle into this "small" Soho "survivor" serving "hearty", "old-style Hungarian" eats; "courteous" staff and "grotesque but absorbing caricatures" of political figures on the "dark-wood" walls complete the picture of the "time-tested" "treat."

Geales *Seafood*   21 | 15 | 18 | £32

NEW **Chelsea** | 1 Cale St., SW3 (Sloane Sq.) | 020-7965-0555
Notting Hill | 2 Farmer St., W8 (Notting Hill Gate) | 020-7727-7528
www.geales.com

"Nothing exotic" is sold at this "been-there-forever" Notting Hill "stalwart", just "generous servings of quintessential fish 'n' chips" and other "well-prepared", "classic" seafood preparations; similarly "reasonable prices", "good wines" and "cheerful" service can also be found at the "cosy" new offshoot, a "welcome addition to Chelsea."

George 🛂 *European*   22 | 23 | 24 | £71

Mayfair | private club | 87-88 Mount St., W1 (Bond St.) | 020-7491-4433 | www.georgeclub.com

"Brilliant" staff make guests feel at "home" at this "cosy", discreet Mayfair townhouse whose "kitchen does a fine job" in preparing "simple" but "sumptuous" (and "very expensive") all-day Modern European eats, which are complemented by "superb" wines and drinks made at the "buzzing downstairs bar"; but "don't get too excited" – "you have to be a member" to get in.

Gessler at Daquise *Polish* | - | - | - | M |

South Kensington | 20 Thurloe St., SW7 (South Kensington) | 020-7589-6117 | www.gesslerlondon.com

Formerly called simply 'Daquise', this modest South Ken Polish stalwart from 1947 has recently raised its profile with new owners, a Warsaw-based restaurant group that's added its name above the door; early word on the revamp is the "fascinating" menu is "enjoyable" and the service is "lovely" – prices, meanwhile, have thankfully remained moderate.

Getti *Italian* ∇ 15 | 13 | 17 | £35 |

Marylebone | 42 Marylebone High St., W1 (Baker St./Regent's Park) | 020-7486-3753
St. James's | 16-17 Jermyn St., SW1 (Piccadilly Circus) | 020-7734-7334 Ⓢ
www.getti.com

"Dependable and filling" sums up the "standard" Italian dishes doled out at these trattorias in Marylebone and St. James's; yes, they're "run-of-the-mill" in every way, yet they attract an "eclectic clientele" because they're "good value" and quite "handy for lunch" or when "working late."

Giaconda Dining Room Ⓢ Ⓜ *European* ∇ 23 | 13 | 20 | £37 |

Soho | 9 Denmark St., WC2 (Leicester Sq./Tottenham Court Rd.) | 020-7240-3334 | www.giacondadining.com

"We should keep this secret" whisper admirers of this Soho "gem" whose "technically accomplished", "deeply flavoured" Modern European cuisine is served in a "tiny", "cramped", minimalist dining room; what's more, the fare is "more affordable" than expected, just like the "good choice of wines."

NEW Gilbert Scott *British* | - | - | - | E |

King's Cross | St. Pancras Renaissance Hotel | Euston Rd., NW1 (King's Cross St. Pancras) | 020-7278-3888 | www.thegilbertscott.co.uk

Chef Marcus Wareing spares time from cheffing at The Berkeley to oversee operations at this pricey Traditional British spot in the St. Pancras Renaissance Hotel (the restaurant is named after the building's 1873 architect); the environs include a high-ceilinged, arc-shaped dining room, plus a handsome bar by the pillared entrance.

Gilgamesh *Asian* 19 | 25 | 18 | £48 |

Camden Town | Stables Mkt. | Chalk Farm Rd., NW1 (Camden Town/ Chalk Farm) | 020-7482-5757 | www.gilgameshbar.com

"Fun, funky", "ornate" and "enormous", this "must see" in Camden's Stables Market proffers a Pan-Asian menu by chef Ian Pengelley, and if the "inventive" eats are not quite as "phenomenal" as the setting, at least they are "prepared to a high standard" (they "come at a price", as do the "great cocktails"); whilst service ranges from "efficient" to "lacking", the "people-watching and celeb-spotting" are "impressive" indeed.

Giovanni's ●⊠ *Italian* | 23 | 19 | 23 | £41 |

Covent Garden | 10 Goodwin's Ct., WC2 (Covent Garden/Leicester Sq.) | 020-7240-2877 | www.giovannislondon.com

"Hard to find" down a "Covent Garden alley", this "charming", "intimate" Italian from 1952 is worth seeking out for its "superb" "standards" served by an owner and staff who "make you feel quite at home"; indeed, the experience is akin to a "dinner party", which many diners "would most definitely repeat."

Giraffe *Eclectic* | 15 | 13 | 16 | £21 |

Marylebone | 6-8 Blandford St., W1 (Baker St./Bond St.) | 020-7935-2333
NEW Soho | 11 Frith St., W1 (Leicester Square) | 020-7494-3491
Shoreditch | Old Spitalfields Mkt. | Crispin St., Unit 1, E1 (Liverpool St.) | 020-3116-2000
South Bank | Royal Festival Hall | Belvedere Rd., Riverside Level 1, SE1 (Waterloo) | 020-7928-2004
Hampstead | 46 Rosslyn Hill, NW3 (Hampstead) | 020-7435-0343
Islington | 29-31 Essex Rd., N1 (Angel) | 020-7359-5999
Battersea | 27 Battersea Rise, SW11 (Clapham Common/Clapham Junction Rail) | 020-7223-0933
Richmond | 30 Hill St., TW9 (Richmond) | 020-8332-2646
Chiswick | 270 Chiswick High Rd., W4 (Turnham Green) | 020-8995-2100
Kensington | 7 Kensington High St., W8 (High St. Kensington) | 020-7938-1221
www.giraffe.net
Additional locations throughout London

The "4 x 4 pushchair brigade" feed their "screaming children" "run-of-the-mill" Eclectic "comfort food" at these "easy-going" all-day cafes whose "frantic" staff remain miraculously "cheery"; even if you're not with the "kids", they're still "useful" for a "quick", "casual bite", because they're "cheap" and people with "very different tastes" can always "find something"; P.S. the new Soho branch offers a more grown-up twist on the concept.

⊠ Glasshouse, The *European* | 26 | 23 | 25 | £53 |

Richmond | 14 Station Parade, TW9 (Kew Gdns.) | 020-8940-6777 | www.glasshouserestaurant.co.uk

"Even if you're not going to the Gardens, it's worth the trip" to this sister of La Trompette by Kew train station whose "outstanding" Modern European dishes boast "original flavours" and are sold at "a price that's right"; the "light, airy" space with lots of "large windows" "can be noisy", but "impeccable service" and an "interesting wine list" make amends.

Golden Dragon ● *Chinese* | 20 | 14 | 15 | £25 |

Chinatown | 28-29 Gerrard St., W1 (Leicester Sq./Piccadilly Circus) | 020-7734-2763

"Just about every Chinese dish you've ever heard of" is listed on the menu of this "reliable", "reasonably priced" Chinatown spot whose "bustling", "slightly garish" "red-and-gold" setting feels like "one of those giant Hong Kong restaurants"; service is "hurried", which is "disappointing" to those seated, but a boon for those "waiting" in the queue, which is "disorganised" "at peak times", such as weekend dim sum service.

Golden Hind 🗷 Seafood
25 | 10 | 19 | £16

Marylebone | 73 Marylebone Ln., W1 (Bond St.) | 020-7486-3644
Despite "extending the premises", this "legendary" Marylebone seafooder is still a "hole-in-the-wall" – but thankfully, it continues to provide the "best fish 'n' chips in London" (maybe "the world"), served "fast and easy" in "generous portions" "with the requisite mushy peas"; there's no alcohol, but "you can bring your own and they don't charge for corkage", which adds to what may be the "best bang for your pound" around.

Goldmine ● Chinese
▽ 24 | 5 | 11 | £23

Bayswater | 102 Queensway, W2 (Bayswater) | 020-7792-8331
"Fantastic" duck is the "house specialty" and "always worth having" at this "reasonably priced" Queensway Chinese, which also prepares some "unusual" Cantonese dishes; "just don't expect anything" in terms of decor and service that's more than "brusque"; P.S. it's "often busy, especially at weekends", but bookings are accepted.

Good Earth, The Chinese
21 | 17 | 20 | £41

Knightsbridge | 233 Brompton Rd., SW3 (Knightsbridge/
South Kensington) | 020-7584-3658
Finchley | 143-145 The Broadway, NW7 (Mill Hill Rail) | 020-8959-7011
www.goodearthgroup.co.uk
"Always a safe bet" for "excellent if not inventive Chinese food", this "civilised" duo in Knightsbridge and Finchley are "equally good for big group celebrations or quick meals for two"; they may be "expensive compared" to other options, but the service is of a "high calibre."

🖪 Goodman 🗷 Chophouse
26 | 20 | 23 | £60

Mayfair | 26 Maddox St., W1 (Oxford Circus) | 020-7499-3776
NEW City | 11 Old Jewry, EC2 (Bank) | 020-7600-8220
www.goodmanrestaurants.com
A "bewildering choice" of "top-quality" American, Irish and Scottish meat is carved into "huge steaks" that are so "delicious", they "don't need sauces" at this "dark-panelled", "clubby", "pricey" chophouse in Mayfair, whose new "business-oriented" City sib exhibits a "softer feel"; staff offer "spot-on suggestions" about the fare and "excellent wine list", making the "macho" venues "fun places to entertain" – "just remember to book well in advance."

Gopal's of Soho ● Indian
22 | 13 | 20 | £28

Soho | 12 Bateman St., W1 (Leicester Sq./Tottenham Court Rd.) |
020-7434-0840 | www.gopalsofsoho.co.uk
Judging by the "interesting, perfectly spiced dishes", there's a "deft hand" in the kitchen of this "reliable", "well-priced" Indian that competes well with "the more touted, hipper places" in Soho; it does a "booming takeaway business", but it's quite "peaceful" for dining in – just "don't let the drab surroundings dissuade you."

	FOOD	DECOR	SERVICE	COST

🛂 Gordon Ramsay
at Claridge's *European*   25 | 26 | 25 | £95

Mayfair | Claridge's Hotel | 45 Brook St., W1 (Bond St.) |
020-7499-0099 | www.gordonramsay.com

A "transporting experience" awaits at Gordon Ramsay's "classy", "stunning" "bastion of fine dining" in Claridge's, where "expertly prepared", "delectable" Modern European cuisine is complemented by an "extraordinary wine list" and presented by "impeccable", "fawning" staff; unless you choose the "terrific value" set lunch menu, you'll need to have "just won a ton of money" to settle the bill, but it's "worth it for a special night out", especially if you're "treated to a tour of the kitchen."

🛂 Gordon Ramsay
at 68 Royal Hospital Rd. Ⓢ *French*   28 | 25 | 28 | £118

Chelsea | 68 Royal Hospital Rd., SW3 (Sloane Sq.) | 020-7352-4441 |
www.gordonramsay.com

"Despite spreading himself thin as a pancake", Gordon Ramsay makes sure the "standards don't slip" at his "temple of haute cuisine" in Chelsea, where chef Clare Smyth's "sublime" New French menu is a "delight from start to finish" and "full of surprises"; in the "sedate", "intimate, luxurious setting", a "wonderful sommelier" (part of the "professional", "gracious" staff) proves "extremely helpful" with the "to-die-for wine list", and whilst everything is "ultraexpensive", it's "worth every penny" for an "unforgettable" experience.

Goring Dining Room *British*   24 | 25 | 26 | £67

Victoria | Goring Hotel | 15 Beeston Pl., SW1 (Victoria) |
020-7396-9000 | www.goringhotel.co.uk

An "old-fashioned venue with modern flair", this "elegant", "expensive" Victoria dining room in "one of the last privately owned hotels" in London presents "well-executed" renditions of "sophisticated" Traditional British classics alongside a "fabulous wine selection"; "long-term staff" provide "excellent" service in a setting that looks sedate, save for the "over-the-top" chandeliers.

Gourmet Burger Kitchen *Burgers*   16 | 10 | 13 | £17

Covent Garden | 13-14 Maiden Ln., WC2 (Covent Garden) |
020-7240-9617

Hampstead | 200 Haverstock Hill, NW3 (Belsize Park) | 020-7443-5335

Hampstead | 331 West End Ln., NW6 (West Hampstead) |
020-7794-5455

Battersea | 44 Northcote Rd., SW11 (Clapham Junction Rail) |
020-7228-3309

Fulham | 49 Fulham Broadway, SW6 (Fulham Broadway) |
020-7381-4242

Putney | 333 Putney Bridge Rd., SW15 (Putney Bridge) |
020-8789-1199

Richmond | 15-17 Hill Rise, TW10 (Richmond) | 020-8940-5440

Wimbledon | 88 The Broadway, SW19 (Wimbledon) | 020-8540-3300

Bayswater | 50 Westbourne Grove, W2 (Bayswater/Royal Oak) |
020-7243-4344

(continued)

(continued)

Gourmet Burger Kitchen

Chiswick | 131 Chiswick High Rd., W4 (Turnham Green) |
020-8995-4548
www.gbk.co.uk
Additional locations throughout London

It's "hardly gourmet", but for "generous, juicy burgers in a variety of guises", accompanied by "fat chips" and "hard-to-resist" milkshakes, this "no-frills" chain is "popular" as a "cheap" "filling stop" as well as a "relaxed place to hang out"; that said, there's a view that, "as the franchise expands, the novelty and quality has faded."

Gravetye Manor *British*   - | - | - | VE

East Grinstead | Gravetye Manor | Vowels Ln., W. Sussex |
01342-810-567 | www.gravetyemanor.co.uk

Enveloped by 1,000 acres of forestry and historic gardens dating back over 400 years, this subdued, oak-panelled Modern British eatery in a Gothic-influenced manor-house hotel near Gatwick Airport in Sussex has been reopened by a new owner, fund manager Jeremy Hosking, after a smart revamp that remains sensitive to its refined architecture; the high-end menu makes much use of produce from the venue's walled garden, and the well-endowed cellar means the wine list is an oenophile's delight.

Great Eastern   ∇ 20 | 19 | 19 | £43
Dining Room ●⑤ *Asian*

Shoreditch | 54-56 Great Eastern St., EC2 (Liverpool St./Old St.) |
020-7613-4545 | www.rickerrestaurants.com

A "great range" of "solid Pan-Asian" alimentation is available at this "buzzy" venue in "funky" Shoreditch, "more reasonably priced than E&O", its higher profile sibling; "friendly service" helps to make it a "worthy place for lunch near the City", whilst the "lively" bar scene is a draw after work – though if you're sensitive to noise, you may want to "take your earplugs."

Great Queen Street *British*   24 | 17 | 21 | £36

Covent Garden | 32 Great Queen St., WC2 (Covent Garden/Holborn) |
020-7242-0622

With a "chameleonlike quality that makes it right for a cosy winter meal or a summer lunch", this "bustling" younger sibling of Anchor & Hope in Covent Garden creates "hearty", "superb" Modern British gastropub fare with "refreshingly novel" preparations and "market-fresh" ingredients; "relaxed surroundings, informed service" and "excellent value" complete the picture.

Green Cottage *Chinese*   ∇ 22 | 7 | 12 | £25

Finchley | 9 New College Parade, Finchley Rd., NW3 (Finchley Rd./
Swiss Cottage) | 020-7722-5305

For "authentic", "reliable" Cantonese fare at "reasonable prices", Finchley locals say this low-key venue "always delivers"; however, "grumpy", "indifferent" staff and "aged decor" mean it's most likely "not worth a special trip."

	FOOD	DECOR	SERVICE	COST

Green Door ● *Chophouse*   ∇ 25 | 19 | 23 | £51

Kensington | 152 Gloucester Rd., SW7 (Gloucester Rd.) | 020-7373-2010 | www.greendoorsteakhouse.co.uk

"Magnificent" meat and "nice people" to serve it – that's the formula of this "relaxed, comfortable", upmarket Gloucester Road chophouse that proves to be a particularly "cosy place" for a "fabulous" "dinner after work."

Greenhouse, The ⊠ *French*   26 | 24 | 25 | £78

Mayfair | 27A Hay's Mews, W1 (Green Park) | 020-7499-3331 | www.greenhouserestaurant.co.uk

"Well hidden from the crowds" in a Mayfair courtyard, this "elegant" New French with "beautiful" "modern decor" offers a "sophisticated" yet "relaxing" ambience, "exquisite", "inventive" cuisine and a wine list "unrivalled in depth"; whilst its "certainly not cheap", "professional", "formal" staff who make sure "every detail of your visit is exceptional" add to the feeling it's "worth it."

Green's Restaurant &   22 | 20 | 23 | £56
Oyster Bar ⊠ *British/Seafood*

St. James's | 36 Duke St., SW1 (Green Park/Piccadilly Circus) | 020-7930-4566
City | 14 Cornhill, EC3 (Bank) | 020-7220-6300
www.greens.org.uk

"The best of the old-fashioned fish dishes" is served in "appropriately clubby", "comfortable" surroundings at this "classic", "expensive" St. James's Traditional British eatery also revered for its "attentive service" and "fabulous wine list with treasures galore"; at the City offshoot, it's "quite the scene" downstairs around the horseshoe-shaped bar (where "superb oysters" tempt), whilst upstairs resides a "quiet dining room" "away from the madding crowd."

Greig's ● *Chophouse*   ∇ 22 | 23 | 22 | £49

Mayfair | 26 Bruton Pl., W1 (Bond St./Green Park) | 020-7629-5613 | www.greigs.com

Low-profile, partly because it's "tucked away behind Berkeley Square", this "charming" chophouse has its share of devotees who "rave about" its "dependable", "good-value" steaks, "friendly" staff that go "out of their way to help" and "beautiful old British decor"; however, it does get a few "mixed reviews", with detractors saying it's "tired."

Grenadier, The *British*   18 | 23 | 19 | £32

Belgravia | 18 Wilton Row, SW1 (Hyde Park Corner) | 020-7235-3074
It's "a hunt" to find, but "when you do", you get "quintessential" Traditional British "pub grub" along with the "possibility of a ghostly visitation" at this "venerable institution" in Belgravia, which once "served as the Duke of Wellington's Grenadiers' mess" (hence, "lots of military memorabilia"); there's a "beautiful pewter bar" in the "small" front area and a "cosy, country-style dining room in the back", where Bloody Marys "with a few bangers" are "a must for a Sunday afternoon."

Groucho Club *British*

18 | 19 | 21 | £45

Soho | private club | 45 Dean St., W1 (Leicester Sq./Piccadilly Circus) | 020-7439-4685 | www.thegrouchoclub.com

"Should you be lucky enough" to get in to this "jolly, media-centric" private club in Soho with a "reasonably priced" brasserie, formal dining room and three bar areas, you'll receive "easy-to-eat" Modern British meals ("all the staples you'd expect, done well") from "friendly" staff; you'll also get a side order of "unrivalled drinking and celeb-gazing", the venue's raison d'être.

Grumbles *British/French*

∇ 17 | 12 | 19 | £29

Pimlico | 35 Churton St., SW1 (Pimlico/Victoria) | 020-7834-0149 | www.grumblesrestaurant.co.uk

Enjoy a "nostalgic" "flashback" and "good vibes" at this "quaint, charming" neighbourhood spot that's been in its rustic "publike" Pimlico premises since 1964; as for the French bistro–Traditional British menu, it seems like even more of a "great value" in light of the "friendly" service.

Guinea Grill ⊠ *Chophouse*

23 | 19 | 22 | £56

Mayfair | 30 Bruton Pl., W1 (Bond St.) | 020-7499-1210 | www.theguinea.co.uk

"Behind the bar" of the same-named "quintessential" Mayfair pub resides this "fine", "old-school" chophouse with "white-clothed" "tables on top of each other", where diners tear into "beautiful steaks" as well as "hearty pies" and other "brilliantly cooked" "standard British favourites"; "cordial", "speedy" staff make recommendations from the "amazing wine list", but be sure to ask them for "a snifter of cognac" at the end of your meal, because the bill "will take your breath away."

Gun, The *British*

20 | 21 | 19 | £43

Canary Wharf | 27 Coldharbour, E14 (Blackwall/Canary Wharf, DLR-South Quay) | 020-7515-5222 | www.thegundocklands.com

Discoverers of this "hip", "cosy" Canary Wharf Modern British gastropub are rewarded with a "roaring fire" in winter, a "waterfront terrace" in summer and "stunning views of the Thames and O2" all year long; though some feel the prices are somewhat "steep for what it is", the fare's uniformly "solid" ("Sunday roast is a better value"), plus there's "hospitable" service and some "seriously good wines" to go with.

Haandi *Indian*

- | - | - | M

Knightsbridge | 7 Cheval Pl., SW7 (Knightsbridge) | 020-7823-7373 | www.haandi-restaurants.com

"Hot or not, all the flavours come through" in the "great food" on offer at this "cosy", "friendly" Knightsbridge North Indian (part of a small international chain spanning Kampala and Nairobi) with Colonial decor and a glass-fronted view into the open kitchen; it's a handy "place to go after trudging through Harrods", not least of all because the prices are moderate; FYI, a haandi is a type of cooking pot.

Haché *Burgers*

20	15	16	£22

Camden Town | 24 Inverness St., NW1 (Camden Town) | 020-7485-9100
Chelsea | 329-331 Fulham Rd., SW10 (South Kensington) | 020-7823-3515
www.hacheburgers.com

"An imaginative range of brilliant burgers" and "great chips" (plus a few "good salads as well") "hit the spot" at this "cool" duo in Camden and Chelsea; "good value for money" and a "family"-friendly atmosphere ensure they're "always busy" (and "noisy"), but staff hustle to take care of everyone "quickly."

☑ Hakkasan ● *Chinese*

26	25	21	£65

Bloomsbury | 8 Hanway Pl., W1 (Tottenham Court Rd.) | 020-7927-7000
NEW **Mayfair** | 17 Bruton St., W1 (Bond St.) | 020-7907-1888
www.hakkasan.com

This "hip", "super-buzzy" Bloomsbury basement and its "calmer" new Mayfair offshoot provide an "orgasmic" experience via "always fantastic" "traditional and nouvelle" Cantonese cuisine (starring "superb dim sum") plus "amazing cocktails" served amidst "stunning", "snazzy" surroundings with "pools of light and shadow"; prices are "steep", but they're easy to swallow for such "high quality" and "sexy", "mysterious vibes."

Halepi ● *Greek*

21	12	24	£37

Bayswater | 18 Leinster Terr., W2 (Lancaster Gate/Queensway) | 020-7262-1070 | www.halepi.co.uk

"Feel like part of a big fat Greek family party" at this "boisterous" taverna in Bayswater, where a "jolly" welcome foreshadows "attentive, friendly service"; portions are so large, you may "struggle to finish" the "delicious" victuals, whose "good value" makes up for decor that "needs a revamp."

Haozhan ● *Chinese*

25	15	16	£34

Chinatown | 8 Gerrard St., W1 (Leicester Sq.) | 020-7434-3838 | www.haozhan.co.uk

"Stylish, flavoursome" Chinese cuisine whose preparation is "a bit different from the usual" sets apart this "real find" on the "Gerrard Street drag"; it's "pricier than most in Chinatown", but most feel it's "worth it" when factoring in the "helpful" service – and despite the "humdrum" setting.

Harbour City ● *Chinese*

∇ 23	18	19	£23

Chinatown | 46 Gerrard St., W1 (Leicester Sq./Piccadilly Circus) | 020-7439-7859

"One of the better" Chinatown options for "fine dim sum" and other "fabulous" Cantonese dishes, this "spacious", "buzzing" venue is also "a good place" for good value; as for service, it's normally "efficient", but it can be "aloof" at times.

Hard Rock Cafe ● *American*

15	21	16	£28

Piccadilly | 150 Old Park Ln., W1 (Green Park/Hyde Park Corner) | 020-7629-0382 | www.hardrock.com

"Feel like a groupie" amongst "rock memorabilia" and "100-plus decibel music" at this "inundated-with-tourists" Hyde Park Corner original of the globe-straddling chain; just "don't go with high expectations" about the "reasonably priced" burgers and other "ordinary" American grub and you'll probably find them "ok."

Harry Morgan's *Deli/Jewish*   16 | 11 | 13 | £24
Highgate | Brent Cross Shopping Ctr. | Prince Charles Dr., NW4 (Brent Cross) | 020-8202-1999
St. John's Wood | 29-31 St. John's Wood High St., NW8 (St. John's Wood) | 020-7722-1869
www.harryms.co.uk
The decor resembles "a school cafeteria", but the setting was "never the point" of this "fair-value" St. John's Wood deli – rather it's the "large portions" of non-kosher Jewish fare, like salt beef and "hearty soups"; P.S. a "self-service" offshoot exists in Highgate's Brent Cross Shopping Centre.

Harry's Bar ●🅏 *Italian*   23 | 24 | 24 | £82
Mayfair | private club | 26 S. Audley St., W1 (Green Park) | 020-7408-0844 | www.harrysbar.co.uk
If you get invited to this "refined" private club in a "beautiful" Mayfair townhouse, "be sure to go" to experience all the "indulgent touches" "impeccable" staff provide as they ferry the "excellent" Northern Italian cuisine (plus, you'll probably "see somebody well known"); and if your hosts offer, "let them pay the bill", because it's "madly expensive."

🅩 Harwood Arms *British*   27 | 19 | 21 | £42
Fulham | 27 Walham Grove, SW6 (Fulham Broadway) | 020-7386-1847 | www.harwoodarms.com
"Brilliance and sheer audaciousness" are the hallmarks of the "addictive" Modern British menu (featuring "exceptional" Scotch eggs and plenty of game) at this "casual", "lively" Fulham gastropub that most find "affordable"; the "wide range of ales and wines" and "charming country" setting add to the "stellar" experience, but "the limited number of tables makes getting a reservation difficult", so plan ahead or try to squeeze in at the bar.

Hawksmoor *Chophouse*   26 | 20 | 21 | £53
NEW Covent Garden | 11 Langley St., WC2 (Covent Garden) | 020-7856-2154
Shoreditch | 157 Commercial St., E1 (Liverpool St./Shoreditch) | 020-7247-7392
www.thehawksmoor.com
"Stupendous steaks" in "massive" sizes take the "serious meatasaurus" to "seventh heaven" at this "bustly" Shoreditch chophouse and its "more glamourous" "little sister" in a "seductively lit former warehouse" in Covent Garden; "superb cocktails" are also specialities, and everything's delivered "*sans* frills", "with charm", by "knowledgeable" staff and at "premium prices."

Haz ● *Turkish*   19 | 16 | 18 | £31
City | 112 Houndsditch, EC3 (Liverpool St.) | 020-7623-8180 🅩
City | 34 Foster Ln., EC2 (St. Paul's) | 020-7515-9467

| | FOOD | DECOR | SERVICE | COST |

(continued)

Haz

City | 6 Mincing Ln., EC3 (Fenchurch St./Monument) | 020-7929-3173
City | 9 Cutler St., E1 (Liverpool St.) | 020-7929-7923
www.hazrestaurant.co.uk

Hazev Canary Wharf ● *Turkish*

Canary Wharf | Discovery Dock W. | 2 S. Quay Sq., E14 (Canary Wharf) |
020-7515-9467 | www.hazev.com

"Escape" from the "mundane" via this "cheerful" chain peppered around the City and Canary Wharf, which beckons with the "tempting exotic smells" of "phenomenal Turkish grills" and other "quality Middle Eastern fare"; it's "pretty good value too", which, when coupled with "charming" service, more than makes up for the "spare", "noisy" settings.

☒ Hélène Darroze at the Connaught ⓜ *French*

24 | 26 | 26 | £100

Mayfair | Connaught | Carlos Pl., W1 (Bond St.) | 020-3147-7200 |
www.the-connaught.co.uk

"Enter 'relaxing, sublime, delicious, refined' in your search engine and Hélène Darroze will undoubtedly appear" gush *amis* of this "epitome of elegance" in the Connaught, where "enticing" Classic French cuisine is "served on beautiful china" amidst "luxurious" decor by an "exquisite" "choreographed staff"; if a few find it all "a bit overwrought", most agree that the experience is "about as good as it gets", with "premium" prices to match.

🆕 Henry Root *British/European*

- | - | - | M

Chelsea | 9 Park Walk, SW10 (South Kensington) | 020-7352-3336 |
www.thehenryroot.co.uk

This "charming, unpretentious" Chelsea bistro joins "excellent-value" Mod Euro–Trad British small and large plates with "great" wines; "friendly, laid-back" service befits the "informal" digs, which are sprinkled with lighthearted memorabilia of William Donaldson, a local habitué and the literary creator of the venue's namesake.

Hereford Road *British*

25 | 20 | 21 | £43

Notting Hill | 3 Hereford Rd., W2 (Bayswater/Queensway) |
020-7727-1144 | www.herefordroad.org

An "emphasis on the lesser-used parts of the animal" makes for some "punchy" dishes at this Modern British bistro off Westbourne Grove, but everything on the menu is "superb"; views on the "minimalist decor" – a white-tiled former Victorian butcher's shop – range from "sophisticated" to "stark", but with "friendly", "accommodating staff" and an ambience that fans "recommend for all types of situations (e.g. groups, couples)", in the end, it's "money well spent."

Hibiscus ⃟ⓜ *French*

26 | 21 | 24 | £78

Mayfair | 29 Maddox St., W1 (Oxford Circus) | 020-7629-2999 |
www.hibiscusrestaurant.co.uk

It "looks expensive, tastes expensive and is expensive", but admirers aver that "no price is too high to pay" for chef Claude Bosi's "amazing repertoire" of "innovative", "ambrosial plates" at this "phenomenal" Mayfair New French; though some do find the beige setting "romantic", others find it too "austere", or at least an "acquired taste" – thankfully, "supreme" service and a "top-hitting wine list" please practically everyone.

High Road Brasserie *European*

18 | 20 | 18 | £35

Chiswick | High Road Hse. | 162-166 Chiswick High Rd., W4 (Turnham Green) | 020-8742-7474 | www.highroadhouse.co.uk

"Still the place to be seen in Chiswick", this "fabulous" all-day brasserie attached to a Nick Jones boutique hotel serves a Modern European menu that "can be relied on" for "great taste" and "good value"; "efficient" staff service the "charming setting", which includes sidewalk seating and is especially "lively" at brunch.

High Timber ⑤ *European*

▽ 21 | 19 | 22 | £53

City | 8 High Timber St., EC4 (Blackfriars/Mansion Hse.) | 020-7248-1777 | www.hightimber.com

It's "not the easiest to find, but worth the effort" say enthusiasts of this Vivat Bacchus sibling near the Millennium Bridge in the City, offering "interesting", "quality" Modern European fare, and though its prices are somewhat high, it's the "extraordinary" wine list that's the real "danger to the wallet"; privacy-seekers enjoy the "good private rooms in the cellar", whilst admirers of "fabulous views" ask for the riverside patio "when the weather allows."

Hinds Head *British*

26 | 20 | 22 | £47

Bray | High St., Berkshire | 01628-626151 | www.hindsheadbray.co.uk

"If you can't get into/afford The Fat Duck", try this "lovely", "historic" Bray pub dating back to the 17th century, where chef Heston Blumenthal's "brilliantly executed" Traditional British menu employs "key elements" of his famed fare, but presents it "without the theatre" and at "better-value" prices; "no snootiness" in the service and a "competent wine list" abet an atmosphere that's "more relaxed" than its parent; P.S. you "can't resist" the triple-cooked chips.

Hix *British*

20 | 19 | 19 | £51

Soho | 66-70 Brewer St., W1 (Piccadilly Circus) | 020-7292-3518 | www.hixsoho.co.uk

"Super-fresh" fare is the signature of the "well-cooked and -presented" Modern British menu at this "trendy", "pricey" Soho venue from chef-owner Mark Hix, which is also blessed with a "sensible wine list" and "plenty of beautiful people"; opinions on the "crowded" setting shift between "stylish" and "dreary", but everyone likes how the downstairs bar "swings", not to mention how "friendly" staff are.

Hix Oyster & Chop House *British*

23 | 19 | 20 | £51

Farringdon | 36-37 Greenhill's Rents, EC1 (Barbican/Farringdon) | 020-7017-1930 | www.hixoysterandchophouse.co.uk

"Spectacular" chops, "outstanding" shellfish, a "varied wine list" – heck, the whole traditionally minded British "menu is desirable" at chef-owner Mark Hix's "crowded", "hip hangout" in Farringdon, which also gets plaudits for a "varied wine list" and "attentive staff"; although "the decor is not the most exciting" (as a matter of fact, it's kind of "austere"), in all other respects, it "seldom disappoints", whether for a "business meal or dinner with friends."

Hix Restaurant & Champagne Bar *British/European*

▽ 23 | 18 | 17 | £37

Marylebone | Selfridges | 400 Oxford St., ground fl., W1 (Bond St.) | 020-7499-5400 | www.hixatselfridges.co.uk

Several Selfridges shoppers say its "always a joy to eat" at chef Mark Hix's somewhat "posh" mezzanine-level British-European due to its "delicious" menu of "elegant comfort food" and the choice of a crustacean counter–blessed dining room or a small, sofa-bedecked bar area; however, there are a few who feel it's "much ado about nothing", let down by "sloppy service."

Hot Stuff ⊠ *Indian*

▽ 24 | 6 | 21 | £20

Kennington | 19 Wilcox Rd., SW8 (Vauxhall) | 020-7720-1480 | www.eathotstuff.com

"Not your ordinary Indian" fare is prepared at this "fantastic" find set amidst a gritty parade of Vauxhall shops, where the "excellent variety" of "interesting" eats arrives via "friendly, helpful" staff and for "bargain prices" (made even more so by its BYO policy); just remember, "one comes here for the food, not the atmosphere" – and one does not come without "booking in advance."

Hoxton Grill ◑ *American*

18 | 19 | 19 | £35

Hoxton | Hoxton Hotel | 81 Great Eastern St., EC2 (Old St.) | 020-7739-9111 | www.hoxtongrill.com

"Hip but relaxed", this "airy" all-day Hoxton Hotel dining room is "recommended" for "decent" American dishes, particularly the "good grills", as well as "attentive" service and "nice" red-and-brick decor; it's a "strong price performer" too, plus there's a bar/lounge that's "perfect" for an "after-work" or "late-night" cocktail.

⊠ Hunan ⊠ *Chinese*

28 | 13 | 22 | £54

Pimlico | 51 Pimlico Rd., SW1 (Sloane Sq.) | 020-7730-5712 | www.hunanlondon.com

At this "characterful Chinese" on Pimlico Green, the father-son chef-owner team ask "what you don't like, then serve course after course" of "amazing" Hunan small plates with "vibrant flavours", some "hot as a pistol", "until you can't take any more"; additionally, the "outstanding", "affordable" wine list is "a great fit with the food", plus it dulls the pain of the "cramped, tired" setting and "pricey" fare (it's "worth it").

Hush ⊠ *European*

19 | 18 | 19 | £46

Mayfair | 8 Lancashire Ct., W1 (Bond St.) | 020-7659-1500 | www.hush.co.uk

Bond Street shoppers find plenty to "choose" from at this "trendy" Mayfair Modern European: a "main restaurant" dubbed the Silver Room, a brasserie, a "lovely bar" and a "charming" cobbled courtyard (the place to be "in warmer months"); service is "well paced", and as for the fare, it's "reliable" and "satisfying", if a bit "overpriced."

Iberica ● *Spanish*

| - | - | - | E |

Marylebone | 195 Great Portman St., W1 (Great Portman St.) | 020-7636-8650 | www.ibericalondon.co.uk

A "terrific combination of traditional and new Spanish dishes" is found at this "lively", somewhat pricey tapas spot near Regents Park; the environs comprise a "friendly" ground floor whose bar attracts a "late-night crowd", and a more discreet upstairs dining room, dubbed Caleya, adorned with works by Iberian artists.

Ikeda ⊠ *Japanese*

| ▽ 28 | 12 | 24 | £68 |

Mayfair | 30 Brook St., W1 (Bond St.) | 020-7629-2730 | www.ikedarestaurant.co.uk

"Wonderfully fresh", "excellent sushi" and "tasty, well-presented" cooked dishes draw "regular customers" to this minuscule Mayfair Japanese; indeed, it's appreciated as an "all-around player" thanks to consistent "quality" and "friendly" service - and in spite of "through-the-nose" pricing and decor that "leaves a lot to be desired."

Il Baretto *Italian*

| 23 | 17 | 16 | £49 |

Marylebone | 43 Blandford St., W1 (Baker St.) | 020-7486-7340 | www.ilbaretto.co.uk

They "must be doing something right" at this "always heaving" Marylebone basement whipping up "wood-oven pizza" and other "upscale" Italian "treats" ("a bit pricey"); service gets "challenged with large crowds", but in general, the crowd and atmosphere are "classy and relaxed"; P.S. it's "a must during truffle season."

Il Bordello *Italian*

| 25 | 16 | 22 | £34 |

Wapping | 81 Wapping High St., E1 (Wapping) | 020-7481-9950

"Even if you live outside Wapping", it's "worth travelling" to this "fun, frenetic" trattoria for "huge portions" of "to-die-for" Italian that "won't break the bank"; the converted-warehouse setting "seems a bit dated", but it's sufficiently "comfortable" thanks largely to "super-friendly" staff and a "lively", "convivial crowd."

Il Convivio ⊠ *Italian*

| 24 | 22 | 21 | £52 |

Belgravia | 143 Ebury St., SW1 (Sloane Sq./Victoria) | 020-7730-4099 | www.etruscarestaurants.com

Fans find it "hard to fault" this "pleasant" Belgravia "gem" serving "outstanding" (and "high-priced") Italian cuisine in an "elegant" townhouse setting with red walls and a conservatory roof that "rolls back in warm weather"; though it may be true that there's a "lack of buzz, even when full", that could make it all the more suitable "for a business dinner" or a "date."

NEW Ilia *Italian*

| - | - | - | E |

Chelsea | 96 Draycott Ave., SW3 (South Kensington) | 020-7225-2555 | www.ilia-london.com

Boasting a chef who previously cooked with Hélène Darroze, this addition to Chelsea offers regionally diverse Italian dishes for upscale

| | FOOD | DECOR | SERVICE | COST |

fees; the bright, window-wrapped corner setting features a comfy lounge that converts into a private dining room.

Il Portico 🖪 *Italian*   23 | 19 | 24 | £40

Kensington | 277 Kensington High St., W8 (High St. Kensington) | 020-7602-6262 | www.ilportico.co.uk

"Regulars" "receive hugs and kisses" from the "welcoming, warm" owners at this "cute", "buzzy (without being overly loud)" Kensington venue that "harks back to the '60s/'70s style of Italian restaurant" with its menu of "great, hearty", "classic" dishes; all in all, it's a "wonderful neighbourhood" "staple", and it's value to boot.

Imli *Indian*   17 | 13 | 15 | £22

Soho | 167-169 Wardour St., W1F (Oxford Circus/Tottenham Court Rd.) | 020-7287-4243 | www.imli.co.uk

Supporters of this often "crowded" Soho spot say it's "worth coming" because the Indian tapas are "incredible value for quantity and quality"; but detractors deem the dishes only "so-so", and they're not fond of the "soulless" decor either.

Imperial China ● *Chinese*   18 | 14 | 16 | £28

Chinatown | 25A Lisle St., WC2 (Leicester Sq./Piccadilly Circus) | 020-7734-3388 | www.imperial-china.co.uk

"Kids love the little footbridge outside" and adults enjoy "experimenting with the wide range" of "reliable" dim sum and other "well-made" Cantonese dishes at this "large", "simple space on three floors" in Chinatown; meanwhile, "friendly" staff and "reasonable prices" ensure everyone's catered for.

Inaho 🖪 *Japanese*   ▽ 25 | 14 | 15 | £37

Bayswater | 4 Hereford Rd., W2 (Bayswater/Queensway) | 020-7221-8495

"Tuck yourself into a little corner" of this "tiny, tiny venue" near Westbourne Grove and "treat" yourself to "high-quality", "excellent-value" sushi and other Japanese eats; "pleasant" staff serve everything "quickly", but you "obviously need to book in advance."

Inamo ● *Asian*   15 | 22 | 14 | £41

Soho | 134-136 Wardour St., W1 (Oxford Circus/Tottenham Court Rd.) | 020-7851-7051

NEW St. James's | 4-12 Regent St., SW1 (Piccadilly Circus) | 020-7484-0500
www.inamo-restaurant.com

"Quirky" and "high-tech", this Soho Asian fusion "gimmick" and its new Regent Street offshoot are "famous" for touch-screen tables on which you can order, "play games and look into the kitchen"; the fare is a "little expensive" for being merely "mediocre", but "for groups" in particular, it's "easy, fun" and "something different."

Incognico 🖪 *French/Italian*   19 | 15 | 19 | £46

Soho | 117 Shaftesbury Ave., WC2 (Leicester Sq./Tottenham Court Rd.) | 020-7836-8866 | www.incognico.com

"Simple but satisfying" French-Italian staples at "reasonable prices" make this "casual", "old-fashioned brasserie" a "reliable go-to" in

Soho; it's especially "wonderful" pre-theatre, as "always-a-joy" staff "get you out the door on time for your show", no matter how "crowded" it is.

NEW Indian Zilla ● *Indian*

–	–	–	E

Barnes | 2-3 Rocks Ln., SW13 (Hammersmith) | 020-8878-3989 | www.indianzilla.co.uk

"Exciting" Indian preparations featuring "delightful" vegetarian options keep this "welcome", "upmarket" Barnes addition "full"; what's more, staff "know their dishes and explain them well", making it an apt choice for novices.

Indian Zing *Indian*

24	18	21	£38

Hammersmith | 236 King St., W6 (Ravenscourt Park) | 020-8748-5959 | www.indianzing.co.uk

Definitely "not your run-of-the-mill" "curry house", this "upmarket", "white-tablecloth" Indian "in the outer reaches of Hammersmith" fills its "something-for-everyone" menu with "much more interesting tastes to savour"; add in "excellent service" and an "interesting wine list", and it's clear to see why it's always "packed to the rafters."

Indigo *European*

22	20	24	£50

Covent Garden | One Aldwych Hotel | 1 Aldwych, WC2 (Charing Cross/Covent Garden) | 020-7300-0400 | www.onealdwych.com

"Cheerful, swift" service, "beautifully prepared" Modern European eats and "a high-quality wine list" (with "prices to match") are what's offered at this dining room on the mezzanine of Covent Garden's One Aldwych Hotel; the generally "low-key" ambience means it's "ideal" for a "quiet" meal or "business meeting", but lest there be hubbub from the "lively bar below", "ask for a seat in the back, away from the lobby overhang."

Inn The Park *British*

17	18	15	£42

St. James's | St. James's Park | off Horse Guards Rd., SW1 (St. James's Park) | 020-7451-9999 | www.innthepark.com

With a location in St. James's Park, the "views are terrific" at this wooden pavilion featuring a snack bar and a full-service dining room where "large portions" of "fair" Traditional British fare are ferried by "passable" staff from breakfast to dinner; though the high prices should be unsurprising given the "wonderful setting", some surveyors admit to a "shock when the bill arrives."

Ishbilia *Lebanese*

25	14	18	£41

Belgravia | 9 William St., SW1 (Knightsbridge) | 020-7235-7788 ●
Knightsbridge | Harrods | 87-135 Brompton Rd., 2nd fl., SW1 (Knightsbridge) | 020-7893-8598
www.ishbilia.com

"Wonderful" Lebanese cuisine is offered in a "huge variety" and for comparative "bargain" prices at this Belgravia venue where the crowd is always "convivial", despite "bland" decor and "variable service"; for "great food in Harrods", check out its offshoot, "oddly located in the middle of the luggage department."

	FOOD	DECOR	SERVICE	COST

Ishtar ● *Turkish* — 20 | 18 | 22 | £29

Marylebone | 10-12 Crawford St., W1 (Baker St.) | 020-7224-2446 | www.ishtarrestaurant.com

Though its set lunch/early-bird dinner is "particularly brilliant", this "large", "upscale" Marylebone "gem" is always "good value" due to the "generous portions" of "quality" Turkish tucker such as "lovely mezze", "wonderful charcoal-grilled meats and delicious sauces"; on weekend evenings, you'll be treated to live music and belly dancing, but whenever you come, service is "friendly."

Itsu *Japanese* — 16 | 13 | 13 | £24

Canary Wharf | Cabot Pl. E., 2nd fl., E14 (Canary Wharf) | 020-7512-5790
Chelsea | 118 Draycott Ave., SW3 (South Kensington) | 020-7590-2400
Notting Hill | 100 Notting Hill Gate, W11 (Notting Hill Gate) | 020-7229-4016
www.itsu.com

"As conveyor-belt places go", this "easy" Japanese chain is a "dependable" "pit stop" for "good-quality sushi", "delicious" soups and "decent value"; folks in a rush should bear in mind that service is "iffy" and "busy times may involve long waits" – on the other hand, parents will want to remember that "kids think it's fun."

⚡ Ivy, The ● *British/European* — 22 | 22 | 23 | £59

Covent Garden | 1-5 West St., WC2 (Leicester Sq.) | 020-7836-4751 | www.the-ivy.co.uk

The "X factor" is palpable at this "glamourous", "energetic" Covent Garden "class act" that attracts "a famous face or four" for its "high-standard", "delish" Modern British–Euro "comfort food"; but "everyone is a star" in the eyes of the "stellar" staff, whose "professionalism" mitigates the "trauma of getting a reservation" and paying the "expensive" bill.

Jak's *Mediterranean* — ∇ 22 | 15 | 11 | £25

Chelsea | 77 Walton St., SW3 (South Kensington) | 020-7584-3441 | www.jakswaltonstreet.com

"From breakfast to late dinner", this "relaxed, communal environment" in Chelsea offers an "amazing display" of "delicious", "healthy" Med eats in a "kind of self-service" format ("you choose and they bring it" to your table); "good value" ensures it's "always packed", but space is tight, so "don't go with someone who has claustrophobia."

Jamie's Italian *Italian* — 19 | 16 | 18 | £33

Covent Garden | St. Martin's Courtyard | 11 Upper St. Martin's Ln., WC2 (Covent Garden/Leicester Sq.) | 020-3326-6390 ●
Canary Wharf | 2 Churchill Pl., Unit 17, E14 (Canary Wharf) | 020-3002-5252
Kingston | 19-23 High St., KT1 (Kingston Rail) | 020-3326-4300
NEW Shepherd's Bush | Westfield Shopping Ctr. | Ariel Way, lower ground fl., W12 (Wood Lane) | 020-8090-9070
Bath | 10 Milsom Pl. | 012-2543-2340
www.jamieoliver.com

"Reasonably priced" fare "beautifully made with high-quality ingredients", aka "just what you expect" from chef Jamie Oliver, is "served amicably" by "attentive, knowledgeable" staff at this ever-growing national chain of "informal" Italians; no reservations for less than six yields queues that can be a "major hassle" (it's the "perfect business lunch" place if you arrive quite early), but once seated, it's all "easy going"; P.S. a branch is slated for Westfield Stratford City, the new shopping centre across from the Olympic Park.

Jenny Lo's Tea House ⊠⇄ *Chinese* ▽ 19 | 9 | 15 | £15

Belgravia | 14 Eccleston St., SW1 (Victoria) | 020-7259-0399 | www.jennylo.co.uk

"If you need a good lunch [or dinner] in a rush", this spartan, "casual" canteen by Victoria Coach Station delivers "solid" Chinese noodle bowls, etc., in "rapid" fashion, and "politely" too; what's more, it's a "bargain" whether you're dining in or taking out.

Jin Kichi Ⓜ *Japanese* 26 | 11 | 20 | £38

Hampstead | 73 Heath St., NW3 (Hampstead) | 020-7794-6158 | www.jinkichi.com

The sushi and yakatori are so "sublime" that whatever's charged "turns out to be a bargain" at this "Hampstead classic" boasting "attentive", "friendly service"; there is a "downside" though: a "pokey", "noisy, tightly packed space" for which "you definitely need a reservation" ("book well in advance").

Joe Allen ❶ *American* 18 | 17 | 19 | £40

Covent Garden | 13 Exeter St., WC2 (Covent Garden) | 020-7836-0651 | www.joeallen.co.uk

"Shades of London's actors' past, present and future" haunt this "theatrical must" in a Covent Garden basement where showgoers come for "people-watching" that gets more "interesting" when the curtains fall and "American comfort food" that's always "good-value" ("those in the know order" the "splendid" "off-menu burger"); service comes "with a dash of wit", however, critics opine the whole production is "living off its past reputation", i.e. in need of a "makeover."

NEW José *Spanish* - | - | - | M

Tower Bridge | 104 Bermondsey St. SE, SE1 (London Bridge) | 020-7403-4902

In a tiny corner site with just 30 covers (and no reservations) near Tower Bridge, José Pizarro (ex Brindisa) evokes the tapas bars of Barcelona with this, his first solo venture where the Spanish plates come from an open kitchen; to complement the moderately priced menu is an impressive, diverse list of wines and sherries.

Joy King Lau ❶ *Chinese* 18 | 9 | 14 | £24

Chinatown | 3 Leicester St., WC2 (Leicester Sq./Piccadilly Circus) | 020-7437-1133 | www.joykinglau.com

Enjoying a "solid reputation", despite decor that "could do with work", this Chinese "staple" in Chinatown reels in a lot of "locals" for "good dim sum"; however, dinner is "not to be ruled out" – though "quieter", the fare is just as "tasty" and the prices are similarly "reasonable."

	FOOD	DECOR	SERVICE	COST

☑ J. Sheekey ◑ *Seafood* — 26 | 22 | 24 | £61

Covent Garden | 28-32 St. Martin's Ct., WC2 (Leicester Sq.) |
020-7240-2565 | www.j-sheekey.co.uk

Though it attracts a "glamourous", "celeb"-dotted crowd, the "real
star is the impeccable fish" offered at this "memorable" Covent
Garden "institution" with a "clubby", "dark-panelled" "labyrinth" of
"nooks and crannies", some "romantic", others with "too many
people sitting too close together"; "warm", "swift service" and a
"delightful wine list" help make the "expense-account" prices seem
"worth it", but remember that it's "always crowded", so a "reservation is a must."

☑ J. Sheekey Oyster Bar ◑ *Seafood* — 26 | 23 | 24 | £46

Covent Garden | 33-34 St. Martin's Ct., WC2 (Leicester Sq.) |
020-7240-2565 | www.j-sheekey.co.uk

"When you want to be a bit more casual, take a bit less time and still
enjoy the great Sheekey seafood", try its "congenial, spirited" next-
door sibling, a "warm, clubby" Covent Garden setting whose "fishy
comfort food" "won't break the bank"; "sublime service" is par for
the course, and though the U-shaped bar is "cramped", there's
"usually no need to book", making it particularly "fun and easy" for
a "before- or after-theatre" caprice.

Julie's *British* — 19 | 22 | 21 | £46

Holland Park | 135 Portland Rd., W11 (Holland Park) | 020-7229-8331 |
www.juliesrestaurant.com

An array of "divine" themed dining rooms (e.g. a "pretty" garden
space) conjures the "quirky", "eccentric" atmosphere at this "venerable", "romantic" Holland Park Modern British option with "relaxed,
friendly service" and an "interesting wine list"; whilst "not always
reaching the gastronomic heights" that the decor and "pricey" fees
portend, the all-day fare is on the whole "nicely prepared."

Just St. James's ☒ *British* — 18 | 19 | 18 | £48

St. James's | 12 St. James's St., SW1 (Green Park) |
020-7976-2222

"Just up from St. James's Palace" resides this "large", "beautiful"
former Edwardian banking hall, now a "pricey" eatery where the
"not-too-close-together tables" are filled with "businesspeople"
downing "solid, reliable" Modern British cuisine; there's also a bar
area, which some "prefer" for its "classic" atmosphere and
"great social scene."

JW Steakhouse *American/Chophouse* — 21 | 20 | 21 | £56

Mayfair | Grosvenor Hse. Hotel | 86 Park Ln., W1 (Bond St./Marble Arch) |
020-7399-8460 | www.jwsteakhouse.co.uk

"Go hungry", because the "portions are American in size" at this
"large", "opulent beef palace" in Mayfair's "elegant" Grosvenor
House Hotel, where all the U.S. chophouse basics are "done well" –
and "expensive"; detractors decry "minimal originality", but even
they might yet return for the "polite", "accommodating" service and
big patio on Park Lane.

	FOOD	DECOR	SERVICE	COST

Kai Mayfair *Chinese*
26 | 22 | 24 | £62

Mayfair | 65 S. Audley St., W1 (Bond St./Marble Arch) | 020-7493-8988 | www.kaimayfair.co.uk

"Ludicrously tasty", "truly amazing fare" is made in "combinations not easily found" at this "comfortable", "luxury Chinese" in Mayfair, which "maintains great standards after so many years"; "sublime service" and an "elegant wine list" add to its reputation as a place "not to be missed" – and for which you should expect to pay "extremely expensive prices" ("apart from the set lunch").

Kazan *Turkish*
20 | 17 | 21 | £31

Pimlico | 93-94 Wilton Rd., SW1 (Victoria) | 020-7233-7100 | www.kazan-restaurant.com

"Delicious Ottoman cuisine at sensible prices" is the "reason why it's full every night" at this Pimlico Turk; "fun, enthusiastic" staff ensure "everyone has a nice time" in a casual environment that "doesn't seem to have changed much", even after a "recent refurb."

Kensington Place *British*
19 | 16 | 16 | £37

Kensington | 201-209 Kensington Church St., W8 (Notting Hill Gate) | 020-7727-3184 | www.kensingtonplace-restaurant.co.uk

Now in its 25th year, this Notting Hill Gate haunt remains a "bustling, gregarious" venue for "reasonably priced" Modern British dishes that are "fine", though "not as good as when it opened" (with a fish market next door, the seafood is the most "reliable" thing offered); though the digs are looking "dated" (particularly the "mural on the back wall"), "people-watching at the large windows is wonderful."

Kensington Square Kitchen *British*
▽ 21 | 17 | 17 | £31

Kensington | 9 Kensington Sq., W8 (High St. Kensington) | 020-7938-2598 | www.kensingtonsquarekitchen.co.uk

Managing to be both "easy-going and classy", this affordable cafe in Kensington Square prepares "delicious" Modern British breakfasts and lunches, plus "out-of-this-world coffee"; the "small", cream-and-pale-green ground-floor space is "often crowded", so "you may need to sit downstairs" in the cellar – that is, if you can't snatch one of the handful of warm-weather pavement tables.

Kensington Wine Rooms *European*
19 | 19 | 22 | £36

Kensington | 127-129 Kensington Church St., W8 (Notting Hill Gate) | 020-7727-8142 | www.greatwinesbytheglass.com

Oenophiles "who love to experiment" adore the "vast" array of varieties "to suit all pockets", which are dispensed from Enomatic machines at this "warm", "buzzing" bar near Notting Hill Gate; though the Modern European small plates are a "side show" to the wine selection, they're suitably "interesting" and "delicious."

Kettner's *French*
16 | 23 | 19 | £37

Soho | 29 Romilly St., W1 (Leicester Sq.) | 020-7734-6112 | www.kettners.com

"There's nowhere quite like" this 1867 "Soho institution" that features "lovely" "private salons" and a "classic" champagne bar where you can "pretend to be Oscar" (Wilde, that is, a former habitué) whilst quaffing pours from a "huge list"; there's also a "buzzing" brasserie, and though the French fare "does not match the decor", it's "acceptable" and "decent value"; P.S. the pianist (Tuesdays-Saturdays) is "a lovely added touch."

	FOOD	DECOR	SERVICE	COST

Khan's ◑ *Indian*   18 | 10 | 14 | £22

Bayswater | 13-15 Westbourne Grove, W2 (Bayswater/Royal Oak) | 020-7727-5420 | www.khansrestaurant.com

Want a "curry in a hurry"? – "surly" "waiters in a flurry" see to it at this "straight-to-the-point", "dependable" Bayswater Indian where "no alcohol makes for an even speedier exit"; the "large", "crowded" digs with "long communal tables" "could do with a face-lift", but at least prices equal a "great bargain."

Khan's of Kensington ◑ *Indian*   19 | 10 | 16 | £26

South Kensington | 3 Harrington Rd., SW7 (South Kensington) | 020-7584-4114 | www.khansofkensington.co.uk

"Convenient if you're on the way" to the nearby South Ken museums, this "old standard" serves up "satisfying", "quick, inexpensive Indian" dishes; like the fare, the "small" setting is "nothing remarkable", but it's "relaxed", making for an experience that's still a "comfort" "after all these years" (more than 20, to be precise).

☒ Kiku *Japanese*   27 | 20 | 24 | £53

Mayfair | 17 Half Moon St., W1 (Green Park) | 020-7499-4208 | www.kikurestaurant.co.uk

"Expensive and worth it" exclaim dinner diners of this "smart", "brightly lit" Mayfair "gem" where "excellent sushi and sashimi" is offered alongside "wonderful" "tempura, shabu-shabu" and other Japanese dishes; lunchtime can be a "bargain" thanks to the set menus, whilst service is "attentive and friendly" at all times.

Kitchen Italia *Italian*   ▽ 14 | 13 | 11 | £27

Covent Garden | 41 Earlham St., WC2 (Covent Garden) | 020-7632-9500
Shepherd's Bush | Westfield Shopping Ctr. | Ariel Way, W12 (Shepherd's Bush) | 020-8749-9133
www.kitchen-italia.com

Akin to "an Italian Wagamama" in both look and concept, this moderately priced duo in Covent Garden and the Westfield Shopping Centre splits commentators: some appreciate the "tasty", "hearty comfort food" and "fun" buzz, whilst others find "no reason to return", citing "ordinary" food, "ragged" service and "bland" decor.

Kitchen W8 *European*   25 | 20 | 22 | £48

Kensington | 11-13 Abingdon Rd., W8 (High St. Kensington) | 020-7937-0120 | www.kitchenw8.com

"Excellent technique" is evident in chef/co-owner Philip Howard's "sophisticated", "innovative" Modern European fare at this Kensington "godsend" whose prices are "incredible" given the "outstanding" quality; the "modern" "decor is pleasing" (there's "some great art on the walls"), as is the "comfortable" atmosphere, smoothed along by "friendly", "attentive service."

	FOOD	DECOR	SERVICE	COST

Z NEW Koffmann's *French*   26 | 21 | 25 | £69

Belgravia | The Berkeley | Wilton Pl., SW1 (Hyde Park Corner/ Knightsbridge) | 020-7235-1010 | www.the-berkeley.co.uk

"Master" chef Pierre Koffmann crafts "sublime" iterations of "rustic" French dishes ("everyone should eat" the "signature" pig's trotters "at least once") at this "smart", earth-toned, tri-tiered "fine-dining" venue in Belgravia's Berkeley Hotel; "unobtrusively attentive service" and a "terrific" wine list further make it a "not-to-miss" "treat", and whilst prices are expectedly "high", the "set lunch is ludicrously good value."

Koi *Japanese*   25 | 21 | 22 | £48

Kensington | 1E Palace Gate, W8 (High St. Kensington) | 020-7581-8778

"Fantastic quality, every time" is the promise of this "friendly", "up-market" Kensington Japanese whose teppanyaki and teriyaki are just as "delicious" as the sushi; maybe due to its "small", "inconspicuous location", it's often "quiet", but "locals" feel "fortunate" that they can dine there "quite frequently" and not have to wait for a table.

NEW Kopapa *Eclectic*   ∇ 17 | 10 | 15 | £36

Covent Garden | 32-34 Monmouth St., WC2 (Covent Garden) | 020-7240-6076 | www.kopapa.co.uk

Providing "all-day bites" to Covent Garden, this "casual", "bustling" spot features "fusion master" Peter Gordon's "interesting" Eclectic menu, much of which is "served tapas-style", all available with a "good selection of New Zealand wines"; service is "erratic", but it "comes with a smile", making the main "drawback" the "deafening noise."

NEW Koya 🍴 *Japanese*   23 | 12 | 15 | £21

Soho | 49 Frith St., W1 (Tottenham Court Rd.) | 020-7434-4463 | www.koya.co.uk

It might take "six tries to get in due to the popularity" (and lack of space) at this ultracasual Soho shop, but it's "definitely worth it" for "brilliant" Japanese noodles that "amaze for their quality" and "bar-gain prices"; "accommodating" service completes the rosy picture.

Kulu Kulu Sushi 🍴 *Japanese*   22 | 9 | 14 | £21

Covent Garden | 51-53 Shelton St., WC2 (Covent Garden) | 020-7240-5687
Soho | 76 Brewer St., W1 (Piccadilly Circus) | 020-7734-7316
South Kensington | 39 Thurloe Pl., SW7 (South Kensington) | 020-7589-2225

"Help yourself" to "mouth-watering" sushi and "other Japanese goodies" off the conveyor belts at this mini-chain of "informal", "cheerful" venues; sure, you'll find "nothing fancy" (particularly in the decor department), but given the "fantastic portion sizes" and "reasonable prices", "what's not to like?"

La Bouchée *French*   ∇ 19 | 15 | 18 | £40

South Kensington | 56 Old Brompton Rd., SW7 (South Kensington) | 020-7589-1929

If "you aren't claustrophobic", you might find the "simple", "cramped quarters" "charming" (still, "avoid the basement") at this

| | FOOD | DECOR | SERVICE | COST |

"down-to-earth French bistro" in South Kensington, a "reliable standby" for all the "classics"; oenophiles sniff that the "wine list is undistinguished", but "that's not why you go there."

La Brasserie *French*

| | 19 | 20 | 18 | £36 |

South Kensington | 272 Brompton Rd., SW3 (South Kensington) | 020-7581-3089 | www.labrasserielondon.com

"Dress up or down, it doesn't matter" at this all-day South Ken "institution" that locals and tourists "count on year after year" for "good" French fare (brunch particularly "never gets old"); what's more, the "old-fashioned brasserie" setting is "wonderful", just like the "smooth" service and reasonable prices.

L'Absinthe Ⓜ *French*

| | 21 | 13 | 22 | £41 |

Primrose Hill | 40 Chalcot Rd., NW1 (Chalk Farm) | 020-7483-4848 | labsinthe.co.uk

"Unpretentious, well-cooked" French bistro "standards" "pull in the crowds" at this "Primrose Hill treat" with "friendly, charming host and servers"; it's "amazing value" too, helped by a "fantastic" set lunch and a "good wine policy" where you choose a bottle from the attached shop and only "a small corkage is added."

Ladurée *French*

| | 23 | 20 | 17 | £33 |

NEW Covent Garden | Covent Garden Piazza | The Market, Unit 1, WC2 (Covent Garden) | 020-7240-0706
Knightsbridge | Harrods | 87-135 Brompton Rd., ground fl., SW1 (Knightsbridge) | 020-3155-0111
Piccadilly | 71-72 Burlington Arcade, W1 (Green Park) | 020-7491-9155 | www.laduree.fr

"Scrumptious, melt-in-the-mouth macarons" are the attraction at this "über-posh", "richly decorated" French cafe/patisserie in Harrods, which also offers a "divine menu of elegant sandwiches, salads" and "fluffy omelets" (all "expensive", all "special"); no reservations mean "long, frustrating queues", but at least there are more tables than at the "shoebox"-sized Burlington Arcade offshoot; P.S. the Covent Garden branch opened post-Survey.

La Famiglia ◗ *Italian*

| | 22 | 18 | 23 | £47 |

Chelsea | 7 Langton St., SW10 (Fulham Broadway/Sloane Sq.) | 020-7351-0761 | www.lafamiglia.co.uk

"You'll be welcomed like one of the family" by "terrific" "Italian waiters" at this "bustling" Chelsea "stalwart" that could be "renamed the Happy Diner from the appearance of the clientele", all smiles as they dig into the "hearty", "rustic, delicious" fare; costs are somewhat high, though the "covered garden out back" is "worth the price of admission alone" – the interior, on the other hand, "needs a face-lift."

La Fromagerie Café *European*

| | 22 | 18 | 15 | £25 |

Marylebone | 2-6 Moxon St., W1 (Baker St.) | 020-7935-0341
Islington | 30 Highbury Park, N5 (Arsenal) | 020-7359-7440
www.lafromagerie.co.uk

"You can buy food to go or sit at the communal tables for a relaxing meal" of "simple", "enjoyable" Modern Euro fare at this "charming", "light-filled" cafe/deli in Marylebone; but really, most people come for the "amazing" array of cheeses ("some of the best in Europe"), presented by "educated cheese mongers"; P.S. the Islington off-shoot is also a "lovely choice", albeit with a smaller menu.

La Genova 🗷 *Italian*   25 | 19 | 24 | £49

Mayfair | 32 N. Audley St., W1 (Bond St./Marble Arch) | 020-7629-5916 | www.lagenovarestaurant.com

"Unimpressive from the street" and as "old school as it gets" inside, this Italian is worth patronising for its "congenial owner" (who "greets everyone"), his "efficient" staff and the "superb" cuisine served with "no gimmicks" and in "healthy portions"; it's a "treat" whether with "business" colleagues or "family", and "surprisingly moderately priced" considering its Mayfair address.

Langan's Bistro 🗷 *British/French*   ∇ 21 | 22 | 24 | £50

Marylebone | 26 Devonshire St., W1 (Baker St.) | 020-7935-4531 | www.langansrestaurants.co.uk

"Solid" Traditional British–French "comfort food" is served in an "intimate", "comfortable setting" with "nice artwork on the walls" at this "handy" Marylebone "standby"; "excellent-value set menus", "fairly priced wines" and "warm service" complete the "charming" picture.

Langan's Brasserie *British/French*   19 | 20 | 20 | £51

Mayfair | Stratton Hse. | Stratton St., W1 (Green Park) | 020-7491-8822 | www.langansrestaurants.co.uk

"Still a safe bet" for "fun", "energy" and "well-prepared", "enjoyable" Traditional British–French fare ("midpriced for London"), this "hectic" yet "classy", "classic" Green Park brasserie also provides "reliable" "old-fashioned service"; whilst it's true that a contingent dubs it the "past-its-prime" "Ivy of the '80s", others hail it as "the once and future king."

L'Anima 🗷 *Italian*   25 | 22 | 22 | £64

City | 1 Snowden St., EC2 (Liverpool St./Old St.) | 020-7422-7000 | www.lanima.co.uk

"Hip" and "brash", this restaurant/bar in a "tucked away" City location is "a magnet" for the sort of "young professionals" who can afford the "expensive" prices charged for the "memorable" "modern" Italian dishes and "excellent" wines; though some find staff "smart", others feel that "service is not up to scratch", e.g. "too casual" for the "sleek", "airy", "minimalist" setting, which is marked by white leather, stone and glass.

Lansdowne, The *European*   ∇ 21 | 15 | 19 | £32

Primrose Hill | 90 Gloucester Ave., NW1 (Chalk Farm) | 020-7483-0409 | www.thelansdownepub.co.uk

"Consistent", daily changing Modern Euro dishes are listed on a value-priced blackboard menu at this Primrose Hill gastropub where staff are "friendly but professional", and they "know their wines too", both in the downstairs bar and upstairs dining room; the vibe is "buzzy" yet "relaxing", except perhaps at weekend brunch, when the "best Bloody Marys" and "chaos" reign.

	FOOD	DECOR	SERVICE	COST

🅐 La Petite Maison *Mediterranean*   27 | 21 | 21 | £65

Mayfair | 54 Brooks Mews, W1 (Bond St.) | 020-7495-4774 |
www.lpmlondon.co.uk

Go with "a group" to "share" and "graze" amongst "exquisite combinations" of "outstanding", "full-of-flavour" Mediterranean small
and large plates at this "big", "inviting" Mayfair "hot spot"; sure, it's
"expensive", "hectic", "noisy" and there's "room for improvement"
in the service department, but those are quibbles – "to call it anything but incredible would be a disservice."

La Porchetta Pizzeria *Pizza*   19 | 10 | 15 | £17

Holborn | 33 Boswell St., WC1 (Holborn) | 020-7242-2434 🛇
Clerkenwell | 84-86 Rosebery Ave., EC1 (Angel) | 020-7837-6060
Camden Town | 74-77 Chalk Farm Rd., NW1 (Chalk Farm) |
020-7267-6822
Muswell Hill | 265 Muswell Hill Broadway, N10 (Highgate) |
020-8883-1500 ◑
Islington | 141-142 Upper St., N1 (Angel/Highbury & Islington) |
020-7288-2488
Stoke Newington | 147 Stroud Green Rd., N4 (Finsbury Park) |
020-7281-2892
www.laporchetta.net

"You get lots, and it's so cheap" at this "relaxed" "neighbourhood"
Italian chain whipping up "solid pizza", "hearty, well-made" pastas,
salads and such; even if "spotty service" can let the side down, it's still
"a fun place to go", though it's sometimes "too noisy" ("eardrums
pop when birthday cake is served", seemingly "twice every visit!").

La Porte des Indes *Indian*   22 | 24 | 21 | £45

Marylebone | 32 Bryanston St., W1 (Marble Arch) | 020-7224-0055 |
www.laportedesindes.com

"The exterior is no way representative of what you will find inside"
this "gorgeous", "exotic" Marble Arch Indian where "splendid"
"food with a twist" is served by "attentive" staff amidst palm trees,
waterfalls, bridges and bamboo accoutrements; ok, it's all a bit
"over-the-top" (and "rather pricey" to boot), but it's all in "good
fun", especially after a few sips of "excellent wine."

La Poule au Pot *French*   21 | 20 | 19 | £51

Pimlico | 231 Ebury St., SW1 (Sloane Sq.) | 020-7730-7763 |
www.pouleaupot.co.uk

"Magic moments" transpire at this "romantic" Pimlico French spot
with a "lovely", "candlelit" main room and "beautiful" outdoor seating ("don't get stuck in the dungeon"); couples coo over the "consistent, comforting" cuisine, "wonderful" wines, mostly "friendly"
service and the fact that, if they get bored, they can easily eavesdrop
on their neighbour, as the "tables are almost on top of one another."

🅐 L'Atelier de Joël Robuchon *French*   27 | 24 | 24 | £79

Covent Garden | 13-15 West St., WC2 (Leicester Sq.) |
020-7010-8600 | www.joel-robuchon.com

"A sublime experience from a sublime chef", this "hip"
Theatrelander stars Joël Robuchon's "artfully presented", "mind-

blowing" New French menu flush with small plates (some find them "too small") sold at "huge prices" (they're "worth it"); "smiley, attentive service" holds sway throughout the tri-tiered space, comprising the "vibrant" red L'Atelier ("sit at the counter" for a "full view" of the "amazing" cooks), the "sleek, quiet", dinner-only La Cuisine and the "even swankier cocktail lounge."

Latium ☒ Italian
24	16	24	£51

Bloomsbury | 21 Berners St., W1 (Goodge St.) | 020-7323-9123 | www.latiumrestaurant.com
Stuffed pasta "in all shapes and forms" makes this somewhat "undiscovered" Fitzrovia Italian a "ravioli-lover's paradise", but the entire menu is a "delight" and features "comparatively modest costs" to boot; the setting is kind of "bland", "sterile" and often "noisy", but "professional, courteous staff" and an "extensive" wine list "more than make up for it."

☑ La Trompette European/French
26	19	24	£58

Chiswick | 5-7 Devonshire Rd., W4 (Turnham Green) | 020-8747-1836 | www.latrompette.co.uk
"Don't let the distance from Central London dissuade you from trying" this "sibling to Chez Bruce" in Chiswick, where the "impeccable" Modern Euro-New French cuisine, backed by an "excellent wine list", is more "reasonably priced"; the owners may have "crammed too many tables" into the "crisp" digs, but "superb" staff put guests at ease.

Launceston Place British
25	23	24	£61

Kensington | 1A Launceston Pl., W8 (High St. Kensington) | 020-7937-6912 | www.launcestonplace-restaurant.co.uk
For a dose of "calm after a busy day" or a "romantic dinner", this Kensington location provides a "chic, soothing" setting divvied into "cosy pockets" where "exquisite", "creative" Modern British fare is "delightfully presented" with "unusual little touches and extra bits"; "impeccable" staff pay "attention to detail", and whilst it's generally "not cheap", the set lunch is "a steal."

L'Autre Pied European
24	18	23	£56

Marylebone | 5-7 Blandford St., W1 (Bond St.) | 020-7486-9696 | www.lautrepied.co.uk
"Cheekier, less formal" but still "worthy" of Pied à Terre, this Marylebone sibling offers "imaginative", "beautifully presented", "satisfying" Modern European dishes alongside an "extensive wine list" and "charming service", all at relatively "reasonable prices" (the prix fixes are "unbelievable bargains"); though some disparage what they deem a "small, crowded", "dated" environment that "lacks atmosphere", others call it "cool."

L'Aventure ☒ French
∇ 26	18	20	£55

St. John's Wood | 3 Blenheim Terr., NW8 (St. John's Wood) | 020-7624-6232 | www.laventure.co.uk
The "fancy, formal French" dishes - "beautifully served" by "friendly" staff (led by a "charming owner") - are so "fabulous" at

| | FOOD | DECOR | SERVICE | COST |

this venue, they're practically a "reason to move" to St. John's Wood; fans "have never been disappointed" with the "intimate" interior, but on clement days, the outdoor seating area is "much in demand."

Le Bouchon Breton *French*   16 | 13 | 13 | £42

Shoreditch | Old Spitalfields Mkt. | 8 Horner Sq., E1 (Liverpool St.) | 020-7377-1839 | www.lebouchon.co.uk

Considering the "expensive prices" they pay, many surveyors are frustrated by this large Spitalfields Market French brasserie's "glitches", including Breton-centric cooking that's "not as good as it should be" and service that fluctuates between "attentive" and "nonexistent"; still, the "amazing cheese selection" wins admirers.

Le Boudin Blanc *French*   24 | 19 | 21 | £48

Mayfair | Shepherd Mkt. | 5 Trebeck St., W1 (Green Park) | 020-7499-3292 | www.boudinblanc.co.uk

Even when they get one of the "surly" members of the otherwise "pleasant" staff, habitués of this Shepherd Market bistro "endure it" for the "wonderful" "traditional" *plats,* which are offered alongside a "strong" wine list in "cosy", "quirky", "kind-of-rustic surroundings"; though it's "on the pricey side", many feel it's "great value for Mayfair", "so go early" or, better yet, "book ahead", because it gets "crowded."

Le Café Anglais *French*   22 | 22 | 21 | £50

Bayswater | Whiteleys Shopping Ctr. | 8 Porchester Gdns., W2 (Bayswater) | 020-7221-1415 | www.lecafeanglais.co.uk

A "haven" for shoppers in Whiteleys and a "huge asset" to Queensway in general, this "grand", "art deco–style setting" features "jovial" chef-owner Rowley Leigh's "well-prepared and -sourced" French brasserie fare that "appeals to gourmets and the casual diner" alike; "warm", "caring service" and "nice house wines" are more pluses, but the best aspect may be the "very good price-to-quality ratio."

Le Café du Marché ⓩ *French*   24 | 22 | 22 | £47

Farringdon | 22 Charterhouse Sq., EC1 (Barbican) | 020-7608-1609 | www.cafedumarche.co.uk

"Ever-reliable" for "informal City lunches" as well as "convivial" suppers with "a discreet jazz pianist playing" nightly, this Smithfield Market "delight" delivers "quality", "well-flavoured" French bistro cuisine; on top of that, respondents find the traditionally turned out setting "beautiful" and the service "friendly and efficient."

ⓩ Le Caprice ❶ *British/European*   23 | 22 | 23 | £63

St. James's | Arlington Hse. | Arlington St., SW1 (Green Park) | 020-7629-2239 | www.le-caprice.co.uk

Whether they're *haute monde* or grandmothers with grandchildren", everyone is "treated well" by "impeccable" servers at this "vibrant", "frenetic" St. James's "institution" whose "superb" "upscale" menu is a "creative blend" of "refined" Modern British–Euro "comfort foods"; though a few feel that the "classic art deco decor"

| | FOOD | DECOR | SERVICE | COST |

now "needs rethinking", the majority say that it's still "sophisticated", with a nightly piano player bolstering the "fine atmosphere."

Le Cercle ⑤Ⓜ French
25 | 23 | 23 | £55

Chelsea | 1 Wilbraham Pl., SW1 (Sloane Sq.) | 020-7901-9999 | www.lecercle.co.uk

An "odd basement location" near Sloane Square belies this Club Gascon offshoot's "beautiful surroundings" (loaded with "cosy nooks"), not to mention its "delicious little tidbits" of New and Southwestern French "delights" prepared with "panache and imagination"; as is usual with "tasting-size dishes", "the bill adds up" – especially if you're "adventurous or hungry" – but the "warm welcome" and "superb wine list" add value.

Le Colombier French
24 | 21 | 23 | £52

Chelsea | 145 Dovehouse St., SW3 (South Kensington) | 020-7351-1155 | www.lecolombier-sw3.co.uk

"Sophisticated tastes" are sated by the "invariably delicious" "classic French bistro" fare that's "well executed" at this somewhat "under-the-radar" Chelsea "standby"; "slick" staffers who run "a tight ship" and an "extensive, varied" wine-and-spirits list also get the thumbs-up, as do "sensible prices."

�Z Ledbury, The French
29 | 25 | 28 | £86

Notting Hill | 127 Ledbury Rd., W11 (Notting Hill Gate/ Westbourne Park) | 020-7792-9090 | www.theledbury.com

The "exhilarating tastes and textures" of "challenging chef" Brett Graham's New French dishes make for "ethereal" meals, which once again earn London's No. 1 Food rating at this Notting Hill destination whose setting is an "attractive, modern" "combination of haute" and "neighbourhood"; "exemplary service" includes a "friendly, passionate" sommelier who "recommends perfect matches" from the "outstanding wine list", and whilst the sum total is "very expensive", it's "worth every penny" (bargain-hunters find the set lunch "excellent value").

Le Deuxième ● European
22 | 18 | 21 | £38

Covent Garden | 65A Long Acre, WC2 (Covent Garden) | 020-7379-0033 | www.ledeuxieme.com

"Delivering the goods for the business-lunch crowd" and "pre- or post-theatre or -opera"–goers, this "lovely" Covent Garden spot is "solid in all respects" thanks to a "good-value", "sure-bet" Modern Euro menu, an "eclectic" wine list and "charming staff"; in fact, there's really only one gripe: at busy times, "it gets noisy beyond belief."

⚡ Le Gavroche ⑤ French
28 | 24 | 27 | £101

Mayfair | 43 Upper Brook St., W1 (Marble Arch) | 020-7408-0881 | www.le-gavroche.co.uk

The imagined "patron saint of fantastic dining" blesses this "magical experience" from Michel Roux Jr in a "plush" Mayfair cellar boasting "old-world charm", "old-fashioned luxury" and "intensely flavoured", "technically spot-on" Classic French cuisine; the "phenomenal service" features a "helpful sommelier" who runs a "deep wine list",

	FOOD	DECOR	SERVICE	COST

and whilst it is "very expensive", most find it ultimately "worth every *centime*", especially the "amazing-value" set lunch.

🗷 Le Manoir aux Quat'Saisons *French*   `28` `28` `28` `£100`

Great Milton | Le Manoir aux Quat'Saisons Hotel | Church Rd., Oxfordshire | 01844-278881 | www.manoir.com

"Flawless" "from start to finish", this "ultimate romantic retreat" in a "gorgeous" Oxfordshire "manor restaurant" employs "impecca-ble" staff to deliver chef-owner Raymond Blanc's "refined" New French fare "par excellence" in an "exquisite" main room and a "huge conservatory" surrounded by "serene" gardens; true, it's a fis-cal "indulgence" (especially if you "stay over") and the location is over an hour from London, but it's "well worth" the money and "the trek" for such an "extraordinary experience."

Le Mercury ❶ *French*   `19` `17` `17` `£27`

Islington | 140A Upper St., N1 (Angel/Highbury & Islington) | 020-7354-4088 | www.lemercury.co.uk

"Extremely popular and with good reason", this "intimate" "Islington institution" spread over three floors of a Victorian build-ing offers "reliably capable" New French fare for "student prices" ("unheard of!"); service is appreciated when it's "attentive", but the majority of the praise is saved for its "prime location", ideal for "be-fore or after a show at the Almeida."

Lemonia ❶ *Greek*   `19` `17` `22` `£34`

Primrose Hill | 89 Regent's Park Rd., NW1 (Chalk Farm) | 020-7586-7454

A "rowdy", "bustling vibe" is achieved "without plate throwing" at this "unfussy", "family-friendly" Primrose Hill taverna doling out "hearty Greek food" at a "reasonable cost"; "efficient", "hospitable" staff who "haven't changed for years" are another reason it's so "popular", so expect "a struggle to get a table."

Leon *Mediterranean*   `17` `12` `15` `£15`

Covent Garden | 73-76 The Strand, WC2 (Covent Garden) | 020-7240-3070
Marylebone | 275 Regent St., W1 (Oxford Circus) | 020-7495-1514
Soho | 35 Great Marlborough St., W1 (Oxford Circus) | 020-7437-5280
NEW Soho | 36-38 Old Compton St., W1 (Tottenham Court Rd.) | 020-7434-1200
Canary Wharf | Cabot Place W., promenade level, E1 (Canary Wharf) | 020-7719-6200
City | 12 Ludgate Circus, EC4 (Blackfriars) | 020-7489-1580 🛇
City | 86 Cannon St., EC4 (Cannon St.) | 020-7623-9699 🛇
Shoreditch | 3 Crispin Pl., E1 (Liverpool St.) | 020-7247-4369
Southwark | Blue Fin Bldg. | 7 Canvey St., SE1 (Southwark) | 020-7620-0035
www.leonrestaurants.co.uk

For "tasty, healthy" Med fare served "fast", you "gotta love" this "bustling" eat-in/takeaway chain that seems to be "popping up everywhere"; even if service is "lacking" and the settings are "basic" at best, you "can't go wrong" with the "cheap" prices.

	FOOD	DECOR	SERVICE	COST

Leong's Legend *Taiwanese* | 23 | 15 | 13 | £22 |

Chinatown | 4 Macclesfield St., W1D (Leicester Sq.) |
020-7287-0288
Bayswater | 82 Queensway, W2 (Bayswater) | 020-7221-2280
www.leongslegend.com

Some call the "atmosphere classier than most Chinatown establishments", others compare it to "a martial-arts movie set", but no one disputes that you get "a huge feast for not a lot of money" at this "interesting", "unusual" Taiwanese eatery; just like its parent, the Queensway offspring offers "solid" eats, "variable" service and "great value."

Le Pain Quotidien *Bakery/Belgian* | 17 | 15 | 14 | £19 |

Holborn | 174 High Holborn, WC1 (Holborn/Tottenham Court Rd.) |
020-7486-6154
Marylebone | 72-75 Marylebone High St., W1 (Baker St./
Regent's Park) | 020-7486-6154
Soho | 18 Great Marlborough St., W1 (Oxford Circus) |
020-7486-6154
South Bank | Royal Festival Hall | Belvedere Rd., Festival Terr., SE1
(Waterloo) | 020-7486-6154
King's Cross | St. Pancras Int'l | 81 Euston Rd., NW1 (King's Cross
St. Pancras) | 020-7486-6154
Chelsea | 201-203 King's Rd., SW3 (Sloane Sq./South Kensington) |
020-7486-6154
South Kensington | 15-17 Exhibition Rd., SW7 (Gloucester Rd./
South Kensington) | 020-7486-6154
Wimbledon | 4-5 High St., SW19 (Wimbledon) | 020-7486-6154
Kensington | 9 Young St., W8 (High St. Kensington) |
020-7486-6154
Notting Hill | 81-85 Notting Hill Gate, W11 (Notting Hill Gate) |
020-7486-6154
www.lepainquotidien.co.uk
Additional locations throughout London

"Get to know your neighbour" around the "big, farmhouse"-style communal tables that fill this "perennially busy" Belgian bakery/cafe chain, a "dependable" "standby" for "quick", "healthy", "light" breakfasts, lunches or dinners; as is to be expected, service is "hit-and-miss" depending on the branch, but the prices, thankfully, are universally "reasonable."

Le Pont de la Tour *French/Seafood* | 21 | 22 | 21 | £55 |

Tower Bridge | Butlers Wharf Bldg. | 36D Shad Thames, SE1
(London Bridge/Tower Hill) | 020-7403-8403 |
www.lepontdelatour.co.uk

"Ask for an outside table", or one near a window inside, for "movie-like views of Tower Bridge" at this "romantic", "posh" Classic French restaurant with a "wonderful" art deco setting and "attentive" service; though surveyors can't agree whether the seafood-centric sustenance is "splendid" or "no great shakes", most find it "expensive" – however, the wine list is generally "sensibly priced" and the separate bar and grill offers "similar quality" "for less" (making it a "reliable business choice").

	FOOD	DECOR	SERVICE	COST

Le Relais de
Venise l'Entrecôte *Chophouse/French* | 23 | 17 | 17 | £32 |

Marylebone | 120 Marylebone Ln., W1 (Bond St./Marylebone) | 020-7486-0878

City | 5 Throgmorton St., EC2 (Bank) | 020-7638-6325 🖾
www.relaisdevenise.com

"Soak in the French brasserie atmosphere" at these "fabulous", "fairly priced" City and Marylebone chophouses that emulate "the Paris original" by "only serving one thing": "simple", "delicious steaks" with an "amazing" "secret sauce" and "yummy fries"; "the downside is you can't book", which means queues can "go around the block", but the "moody" staff "try to turn over the tables" "fast."

L'Escargot ● 🖾 *French* | 22 | 24 | 20 | £52 |

Soho | 48 Greek St., W1 (Leicester Sq./Tottenham Court Rd.) | 020-7437-6828 | www.lescargotrestaurant.co.uk

"Mirrors and Miros", Picassos and Chagalls fill the "beautiful interior" of this somewhat "formal" "old favourite" in Soho, which "continues a long tradition" (since 1927) of providing "reliably well-prepared and delicious" Classic French fare and "a long wine list" at "high prices"; "attentive" staff help make it a "pre-theatre tradition", as they'll get you to the show on time, but they'll "never rush" you either if you want to linger.

🆕 **Les Deux Salons** *French* | 19 | 22 | 18 | £46 |

Covent Garden | 40-42 William IV St., WC2 (Charing Cross) | 020-7420-2050 | www.lesdeuxsalons.co.uk

"Brought to you by the owners of Arbutus and Wild Honey", this "worthy newcomer" by Trafalgar Square offers two "beautiful" floors with "lively, fun" atmospheres and "uncomplicated, accomplished" French fare for "reasonable" prices; some say service "hasn't got its act together" yet, but a round of applause goes to the "genius" "carafes of great wines" that "liberate you" from "your comfort zone."

Les Trois Garçons 🖾 *French* | 20 | 26 | 20 | £59 |

Shoreditch | 1 Club Row, E1 (Liverpool St.) | 020-7613-1924 | www.lestroisgarcons.com

With "amazing", "eccentric" bric-a-brac, bling and baubles hanging on the walls and from the ceiling, "there is nothing like" this "wonderful extrovert" in Shoreditch; the "solid", "expensive" Classic French cuisine makes for an overall "enjoyable" meal – but "if the food were a little better", the entire experience "would be superb."

Le Suquet ● *French/Seafood* | 23 | 17 | 22 | £52 |

Chelsea | 104 Draycott Ave., SW3 (South Kensington) | 020-7581-1785

"It keeps a steady course and will sail forever" say *amis* of this "charming" Chelsea French offering "delightful", "pricey" "classic" seafood dishes and "lovely" service; if the "old-fashioned" setting is "in need of a pick-me-up", it's nevertheless a "welcoming" "ray of sunshine", particularly on "a cold winter's night."

L'Etranger *French/Japanese*

| 24 | 19 | 21 | £58 |

South Kensington | 36 Gloucester Rd., SW7 (Gloucester Rd.) | 020-7584-1118 | www.etranger.co.uk

"Strikingly interesting dishes" are composed via a "wonderful fusion" of French and Japanese cuisines (including sushi) at this "expensive" South Ken venue; whilst it's "a bit gloomy inside", a "terrific wine list" and "expert, unstuffy" service ensure it works for both "business or social" engagements.

Le Vacherin *French*

| 23 | 19 | 21 | £47 |

Chiswick | 76-77 South Parade, W4 (Chiswick Park) | 020-8742-2121 | www.levacherin.com

"You're lucky if you live near" this "super neighbourhood restaurant", but if not, it's still "worth the trek to Chiswick" for the "accomplished" French bistro cooking and "great selection of wines"; "pleasant ambience and discreet service" further warrant costs that are on the high side, unless you go for the "excellent-value" lunch or dinner prix fixes.

Light House *Eclectic*

| ▽ 19 | 18 | 20 | £37 |

Wimbledon | 75-77 Ridgway, SW19 (Wimbledon) | 020-8944-6338 | www.lighthousewimbledon.com

"Compared to the plethora of chain eateries in Wimbledon Village", this "interesting" Eclectic is a "refreshing" alternative, and "fab value" to boot, especially for weekday and Sunday lunch; though the setting is simple, it's warmed up with "friendly" service.

Little Bay ◑ *European*

| 19 | 16 | 20 | £21 |

Farringdon | 171 Farringdon Rd., EC1 (Farringdon) | 020-7278-1234
Kilburn | 228 Belsize Rd., NW6 (Kilburn Park) | 020-7372-4699 ⊅ www.little-bay.co.uk

"Overdone decor" (sort of a "sensuous Moorish boudoir") is "part of the charm" at this "quaint", "eccentric" duo in Farringdon and Kilburn, whose "tasty, large portions" of Modern Euro fare are priced for those on a "limited budget"; "smiling staff" and "late" hours are two more reasons it's "always full."

Livebait *Seafood*

| 17 | 13 | 16 | £34 |

Covent Garden | 21 Wellington St., WC2 (Covent Garden) | 020-7836-7161
Waterloo | 43 The Cut, SE 1 (Waterloo) | 020-7928-7211 www.livebaitrestaurants.co.uk

"Quality fish in a variety of non-fussy preparations" is the "simple" mantra of this "quick", "good-value" seafood duo in Covent Garden (a pre-theatre "standby") and Waterloo ("convenient for the Old Vic"); whilst "the white-tile decor is cold, the service is warm" – except when it's "rude."

Living Room *European*

| - | - | - | M |

Piccadilly | 3-9 Heddon St., W1 (Oxford Circus/Piccadilly Circus) | 020-7292-0570 | www.thelivingroom.co.uk

"Part nightclub, part eating house", this "great spot for meeting friends for a drink or two" off Regent Street "gets very loud" with live performances Thursday–Sunday; foodwise, the "reasonably priced" Modern Euro fare gets "solid" comments, though sticklers say the "varied" menu "could use some culling."

🛛 Locanda Locatelli *Italian*   25 | 22 | 23 | £71

Marylebone | Hyatt Regency London - The Churchill | 8 Seymour St., W1 (Marble Arch) | 020-7935-9088 | www.locandalocatelli.com

"Exquisite" dishes that "constantly amaze" fill chef Giorgio Locatelli's "well-presented" Italian menu at this "stylish, elegant" dining room attached to a Marylebone hotel; if a few baulk at the "break-the-bank prices" and "visible preference" given "celebrities" from the otherwise "efficient staff", the majority claim "nothing disappoints", including the "helpful" sommelier's "spot-on" recommendations from the "phenomenal wine list."

Locanda Ottoemezzo 🛽 *Italian*   25 | 20 | 23 | £53

Kensington | 2-4 Thackeray St., W8 (High St. Kensington) | 020-7937-2200 | www.locandaottoemezzo.co.uk

"Close to but removed from the hustle and bustle of Kensington High Street", this "romantic", "intimate Italian" "makes up for" its "cramped space" with "fantastic" fare and "engaging", "attentive staff"; for some, the prices can cause "indigestion", but the wares are cheaper in the "casual next-door deli"; P.S. the name and decor pay homage to Fellini's movie *8 ½*.

Loch Fyne *Seafood*   19 | 15 | 17 | £37

Covent Garden | 2-4 Catherine St., WC2 (Covent Garden) | 020-7240-4999

City | Leadenhall Mkt. | 77-78 Gracechurch St., EC3 (Monument) | 020-7929-8380 🛽

www.lochfyne.com

"Reliable seafood" and "reasonable prices" trump the "Ikea decor" and "informal service" at these "unpretentious", "bustling" outposts of the national chain; sure, it's "nothing to sing about", but for an "easy business lunch" in the City or "pre-theatre dinner" in Covent Garden, they're "hard to beat."

🛛 L'Oranger 🛽 *French*   27 | 25 | 27 | £73

St. James's | 5 St. James's St., SW1 (Green Park) | 020-7839-3774 | www.loranger.co.uk

For "special nights out" and "relaxing" lunches, this "elegant", "charming" St. James's "standard" "stays on top" with "wonderful" Classic French cuisine and "formal", "gracious service"; just know that such "mature dining" comes at a grown-up price; P.S. in clement weather, try for the "lovely private courtyard in the back."

Lucio *Italian*   24 | 22 | 26 | £55

Chelsea | 257-259 Fulham Rd., SW3 (South Kensington) | 020-7823-3007 | www.luciorestaurant.com

Even if Chelsea is a foreign land, you'll "feel as though you've come home" at this "elegant", "relaxing" Italian where the eponymous host-owner greets everyone with "a smile" while ensuring "everything runs like clockwork"; though some folks feel it's a bit "pricey" for a "neighbourhood joint", others say it's "great value for money" considering the "consistent", "superb" cuisine.

Lucky 7 *American*

19	17	16	£23

Notting Hill | 127 Westbourne Park Rd., W2 (Royal Oak/ Westbourne Park) | 020-7727-6771 | www.lucky7london.co.uk

"Mighty fine" eats, from pancakes and eggs to burgers, shakes and malts, make this "hip, fun", "budget"-priced "U.S.-style diner" an all-day destination for Notting Hill "trustafarians" and "celebs"; with just 36 seats and a "no-booking policy", you should "be prepared to queue" and possibly "share" one of the "cosy" booths.

Luc's Brasserie 🅱 *French*

–	–	–	E

City | 17-22 Leadenhall Mkt., EC3 (Bank/Monument) | 020-7621-0666 | www.lucsbrasserie.com

Decked out like a traditional Parisian brasserie with a zinc-topped bar, this first-floor Leadenhall Market venue proffers pricey French fare that "does not disappoint"; it's "excellent for an informal" meal in the City, thanks in part to the "quick, attentive staff" and a well-chosen selection of Gallic wines, so no surprise, it's "always packed at lunchtime."

Lutyens Restaurant, Bar & Cellar Rooms 🅱 *French*

23	21	22	£50

City | 85 Fleet St., EC4 (Blackfriars) | 020-7583-8385 | www.lutyens-restaurant.com

"Bankers, lawyers and other suited-and-booted types" "pack" the "large, buzzy dining rooms" of this "well-executed" Terence Conran venture whose "competent" though "uncontroversial" New French fare is ferried by "attentive yet discreet" staff; indeed, it's a "solid" choice to "take clients" for breakfast, lunch or supper because the food-and-wine selection is "well balanced" and the bill is best put on an expense account.

Luxe, The *British*

12	16	12	£40

City | 109 Commercial St., E1 (Liverpool St.) | 020-7101-1751 | www.theluxe.co.uk

At this Spitalfields Modern British spot, the "busy", "cafelike" ground floor (whose offerings include "a nice burger and chips") is "better" than the formal first level with tables surrounding an open kitchen; however, the list of grievances is addressed to the entire endeavour, and it includes food execution that's "a little careless", "noisy" acoustics due to "wooden floors and high ceilings" and some "rude" servers.

NEW Made in Camden *European*

–	–	–	M

Camden Town | The Roundhouse | Chalk Farm Rd., NW1 (Chalk Farm) | 020-7424-8495 | www.madeincamden.com

Reflecting the "colour and atmosphere of Camden", this newcomer at performing-arts landmark The Roundhouse offers "delicious, inventive" Modern European small and large plates that are "well priced" (particularly the pre-show prix fixe) and served by "terrific" staff in a space with floor-to-ceiling windows; philanthropists take note: profits make their way to the venue's charitable trust.

	FOOD	DECOR	SERVICE	COST

Made in Italy ● *Italian* — 20 | 14 | 14 | £28

Marylebone | 50 James St., W1 (Bond St.) | 020-7224-0182
NEW **Soho** | 14A Old Compton St., W1D (Leicester Sq./
Piccadilly Circus) | 020-0011-1214
Chelsea | 249 King's Rd., SW3 (Sloane Sq./South Kensington) |
020-7352-1880
www.madeinitalygroup.co.uk

"Generous helpings" of "well-priced" Italian standards plus "terrific
pizza" by the meter keep this "rustic" King's Road spot "busy";
whilst some whinge that the "awkward layout" makes the inevitable
"wait for a table" "uncomfortable", once seated, "friendly staff"
smooth things over; P.S. offshoots exist in Marylebone and Soho.

Madsen *Scandinavian* — ∇ 16 | 13 | 19 | £33

South Kensington | 20 Old Brompton Rd., SW7 (South Kensington) |
020-7225-2772 | www.madsenrestaurant.com

"Helpful staff" create a "warm ambience" that belies the cooler
Scandinavian origins of this "wee" South Ken venue serving "tasty,
hearty" nosh amidst "sensible" decor (with "hard seating"); what's
more, the "reasonable prices" go down as easy as a shot of aquavit.

Magdalen ⊠ *European* — 24 | 19 | 22 | £47

Borough | 152 Tooley St., SE1 (London Bridge) | 020-7403-1342 |
www.magdalenrestaurant.co.uk

"Fabulous" Modern European fare is "done with flair" at this Borough
venue where "welcoming" staff lavish "a lot of care and attention"
on both diners and dishes; the "not-outrageous wine list" helps keep
it "excellent value for money", and with such "warm", "lovely" surroundings, it's no wonder most feel it "always hits the mark."

Maggie Jones's *British* — 19 | 20 | 19 | £37

Kensington | 6 Old Court Pl., W8 (High St. Kensington) | 020-7937-6462 |
www.maggie-jones.co.uk

"Twee and cosy", this "rustic" "farmhouse" facsimile in Kensington is
"unashamedly British" in both its traditional cuisine and style, and
"just the thing on a cold winter's day" when the "warm atmosphere"
encourages patrons ("especially big eaters") to linger over the
"delicious" "comfort food" and house wine measured by the ruler.

Malabar ● *Indian* — 20 | 13 | 18 | £33

Notting Hill | 27 Uxbridge St., W8 (Notting Hill Gate) | 020-7727-8800 |
www.malabar-restaurant.co.uk

"Stimulating spicing" is the star of the show at this Indian near Notting
Hill's cinema, and while critics carp that the portions are "small for the
price", the Sunday lunch buffet is a pre-matinee bargain; the space
"needs a bit of modernisation", but a "vibrant atmosphere" prevails
thanks to the efforts of the "accommodating", "friendly" staff.

Malabar Junction *Indian* — 19 | 17 | 18 | £27

Bloomsbury | 107 Great Russell St., WC1 (Tottenham Court Rd.) |
020-7580-5230 | www.malabarjunction.com
Even with a "bright" atrium at the back, it's looking "a little tired",
but this Bloomsbury stalwart is worth it for "wonderful Southern

Indian cuisine", which comes via "attentive, knowledgeable" staff; while it's always well priced, budgeters will especially appreciate the prix fixe weekday lunches and Sunday 'wonder meal.'

Mall Tavern British   ▽ 20 | 21 | 22 | £28

Notting Hill | 71-73 Palace Gardens Terr., W8 (Notting Hill Gate) | 020-7229-3374 | www.themalltavern.com

It's "off-the-beaten-track, so it's mainly locals" who patronise this "relaxed" Notting Hill gastropub whose Traditional British leanings are evident in both the "beautifully redecorated" Victorian interior and the "delicious" dishes; it "remembers to be a good pub as well", with a selection of malts, beers and wines, all administered by "helpful" staff.

Mandarin Kitchen ● Chinese/Seafood   25 | 14 | 19 | £36

Bayswater | 14-16 Queensway, W2 (Bayswater/Queensway) | 020-7727-9012

"Enjoy the ocean's treasures" in "gourmet" Chinese fare, particularly the "nothing-short-of-heaven" lobster noodles, at this "always-full" Bayswater kitchen; despite the "good value" offered, aesthetes still complain that the "funky" "decor needs livening up" – and a scheduled late-2011 renovation should quell their grumblings.

Mango Tree Thai   21 | 20 | 18 | £39

Victoria | 46 Grosvenor Pl., SW1 (Hyde Park/Victoria) | 020-7823-1888 | www.mangotree.org.uk

"Sophisticated" Thai renditions, "cool" "high-end decor" and "expensive" prices sum up this Victoria venue; "brisk" service is a selling point, however, some folks find it "hard to overcome the unpleasantries" born of "barnlike" digs that get "extremely noisy."

Manicomio Italian   15 | 13 | 14 | £38

City | Gutter Ln., EC2 (St. Paul's) | 020-7726-5010 Ⓢ
Chelsea | 85 Duke of York Sq., SW3 (Sloane Sq.) | 020-7730-3366
www.manicomio.co.uk

"For lunch outside in the summer or an early evening Prosecco", these Chelsea and City Italians can be "oases", and they're "useful" for takeaway too; however, quite a few find the fare "a bit on the expensive side for what it is": "nothing special."

Manson European   - | - | - | M

Fulham | 676 Fulham Rd., SW6 (Parsons Green) | 020-7384-9559 | www.mansonrestaurant.co.uk

Fulham folk who say they "badly needed a fine restaurant" in the area feel this Modern European "fits the bill"; indeed, in just its second year, it's "hitting its stride" with "consistent", well-priced Gallic-influenced eats listed on a "variable" menu, which is proffered in traditional brasserie-style surroundings.

Mao Tai ● Asian   ▽ 20 | 18 | 18 | £44

Fulham | 58 New King's Rd., SW6 (Parsons Green) | 020-7731-2520 | www.maotai.co.uk

"Quality" Pan-Asian chow including dim sum is served amidst sleek, stylised decor at this Fulham eatery; however, a couple of penny-

| | FOOD | DECOR | SERVICE | COST |

pinchers say that neither the fare nor the "fabulous staff" nor the "good vibes" warrant such "outrageous prices."

Marco Pierre White
Steak & Alehouse *Chophouse*

| 19 | 19 | 19 | £61 |

City | East India House | 109-117 Middlesex St., E1 (Liverpool St.) | 020-7247-5050 | www.mpwsteakandalehouse.org

Diners are divided over the eponymous chef's City chophouse: some applaud "wonderful red meat", "eager-to-please" staff and a "classy", wood-floored ambience, while others lament that, at most, everything "suffices" but leaves them ultimately "disappointed" considering "the name"; one thing everyone agrees on is the price: "quite expensive."

☑ Marcus Wareing at
The Berkeley ☒ *French*

| 27 | 26 | 26 | £107 |

Belgravia | The Berkeley | Wilton Pl., SW1 (Hyde Park Corner/ Knightsbridge) | 020-7235-1200 | www.marcus-wareing.com

Advocates aver it's "difficult to imagine a more satisfying dining experience" than that offered at this "sumptuous" setting within Belgravia's Berkeley Hotel, where "unobtrusive, knowledgeable" staff convey Marcus Wareing's "stylishly presented", "breathtaking" New French fare, and "a sommelier worth listening to" offers advice on the "extensive" wine list; unsurprisingly, this brand of "out-of-this-world" "excellence" is "expensive", which is why the "faint of credit card" opt instead for the "fantastic-value" set lunch.

☑ Mark's Club ☒ *British/French*

| 24 | 28 | 28 | £97 |

Mayfair | private club | 46 Charles St., W1 (Green Park) | 020-7499-2936 | www.marksclub.co.uk

"Warm" colours, "handsome paintings" and "hushed" tones describe the atmosphere of this "very British" Mayfair private club that provides an "exclusive" "upscale" "'in' crowd" with "wonderful" Franco-British fare and "discreet" service; indeed, the "simply wonderful" experience is "worth the heavy price" – "if you can get in" (as a member of a guest of one).

Maroush ● *Lebanese*

| 22 | 14 | 17 | £30 |

Knightsbridge | 38 Beauchamp Pl., SW3 (Knightsbridge) | 020-7581-5434
Marylebone | 1-3 Connaught St., W2 (Marble Arch) | 020-7262-0222
Marylebone | 21 Edgware Rd., W2 (Marble Arch) | 020-7723-0773
Marylebone | 4 Vere St., W1 (Bond St.) | 020-7493-5050
Marylebone | 68 Edgware Rd., W2 (Marble Arch) | 020-7224-9339
www.maroush.com

For "significant portions" of "succulent" Lebanese fare, these "reliable" West End "oases" are "excellent value for money" ("the bowl of fresh vegetables on every table is a special touch"); the settings are "somewhat dated" and service is "patchy", nevertheless it's always "buzzy" and a "fave late-night-falafel-and-schwarma hangout" too, especially in Knightsbridge and Vere Street, which are open until 5 AM (the former nightly, the latter Thursday–Saturday).

Masala Zone *Indian* | 19 | 16 | 18 | £23 |

Covent Garden | 48 Floral St., WC2 (Covent Garden) | 020-7379-0101
Soho | 9 Marshall St., W1 (Oxford Circus/Piccadilly Circus) |
020-7287-9966
Camden Town | 25 Parkway, NW1 (Camden Town) | 020-7267-4422
Islington | 80 Upper St., N1 (Angel) | 020-7359-3399
Earl's Court | 147 Earl's Court Rd., SW5 (Earl's Ct.) | 020-7373-0220
Fulham | 583 Fulham Rd., SW6 (Fulham Broadway) | 020-7386-5500
Bayswater | 75 Bishop's Bridge Rd., W2 (Bayswater) | 020-7221-0055
www.masalazone.com

"Curry in a hurry without the chintz" is the stock-in-trade of these
"cheap" Indians specialising in "fantastic Thalis" ("mixed plates")
and other "well-rendered" street food; with "convenient" locations
throughout the capital, each "bright, colourful" branch is "themed
differently" decorwise (with everything from modern paintings to
"amusing" tribal art to "scary" puppets), while staff are universally
"welcoming" and "attentive."

NEW Massimo 🅱 *Mediterranean* | - | - | - | VE |

Westminster | Corinthia Hotel London | 16 Northumberland Ave., SW1
(Embankment) | 020-7998-0555 | www.massimo-restaurant.co.uk
Bulbous brass-and-glass chandeliers framed by grand pillars strike
an opulent tone at this high-end Med inside the imposing new
Corinthia Hotel on Northumberland Avenue; Italian chef Massimo
Riccioli evokes his celebrated venture in Rome, La Rosetta, with an
oyster and crustacean bar on one side, a formal dining room on the
other and a cafe-style section in between.

Matsuri *Japanese* | 24 | 17 | 20 | £55 |

St. James's | 15 Bury St., SW1 (Green Park) | 020-7839-1101 |
www.matsuri-restaurant.com
It's "fun to watch the chefs cook and do their little show" at this "fantastic" basement teppanyaki specialist in St. James's, which also
prepares "quality" sushi; "if your wallet can manage it", try the
"melt-in-your-mouth" Wagyu beef, but if you're hunting for a "bargain", come for lunch and get the bento box.

Maze *French* | 24 | 22 | 22 | £73 |

Mayfair | Marriott Grosvenor Sq. | 10-13 Grosvenor Sq., W1 (Bond St.) |
020-7107-0000 | www.gordonramsay.com
"Imaginative", Asian-influenced New French "small plates of explod-
ing flavours" are the métiers of this "divine" Gordon Ramsay operation
("one of his better efforts") in the Marriott Grosvenor Square, where
"polished staff" patrol the "modern" setting; those who've left
"broke" and "hungry" snipe that it "trades on its celebrity rep", but the
majority call it a "wonderful" experience that's "worth the price."

Maze Grill *Chophouse* | 22 | 20 | 21 | £59 |

Mayfair | Marriott Grosvenor Sq. | 10-13 Grosvenor Sq., W1 (Bond St.) |
020-7495-2211 | www.gordonramsay.com
"Flavourful" charcoal-grilled chops are "prepared as you prefer" and
delivered by "professional, attentive" staff at Gordon Ramsay's

"slightly more casual version of the adjacent Maze" in the Marriott Grosvenor Square; plenty of punters beef about the "huge bill", but they might not have tried the "early supper seating", a real "bargain."

Mediterraneo ● *Italian* | 22 | 15 | 18 | £38

Notting Hill | 37 Kensington Park Rd., W11 (Ladbroke Grove) | 020-7792-3131 | www.mediterraneo-restaurant.co.uk

Notting Hill diners "rely" on this "relaxing" ristorante for "tasty" Italian "basics" at decent prices; though it "lacks atmosphere" when compared to its older sib, Osteria Basilico (despite similarly rustic decor), on the upside, it's "quiet enough for conversation."

Mela ● *Indian* | 21 | 15 | 15 | £29

Covent Garden | 152-156 Shaftesbury Ave., WC2 (Leicester Sq.) | 020-7836-8635 | www.melarestaurant.co.uk

"In a city where there's a curry 'round every corner", this Covent Garden Indian stands out with "distinct" dishes and "well-trained staff"; prices are always "good value", but the "pre-theatre special is an amazing bargain for such quality."

Memories of China *Chinese* | 23 | 18 | 20 | £46

Belgravia | 65-69 Ebury St., SW1 (Victoria) | 020-7730-7734
Kensington | 353 Kensington High St., W8 (High St. Kensington) | 020-7603-6951
www.memories-of-china.co.uk

"Dress smart" for this "classy" Belgravia "escape" to China and its similarly "pleasant" Kensington offshoot offering "sensational" "gourmet" Cantonese and Mandarin fare; it's a bit "more costly than you'd think" and staff swing between "friendly" and "surly", but you can save some pennies and possible aggravation by utilising take-away, "an unexploited secret."

Mennula *Italian* | 26 | 18 | 23 | £52

Bloomsbury | 10 Charlotte St., W1 (Goodge St.) | 020-7636-2833 | www.mennula.com

A Sicilian chef-patron prepares "fantastic" fare whilst taking "a personal interest in his guests" at this Bloomsbury Italian; "friendly, accommodating" staff abet "cosy", "charming" vibes in the somewhat "awkward", white-and-lavender-hued space, and both the menu and "fun wine list" are "reasonably priced for this sort of experience."

Mercer, The 🅢 *British* | ▽ 20 | 21 | 20 | £61

City | 34 Threadneedle St., EC2 (Bank) | 020-7628-0001 | www.themercer.co.uk

"A fine lunch in a lovely venue" is what's on offer at this old banking hall in the City, where "wonderful" Trad British tucker is prepped for breakfast and dinner too; a "good wine list", "impeccable service" and "chic" decor are part of the deal – just don't expect a bargain.

Meson Don Felipe 🅢 *Spanish* | ▽ 21 | 17 | 16 | £24

Waterloo | 53 The Cut, SE1 (Southwark/Waterloo) | 020-7928-3237
Enthusiasts say it's "worth the trip south of the river" for the "fantastic tapas" doled out at this moderately priced Waterloo watering

hole that also harbours an "interesting Spanish wine" and beer selection in its "cramped quarters"; despite "rushed" service, it's often "impossible to get a table", possibly due to the added allure of a nightly Flamenco guitarist.

Mestizo *Mexican*
22 | **17** | **16** | **£32**

Camden Town | 103 Hampstead Rd., NW1 (Warren St.) | 020-7387-4064 | www.mestizomx.com
"Wonderfully authentic", "mouthwatering" Mexican dishes plus "great cocktails", tequilas and beers make this a "genuinely interesting" option in Camden Town; service that's "haphazard" doesn't detract from the "good value" offered, especially at the all-you-can-eat brunch, "something different for a Sunday."

Mews of Mayfair *British*
17 | **20** | **18** | **£47**

Mayfair | 10-11 Lancashire Ct., New Bond St., W1 (Bond St./ Oxford Circus) | 020-7518-9388 | www.mewsofmayfair.com
Modern British cuisine "ranging from burgers to more sophisticated dishes" is served by "attentive, courteous staff" on all four floors of this "light and airy" restaurant, bar and lounge down a "little cobbled street" in Mayfair; it's "good for quiet conversation" and "you can always get a reservation", however, those who find the food only "so-so" say it's "not worth the price" regardless.

Mien Tay *Vietnamese*
∇ **19** | **10** | **13** | **£17**

Shoreditch | 122 Kingsland Rd., E2 (Hoxton) | 020-7729-3074
Battersea | 180 Lavender Hill, SW11 (Clapham Junction) | 020-7350-0721
www.mientay.co.uk
"Diners are treated to a hypnotic array of flavours and sensations at impossibly low prices" at this "always packed" Battersea Vietnamese and its Shoreditch sibling; true, they have to put up with "dingy settings", "tight tables" and mostly "terrible" service, but "who cares?" – it's "delicious."

Milroy, The 🗷 *British/European*
- | **-** | **-** | **VE**

Mayfair | Les Ambassadeurs Club | 5 Hamilton Pl., W1 (Hyde Park Corner) | 020-7317-6108 | www.themilroy.com
On a historic Mayfair site that once housed King Henry VIII's hunting lodge, the "beautiful surroundings" of the exclusive Les Ambassadeurs casino now include a very expensive Traditional British–Modern Euro dining room with huge, roulette-sized tables, open to members and non-members alike (for weekday lunch only); the serene space blends plush period features with slick upholsteries, plus there's a "fantastic selection of wines."

Min Jiang *Chinese*
23 | **23** | **20** | **£56**

Kensington | Royal Garden Hotel | 2-24 Kensington High St., 10th fl., W8 (High St. Kensington) | 020-7937-8000 | www.minjiang.co.uk
"Soigné Chinese" dishes starring "excellent dim sum" and "outstanding" Beijing duck are served with "aplomb" at this Royal Garden Hotel spot; its perch on the 10th floor affords "spectacular views" of Kensington Palace and Gardens, and the prices are just as "sky high."

	FOOD	DECOR	SERVICE	COST

Mint Leaf *Indian*

22 | 20 | 20 | £44

St. James's | Haymarket & Suffolk Pl., SW1 (Piccadilly Circus) | 020-7930-9020 | www.mintleafrestaurant.com

"Sophistication" is evident in both the "creative Indian" cuisine and "sleek, modern" basement setting of this "trendy" hideout with "attentive staff" in Haymarket in St. James's; "excellent cocktails" from the "lively" bar add to the overall "clubby atmosphere", which some aurally sensitive types say is "a bit noisy" for their liking.

Ⓩ Miyama *Japanese*

26 | 12 | 21 | £42

Mayfair | 38 Clarges St., W1 (Green Park) | 020-7499-2443
City | 17 Godliman St., EC4 (St. Paul's) | 020-7489-1937 Ⓩ
www.miyama.co.uk

Diplomats from the Japanese embassy need only go "around the corner" to this Mayfair venue for "exquisite", "fresh-off-the-boat" sushi coupled with "attentive" service; whilst it's true that the "shabby interior needs a shake-up", a refurb would most likely raise the "reasonable" prices; P.S. the "convenient" City sibling sates bankers on budget.

Modern Pantry *Eclectic*

22 | 19 | 19 | £35

Clerkenwell | 47-48 St. John's Sq., EC1 (Farringdon) | 020-7553-9210 | www.themodernpantry.co.uk

Whether you dine on the "inventive", "hearty" Eclectic eats in the "buzzy" all-day ground-floor cafe or the "quieter, prettier" upstairs dining room (where only lunch and dinner are offered), you'll "never feel rushed" at this "light, welcoming" Clerkenwell kitchen; a "well-chosen wine list" and "legendary" brunch are two more pluses, making the whole endeavour "worth every penny" (and you won't even need that many); P.S. "connoisseurs' ingredients" are sold in the "adjacent grocery."

Momo ◑ *Moroccan*

21 | 25 | 20 | £48

Piccadilly | 25 Heddon St., W1 (Piccadilly Circus) | 020-7434-4040 | www.momoresto.com

Piccadilly pals wash down "to-die-for" Moroccan morsels with "killer" cocktails at this "decadent, glamorous" den that's as "heavy on atmosphere" as it is "the wallet"; authentically "low chairs" and "patchy" service can be a pain, but for a "fun night", souk-style, it's usually "enjoyable."

Mon Plaisir Ⓩ *French*

18 | 16 | 18 | £40

Covent Garden | 21 Monmouth St., WC2 (Covent Garden/Leicester Sq.) | 020-7836-7243 | www.monplaisir.co.uk

The "higgledy piggledy collection" of "cosy" rooms is "always busy" and "loud", particularly on a "rainy day" or before a show, at this "long-established" (since 1942) Covent Garden bistro where the "old-time French cuisine" is "comfortable" and "consistent"; "friendly" *serveurs* help to keep the atmosphere "convivial", and your fellow diners recommend you "go for the prix fixes" to avoid a "surprising" bill.

Montpeliano ● *Italian*   16 | 17 | 19 | £48

Knightsbridge | 13 Montpelier St., SW7 (Knightsbridge) |
020-7589-0032 | www.montpelianorestaurant.com

"The food just gets by, the service is ok and the pricing is based on a
knowledge of the locals' deep pockets" carp critics of this
Knightsbridge conservatory simulacrum, which has been serving
Italian staples since 1975; despite such cynicism, for many, the
ambience (or at least the "good memories") "justifies the experience."

Morgan M ⓜ *French/Vegetarian*   26 | 17 | 25 | £67

Islington | 489 Liverpool Rd., N7 (Highbury & Islington) |
020-7609-3560 | www.morganm.com

In an "unexpected", "far-off corner of Islington", this "cosy", "understated" endeavour delights with "beautifully crafted", practically
"magical" New French cuisine that includes an "excellent vegetarian
menu", all served by "seamless" staff; though it's at the "top end"
costwise, when factoring in value, the "price puts some more august
establishments to shame."

NEW Morito Ⓢ *African/Spanish*   ▽ 26 | 14 | 16 | £27

Clerkenwell | 32 Exmouth Mkt., EC1 (Angel/Farringdon) | 020-7278-7007

Serving up the same "fantastic" Moorish (i.e. Spanish–North African)
tapas as daddy Moro next door, this Clerkenwell haunt is nevertheless "different in style", with "cramped", funkier quarters; but that
only makes it feel more "authentic", as do the "inexpensive" prices

Moro Ⓢ *African/Spanish*   26 | 18 | 23 | £45

Clerkenwell | 34-36 Exmouth Mkt., EC1 (Angel/Farringdon) |
020-7833-8336 | www.moro.co.uk

"A revelation" cry even "the most jaded palates" about the "beautifully executed", "exquisitely unusual" Moorish tapas - not to
mention the "fascinating wines" and "superb sherries" - at this
"good-value" Spanish–North African in Clerkenwell; "hard-working"
staff service the "crisp, uncluttered" digs, whose "clattery, chattery"
"buzz" is "fantastic."

Morton's Ⓢ *Mediterranean*   23 | 23 | 22 | £61

Mayfair | private club | 28 Berkeley Sq., W1 (Bond St./Green Park) |
020-7499-0363 | www.mortonsclub.com

Many a member of this Berkeley Square private club with a ground-
floor bar and a basement nightclub feel its restaurant is the "best
part", as the Med menu "never disappoints", the decor is light and airy
(thanks in part to "lots of natural light streaming through big windows") and the atmosphere is "suave yet not stuffy"; just be sure to
bring lots of money, because "dining at its finest" doesn't come cheap

Ⓩ Mosimann's Ⓢ *Eclectic*   23 | 27 | 26 | £78

Belgravia | private club | The Belfry | 11B W. Halkin St., SW1
(Knightsbridge) | 020-7235-9625 | www.mosimann.com

A former Belgravia church is the "fantastic, unusual" setting of this
members' club, where "ambitious", "delightful" Eclectic dishes are
"beautifully presented" by "exquisite" staff; those who were "lucky

enough to be invited" as a guest muse "too bad it's private" – but then again, "perhaps that's what makes it so special."

Motcombs *Eclectic*   21 | 18 | 21 | £47

Belgravia | 26 Motcomb St., SW1 (Knightsbridge/Sloane Sq.) | 020-7235-6382 | www.motcombs.co.uk

"Charming" management and staff help craft a "warm feeling" at this "casual" Belgravia "comfort-food haven" where "delicious" Eclectic eats and "fab wine" are offered in a "busy" ground-floor brasserie and a "cosy" basement; in fact, there's only one "problem": "you will not want to leave."

Moti Mahal ⊠ *Indian*   25 | 20 | 23 | £48

Covent Garden | 45 Great Queen St., WC2 (Covent Garden/Holborn) | 020-7240-9329 | www.motimahal-uk.com

"Fantastic", "innovative" dishes from a "historically interesting" Silk Road "concept" menu make this "mod" Covent Garden Indian "worth visiting even if you aren't going to the theatre"; "warm, accommodating" staff, "upscale" decor and a glass-encased kitchen add to the sense that it's a "cut above the usual"; P.S. for a "culinary journey" at less "pricey" fees, try the "good-value set lunch."

Mr. Chow ◐ *Chinese*   22 | 20 | 20 | £60

Knightsbridge | 151 Knightsbridge, SW1 (Knightsbridge) | 020-7589-7347 | www.mrchow.com

Since 1968, this "elegant" Knightsbridge Chinese with mostly "wonderful service" has been dishing out "gourmet" Mandarin meals to "celebs" and other "high-end" types; though some take issue with the fact it's "fading" and "expensive", as long as it "hangs in there", it's "worth a visit from time to time."

Mr. Kong ◐ *Chinese*   22 | 12 | 20 | £26

Chinatown | 21 Lisle St., WC2 (Leicester Sq.) | 020-7437-7341 | www.mrkongrestaurant.com

"Don't let the lack of decor" deter you, because amongst Chinatown's "myriad restaurants", this Cantonese "stands out", with an "extensive" selection of "superb" "value-for-money" fare; furthermore, staff are "amongst the friendliest in the area", which is "amazing" considering that they work until after 2 AM.

Mulberry Street ◐ *Italian*   ∇ 16 | 12 | 17 | £19

Notting Hill | 84 Westbourne Grove, W2 (Notting Hill Gate) | 020-7313-6789 | www.mulberrystreet.co.uk

"Gigantic" pizzas and other Big Apple–style Italian foodstuffs are cheap and "good for groups" or takeaway at this two-storey Notting Hill haunt; but it's "a far cry from New York" scoff connoisseurs, who also pick at the "plain" decor.

🄩 Murano ⊠ *European*   27 | 22 | 26 | £84

Mayfair | 20 Queen St., W1 (Green Park) | 020-7495-1127 | www.angela-hartnett.com

From "wonderful" amuse bouches to "mind-blowing" desserts, with seemingly "endless" "extras" throughout, everything at chef Angela

Hartnett's "Italian-inspired" Modern European in Mayfair is "divine" (foodies "highly recommend treating yourself to the tasting menu"); the "intimate", "graceful" white room is "a little too formal" for some, but "exemplary" staff convey "warmth", and whilst prices are "very expensive", "you get what you pay for."

My Dining Room *French*

`-` `-` `-` `M`

Fulham | 18 Farm Ln., SW6 (Fulham Broadway) | 020-7381-3331 | www.mydiningroom.net

Fulham parents approve of the "fantastic" "twists" on "French bistro fare" dreamt up at this affordable, art-bedecked eatery, while *les enfants* are kept happy via the "good kids' menu"; if it's "more a neighbourhood spot than a destination", the experience is wholly "enjoyable", with "enthusiastic" service another selling point.

Nahm *Thai*

`25` `21` `24` `£65`

Belgravia | Halkin Hotel | 5 Halkin St., SW1 (Hyde Park Corner) | 020-7333-1234 | www.nahm.como.bz

Chef David Thompson takes Thai cuisine to an "inspirational" level at this "intimate", "artful" Belgravia dining room in the Halkin Hotel; expect to dine amongst "hotel guests", "businessmen" and "polished, attentive" servers, but "don't look" at the bill if possible – it's "about as expensive as flying" to Bangkok.

Nando's *Portuguese*

`16` `12` `13` `£17`

Bloomsbury | 57-59 Goodge St., W1T (Goodge St.) | 020-7637-0708
Covent Garden | 66-68 Chandos Pl., WC2 (Charing Cross/ Covent Garden) | 020-7836-4719 ◐
Marylebone | 113 Baker St., W1 (Baker St.) | 020-3075-1044 ◐
Blackheath | 16 Lee High Rd., SE13 (Lewisham Rail) | 020-8463-0119
Bethnal Green | 366 Bethnal Green Rd., E2 (Bethnal Green) | 020-7729-5783
Hampstead | 252-254 West End Ln., NW6 (West Hampstead) | 020-7794-1331
Camden Town | 57-58 Chalk Farm Rd., NW1 (Chalk Farm) | 020-7424-9040 ◐
Islington | 324 Upper St., N1 (Angel) | 020-7288-0254 ◐
Brixton | 59-63 Clapham High St., SW4 (Clapham Common/ Clapham N.) | 020-7622-1475 ◐
Bayswater | 63 Westbourne Grove, W2 (Bayswater/Royal Oak) | 020-7313-9506 ◐
www.nandos.co.uk
Additional locations throughout London

When it comes to "fast food" (albeit with "table service and alcohol"), this "cheery" Portuguese chain is "top of the pecking order" thanks to its "succulent" peri-peri chicken, flame-grilled and served at a "level of heat to match your mood"; there's "tremendous value" too, hence everyone from "families with kids" to "late-night" "hipsters" leave "quite impressed."

Napket *Eclectic/Sandwiches*

`14` `16` `10` `£28`

Mayfair | 6 Brook St., W1 (Bond St./Oxford Circus) | 020-7495-8562 🗷
Mayfair | 61 Piccadilly, W1 (Green Park) | 020-7493-4704
Piccadilly | 5 Vigo St., W1 (Piccadilly Circus) | 020-7734-4387

(continued)

Napket

City | 34 Royal Exchange, EC3 (Bank) | 020-7621-1831 🗷
Chelsea | 342 King's Rd., SW3 (South Kensington) | 020-7352-9832
www.napket.com

"Too-good-to-miss pastries" are "great for breakfast" at this "industrial-chic" cafe chain, while swanky Eclectic sandwiches and salads make for "decent" lunches and early dinners; just know that it's somewhat "expensive" for what it is, and service is usually "frazzled."

Narrow, The *British* `21` `20` `20` `£38`

Wapping | 44 Narrow St., E14 (Limehouse DLR) | 020-7592-7950 | www.gordonramsay.com

"Friendly staff" make Gordon Ramsay's "subtly upscale" Wapping gastropub feel like "a proper local", albeit one with "gorgeous" river views and the sort of "uncomplicated but delicious" Trad British "comfort" grub that's worth travelling for; best of all, there's "real value for money."

National Dining Rooms *British* `17` `19` `16` `£30`

Soho | National Gallery, Sainsbury Wing | Trafalgar Sq., WC2 (Charing Cross) | 020-7747-2525 | www.thenationaldiningrooms.co.uk

"Location, location, location" is the main selling point of this Modern British eatery in the National Gallery, overlooking Trafalgar Square; that said, the "respectable" dishes are apropos for a "comfortable", "relaxed lunch" or "a spot of tea" after "soaking up the culture", even if "spotty" service abets the feeling that it's "overpriced for what it is."

Nautilus Fish 🗷 *Seafood* ∇ `25` `8` `19` `£21`

Hampstead | 27-29 Fortune Green Rd., NW6 (West Hampstead) | 020-7435-2532

"Fantastic" fish comes fried with chips or grilled with "a decent salad, for the diet conscious" at this "friendly" Hampstead spot; whatever you're angling for, everything's "reliable", and if the "down-to-earth decor" doesn't suit, there's "easy access to the Heath" for a piscatorial picnic.

New Culture Revolution *Chinese* `16` `9` `14` `£19`

Islington | 42 Duncan St., N1 (Angel) | 020-7833-9083
Chelsea | 305 King's Rd., SW3 (Sloane Sq.) | 020-7352-9281
Notting Hill | 157-159 Notting Hill Gate, W11 (Holland Park/ Notting Hill Gate) | 020-7313-9688
www.newculturerevolution.co.uk

"Tasty dumplings" and "hearty" noodles are the stock-in-trade of this "cheap and cheerful", "quick and simple" Mandarin trio, the kind of place that's "perfect before a movie"; service is "a bit hit-and-miss", but "kind" staff "do try."

New World ❶ *Chinese* `18` `8` `12` `£21`

Chinatown | 1 Gerrard Pl., W1 (Leicester Sq.) | 020-7434-2508

"Get there early for Sunday lunch" and "feast on authentic dim sum for next to nothing" at this colossal Chinatown Cantonese where the "goodies" are rolled around on carts by "ok" staff; just try to focus on the fare and not the "fairly tatty" decor.

1901 Restaurant *British*　21 | 23 | 20 | £58

City | Andaz Liverpool St. Hotel | 40 Liverpool St., EC2 (Liverpool St.) | 020-7618-7000 | www.andazdining.com

"Beautiful", "interesting" "modern decor" is the "highlight" of this "airy" City hotel eatery where "upscale" Modern British fare is ferried by mostly "attentive" servers to "well-spaced" tables that allow for a "private feeling"; if "some dishes are better than others", the "extensive" wine list and cocktails are roundly praised.

☑ Nobu Berkeley St ◑ *Japanese*　25 | 21 | 20 | £70

Mayfair | 15 Berkeley St., W1 (Green Park) | 020-7290-9222 | www.noburestaurants.com

"Footballers", "twentysomething bankers" and "models" ("probably the only people that can afford it") "eavesdrop" on one another at "too-close-together" tables whilst nibbling on Nobu Matsuhisa's "to-die-for" Japanese-Peruvian fare, starring "fresh, flavourful" sushi, at this "beautiful", "more-happening" Berkeley Square sibling of the Old Park Lane outpost; as for the "great-looking staff", some are "keen to help the beginner navigate the comprehensive menu" and others "need to relax the attitude."

☑ Nobu London *Japanese*　27 | 21 | 23 | £76

Mayfair | Metropolitan Hotel | 19 Old Park Ln., W1 (Hyde Park Corner) | 020-7447-4747 | www.noburestaurants.com

Despite a "rather simple" Old Park Lane setting and competition from "brash, younger rivals", Nobu Matsuhisa's "distinguished" "dining experience" is still pretty much "unbeatable" thanks to its "fabulous" "fresh-from-the-sea" sushi and "phenomenal" Japanese-Peruvian plates; though generally "pleasant", staff tend to be strict about the "table limits", so best to come with a "menu plan" – not to mention "a lot" of money.

Noor Jahan *Indian*　20 | 12 | 17 | £32

South Kensington | 2A Bina Gdns., SW5 (Gloucester Rd./ South Kensington) | 020-7373-6522
Paddington | 26 Sussex Pl., W2 (Lancaster Gate) | 020-7402-2332 www.noorjahanrestaurants.co.uk

"For many decades", this South Kensington kitchen has sated locals with "traditional Indian" fare that's "great for the price" in digs where the downstairs is "more comfortable than upstairs" (though both floors are "a bit tired"); service can be a bit "pushy" here and at the Paddington offshoot, so it may be best to utilise the takeaway service.

NEW Nopi ◑ *Asian/Mideastern*　- | - | - | M

Soho | 21-22 Warwick St., W1 (Piccadilly Circus) | 020-7494-9584 | www.nopi-restaurant.com

The team behind Ottolenghi adds a new string to its bow with this energetic all-day Soho brasserie (the name refers to its location north of Piccadilly) featuring whitewashed walls and golden-spider marble flooring; the midpriced menu spans an exotic mélange of Asian and Middle Eastern influences, served both in the glam ground-floor dining room and casual basement where barstools are set around communal tables and an open kitchen.

Northbank ☒ *British* — | — | — | M

City | 1 Paul's Walk, EC4 (Mansion Hse.) | 020-7329-9299 | www.northbankrestaurant.com

Take in "lovely views" "across the Thames" to the Globe Theatre and Tate Modern from this Modern British venue on the river's north bank (hence the name) near the Millennium Bridge in the City, and be sure to "check out the wallpaper depicting homeless people, drug addicts and police raids"; as for the fare, it's "well presented" by "superb" staff, "wonderful" tasting and "affordably priced."

NEW North Road ☒ *European* — | — | — | E

Clerkenwell | 69-73 St. John St., EC1 (Farringdon) | 020-3217-0033 | www.northroadrestaurant.co.uk

Early visitors to this sleek, spare new Clerkenwell address swear they've seen every one of the "innovative" Scandinavian-centric Modern European dishes (from a Danish chef) "licked clean"; "gracious, unobtrusive service" reigns both at dinner, when the prices are somewhat high, and lunch, featuring a "bargain" three-course set menu.

North Sea ☒ *Seafood* 24 | 12 | 19 | £21

Bloomsbury | 7-8 Leigh St., WC1 (King's Cross/Russell Sq.) | 020-7387-5892 | www.northseafishrestaurant.co.uk

"Huge portions of the freshest fish" come "expertly" fried, sautéed or grilled at this "plain little shop" in Bloomsbury; "counter service and bench seating" are "functional" at best, but everyone's "hospitable" and everything's "reasonably priced", making for a "refreshing" step "back in time."

NEW Nottingdale *French/Italian* — | — | — | M

Shepherd's Bush | 11 Evesham St., W11 (Latimer Rd.) | 020-7221-2223 | www.nottingdale.com

In the shadow of the striking new Talk Talk HQ near Latimer Road tube station in Shepherd's Bush lies this idiosyncratic, glass-fronted endeavour spread over two floors, with chunky wooden dining furniture and a suntrap terrace; the open kitchen doles out gutsy, fairly priced provincial Italian and French dishes from a Boot-born chef.

Notting Hill Brasserie *European* 22 | 20 | 20 | £55

Notting Hill | 92 Kensington Park Rd., W11 (Notting Hill Gate) | 020-7229-4481 | www.nottinghillbrasserie.com

The "compact menu" of this "refined" Notting Hill brasserie "surprises and pleases with its original take" on Modern European dishes, served in "intimate" rooms that are "great for dates or Sunday lunches" with live jazz; furthermore, with "long-serving staff" who "make you feel welcome from the moment you set foot in the door", diners would happily "move here" – were it not for the "steep prices."

	FOOD	DECOR	SERVICE	COST

Noura *Lebanese*   21 | 16 | 18 | £40

Belgravia | 12 William St., SW1 (Knightsbridge) | 020-7235-5900

Mayfair | 16 Curzon St., W1 (Green Park) | 020-7495-1050 ◑

Piccadilly | 122 Jermyn St., SW1 (Piccadilly Circus) | 020-7839-2020 ◑

Victoria | 16 Hobart Pl., SW1 (Victoria) | 020-7235-9444 ◑

www.noura.co.uk

"Reliable mezze", "delicious" kebabs, "wonderful" vegetarian options and "excellent" Middle Eastern wines are the highlights of these "simple" Lebanese eateries that are as "great for groups" as they are "gracious for single diners"; but stray beyond the "good-value lunches" at your peril, as plum locations mean plump prices.

Nozomi ◑ *Japanese*   21 | 17 | 15 | £67

Knightsbridge | 15 Beauchamp Pl., SW3 (Knightsbridge) | 020-7838-1500 | www.nozomi.co.uk

A "vibrant" "scene" is virtually guaranteed at this "trendy", multi-floored Knightsbridge spot with a menu of "delicious" Japanese small plates and sushi; but with "so-so service", "blindingly expensive" prices and "loud" DJ-provided soundtrack, some night owls feel it's "a better choice for drinks rather than dinner."

Odette's *European*   18 | 17 | 18 | £59

Primrose Hill | 130 Regent's Park Rd., NW1 (Chalk Farm) | 020-7586-8569 | www.odettesprimrosehill.com

"Fancy presentations" of Modern European eats are matched by fancy wallpaper (some call the setting "beautiful", some "overdecorated") at this Primrose Hill haunt that employs "knowledgeable" "friendly" staff; however, an across-the-board slide in scores supports suspicions that it has "slipped", with "underwhelming food" at "West End prices."

Odin's ⊠ *British/French*   21 | 24 | 24 | £55

Marylebone | 27 Devonshire St., W1 (Baker St.) | 020-7935-7296 | www.langansrestaurants.co.uk

"Some things never change, and sometimes you don't want them to" muse the many "charmed" by this 1966 Marylebone "stalwart" whose "professional" staff convey "elegant" Franco-British classics also on hand is an "eclectic" list of "well-priced wines", but perhaps most intoxicating is the "beautiful" space, with an impressive array of paintings that include some Hockneys.

Old Brewery *British*   ▽ 18 | 25 | 18 | £27

Greenwich | Pepys Bldg. | Old Royal Naval College, SE10 (Greenwich Rail) | 020-3327-1280 | www.oldbrewerygreenwich.com

Hops-hounds boggle at the "killer" setting – centred around eight 1,000-litre copper vats in which an "interesting range" of beers is "well made" – of this Modern British microbrewery on the grounds of Greenwich's Old Royal Naval College; in the main hall, "attentive" servers deliver "enjoyable" bistro-style bites by day and less-dainty eats at night, while after-work pint-seekers drop into the adjacent pub and its attached courtyard garden.

	FOOD	DECOR	SERVICE	COST

Old Bull & Bush *European* 14 | 15 | 12 | £31

Hampstead | Northend Rd., NW3 (Golders Green/Hampstead) |
020-8905-5456 | www.thebullandbush.co.uk

"For a drink and a bite after a walk on the Heath", this "upmarket"
Hampstead pub has an "almost-monopoly" – too bad then that the
"location is better" than the merely "adequate" Modern Euro eats;
on the upside, the atmosphere is "relaxed" – but unfortunately, that
extends to the staff, meaning "service can be slow, especially at
weekends" when "it gets very busy."

Oliveto *Italian* 24 | 14 | 19 | £34

Belgravia | 49 Elizabeth St., SW1 (Sloane Sq./Victoria) | 020-7730-0074 |
www.olivorestaurants.com

If you're "missing Sardinia", hit this "informal" Belgravia offshoot of
Olivo, whose "yummy" Italian eats include "perfectly cooked thin-
crust pizzas with wonderful toppings"; affordable prices and "friendly"
service are part of the package, so little wonder it's "always packed."

Olivo *Italian* 23 | 16 | 21 | £40

Victoria | 21 Eccleston St., SW1 (Victoria) | 020-7730-2505 |
www.olivorestaurants.com

A "loyal clientele affirms the quality" of the "simple", "superb"
Sardinian standards prepared at this "bustling" "big brother to
Oliveto" in Victoria; a "relaxed", rustic atmosphere, service "without pretension" and prices that are "not wildly expensive" are a few
more reason's it's a "neighbourhood favourite."

Olivomare *Italian/Seafood* 24 | 17 | 21 | £49

Belgravia | 10 Lower Belgrave St., SW1 (Victoria) | 020-7730-9022 |
www.olivorestaurants.com

"Tasty Italian with a seafood twist" is "efficiently" delivered to
Belgravia's "diplomats" and "hedge-fund managers" at this member
of the Olivo stable; those who report "psychedelic nightmares" from
the "bit-strange" fish mural that dominates the "cold, modern" interior say "make sure you sit outside when possible" – it's not as
"noisy" there either.

1 Lombard Street ⊠ *French* 22 | 21 | 21 | £52

City | 1 Lombard St., EC3 (Bank) | 020-7929-6611 |
www.1lombardstreet.com

"An oasis of elitist calm amidst the bustle of Lombard Street", this
"formal" "power-lunch" and dinner spot at the rear of the same-
named City brasserie offers "fancy", "reliable" New French cuisine
at "commensurate prices"; service is "prompt without being
rushed", and it includes a "knowledgeable" sommelier to assist with
the "eye-wateringly expensive wine list."

1 Lombard Street Brasserie ⊠ *European* 21 | 20 | 19 | £40

City | 1 Lombard St., EC3 (Bank) | 020-7929-6611 |
www.1lombardstreet.com

In a former banking hall "steeped in City history", this "spacious",
"buzzy" venue offers "good-quality", "creative" Modern European

FOOD DECOR SERVICE COST

dishes along with "fantastic" wines; service fluctuates from "efficient" to "lost", but it's nevertheless a "great choice" for a "relaxed" "business lunch, dinner" or an after-work cocktail, plus "breakfast is worthy of mentioning" as well.

108 Marylebone Lane *British*   19 | 19 | 20 | £42

Marylebone | Marylebone Hotel | 108 Marylebone Ln., W1 (Bond St.) | 020-7969-3900 | www.108marylebonelane.com

"Tucked away from the overpriced, over-trafficked venues" on Marylebone High Street, this "casual" hotel dining room prepares Traditional British food that's "nothing to write home about but never disappointing either"; though a few have found it a "little quiet and lacking in atmosphere", many deem it a "stylish", "charming place" for meals with "friends or lovers."

One-O-One *French/Seafood*   22 | 17 | 20 | £63

Knightsbridge | Sheraton Park Tower | 101 Knightsbridge, SW1 (Knightsbridge) | 020-7290-7101 | www.oneoonerestaurant.com

Supporters say the "beautiful food and beautiful service" at this New French seafood purveyor in Knightsbridge's Sheraton Park Tower mean the "high" prices are "justified"; however, detractors who "expected more" from both the fare and the "corporate-ish", wavy-walled decor deem it "overpriced."

Only Running Footman *British*   19 | 16 | 18 | £42

Mayfair | 5 Charles St., W1 (Green Park) | 020-7499-2988 | www.therunningfootman.biz

Whether you come for a pint and casual eats downstairs or a "posh" meal upstairs, the Traditional British dishes are equally "solid and hearty" at this "minimalist" gastropub off Berkeley Square; "attentive but relaxed" service abets a "great atmosphere" throughout, but what really makes it an "all-round fun" place are the "fair prices."

NEW Opera Tavern *Italian/Spanish*   - | - | - | M

Covent Garden | 23 Catherine St., WC2 (Covent Garden) | 020-7836-3680 | www.operatavern.co.uk

From the Dehesa and Salt Yard crew comes this "new jewel in Covent Garden" set in a landmark boozer that's been gutted save for wood panelling and some original theatrical features; the "fabulous", mid-priced Spanish-Italian tapas menu – majoring on charcoal-grilled Ibérico meat, charcuterie and specialty cheeses – is served in a "lively" ground-floor bar area and a "classy, stylish" upstairs dining room with a gilded ceiling and Murano chandelier; "good-value" wines and "charming service" complete the picture.

Orange, The ● *European*   22 | 22 | 18 | £36

Pimlico | The Orange | 37-39 Pimlico Rd., SW1 (Sloane Sq.) | 020-7881-9844 | www.theorange.co.uk

"The Orange is a peach" declare pun-sters of this "beautiful", "faux-rural-chic" gastropub in Pimlico, whose reasonably priced Modern European menu lists everything from "wonderful breakfasts" to "superb dinners" to a Sunday roast that "makes you question cooking

128   Vote at ZAGAT.com

at home" ever again; service can be "slow", though in all other respects, it's "lovely" – but peace-seekers should know that it can get quite "noisy" in here.

Original Lahore Kebab House ❂ *Pakistani* | 25 | 7 | 14 | £20 |

Whitechapel | 2-10 Umberston St., E1 (Aldgate E./Whitechapel) | 020-7481-9737

Hendon | 148-150 Brent St., NW4 (Hendon Central) | 020-8203-6904

NEW **Streatham** | 668 Streatham High Rd., SW16 (Norbury Rail) | 020-8679-9980

www.lahore-kebabhouse.com

It's "all about the food" at this "legendary" Whitechapel BYO where "City boys, Hoxton bohos" and everyone else join "long queues" for "sublime", "great-value" halal Pakistani plates ("the lamb chops are the dish of choice"); indeed, it's certainly not about the "noisy, scruffy" setting or the "not-always-friendly" service (to be fair, it's usually "quick"); P.S. there's a Hendon branch and a new Streatham iteration.

Original Tagines ❂ *Moroccan* | - | - | - | M |

Marylebone | 7A Dorset St., W1 (Baker St.) | 020-7935-1545 | www.original-tagines.com

Arabic calligraphy and artwork–festooned decor plus "reliable" tagines, couscous and grills "transport you from busy Baker Street to North Africa" at this Marylebone Moroccan; "the space is small and a bit cramped", but service is "gracious" and, best of all, the prices, even on the "good wine list", are "reasonable."

Orrery *French* | 25 | 23 | 25 | £59 |

Marylebone | 55 Marylebone High St., W1 (Baker St./Regent's Park) | 020-7616-8000 | www.orreryrestaurant.co.uk

"Simply wonderful" sigh fans of this Marylebone *maison* that's "first class all around", from the "inspired" New French cuisine laden with "foie gras and truffles" to the "lovely", light-filled setting and "extremely attentive" treatment; it's "expensive", and some find the Gallic service a touch "overbearing", but for "a special occasion" "you really get what you pay for"; P.S. try the "wonderful prix fixe lunch."

Orso ❂ *Italian* | 21 | 17 | 21 | £44 |

Covent Garden | 27 Wellington St., WC2 (Covent Garden) | 020-7240-5269 | www.orsorestaurant.co.uk

Particularly "handy" "before heading off to the theatre", this "steady" Covent Garden Italian offers a "tasty" menu doled out by "sharp" staff that get you out in time for curtain; sure, the "dated" basement digs "could use some refreshing", but there's always the "the possibility of eying a celeb", so overall it's an "enjoyable night out", and open late too.

❷ Oslo Court ⧉ *French* | 26 | 19 | 26 | £53 |

St. John's Wood | Charlbert St., off Prince Albert Rd., NW8 (St. John's Wood) | 020-7722-8795

"Marvellous" beef Wellington, duck à l'orange and other "unapologetically" "retro" French dishes "never disappoint" at this 30-year-old "gem" in St. John's Wood, "off the beaten track near Regent's Park"; the "wonderful" service and "bright"-"pink" setting are appropriately "old school", and whilst it's not cheap, for a "celebration", it's "always a delight"; P.S. save room for the "cream-laden" desserts peddled from the "legendary" sweets trolley.

Osteria Basilico ● *Italian* | 25 | 18 | 19 | £39 |

Notting Hill | 29 Kensington Park Rd., W11 (Ladbroke Grove/ Notting Hill Gate) | 020-7727-9957 | www.osteriabasilico.co.uk

Ever "popular", this well-priced Notting Hill Italian puts out "mouth-watering" pastas and "fantastic" "thin-crust" pizzas in a "quaint", candlelit interior that's "as crowded as Rome at Easter, and as noisy as Venice in July"; indeed, "the tables are so close your neighbours may be in your lap", but "accommodating" service eases the crush, and seats near the open windows in summer afford for some primo "people-watching."

Osteria Dell'Angolo ⌸ *Italian*   ∇ | 22 | 18 | 22 | £40 |

Westminster | 47 Marsham St., SW1 (St. James's Park/ Westminster) | 020-3268-1077 | www.osteriadellangolo.co.uk

Politicos bemoaning the "sparse choice" of venues in Westminster especially appreciate this "swish" yet somewhat "quiet" Italian offering "simple", "quality" dishes; whilst there's no knocking the "friendly staff", surveyors can't agree on whether it's "good value" or "overpriced."

Osteria dell'Arancio *Italian* | 19 | 21 | 22 | £45 |

Chelsea | 383 King's Rd., SW10 (Sloane Sq./South Kensington) | 020-7349-8111 | www.osteriadellarancio.co.uk

"Italian wines to die for" complement a "solid" menu selection at this Chelsea spot with a "cute and quirky", "rustic" ground floor and classier upstairs, both bedecked with colourful art; though a slide in scores supports the feeling that it's "not as wonderful" as it once was (and therefore "overpriced"), the service remains "knowledgeable" and "friendly."

Ottolenghi *Bakery/Mediterranean* | 25 | 17 | 18 | £31 |

Belgravia | 13 Motcomb St., SW1 (Knightsbridge) | 020-7823-2707
Islington | 287 Upper St., N1 (Angel) | 020-7288-1454
Notting Hill | 63 Ledbury Rd., W11 (Notting Hill Gate) | 020-7727-1121
www.ottolenghi.co.uk

"Piled-high" salads, "novel" tapas and other "out-of-this-world", "forward-thinking" Med dishes bring the masses into these "stylishly minimal" cafe/bakeries also crafting "divine pastries" "worth breaking the diet for"; regulars forgo the "cramped" communal tables and sometimes "slow" service in favour of "takeaway" – just be aware that the bill can mount quickly.

Oxo Tower *European* | 21 | 24 | 19 | £57 |

South Bank | Oxo Tower Wharf | Barge House St., 8th fl., SE1 (Waterloo) | 020-7803-3888 | www.harveynichols.com

"It's all about the view of the Thames" at this "expense-account" standby on the eighth floor of the "iconic" South Bank building,

	FOOD	DECOR	SERVICE	COST

where the Modern European cuisine, though "well executed", takes a backseat to the "spectacular" vista; given the "hit-or-miss" service and "expensive" prices, some stick to "cocktails at the bar."

Oxo Tower Brasserie *Asian/Mediterranean* | 19 | 23 | 19 | £47 |

South Bank | Oxo Tower Wharf | Barge House St., SE1 (Waterloo) | 020-7803-3888 | www.harveynichols.com

This "informal alternative" to next-door's Oxo Tower boasts the same "enchanting" view over the Thames and high prices, but a more "relaxed" atmosphere; the "original" Mediterranean and Pan-Asian menu is "tasty" enough and delivered in a "timely" fashion by "polite" people, whilst nightly jazz completes the package.

Özer Restaurant & Bar ● *Turkish* | ▽ 20 | 21 | 19 | £47 |

Marylebone | 5 Langham Pl., W1 (Oxford Circus) | 020-7323-0505 | www.ozerrestaurant.com

A "corner of Turkey" near Oxford Circus, this red-walled, grown-up sibling of Sofra is frequently "full" with folks enjoying its mezze and mains; indeed, many find it a "nice change" from the ordinary, with lunch and dinner prix fixes that help keep costs affordable.

Pacific Oriental ☒ *Asian* | ▽ 18 | 18 | 15 | £46 |

City | 52 Threadneedle St., EC2 (Bank) | 0871-704-4060 | www.orientalrestaurantgroup.co.uk

City slickers hit this "elegant" art deco-style banking hall-turned eatery for "original" "East-meets-West" Asian fusion fare; but though it's "highly regarded" by some, others deem it "expensive for what it is" and stick to drinks at the bar, which "can be rowdy in the evening."

Painted Heron *Indian* | 24 | 20 | 20 | £49 |

Chelsea | 112 Cheyne Walk, SW1 (Sloane Sq.) | 020-7351-5232 | www.thepaintedheron.com

"Nontraditional ingredients" (e.g. pheasant) pair with "traditional spices" to create "modern" dishes that are "not-to-be-missed" at this "friendly" Thames-side Indian in Chelsea; as for the decor, the minimalist digs are dotted with contemporary artworks whose sophistication matches the generally "upscale" pricing.

Palm, The *American/Chophouse* | 23 | 20 | 22 | £64 |

Belgravia | 1 Pont St., SW1 (Knightsbridge/Sloane Sq.) | 020-7201-0710 | www.thepalm.com

"Red-blooded" types tuck into "outstanding" prime-aged steaks "cooked to perfection" at this "classy, wood-panelled", celebrity-caricature-filled Belgravia outpost of the American chophouse chain; also "U.S.-style" are "gargantuan" portions (in the "yummy" sides and "exquisite" Nova Scotia lobsters as well) and "knowledgeable" staff, all of which may "actually make it worth the crazy prices."

Pantechnicon Rooms *European* | 20 | 19 | 16 | £38 |

Belgravia | 10 Motcomb St., SW1 (Hyde Park Corner/Knightsbridge) | 020-7730-6074 | www.thepantechnicon.com

"Comfy leather seats" cosset Belgravian bottoms as their owners "enjoy every bite" of "well-cooked and -presented" Modern

European fare (particularly "terrific" for Sunday lunch) at this spot with a "buzzy" pub downstairs and a more "elegant" dining room upstairs; however, the consensus about the cost is that it's "pricey for what it is", whilst the general feeling about staff is it's a "shame" they're "more interested in chatting than looking after customers."

Paradise by way of Kensal Green British   — | — | — | M

Kilburn | 19 Kilburn Ln., W10 (Kensal Green) | 020-8969-0098 | www.theparadise.co.uk

"Quirky" Victorian Gothic touches ("large angel statue", "taxidermy") are as "interesting" as the "reliable", reasonably priced Modern British menu at this "lively" Kilburn gastropub that also features a "swanky bar" and a roof terrace; everything's served in an "efficient and pleasant" fashion, whilst occasional live music, comedy and a private karaoke room further make it a "desirable place to be."

Paramount 🗷 British   ∇ 16 | 21 | 15 | £53

Soho | Centre Point | 101-103 New Oxford St., 32nd fl., WC1 (Tottenham Court Rd.) | 020-7420-2900 | www.paramount.uk.net

"Spectacular" 360-degree views "impress dates" and "overseas business contacts" at this "dark, buzzy" Modern British perch on the 32nd floor of Soho's Centre Point; if the "food can't achieve the same heights", the "jaw-dropping" sight of "the lights of London sparkling in the dark" make the "expensive" bill "worth it."

Pasha Turkish   ∇ 20 | 20 | 22 | £28

Islington | 301 Upper St., N1 (Angel/Highbury & Islington) | 020-7226-1454 | www.pashaislington.co.uk

At this "peaceful", "elegant" Islington retreat, you'll find "upmarket Turkish without the upmarket price", including "yummy" mezzes and "reliable" grills; the "smart surroundings" are matched by "slick service", making for an experience that "never disappoints."

Pasha ● Moroccan   18 | 22 | 18 | £41

South Kensington | 1 Gloucester Rd., SW7 (Gloucester Rd.) | 020-7589-7969 | www.pasha-restaurant.co.uk

"Tasty" Moroccan meals and "intriguing" belly dancing make for a "fantastic evening out" at this "sumptuous" "sunken dining room" and its "absolutely fabulous" alcoves in South Kensington; it's usually filled with a "noisy young crowd", the kind that doesn't mind leaving "considerably poorer."

Patara Thai   24 | 20 | 20 | £39

Knightsbridge | 9 Beauchamp Pl., SW3 (Knightsbridge/ South Kensington) | 020-7581-8820
Mayfair | 3-7 Maddox St., W1 (Oxford Circus) | 020-7499-6008
Soho | 15 Greek St., W1 (Leicester Sq./Tottenham Court Rd.) | 020-7437-1071
South Kensington | 181 Fulham Rd., SW3 (South Kensington) | 020-7351-5692
www.patarauk.com

The "terrific", "authentic" Thai menu is "packed with temptations" at this "fashionable" quartet set in "chic", "serene" quarters offering

	FOOD	DECOR	SERVICE	COST

"skillful", "darn-tasty" specialties crafted from "top-quality" ingredients; perhaps prices are "a little expensive" for the genre, but the service is "gracious" and, overall, it's "amazingly consistent."

Paternoster Chop House *Chophouse* ▽ 15 | 16 | 16 | £43

City | Warwick Ct., Paternoster Sq., EC4 (St. Paul's) | 020-7029-9400 | www.paternosterchophouse.com

With a "wonderful view of St. Paul's from the tables outside" and an upscale marble-and-wood interior, this City chophouse "packs them in" and sates them with an "interesting variety of meat dishes", "some unusual" (including a 'beast of the day'); whilst some sniff that it "feels like a chain", on the whole, it "keeps the punters happy."

Patisserie Valerie *French* 16 | 13 | 13 | £20

Belgravia | 17 Motcomb St., SW1 (Knightsbridge) | 020-7245-6161
Covent Garden | 15 Bedford St., WC2 (Charing Cross/Royal Opera Hse.) | 020-7379-6428
Covent Garden | 8 Russell St., WC2 (Covent Garden) | 020-7240-0064
Knightsbridge | 32-44 Hans Cres., SW1 (Knightsbridge) | 020-7590-0905
Marylebone | 105 Marylebone High St., W1 (Baker St./Bond St.) | 020-7935-6240
Piccadilly | 162 Piccadilly, W1 (Green Park) | 020-7491-1717
Soho | 44 Old Compton St., W1 (Leicester Sq.) | 020-7437-3466
City | Pavillion Bldg. | 37 Brushfield St., E1 (Liverpool St.) | 020-7247-4906
Chelsea | 81 Duke of York Sq., SW3 (Sloane Sq.) | 020-7730-7094
Kensington | 27 Kensington Church St., W8 (High St. Kensington) | 020-7937-9574
www.patisserie-valerie.co.uk
Additional locations throughout London

"Sweet-toothed" surveyors "drool just looking in the windows" of these cafes "located all over town", which are "fair value for a breakfast" of "flaky croissants", "wonderful pastries", "cracking coffee" and the like and a "convenient" stop for "basic" French bistro lunches; however, for quite a few folks, "indolent staff" and "decaying" decor spell the "end of a love affair."

Patterson's 🛇 *European* 24 | 20 | 22 | £51

Mayfair | 4 Mill St., W1 (Oxford Circus) | 020-7499-1308 | www.pattersonsrestaurant.com

"Smashing" dishes celebrate "the best of the season and the market" at this Modern European in Mayfair, with "smooth" service and a "nicely understated" design featuring pine floors and marble walls; just "forget about having a conversation" "if you have a couple of jovial tables around you" – which, with such "reasonably priced" wines thrown into the mix, you probably will.

Pearl *French* 26 | 25 | 24 | £66

Holborn | Renaissance Chancery Court Hotel | 252 High Holborn, WC1 (Holborn) | 020-7829-7000 | www.pearl-restaurant.com

"Genius" chef Jun Tanaka's "innovative", "beautifully presented" French menu is the pearl of this "sleek, chic" oyster, a "grand", chandelier-bedecked dining room in a Holborn hotel; "wonderful" staff featuring "a knowledgeable sommelier" plus "expensive" prices mean its "hits all the right buttons" "for a special occasion", but it's also an "excellent spot for breakfast" and lunch, the latter offering some "great deals."

Pearl Liang *Chinese*   23 | 19 | 18 | £36

Paddington | 8 Sheldon Sq., W2 (Paddington) | 020-7289-7000 | www.pearlliang.co.uk

"You need a map and a guide dog to find" this fuchsia-hued Chinese venue in a "random" part of Paddington, where the adventurous are rewarded with an "extensive" range of "delicious dim sum" and "innovative", affordable mains; unlike many of its ilk, you can actually "book a table" for "a Sunday afternoon" – "great if you're on a schedule."

Pellicano *Italian*   ∇ 19 | 18 | 20 | £42

Chelsea | 19-21 Elystan St., SW3 (South Kensington) | 020-7589-3718 | www.pellicanorestaurant.co.uk

In a "quiet" Chelsea street, this "upscale neighbourhood Italian" proves "popular with locals" with a penchant for "varied" Sardinian-accented specials; lunch is the time to come for "good value" (it's "otherwise expensive"), whilst in summer, fresh-air-seekers ask to sit outside under the blue canopy.

NEW Penny Black Ⓜ *British*   - | - | - | M

Chelsea | 212 Fulham Rd., SW10 (Fulham Broadway/ South Kensington) | 0845-838-8998 | www.thepennyblack.com

Retro British faves such as beef Wellington, toad in the hole and rice pudding are among the fairly priced offerings at this quietly sophisticated Fulham Road newcomer; red, black and grey hues lend a dark, discreet air to the narrow premises, which include a small lounge at the front, with comfy sofas and a meandering cocktail list.

Pepper Tree *Thai*   - | - | - | M

Clapham | 19 Clapham Common S., SW4 (Clapham Common) | 020-7622-1758 | www.thepeppertree.co.uk

"It might not be the trendiest-looking venue", with communal benches that can be "a bit bum-numbing", but this canteen is usually "busy" because its "great Thai food" is sold for "reasonable prices"; in sum, for a "quick, informal" meal, it's a "solid" choice in Clapham.

Pescatori Ⓢ *Italian/Seafood*   22 | 19 | 24 | £41

Bloomsbury | 57 Charlotte St., W1 (Goodge St.) | 020-7580-3289
Mayfair | 11 Dover St., W1 (Green Park) | 020-7493-2652
www.pescatori.co.uk

Bring the "whole family" to one of these "smart" Italians in Fitzrovia and Mayfair, where the "long list of fish" is prepared in "straightforward", "reliable" fashion; "attentive staff" are on hand to facilitate an experience that "relaxes", even though some surveyors feel as if they've "paid a bit too much"; P.S. it's "lovely outside on a summer day" in Charlotte Street.

	FOOD	DECOR	SERVICE	COST

Petersham, The *European* — — — E

Richmond | Petersham Hotel | Nightingale Ln., TW10 (Richmond) |
020-8940-7471 | www.petershamhotel.co.uk

"Beautiful views out over Richmond Park and the Thames" "domi-
nate the dining room" of this handsome hotel that's "a little formal",
therefore popular for special occasions as well as weddings and
functions; service is "excellent", whilst the "flavoursome" Modern
European cuisine, accompanied by a "conservative wine list", is
pricey, save for the "incredible value" set lunch.

Petersham Nurseries Café Ⓜ *European* 24 24 20 £49

Richmond | Petersham Nurseries | Church Ln., off Petersham Rd., TW10
(Richmond) | 020-8605-3627 | www.petershamnurseries.com

On paper, this Richmond destination "shouldn't work", with "expensive" dishes served on "rickety" furniture in a dirt-floored greenhouse; but on the contrary, it "amazes", with "phenomenal"
seasonal produce punctuating "sophisticated" Modern European eats
and a setting that's "charming", "surrounded by exotic plants and
antique wall-hangings"; in fact, the only thing wanting is longer hours –
"please open for dinner!" (it's lunch-only, Wednesday–Sunday).

Petrus Ⓩ *French* 25 24 26 £86

Belgravia | 1 Kinnerton St., SW1 (Hyde Park Corner/Knightsbridge) |
020-7592-1609 | www.gordonramsay.com

"In a word, superb" sigh the "rich clientele" who habituate Gordon
Ramsay's "sumptuous" Modern French in Belgravia, where staff go
"above and beyond" as they present the "sublime" dishes; 1,500
"unbelievable wines" are stored in a glass-enclosed, central storage
section, and whilst it's "expensive", "every now and again, who cares?"

NEW Phene, The *European* ▽ 13 21 14 £36

Chelsea | 9 Phene St., SW3 (Sloane Sq.) | 020-7352-9898 |
www.thephene.com

An iconic Chelsea boozer has been turned into this "poncey but
fun", moderately priced haunt with a library-themed room serving
"serviceable", "pub-quality" Modern European grub and an all-day,
organic-oriented deli/cafe; outside is a large terrace decked out like
a cool beach bar (canvas canopies, swinging basket seats), whilst
upstairs is a "convivial", purple-velvet-clad lounge bar.

Pho *Vietnamese* 20 12 16 £18

Bloomsbury | 3 Great Titchfield St., W1 (Oxford Circus) |
020-7436-0111 Ⓢ
NEW Soho | 163-165 Wardour St., W1 (Tottenham Court Rd.) |
020-7434-3938
Farringdon | 86 St. John St., EC1 (Barbican/Farringdon) |
020-7253-7624 Ⓢ
Shepherd's Bush | Westfield Shopping Ctr. | Ariel Way, balcony, W12
(Shepherd's Bush) | 020-7824-662320
www.phocafe.co.uk

The "street food of Saigon" comes in "colourful, fun combinations",
with "zingy flavours" and for "bargain" prices at this growing

Vietnamese chain; while the "low-rent settings" and "scatty" service are deterrents pho some, "on a cold day", "it's hard to imagine healthier, more satisfying" "fast food."

Phoenix Palace ● *Chinese* | 25 | 18 | 17 | £31 |
Marylebone | 5-9 Glentworth St., NW1 (Baker St.) | 020-7486-3515 | www.phoenixpalace.co.uk

"Large families" "savouring" "tasty" daily dim sum and "some not-so-run-of-the-mill" Cantonese dishes fuel the "buzzy atmosphere" at this spacious, moderately priced Marylebone Chinese; traditional trappings add to the "authenticity", and if "service can be a little slow when busy", it's still "a cut above" many others.

NEW Picasso *Chophouse* | - | - | - | M |
Chelsea | 127 King's Rd., SW3 (Sloane Sq.) | 020-7351-1661 | www.blackandbluerestaurants.com

This iconic 1980s bastion of King's Road cafe culture has been adopted by the Black & Blue family, which has bestowed its signature formula of well-priced chophouse fare served in a stylish setting of leather banquettes and abstract wall art; breakfast is a big deal in the AM, whilst at night, the small bar presents a large cocktail list.

☑ Pied à Terre ⑤ *French* | 28 | 22 | 27 | £83 |
Bloomsbury | 34 Charlotte St., W1 (Goodge St.) | 020-7636-1178 | www.pied-a-terre.co.uk

An absolute "must" declare devotees of this Charlotte Street "favourite" where "exquisite", "conversation-stopping" New French cuisine comes "beautifully presented", and the infamous "bacon-brioche rolls alone are worth a transatlantic flight"; perhaps the Bloomsbury setting's "nothing to write home about", but it's "comfortable and discreet", whilst a "responsive", "engaged" crew "make you feel [so] special" that you "never regret" the not-inconsiderable expense.

Pig's Ear *British/French* | 22 | 19 | 19 | £37 |
Chelsea | 35 Old Church St., SW3 (Sloane Sq.) | 020-7352-2908 | www.thepigsear.info

It might "look like an average pub", but "those in the know in Chelsea" know the Traditional British and French brasserie fare at this gastropub is "interesting", "high quality" and reasonably priced; it's particularly "excellent for a lazy, long Sunday lunch", and whilst downstairs is usually the site of "noise and queuing", the oak-panelled dining room upstairs can feel more "romantic."

Pinchito Tapas *Spanish* | - | - | - | M |
Bloomsbury | 11 Bayley St., Bedford Sq., WC1 (Tottenham Court Rd.) | 020-7637-3977
City | 32 Featherstone St., EC1 (Old St.) | 020-7490-0121 ⑤
www.pinchito.co.uk

"Funky" settings set the stage for "fun" at these "excellent" joints in the City and Bloomsbury, where "friendly" staff ferry "delicious" Barcelona-style tapas alongside "great drinks"; whilst fees are always reasonable, groups of four or more can "pre-book the set menu" for even "better value."

Ping Pong *Chinese* | 16 | 15 | 14 | £27 |

Bloomsbury | 48 Eastcastle St., W1 (Oxford Circus) | 020-7079-0550
Bloomsbury | 48 Newman St., W1 (Goodge St.) | 020-7291-3080
Marylebone | 10 Paddington St., W1 (Baker St.) | 020-7009-9600
Marylebone | 29A James St., W1 (Bond St.) | 020-7034-3100
Soho | Royal Festival Hall | 45 Great Marlborough St., W1 (Oxford Circus) | 020-7851-6969 ◑
City | Bow Bells Hse. | 1 Bread St., EC4 (Mansion Hse.) | 020-7651-0880 ◪
South Bank | Belvedere Rd., Festival Terr. | Royal Festival Hall, SE1 (Waterloo) | 020-7960-4160 ◑
Tower Bridge | St. Katherine Docks | 50 St. Katharine's Way, E1 (Tower Hill) | 020-7680-7850
Hampstead | 83-84 Hampstead High St., NW3 (Hampstead) | 020-7433-0930
Notting Hill | 74-76 Westbourne Grove, W2 (Notting Hill Gate) | 020-7313-9832
www.pingpongdimsum.com
Additional locations throughout London

"Amazing" flowering teas and "creative" "cocktails are the best bit" about this "lively" Chinese chain that draws "young, hip" people; as far as the "wide variety of dim sum" goes, sure, it's "not authentic", merely "adequate" and "overpriced" – not to mention served at "uncomfortable", "close" tables by "erratic" staff – yet all branches remain "busy" because, all in all, they're "fun."

Pix Pintxos *Spanish* | ▽ 16 | 18 | 15 | £27 |

Covent Garden | 63 Neal St., WC2 (Covent Garden/ Tottenham Court Rd.) | 020-7836-9779
Notting Hill | 175 Westbourne Grove, W11 (Notting Hill Gate) | 020-7727-6500 ◑
www.pix-bar.com

Notting Hill and Covent Garden snackers like the "casual sophistication" of these "light, airy", rustic Spaniards whose skewered tapas are laid out buffet-style and the price is tallied per stick; unfortunately, some fume that the fare tastes like it was "made hours before it's served."

Pizza East *Pizza* | 20 | 22 | 17 | £30 |

Shoreditch | Tea Bldg. | 56 Shoreditch High St., E1 (Liverpool St./Old St.) | 020-7729-1888 | www.pizzaeast.com ◑
NEW **Notting Hill** | 310 Portobello Rd., W10 (Ladbroke Grove/ Westbourne Park) | 020-8969-4500 | www.pizzaeastportobello.com

Whether you're trying to "impress a date" or manage "a table of 10-year-olds", this "achingly trendy", "massive" Shoreditch parlour does the trick via "awesome", "crispy, light" pizzas with "unusual toppings" like rabbit and sprouting broccoli; in short, it's a "refreshing" "break-away from the usual", despite service that can occasionally be a "bit too cool"; P.S. the rustic Notting Hill offshoot premiered post-Survey.

	FOOD	DECOR	SERVICE	COST

Pizza Express *Pizza* | 16 | 14 | 16 | £20 |

Covent Garden | 9-12 Bow St., WC2 (Covent Garden) | 020-7240-3443 ❷
Knightsbridge | 7 Beauchamp Pl., SW3 (Knightsbridge) | 020-7589-2355
Soho | 29 Wardour St., W1 (Leicester Sq./Piccadilly Circus) | 020-7437-7215
City | 125 Alban Gate, London Wall, EC2 (Moorgate/St. Paul's) | 020-7600-8880
Battersea | 46-54 Battersea Bridge Rd., SW11 (Imperial Wharf) | 020-7924-2774
Chelsea | The Pheasantry | 152-154 King's Rd., SW3 (Sloane Sq.) | 020-7351-5031
Fulham | 363 Fulham Rd., SW10 (Fulham Broadway) | 020-7352-5300 ❷
Fulham | 895-896 Fulham Rd., SW6 (Parsons Green) | 020-7731-3117 ❷
Kensington | 35 Earl's Court Rd., W8 (Earl's Ct.) | 020-7937-0761
Notting Hill | 137 Notting Hill Gate, W11 (Notting Hill Gate) | 020-7229-6000
www.pizzaexpress.com
Additional locations throughout London

"Snob appeal be damned!" – this "contemporary" pizza chain does a "solid" job with a "diverse choice" of options suitable for a "hungry group" or parents with "kids", not least of all because it's "easy on the wallet"; purists maintain that they're "nothing to write home about", but even they utilise them as a "fallback" when they "don't want to make a decision."

PJ's Bar & Grill ❷ *American* | 17 | 19 | 18 | £34 |

Covent Garden | 30 Wellington St., WC2 (Covent Garden) | 020-7240-7529 | www.pjscoventgarden.co.uk
Chelsea | 52 Fulham Rd., SW3 (South Kensington) | 020-7581-0025 | www.pjsbarandgrill.co.uk

"When you're too tired to walk elsewhere", this "preppy" Chelsea spot and its "theatrical", separately owned Covent Garden cousin "shoe-horn you in" so you can shovel down "simple", "reliable", "quite inexpensive" American eats; it's all "unpretentious", "lively" "fun", but possibly with the exception of a "great" Bloody Mary, a little "uninspiring."

Planet Hollywood ❷ *American* | 12 | 15 | 14 | £26 |

Piccadilly | 57-60 Haymarket, SW1 (Piccadilly Circus) | 020-7437-7639 | www.planethollywoodlondon.com

Attempting Hollywood "razzamatazz" in the Haymarket, this "noisy", "tourist"-heavy American chain outpost's highlights are "huge drinks" and "massive" puddings; the grub, however, is "expensive for the quality", and critics also knock the "inattentive service" and "stale" "diner atmosphere."

Plateau ⧄ *French* | 19 | 20 | 19 | £52 |

Canary Wharf | Canada Pl., 4th fl., E14 (Canary Wharf) | 020-7715-7100 | www.plateaurestaurant.co.uk

If ever there were an "expense-account venue", it's this "light, bright" New French venture where "Canary Wharf bankers, traders" and other people with "money to burn" dine on "pleasant" *plats* and wines whilst admiring the "good views"; it probably goes without saying that "the restaurant peaks during lunch, the bar peaks for after-work drinks" and it's "not very thrilling" at other times.

Plum Valley ● *Chinese*

FOOD	DECOR	SERVICE	COST
21	20	15	£35

Chinatown | 20 Gerrard St., W1 (Piccadilly Circus) | 020-7494-4366

In a sea of "overly brightly lit" eateries, this Chinatown plum offers its "well-prepared" fare – including "lovely choices for vegetarians" and "delicious" dim sum – in "dark", "stylish", slate-walled environs; whilst it's always affordable, insiders recommend the specials for "the best value."

Poissonnerie de L'Avenue ● *French/Seafood*

FOOD	DECOR	SERVICE	COST
22	17	20	£57

Chelsea | 82 Sloane Ave., SW3 (South Kensington) | 020-7589-2457 | www.poissonneriedelavenue.com

"It feels like 1960", in terms of both the "dated decoration" and "well-dressed, sophisticated neighbourhood regulars", at this "civilised, reliable" Chelsea "classic" providing "wonderful French-style seafood" for "expensive" prices; it may be "a little old fashioned" for younger diners, and possibly even "flagging", but nostalgists forgive much because it's been here "for decades" – and "long may it continue to serve."

NEW Pollen Street Social 🅩 *British*

FOOD	DECOR	SERVICE	COST
–	–	–	E

Mayfair | 8-10 Pollen St., W1 (Oxford Circus) | 020-7290-7600 | www.jasonatherton.co.uk

For the first time, ex-Maze chef Jason Atherton is calling all the shots, presiding over this stylish, oak-lined Modern British venture in Mayfair offering a relaxed tapas bar (called the Social Room) and a bright, airy dining room boasting a novel dessert bar with stools and a prime kitchen view; P.S. diners get a key to unlock their own little gift box on leaving.

NEW Polpetto 🅩 *Italian*

FOOD	DECOR	SERVICE	COST
∇ 22	19	20	£37

Soho | The French House | 49 Dean St., 1st fl., W1 (Leicester Sq.) | 020-7734-1969 | www.polpetto.co.uk

Zinc-topped tables groan with a "variety" of "delicious" Venetian tapas at this "tiny" (28 seats), "atmospheric" sister of Polpo in Soho; those who brave the wait (no reservations in the evenings) are also rewarded with wines available by the glass, carafe or bottle and a bill that's as "unpretentious" as the service.

Polpo *Italian*

FOOD	DECOR	SERVICE	COST
23	19	18	£32

Soho | 41 Beak St., W1 (Oxford Circus/Piccadilly Circus) | 020-7734-4479 | www.polpo.co.uk

"One of the most authentic Venetian bars this side of Lake Como" swear Sohoites of this "industrial-chic" *bacaro* whose small plates are "fantastic", "inventive" and "terrific value"; "enjoyable though limited Italian wines" fuel the "buzzing" atmosphere, and whilst the "no-reservations policy" in the evening is "irritating", the "friendly" staff keep you watered "while you wait" in the new Campari bar downstairs.

Porters *British*

15	14	16	£24

Covent Garden | 17 Henrietta St., WC2 (Covent Garden) | 020-7836-6466 | www.porters-restaurant.com

If you're a show-going "traveller looking" to "dip your toes in the pond" of Traditional British tucker – of the "pie and pint" variety – you'll find "good bang for the buck" and "reliable" quality at this wood-panelled Covent Garden "standby"; and if you're not entirely sure what "bubble and squeak or spotted dick" are, "friendly staff are usually standing by to assist."

NEW Portman, The *European*

-	-	-	M

Marylebone | 51 Upper Berkeley St., W1 (Marble Arch) | 020-7723-8996 | www.theportmanmarylebone.com

The Only Running Footman team have spruced up a Victorian boozer in Marylebone to make this "friendly" Modern European gastropub with a ground-floor bar and a first-floor dining room; the down-to-earth menu is served from breakfast onward, majored on game sourced from an upscale farm in Northamptonshire and accompanied by an "experimental wine list"; P.S. open 365 days a year.

Portrait *British*

21	23	21	£37

Soho | National Portrait Gallery | 2 St. Martin's Pl., 3rd fl., WC2 (Charing Cross/Leicester Sq.) | 020-7312-2490 | www.searcys.co.uk

Views of nearby Trafalgar Square, Big Ben and beyond are "to-die-for" at this eatery in the National Portrait Gallery; the all-day Modern British menu is rather "lovely" too, especially for a weekend brunch when the "bright young things" that "fill the bar on Fridays" have fled and you have "superb" staff to yourself.

Princess Garden ● *Chinese*

25	21	22	£53

Mayfair | 8-10 N. Audley St., W1 (Bond St./Marble Arch) | 020-7493-3223 | www.princessgardenofmayfair.com

Backers believe you "never go wrong" at this "fine" Mayfair Mandarin where the "excellent" fare includes "lovely dim sum", all brought by "helpful staff" in "spacious" contemporary environs; too bad then that some folks, especially Americans from the nearby embassy, find the portions "small", and therefore, "expensive."

Princess of Shoreditch *British*

-	-	-	M

Shoreditch | 76 Paul St., EC2 (Old St.) | 020-7729-9270 | www.theprincessofshoreditch.com

If "grown-up" Modern British grub accompanied by "wonderful wines" is your thing, this Shoreditch gastropub is "the sort of place you could become a regular" easily; the "gorgeously renovated" space comprises a "lively" pub downstairs and a "quieter restaurant upstairs", both boasting "good service" and reasonable prices.

Princess Victoria *British*

-	-	-	M

Shepherd's Bush | 217 Uxbridge Rd., W12 (Goldhawk Rd./Shepherd's Bush) | 020-8749-5886 | www.princessvictoria.co.uk

Surveyors say this Shepherd's Bush gastropub just "gets better and better", with a "lovely, somewhat upscale" Traditional British menu on which there are "always interesting new dishes"; a "cavernous dining area, plentiful seating in the bar" and "attentive" staff mean there's usually no hindrance to an "enjoyable" meal.

Princi London ● *Bakery/Italian* | 22 | 19 | 13 | £16 |

Soho | 135 Wardour St., W1 (Leicester Sq./Piccadilly Circus) | 020-7478-8888 | www.princi.co.uk

Soho's "bright young things" make this "stone-and-copper"-filled Italian bakery their "go-to" for "sensational" Italian breads, pizza and desserts, washed down with Prosecco and espresso done "right"; "be warned", "ordering from the canteen-style counter" with "no discernable" queue "can be chaotic", as is "finding a table", but for such "delectable", "great-value" vittles, it's worth having "patience."

Prism ⓩ *British* | ∇ 18 | 18 | 20 | £50 |

City | 147 Leadenhall St., EC3 (Bank/Monument) | 020-7256-3888 | www.harveynichols.com

City suits seeking a "good business lunch" in a "fine-dining" atmosphere patronise this Modern British option based in an "attractive" "old bank building" with "helpful staff"; however, some dinner diners quip "refracting on our evening there, we were not impressed", perhaps because of the high prices.

Providores *Eclectic* | 25 | 17 | 18 | £42 |

Marylebone | 109 Marylebone High St., W1 (Baker St./Bond St.) | 020-7935-6175 | www.theprovidores.co.uk

Chef Peter Gordon's "unique combinations of ingredients" yield "amazing flavours" at this Marylebone Eclectic, which marries its small-plates menu with an "astonishing" New Zealand–heavy wine list; bookings are only accepted for Providores upstairs, but most folks want to be in the "better-atmosphere" (though "cramped") Tapa Room downstairs, which offers breakfast and "possibly the best brunch in London" (the queue is "out of control").

Quadrato *Italian* | ∇ 22 | 21 | 22 | £64 |

Canary Wharf | Four Seasons Canary Wharf | 46 Westferry Circus, E14 (Canary Wharf) | 020-7510-1857 | www.fourseasons.com

Business types escaping Canary Wharf's bustle "look forward to every visit" at this "calm and relaxed" hotel eatery boasting a "pleasant" Thames-side location (though its "views are not exactly riverfront", except maybe from the terrace); considering it's a Four Seasons' property, the service is as "excellent" as expected, just like the Northern Italian fare, making it "worth every penny."

Quaglino's ⓩ *European* | 18 | 21 | 18 | £55 |

St. James's | 16 Bury St., SW1 (Green Park) | 020-7930-6767 | www.quaglinos.co.uk

St. James's "upper classes" are "still impressed" by this "grand" "stalwart" with a "sweeping" "Hollywood" staircase, loads of "buzz", nightly live music and "great" people-watching; however, quite a few of them admit the "show" is "better" than the "tired" Modern European fare, which when coupled with sometimes "sloppy" service, makes it seem "too expensive."

	FOOD	DECOR	SERVICE	COST

Quilon *Indian*
26 | 19 | 25 | £50

Victoria | Crowne Plaza St. James Hotel | 41 Buckingham Gate, SW1 (St. James's Park/Victoria) | 020-7821-1899 | www.quilon.co.uk

Subcontinental connoisseurs say this Victoria hotel eatery is "the place to take people who say they don't like Indian food", as its "intense", "innovative" flavours from the country's Southwest coast "make one see it in a different light"; although "a bit pricey", the "stupendous" cuisine quality coupled with "incredibly attentive", "caring service" make it "worth it" – it's just too bad the "forgettable" decor is "out of keeping with the rest of the experience."

NEW Quince *Mediterranean*
- | - | - | E

Mayfair | The May Fair | Stratton St., W1 (Green Park) | 020-7915-3892 | www.quincelondon.com

From a wide-open kitchen set behind a copper-and-onyx-topped counter, TV chef Silvena Rowe prepares pricey, sharing-style Mediterranean dishes laced with exotic Ottoman influences in this new May Fair Hotel haunt whose glossy, low-ceilinged dining room is rich in deep colours and evocative lighting; also on premises are a comfy bar and windowless tea salon that doubles up as the weekend breakfast room.

Quirinale ⊠ *Italian*
∇ 23 | 17 | 23 | £48

Westminster | 1 Great Peter St., SW1 (Westminster) | 020-7222-7080 | www.quirinale.co.uk

"Pasta reigns supreme", and fish is of a "high standard" too, at this "quiet, classy" basement Italian in Westminster; politicos also praise "precise" service that ensures a "feeling of pampered luxury", exceeding what one might expect, given the "moderate" pricing for the locale.

Quo Vadis ⊠ *British*
21 | 21 | 21 | £58

Soho | 26-29 Dean St., W1 (Leicester Sq./Tottenham Court Rd.) | 020-7437-9585 | www.quovadissoho.co.uk

A "comfortable, clubby" ambience pervades this "attractive" Soho haunt that's beloved of the "media crowd", aka "pretty people" who pick at "high-calibre" Modern British morsels furnished by "friendly" staff; tipplers warn it can be "expensive if you're not careful with the drinks" and "great wines", though post-Survey changes have relaxed the atmosphere and food prices (possibly outdating some scores).

Racine *French*
23 | 19 | 22 | £52

Knightsbridge | 239 Brompton Rd., SW3 (Knightsbridge/ South Kensington) | 020-7584-4477 | www.racine-restaurant.com

"Wonderful", "hearty" "soul food from across the Channel" and "cosy" quarters yield a "real French atmosphere" at this "convivial" Brompton Road brasserie; staff who "know what they're doing" give a "gracious welcome" to "regulars" and "first-time visitors" alike, and best of all, it's "better value than most at this end of town", especially if you go for the "fantastic" prix fixe.

Randall & Aubin *British/Seafood*

FOOD	DECOR	SERVICE	COST
19	15	18	£50

Soho | 14-16 Brewer St., W1 (Piccadilly Circus) | 020-7287-4447 | www.randallandaubin.com

Fruits de mer so "fresh" they're "practically still swimming" are some of the "great food options" at this Modern British place that's a perfect "loud" and "campy" fit for its "bawdy Soho" location; "industrial decor" and "sexy lighting (and staff)" add to the "fabulous fun", for which fans have no issue queuing up, then squeezing onto shared benches at marble counters in the "cramped quarters."

Ransome's Dock *British/Eclectic*

FOOD	DECOR	SERVICE	COST
▽ 19	15	20	£48

Battersea | 35-37 Parkgate Rd., SW11 (Sloane Sq./South Kensington) | 020-7223-1611 | www.ransomesdock.co.uk

Wine buffs wax lyrical about the "excellent", "fairly priced" wine list at this "casual, relaxing" dockside eatery in Battersea; but the solids are just as "solid", with a "super" menu blending Modern British-Eclectic eats, brought by "good folks" who add to the "sheer enjoyment."

Raoul's *Mediterranean*

FOOD	DECOR	SERVICE	COST
18	12	13	£27

St. John's Wood | 13 Clifton Rd., W9 (Warwick Ave.) | 020-7289-7313

NEW **Hammersmith** | 111-115 Hammersmith Grove, W6 (Hammersmith) | 020-8741-3692

Notting Hill | 105-107 Talbot Rd., W11 (Westbourne Park) | 020-7229-2400

www.raoulsgourmet.com

Though it makes Med meals all day, morning fare is the highlight (expect a "queue if you come anywhere near brunchtime") of these cafes due to the "fantastic", "special" free-range eggs imported from Tuscany; the rest of the offerings are equally "solid and reliable", as opposed to service that's usually "slow and unfriendly" – and the decor's "nothing to write home about" either; P.S. "very good deli" offshoots reside across the street in St. John's Wood and Hammersmith.

Rasa *Indian*

FOOD	DECOR	SERVICE	COST
24	16	20	£29

Bloomsbury | 5 Charlotte St., W1 (Tottenham Court Rd.) | 020-7637-0222

Mayfair | 6 Dering St., W1 (Bond St./Oxford Circus) | 020-7629-1346 🗷

Islington | Holiday Inn King's Cross | 1 King's Cross Rd., WC1 (Farringdon/King's Cross) | 020-7833-9787 🗷

Stoke Newington | 55 Stoke Newington Church St., N16 (Stoke Newington Rail) | 020-7249-0344

www.rasarestaurants.com

Once you've tasted the "fragrant", "ambrosial" Keralan dishes (vegetarian and seafood are "specialities") at this distinctively pink Indian mini-chain, supporters suspect "you'll never put up with a shabby takeaway curry again"; whether you favour "subtle" or "aggressive" spicing, the "friendly" servers can offer "recommendations", and everything comes at "fair prices."

☒ Rasoi Vineet Bhatia *Indian* — 26 | 22 | 25 | £68

Chelsea | 10 Lincoln St., SW3 (Sloane Sq.) | 020-7225-1881 |
www.rasoirestaurant.co.uk

Devotees of Vineet Bhatia's "unique" take on "upscale" Indian
cuisine find "nirvana" at this "elegant", "old-world", "comfortable" Chelsea townhouse, where the chef crafts his "memorable,
dazzling" dishes; "perfectly paced" service with "flair" helps pair
pours from the "diverse", "thoughtful" wine list, all of which adds
up to a "sensational" experience that most feel warrants
the "obscene price."

Real Greek *Greek* — 14 | 13 | 14 | £27

Covent Garden | 60-62 Long Acre, WC2 (Covent Garden) |
020-7240-2292
Marylebone | 56 Paddington St., W1 (Baker St.) | 020-7486-0466
Hoxton | 14-15 Hoxton Mkt., N1 (Old St.) | 020-7739-8212
Shoreditch | Old Spitalfields Mkt. | 6 Horner Sq., E1 (Liverpool St.) |
020-7375-1364
Borough | Riverside Hse. | 2A Southwark Bridge Rd., SE1
(London Bridge/Southwark) | 020-7620-0162
Shepherd's Bush | Westfield Shopping Ctr. | Ariel Way, ground fl., W12
(Shepherd's Bush) | 020-8743-9168
www.therealgreek.com

It's "not Downtown Athens" by any stretch of the imagination, but
the "familiar" mezze-centric Greek eats sold at this "cheap", "quick"
chainlet are "filling" and "tasty enough"; "sampler combinations"
equal the "best value", but at these prices, don't expect much more
than "lacklustre" service.

Red Fort ● *Indian* — 24 | 21 | 22 | £47

Soho | 77 Dean St., W1 (Leicester Sq./Tottenham Court Rd.) |
020-7437-2525 | www.redfort.co.uk

"Inspired" Indian dishes that "look as wonderful as they taste"
("perfectly spiced" and "bright with flavours") are what's for sale at
this "sophisticated", "plush" Soho "standard"; an "excellent choice
of wines" adds to the sense of "refinement", as does the "suave
service"; P.S. it's "pricey", but "the lunch and pre-theatre set menus
are terrific bargains."

Red 'n' Hot *Chinese* — - | - | - | M

Chinatown | 59 Charing Cross Rd., WC2 (Leicester Sq.) | 020-7734-8796 |
www.rednhotgroup.com

For a hot pot just like you "had in Taipei" – a *very* hot pot – plus other
"brilliant" renditions of "spicy" Sichuan dishes, come to this traditionally clad, moderately priced place on the outskirts of
Chinatown; if you're Caucasian, you might be "the only" one there,
but if you can stand the heat, it's the kitchen for you.

Red Pepper *Italian* — ∇ 23 | 14 | 17 | £29

St. John's Wood | 8 Formosa St., W9 (Warwick Ave.) | 020-7266-2708 |
www.theredpepper.net

"Excellent" wood-fired pizzas and other "consistent quality" Italian
eats get "locals" to "pack" into this "reliable" St. John's Wood trat-

...toria; downstairs is "cosy", upstairs is "noisy" and "cramped", with "barely any elbow room between the tables", whilst "friendly" staff and "decent prices" reign throughout.

Refettorio ☒ *Italian* ▽ 21 | 19 | 22 | £49

City | Crowne Plaza London | 19 New Bridge St., EC4 (St. Paul's/Temple) | 020-7438-8052 | www.refettorio.com

During the week, City folk slide into "huge booths" to down "good-sized" portions of "delicious" homemade pasta and other Italian dishes, washed down with "interesting" wines and ferried by "attentive" staff at this "expensive", minimalist Crowne Plaza Hotel refectory; however, don't expect any buzz after the drones have gone home, as this is "a neighbourhood that's virtually dead at weekends."

Refuel *European* ▽ 20 | 18 | 20 | £50

Soho | Soho Hotel | 4 Richmond Mews, W1 (Tottenham Court Rd.) | 020-7559-3000 | www.sohohotel.com

"Even without having an entourage in tow", you'll be "made to feel important" at this "chic" Soho Hotel refueling spot where "beautiful people" "see and be seen" over "satisfying" Modern European eats; this sort of "high energy" "certainly doesn't come cheaply", but if you choose the set lunch or dinner menu, it's an "affordable luxury."

NEW Restaurant at the Royal Academy of Arts *British* - | - | - | E

Piccadilly | Burlington House, Piccadilly, W1 (Green Park/Piccadilly Circus) | 020-7300-5608 | www.royalacademy.org.uk

Oliver Peyton adds another illustrious cultural landmark to his portfolio (including The Wallace and The National Dining Rooms) with the unveiling of this striking, "charming" all-day Modern British eatery in the Royal Academy of Arts; the setting features sculptures and a bar made from Mount Etna lava stone, while the "tasty", upscale fare is less cautious than might be expected from such a traditional institution.

Reubens *Deli/Jewish* 19 | 13 | 15 | £29

Marylebone | 79 Baker St., W1 (Baker St.) | 020-7486-0035 | www.reubensrestaurant.co.uk

"Hearty", "homestyle" glatt "classics" like a "cure-all" matzo ball soup and salt beef that "lives up to NY standards" are what's on offer at this Jewish spot in Marylebone with a "self-service" upstairs deli (where there's "not much ambience") and a downstairs dining room (where staff are "variable"); some kvetch that fees "seem overpriced" all things considered, but "if you want kosher" in Central London "this is the place to go."

Rhodes Twenty Four ☒ *British* 23 | 24 | 22 | £59

City | Tower 42 | 25 Old Broad St., 24th fl., EC2 (Bank/Liverpool St.) | 020-7877-7703 | www.rhodes24.co.uk

"Over the top" in so many ways, this Traditional British perch on the 24th floor of a City skyscraper complements its "fantastic views"

	FOOD	DECOR	SERVICE	COST

with "beautiful decor" and chef Gary Rhodes' "fine" food; "nose-bleed"-triggering prices have some crying "overrated", but for most, it's a "joyous" experience made even more so by "excellent service."

Rhodes W1 Restaurant ⌧ Ⓜ *French* | 24 | 21 | 21 | £48 |

Marylebone | Cumberland Hotel | Great Cumberland Pl., W1 (Marble Arch) | 020-7616-5930

Rhodes W1 Brasserie *European*

Marylebone | Cumberland Hotel | Great Cumberland Pl., W1 (Marble Arch) | 020-7616-5930
www.rhodesw1.com

"Brilliant flavours and textures" fill an "interesting" Modern European menu that's "fairly priced" and "extensive enough" to appeal to all comers at this "busy" brasserie in a Marble Arch hotel; meanwhile, the abutting restaurant specialises in equally "excellent" Classic French fare, which is served in Swarovski-encrusted environs by "accommodating" staffers and priced "for special occasions."

Rib Room *Chophouse* | 22 | 19 | 22 | £68 |

Belgravia | Jumeirah Carlton Tower Hotel | 2 Cadogan Pl., SW1 (Knightsbridge/Sloane Sq.) | 020-7858-7255 | www.jumeirahcarltontower.com

In "classy, old-world" surroundings reminiscent of a "gentlemen's club", this Belgravia hotel eatery employs staff who've been here "year in, year out", proffering an "extensive, traditional" menu of "well-prepared", "melt-on-the-tongue" chophouse choices; just know that it's "outrageously expensive", so if you "have a rich uncle", bring him.

Riccardo's *Italian* | ∇ 16 | 11 | 14 | £35 |

Chelsea | 126 Fulham Rd., SW3 (Gloucester Rd./South Kensington) | 020-7370-6656 | www.riccardos-italian-restaurant.co.uk

Turning out "simply prepared" Tuscan fare, this rustic Chelsea locale has a loyal following who feel it's "just the place" for a quick bite; however, foes feel it's slipped, wondering "what would mamma say" about the "expensive" prices being charged for "nouvelle cuisine-size" portions?

Richoux *British* | 17 | 16 | 16 | £27 |

Knightsbridge | 86 Brompton Rd., SW3 (Knightsbridge) | 020-7584-8300
Mayfair | 41A S. Audley St., W1 (Bond St.) | 020-7629-5228
St. James's | 172 Piccadilly, W1 (Green Park/Piccadilly Circus) | 020-7493-2204
St. John's Wood | 3 Circus Rd., NW8 (St. John's Wood) | 020-7483-4001
www.richoux.co.uk

"Take mum" and your "aunt" to this red-hued, "old-fashioned", "competently run small chain" whose "casual", "simple" Traditional British menu is "reliable" all day, but is "best for breakfast", tea with "wonderful" "scones galore" or a "quick pick-me-up" after "a hard day of shopping or touring"; "service is erratic, but never terrible" and more tolerable when considering the affordable prices.

	FOOD	DECOR	SERVICE	COST

NEW Riding House Café *European* — | — | — | M

Bloomsbury | 43-51 Great Titchfield St., W1 (Goodge Street/
Oxford Circus) | 020-7927-0840 | www.ridinghousecafe.co.uk

At this glass-wrapped, bohemian Modern European newcomer on
the corner of Riding House Street in the Fitzrovia section of
Bloomsbury, a large, easy-going brasserie with rickety communal
tables is sandwiched between a cosy dining room with bright-
orange seating and a comfy lounge with bright-blue seating; the
moderately priced menu, which is offered throughout all areas,
serves from breakfast through dinner and swings from small plates
to gutsy grills.

☑ Ritz, The *British/French* 25 | 28 | 26 | £79

St. James's | Ritz Hotel | 150 Piccadilly, W1 (Green Park) |
020-7300-2370 | www.theritzlondon.com

"Feel aristocratic" at this "magnificent" "classic" in St. James's Ritz
Hotel whose "stunning" frescoes, chandeliers and "gilded" accoutrements set the stage for "wonderful", "expensive" Traditional
British-French dishes, many prepared tableside by "solicitous",
"dignified" staff in "tailcoats"; if you're not the "jacket-and-tie" type,
you may find it "stuffy", but to most, it's a "fun" trip to a more
"noble", "elegant" era; P.S. "fabulous afternoon tea" is served in
the "glamourous" Palm Court next door (be sure to "book
way in advance").

☑ River Café *Italian* 27 | 24 | 25 | £71

Hammersmith | Thames Wharf | Rainville Rd., W6 (Hammersmith) |
020-7386-4200 | www.rivercafe.co.uk

From "simple pastas" to "wood-grilled specialities" and everything in between, "exquisite" flavours infuse each "divine" daily
changing dish at this "vibrant" "bastion" of "cutting-edge-
creative" Italian cuisine, which is "worth the trek" all the way to
Hammersmith and the "eye-watering" prices; though the "modern" dining room offers "no view of the river", there are "fascinating" sights to behold in the open kitchen, home to "efficient"
staff who toil "with style and a smile"; P.S. in summer, book a terrace
table ("well in advance").

Rivington Grill Bar *British* 18 | 18 | 17 | £36

Greenwich | Greenwich Picturehouse Cinema | 178 Greenwich High Rd.,
SE10 (Greenwich) | 020-8293-9270 Ⓜ
Shoreditch | 28-30 Rivington St., EC2 (Old St.) | 020-7729-7053
www.rivingtongrill.co.uk

Whilst "large groups" of pork-lovers indulge in "the whole suckling
pig meal deal", this "quirky" Traditional British locale in Shoreditch
offers a menu "varied enough" to satisfy "whatever it is you're
craving", be it for breakfast, lunch or dinner; the "informal" accom-
modations are brightened by works from local artists, and whilst a
few feel it's "more pricey" than it should be, the experience is "nice
all the same"; P.S. the dinner-only sibling in the Greenwich
Picturehouse sates cinema-goers.

	FOOD	DECOR	SERVICE	COST

Roast *British*
24 | 24 | 22 | £49

Borough | Borough Mkt. | Floral Hall, Stoney St., SE1 (London Bridge) | 0845-034-7300 | www.roast-restaurant.com

"Fat cat bankers" and shoppers find a "warm welcome" at this "light, airy", "lively" and "striking" "pleasure palace" "up in the eaves of Borough Market", where the "rich, satisfying" all-day Modern British eats star "succulent roasted meats"; "creatively paired wines" and a "wonderful" bar add to the attraction, which helps make the "bit-pricey" bill seem "worth every penny."

Rocca *Italian*
- | - | - | M

NEW Dulwich | 75-79 Dulwich Village, SE21 (North Dulwich Rail) | 020-8299-6333

South Kensington | 73 Old Brompton Rd., SW7 (South Kensington) | 020-7225-3413 ◑

www.roccarestaurants.com

Named after a small village in the hills near Rome, this "popular" South Kensington restaurant in a space formerly part of Christie's auction house harbours "solid Italian" cuisine (like "value" pizza), "energetic staff", "friendly" vibes and a heated front terrace for alfresco people-watching; in Dulwich Village, the new sibling offers similar wares, plus it has a wood-fired oven and its own herb garden.

Rock & Sole Plaice *Seafood*
24 | 10 | 16 | £18

Covent Garden | 47 Endell St., WC2 (Covent Garden) | 020-7836-3785

"Awesome fish 'n' chips" for "cheap" prices keep this "reliable" Covent Garden seafooder "crowded"; "the digs here are quite awful" and service is at best "adequate", which explains why eating on a "bench outside" or "takeaway" are more "popular" choices.

Rocket *Mediterranean*
20 | 17 | 18 | £30

Mayfair | 4-6 Lancashire Ct., W1 (Bond St.) | 020-7629-2889 ◑

Canary Wharf | 2 Churchill Pl., E14 (Canary Wharf) | 020-3200-2022 🗷

City | 6 Adams Ct., EC2 (Bank/Liverpool St.) | 020-7628-0808 🗷

www.rocketrestaurants.co.uk

Feel free to "take your date or your parents", because this "friendly", "relaxed", colourful Med trio charm all with its "huge", "interesting pizzas" and salads "big enough to be a proper meal", not to mention "spot-on" wines at the "perennially fun" bar; best of all, it's amply "affordable" to suit all budgets.

Rodizio Rico ◑ *Brazilian*
15 | 11 | 14 | £36

Greenwich | O2 Arena | Peninsula Sq., SE10 (North Greenwich) | 020-8858-6333

Islington | 77-78 Upper St., N1 (Angel) | 020-7354-1076

Bayswater | 111 Westbourne Grove, W2 (Bayswater) | 020-7792-4035

www.rodiziorico.com

A "good idea" if you're "really hungry", these "festive" Brazilian churrascarias feature "all-you-can-eat" meats sliced straight onto your plate "nonstop" – well, at least until you call a halt; but more discerning palates claim the fare's a "real let down", and "not-great decor" doesn't help matters.

	FOOD	DECOR	SERVICE	COST

❷ Roka *Japanese* — 26 | 23 | 21 | £65

Bloomsbury | 37 Charlotte St., W1 (Goodge St./Tottenham Court Rd.) | 020-7580-6464 ●

Canary Wharf | 4 Park Pavilion, 40 Canada Sq., E14 (Canary Wharf) | 020-7636-5228

www.rokarestaurant.com

The "large, wooden" sushi bar with "an unobstructed view" of the central robata grill is the "best place" to sample the "divine", "imaginative", "high-priced" cooked and raw fare at this "energy-filled" Japanese sibling of Zuma on Charlotte Street, where the crowd is "über-hip" and the tipples feature "well-chosen" wines and sake-based cocktails in the "fantastic" Shochu Lounge downstairs; if service is "inconsistent", it's mostly "fast", here and at the "more-corporate" Canary Wharf version.

Rotunda *British* — - | - | - | M

King's Cross | Kings Pl. | 90 York Way, N1 (King's Cross St. Pancras) | 020-7014-2840 | www.rotundabarandrestaurant.co.uk

If you're "visiting the Kings Place concert hall", make time for this "attractive, minimalist" Traditional British spot where the "pleasant", sometimes "unusual dishes" bend to beef and lamb reared on its "own farm" in Northumberland; though it "feels overpriced" to a few, you really get your money's worth in warm weather when you can "people-watch passers-by" from the canalside terrace.

❷ Roussillon Ⓩ *French* — 26 | 22 | 25 | £70

Pimlico | 16 St. Barnabas St., SW1 (Sloane Sq./Victoria) | 020-7730-5550 | www.roussillon.co.uk

"You feel pampered from the moment" you enter this "quiet", "sophisticated" New French "treasure" in Pimlico, which is "happily thriving" under the auspices of a new chef whose "deep knowledge of ingredients" and "serious technical skill" are evident even in the vegetarian preparations; an "impressive" wine list with some "unusual finds" adds to the "sublime" time – for which you should be prepared to "spend" ("it's worth it").

Roux at Parliament Square Ⓩ *European* — ▽ 24 | 18 | 20 | £70

Westminster | Royal Institution of Chartered Surveyors | 1 Parliament Sq., SW1 (Westminster) | 020-7334-3737 | www.rouxatparliamentsquare.co.uk

"At a time when MPs are being careful not to look extravagant", premiering a swanky eatery so "close to Parliament" is a bit of "a gamble" – but it's paying off at this Modern European, where Michel Roux Jr's "enjoyable" seasonal menu is ferried by "caring" staff in cream-coloured digs; as previously implied, it's "super expensive", but there are some "reasonably priced wines", plus "real-value" prix fixes.

ᴺᴱᵂ Roux at The Landau *European* — - | - | - | VE

Marylebone | The Langham Hotel | 1 Portland Pl., W1 (Oxford Circus) | 020-7973-7560 | www.thelandau.com

Albert and Michel Roux Jr have taken over The Langham Hotel's suave, wood-panelled, very expensive Modern European eatery and installed Chris King (ex Le Gavroche) as chef; early diners say the results are "impressive" and matched by a "phenomenal wine list" - in short, everything you desire for "a proper night out."

Rowley's British

| 18 | 19 | 19 | £44 |

St. James's | 113 Jermyn St., SW1 (Piccadilly Circus) | 020-7930-2707 | www.rowleys.co.uk

"Steak and unlimited chips" is still the dish to order at this "low-key", "old-school" Traditional British dining room bedecked with art nouveau mirrors in St. James's, where "big appetites" are sated for not-too-expensive prices; it may be "nothing spectacular", but it's "friendly" and "reliable", and that's "nothing to sneeze at."

Royal China Chinese

| 23 | 15 | 15 | £35 |

Marylebone | 24-26 Baker St., W1 (Baker St.) | 020-7487-4688
Canary Wharf | 30 Westferry Circus, E14 (Canary Wharf) | 020-7719-0888
Fulham | 805 Fulham Rd., SW6 (Parsons Green) | 020-7731-0081
Bayswater | 13 Queensway, W2 (Queensway) | 020-7221-2535
www.royalchinagroup.co.uk

A seemingly "unlimited" selection of "exceptional dim sum" is served daily until 4.45 PM at this "well-priced" chainlet, after which "heaped" dishes of "reliable" Cantonese "classics" take over; "go early" (especially on Sunday) or risk "a long queue" for seats in the "noisy", "crowded", "funky" black-and-gold settings – like the "notoriously indifferent" service, it's "part of the experience."

Royal China Club Chinese

| 25 | 16 | 18 | £45 |

Marylebone | 40-42 Baker St., W1 (Baker St.) | 020-7486-3898 | www.royalchinagroup.co.uk

A little further down Baker Street from Royal China, this "upmarket sibling" provides "greater finesse and some more interesting dishes" - including seafood plucked live from a tank and "superb" dim sum - for "extra money"; still, some reckon that it's "overpriced" especially when factoring in the sometimes "spotty" service.

Royal Exchange
Grand Café & Bar ⓢ European

| ▽ 15 | 23 | 19 | £36 |

City | Royal Exchange, EC3 (Bank) | 020-7618-2480 | www.royalexchangegrandcafeandbar.com

The "spectacular", "roomy" setting of this Modern European set in the old Royal Exchange is "the real reason" "business-lunchers" eschew the City's "sandwich bars and expense-account" options; it certainly isn't the seafood-heavy all-day menu, which though not exorbitant, seems to some "overpriced" for being merely "ok", although "slick service" compensates somewhat.

Royal Oak British

| ▽ 22 | 19 | 21 | £47 |

Maidenhead | Paley St., Berkshire | 01628-620541 | www.theroyaloakpaleystreet.com

Maidenhead diners "can't get enough of the famous Scotch eggs" or any of the "tempting", "thoughtful" Traditional British dishes, at Sir Michael Parkinson's "smart, old-fashioned", "upscale" gastropub; oenophiles applaud the "huge" wine list, for which a sommelier provides "spot-on suggestions."

R.S.J. ⓩ *British* | 20 | 14 | 19 | £39

Waterloo | 33 Coin St., SE1 (Waterloo) | 020-7928-4554 |
www.rsj.uk.com

National Theatre pre- or post-showgoers "count on" this "friendly" Modern British "delight" for "interestingly varied dishes" at "value" costs; but what really accounts for its "cult following" is the "amazing wine list at awesome prices" ("if you like Loire wines, there's nowhere better") – drink enough, and you won't mind that the "decor could do with refreshing."

ⓩ Rules *Chophouse* | 23 | 25 | 23 | £57

Covent Garden | 35 Maiden Ln., WC2 (Covent Garden) | 020-7836-5314 |
www.rules.co.uk

"Velvet chairs and country-estate decor" craft a "clubby Edwardian" feel at this "expensive but marvellous" Covent Garden chophouse that's "as old as Dickens" (older actually, since 1798) and "owns its own manor" where a "wild assortment of game" is raised ("watch out for buckshot") and served by "cosseting" staff alongside "outstanding" beef; if some tut it's "too touristy", addicts counter that you go once so you can say you did, but then you go back and back for the fun of it."

Sabor ◑ *S American* | – | – | – | M

Islington | 108 Essex Rd., N1 (Angel) | 020-7226-5551 | www.sabor.co.uk

"Something different" is offered at this "fun, lively", "little" Islington "gem", namely "South American spice" and "superb", "huge" Argentinean steaks, which are "good value" and complemented by "bright, colourful" Latin-tinged digs; "brilliant cocktails" are also on hand, and everything comes from "warm, attentive" staff.

Saf *Eclectic/Vegan* | 20 | 18 | 22 | £37

Shoreditch | 152-154 Curtain Rd., EC2 (Old St./Liverpool St.) |
020-7613-0007

NEW Kensington | The Barker's Bldg., Whole Foods Mkt. | 63-97 Kensington High St., 5SE (High St. Kensington) | 020-7368-4555 | www.safrestaurant.co.uk

"Even meateaters salivate over" the "stylish, inventive" vegan delights whipped up at this "lovely" eco-friendly Shoreditch Eclectic; "yummy" botanic cocktails and biodynamic wines enhance an experience that fans faun is "impossible to leave without feeling better about yourself" – however, cost-calculators think it's "too expensive for the size of the portions"; P.S. there's a new Kensington offshoot.

Sake No Hana ⓩ *Japanese* | 23 | 22 | 20 | £64

St. James's | 23 St. James's St., SW1 (Green Park/Piccadilly Circus) |
020-7925-8988 | www.sakenohana.com

After a stroll in St. James's, "go up the escalator" to this "chic, modern" Japanese promising "superb sourcing" of its fish, which is sliced into "precise" preparations of "melt-in-the-mouth" sushi and paired with a "wide selection of sake"; service that's "discreet and

attentive" adds to the "treat", but make sure you "bring your bank
manager" to approve the "expensive" charges.

Sakura *Japanese*

▽ 19 | 9 | 10 | £27

Mayfair | 23 Conduit St., W1 (Oxford Circus) | 020-7629-2961

Mayfair Japanese junkies descend on this haunt for a "quick", well-
priced meal of "delicious" sushi and "cooked dishes you won't find
on most menus"; as for the "appalling tatty decor and brusque
service", they're "beside the point."

Sale e Pepe ●🗷 *Italian*

21 | 18 | 23 | £50

Knightsbridge | 9-15 Pavilion Rd., SW1 (Knightsbridge) |
020-7235-0098 | www.saleepepe.co.uk

A real "riot", this "bustling" Knightsbridge Italian employs "boisterous" staff who "sing" when they're not doling out "fabulous" dishes
that are "on the expensive side" but still "great value"; "tight" tables
add to the "crazy" atmosphere, which tourists particularly deem
"thoroughly enjoyable" because they're "treated as friends."

Salloos ●🗷 *Pakistani*

24 | 18 | 20 | £46

Belgravia | 62-64 Kinnerton St., SW1 (Hyde Park Corner/
Knightsbridge) | 020-7235-4444

"Tandoori lamb chops" that are "a religious experience" and "rich
spices" that internationals "dream of from across the world" are
highlights of this Pakistani "standby" in Belgravia; if "not everything
quite warrants the price", at its best, it's "spectacular", bolstered by
"good" service and a setting with "nicely spaced" tables.

Salt Yard 🗷 *Italian/Spanish*

23 | 18 | 20 | £38

Bloomsbury | 54 Goodge St., W1 (Goodge St.) | 020-7637-0657 |
www.saltyard.co.uk

Always "busy, sometimes frenetic", this "cosy" Bloomsbury venue
offers "unique" Italian-Spanish tapas whose "top-notch ingredients" are whipped into a "revelation for the senses" ("yes, you
should try the stuffed courgette flowers" – they're "the centrepiece
of the menu and fabulous"); "excellent wines" also excite – it's only
the somewhat "steep" prices that disappoint.

NEW Samarqand ● *Central Asian*

- | - | - | M

Marylebone | 18 Thayer St., W1 (Bond St.) | 020-7935-9393 |
www.samarqand-restaurant.com

A culinary "revelation", this subterranean Marylebone newcomer
presents "novel, tasty" Uzbeki, Kazakhstani and Turkmen fare,
some of it cooked in the open kitchen's two huge clay tandoori ov-
ens, all of it moderately priced; the "gorgeous" silk-walled setting is
sprinkled with traditional artefacts in multiple spaces, which include a discrete lounge and feature "charming service."

Sam's Brasserie & Bar *European*

▽ 20 | 20 | 21 | £38

Chiswick | Barley Mow Ctr. | 11 Barley Mow Passage, W4 (Chiswick Park) |
020-8987-0555 | www.samsbrasserie.co.uk

By day, this "comfortable", "family-friendly" Chiswick brasserie is
"often jam-packed" with locals lingering over "large amounts" of

"reasonably priced" Mod Euro breakfasts, brunches and lunches; at dinner and beyond, it's just as "buzzy" thanks to the "lively bar scene" fuelled by "oh-so-delicious" cocktails and occasional live music.

San Lorenzo ⊠ Italian

FOOD	DECOR	SERVICE	COST
21	19	21	£64

Knightsbridge | 22 Beauchamp Pl., SW3 (Knightsbridge) | 020-7584-1074

San Lorenzo Fuoriporta Italian

Wimbledon | 38 Wimbledon Hill Rd., SW19 (Wimbledon) | 020-8946-8463
www.sanlorenzo.com

Adding to "the hustle of Knightsbridge", this "elegant" Italian "staple" provides a "reliable", "yummy" "pasta fix" to "royals, Eurotrash" and the resulting "people-watchers"; however, a few feel that the fare's only "satisfactory" with an ambience that's "not quite what it was in its '90s heyday", leading to accusations of "overpriced"; P.S. the Wimbledon cousin's "garden area is nice in the summer."

Santa Maria del Sur ● Argentinean

FOOD	DECOR	SERVICE	COST
24	14	20	£42

Battersea | 129 Queenstown Rd., SW8 (Clapham Common) | 020-7622-2088 | www.santamariadelsur.co.uk

Garufa Grill Argentinean

Islington | 104 Highbury Pk., N5 (Arsenal) | 020-7226-0070 | www.garufa.co.uk

At this bare-brick-and-wood Battersea "meatfest", "gorgeous steaks" are "flown in from Argentina", "well seasoned", grilled to a "moo-vellous" finish and served by "friendly staff"; the Islington sibling offers similar atmosphere and "charm", not to mention "value for money."

Santini Italian

FOOD	DECOR	SERVICE	COST
▽ 26	23	25	£69

Belgravia | 29 Ebury St., SW1 (Victoria) | 020-7730-4094 | www.santini-restaurant.com

"Modern and stylised" but retaining a "family" feel, this "excellent" Belgravia Italian softens its starchy white decor with "warm, welcoming service"; if some deem it "overpriced", "romantics" rate it "terrific", particularly in summer when they can whisper their sweet nothings alfresco.

Sardo ⊠ Italian

FOOD	DECOR	SERVICE	COST
▽ 22	16	22	£39

Bloomsbury | 45 Grafton Way, W1 (Warren St.) | 020-7387-2521 | www.sardo-restaurant.com

With a "bright" and "homey" setting, this "inviting" Bloomsbury Italian specialises in "wonderful" dishes from Sardinia; "vibrant" wines add to the "interesting" experience, and when you factor in the "friendly" service and "fair" prices, it's obvious why supporters say this one's "a keeper."

Sardo Canale Ⓜ Italian

FOOD	DECOR	SERVICE	COST
19	18	16	£41

Primrose Hill | private club | 42 Gloucester Ave., NW1 (Camden Town/Chalk Farm) | 020-7722-2800 | www.sardocanale.com

A "romantic" slice of Sardinia exists on Primrose Hill's Regent Canal at this "sweet" little sister of Sardo, whose "tasty" dishes are served in an "intimate", brick-bedecked, "cave"-like interior and an "amazing" olive tree–adorned courtyard; if some gripe that you "spend a bit extra" here for service that vacillates between "friendly" and "snooty", all are satisfied with the "excellent wine list."

Sartoria ☒ *Italian*   22 | 21 | 22 | £50

Mayfair | 20 Savile Row, W1 (Oxford Circus/Piccadilly Circus) | 020-7534-7000 | www.sartoriabar.co.uk

Whether on a date or dallying with friends, smart-suited sorts feel at home in this "grown-up", art-festooned Saville Row "staple"; the "delicious" Italian dishes, accompanied by a "good wine list" and 20 types of grappa, just whisper "class", as does the "discreet" service, and whilst prices are high, the "set-meal offers are fabulous value."

Sauterelle ☒ *French*   ▽ 18 | 13 | 18 | £46

City | Royal Exchange, EC3 (Bank) | 020-7618-2483 | www.restaurantsauterelle.com

City sophisticates escape the "chattering classes in the bar below" in favour of this "intimate" aerie (some feel like they're "in a corridor") in the Royal Exchange, where "attentive" staff serve "beautifully cooked" Classic French fare that aesthetes exclaim is "almost too pretty to eat"; unsurprisingly, such "elegance" commands prices that are "geared to the corporate purse."

Savoy Grill *British/French*   23 | 25 | 23 | £71

Covent Garden | Savoy Hotel | The Strand, WC2 (Charing Cross) | 020-7592-1600 | www.gordonramsay.com

After a "beautifully done" refurb, this "grand", "glorious" and "storied" Covent Garden art deco destination is back in action as part of the Gordon Ramsay group; on the menu, "impressive", often "fantastic" Classic French dishes mingle with "reliable", roast-centric British fare that, at lunch, comes from trolleys manned by "professional" staff; some surveyors complain that it's "overpriced for routine food", but for those on "big expense accounts", it's nothing but "sublime."

Savoy River Restaurant *French*   21 | 24 | 23 | £82

Covent Garden | Savoy Hotel | 100 Strand, WC2 (Charing Cross) | 020-7420-2111 | www.fairmont.com

With "beautiful views of the Thames" and "elegant" art deco deco in "extensively made-over" digs, plus mostly "excellent service" and "sky-high" prices, this Covent Garden hotel eatery fits the bill for a "special occasion"; the Modern French fare is "not bad at all", just "not the best", which is why some recommend coming for breakfast when the bill's "cheaper."

Scalini *Italian*   23 | 18 | 22 | £55

Chelsea | 1-3 Walton St., SW3 (Knightsbridge/South Kensington) | 020-7225-2301

The "wealthies" of Chelsea check into this "warhorse" "behind Harrods" for "bountiful", "outstanding" Italian sustenance sold at "expensive" fees; the setting's "crowded", tables are "close together" and "the monkey house at London Zoo is quieter", but "you're sure to leave with a smile on your face" anyway, thanks in part to "lots of laughs from the staff."

		FOOD	DECOR	SERVICE	COST

☑ Scott's *Seafood*

27 | 24 | 25 | £72

Mayfair | 20 Mount St., W1 (Bond St./Green Park) | 020-7495-7309 | www.scotts-restaurant.com

"Flawless shellfish" plucked from an "iced display" behind the "convivial bar" and "divine seafood" preparations are snapped up by "chic", "upper-crust" clientele at this "posh", "contemporary" Mayfair "piscatorial palace" known for its "major buzz factor" and "nosebleed prices"; though a few folks say they were "made to feel like commoners" because they're not on the "A-list", the vast majority recall "feeling special and appreciated" by "impeccable" staff.

Semplice Bar
Trattoria *Italian*

21 | 14 | 18 | £37

Mayfair | 22-23 Woodstock St., W1 (Bond St.) | 020-7491-8638 | www.bartrattoriasemplice.com

For "Semplice on the cheap", check out its "little sister" across the street in Mayfair, where the "simple but tasty" Italian menu is highlighted by "salumi to die for"; service seems to be sometimes "great", sometimes "lackadaisical", whilst the "rustic", stripped-wood surrounds are always "a bit crowded and noisy."

Semplice Ristorante ☒ *Italian*

23 | 20 | 22 | £55

Mayfair | 9-10 Blenheim St., W1 (Bond St.) | 020-7495-1509 | www.ristorantesemplice.com

"As the name suggests", this "accomplished" Mayfair haunt specialises in Italian fare that's "simple, but elegant" too, plus it's served by "polished" staff who can make recommendations from the "excellent wine list"; it's "on the expensive side", which irks aesthetes who think the "dark" "decor could use updating", but in all other respects, it's "perfect for business lunches" and "eventful evenings" with loved ones alike.

Seven Park Place ☒Ⓜ *British/French*

- | - | - | VE

St. James's | St. James's Hotel & Club | 7-8 Park Pl., SW1 (Green Park) | 020-7316-1600 | www.stjameshotelandclub.com

In "a gorgeous jewel box of a room" inside the St. James's Hotel, chef William Drabble creates "complex", "sublime" New French dishes from British seasonal ingredients of "amazing quality"; and with such "highly skilled" staff, "extensive, well-thought-out" wine list and "serene" ambience, it's clear why supporters "can't recommend it enough", despite very high prices.

NEW Shaka Zulu *S African*

- | - | - | E

Camden Town | Stables Mkt. | Chalk Farm Rd., NW1 (Camden Town/Chalk Town) | 020-3376-9911 | www.shaka-zulu.com

"Impressive" tribal masks, mosaics, tall statues and acres of "elaborate", handcrafted wood panelling pack this "huge" tribute to King Shaka Zulu in Camden's hip Stables Market; "exotic meats" (zebra, ostrich, springbok) fill its premium South African menu, whilst "nice" cocktails come from the cavernous bar, hosting live music and floor shows nightly.

	FOOD	DECOR	SERVICE	COST

Shanghai Blues ❍ *Chinese*
22 | 21 | 19 | £47

Holborn | 193-197 High Holborn, WC1 (Holborn) | 020-7404-1668 | www.shanghaiblues.co.uk

"Go conservative or try some of the more exotic dishes, both will please" assure advocates of this Holborn Chinese whose "stunning", "flashy" Far East setting features a "great cocktail bar"; just remember that you'll need "deep pockets" for the bill, unless you come for the "bargain" set lunch or early-bird dinner; P.S. dim sum is also offered.

Shepherd's ⊠ *British*
19 | 19 | 19 | £51

Westminster | Marsham Ct., Marsham St., SW1 (Pimlico) | 020-7834-9552 | www.langansrestaurants.co.uk

"In the shadow of Parliament", this "gracefully ageing" Traditional British spot "soothes" by employing "accommodating" staff to convey the "basic" menu of "high-quality" dishes (akin to "school dinners", some say); like the fare, the clubby, art-filled digs hold "no surprises", as opposed to the bill, which is quite "pricey these days."

Signor Sassi ❍ *Italian*
21 | 18 | 21 | £46

Knightsbridge | 14 Knightsbridge Green, SW1 (Knightsbridge) | 020-7584-2277 | www.signorsassi.co.uk

"Take your time" over "generous servings" of "impressive" Italian fare at this bright, "tight", mirror-filled Knightsbridge ristorante, as "warm and welcoming" staff won't rush you; whilst some find it "pricey" others insist that they're actually quite "reasonable for the area."

⊠ Simpson's-in-the-Strand *British*
22 | 24 | 24 | £58

Covent Garden | Savoy Hotel | 100 The Strand, WC2 (Charing Cross) | 020-7836-9112 | www.simpsonsinthestrand.co.uk

"Dickens, Trollope and Disraeli all dined" at this Traditional British stalwart on the Strand, and the wood-panelled setting "doesn't appear to have changed much since"; these days it's mostly "tourists" tucking into the "excellent roast beef" rolled to your table on "silver trolleys" and carved into "big, fat slabs" by "masterly" gentlemen, and if some find it all "too stuffy", most just don an imaginary "top hat", "pretend it's 125 years ago" and "enjoy"; P.S. breakfast is "less expensive."

Singapore Garden *Malaysian/Singaporean*
19 | 15 | 18 | £35

Swiss Cottage | 83 Fairfax Rd., NW6 (Swiss Cottage) | 020-7328-5314
Chiswick | 474 Chiswick High Rd., W4 (Chiswick Park) | 020-8994-2222
www.singaporegarden.co.uk

"Locals" who "first went" to this black-and-red Swiss Cottage bolthole "in the '80s" keep returning for its "wide variety" of "terrific" Malaysian and Singaporean specialities; it's also "popular" for its "friendly" staff and decent prices, "so best to book"; P.S. the Chiswick offshoot does delivery and takeout only.

⊠ Sketch – The Gallery ⊠ *European*
21 | 27 | 21 | £69

Mayfair | Sketch | 9 Conduit St., W1 (Oxford Circus) | 020-7659-4500 | www.sketch.uk.com

To "impress guests from out of town", "pencil Sketch in to your diary" advise groupies of this "hip", "surreal, magical" Modern European in a Mayfair town house, where even the "amazing bathrooms" resemble a "Salvador Dalí painting"; if the fare "tries a little too hard" to match the "dynamic" digs but winds up being "nothing special" (therefore, "overpriced"), it's "pretty good" nonetheless.

⚄ Sketch – The Lecture Room & Library 🅂Ⓜ European | 24 | 28 | 24 | £94 |

Mayfair | Sketch | 9 Conduit St., W1 (Oxford Circus) | 020-7659-4500 | www.sketch.uk.com

"Fabulous", opulent claret-coloured "decor to marvel" at (rated London's No. 1) sets a "beautiful" stage at this "masterpiece" in a Mayfair town house, a "magical experience" for the palate as well as the eyes thanks to consulting chef Pierre Gagnaire's "unique" Modern European "works of art", which are brought to table by staff who treat everyone like a "VIP"; you'll have to "sell the kids to fund the meal", but that's to be expected for this sort of "not-to-be-missed experience."

⚄ Sketch – The Parlour 🅂 British | 23 | 28 | 22 | £51 |

Mayfair | Sketch | 9 Conduit St., W1 (Oxford Circus) | 020-7659-4500 | www.sketch.uk.com

Located in a Mayfair town house "amidst the luxury shops" of Conduit Street, this "*Alice in Wonderland*"-meets–Louis XV tearoom is perfect for post-retail "refueling" via "super-expensive sandwiches", "delicious" pastries and other light English bites; after 5 PM, the cakes give way to cocktails, and "quick drinks" often turn into "dancing until 2 AM" (members only after 9 PM).

Skylon European | 19 | 24 | 20 | £44 |

South Bank | Royal Festival Hall | Belvedere Rd., SE1 (Waterloo) | 020-7654-7800 | www.skylonrestaurant.co.uk

"Grab a window table", because the "spectacular vista of the Thames" "never ceases to impress" at this "cavernous" South Bank Modern European; whether opting for a "quality" "lunch on a budget" in the "relaxed" grill, "pricier" fare with "flair" in the "fine dining room" or tipples at the "fabulous cocktail bar", a "laid-back atmosphere", "fun crowd" and "attentive service" are found throughout.

Smiths of Smithfield – Dining Room 🅂 British | 23 | 21 | 20 | £47 |

Farringdon | 67-77 Charterhouse St., 2nd fl., EC1 (Barbican/Farringdon) | 020-7251-7950 | www.smithsofsmithfield.co.uk

Smithfield Market meatlovers feel they're "guaranteed" a "satisfying feed" of "juicy, delicious" chops and burgers at this pricey second-floor Modern British from chef John Torode; service "varies" and the brick-walled setting "can get noisy", especially due to the "animated" crowd in "the bar below" (which offers breakfast in the AM), but that's all part of its charms.

Smiths of Smithfield – Top Floor British | 21 | 19 | 17 | £56 |

Farringdon | 67-77 Charterhouse St., 3rd fl., EC1 (Barbican/Farringdon) | 020-7251-7950 | www.smithsofsmithfield.co.uk

"Fabulous" "views of St. Paul's" and what oenophiles feel is "a better wine list than downstairs" draw "noisy" crowds to the roof of chef

John Torode's Smithfield Market Modern British venture where "big
steaks" get top billing; but "subpar service detracts from the experience", making it possibly "not worth the money."

Smollensky's *American/Chophouse*

14	14	13	£43

Covent Garden | 105 The Strand, WC2 (Charing Cross/
Covent Garden) | 020-7497-2101
Canary Wharf | 1 Reuters Plaza, E14 (Canary Wharf) | 020-7719-0101 ⊠
www.smollenskys.com

"Cordon Bleu it isn't", but this American-style chophouse duo is "in
the right place" (i.e. Canary Wharf and Covent Garden) to attract
"boozy office parties", "business-lunchers" and tourists "with children" willing to down "run-of-the-mill" meals; however, when you
factor in the "slow", sometimes "rude" service, it's easy to see why
some say they're "best avoided."

Sofra *Turkish*

19	14	18	£29

Covent Garden | 36 Tavistock St., WC2 (Covent Garden) | 020-7240-3773
Marylebone | 1 St. Christophers Pl., W1 (Bond St.) | 020-7224-4080 ●
Mayfair | 18 Shepherd St., W1 (Green Park) | 020-7493-3320
St. John's Wood | 11 Circus Rd., NW8 (St. John's Wood) |
020-7586-9889
www.sofra.co.uk

"Tasty Turkish dishes awaken jaded taste buds" at this "fast and
frantic" mini-chain that makes choosing amongst its "well-
prepared" mezze and "tender grilled meats" "easy" thanks to
"excellent-value" prix fixes for lunch, pre-theatre and dinner;
"charming staff" will "always squeeze you in" inside (it's sometimes
"a tight fit"), but the most "pleasant" spots are outside "on a warm
summer's day" at all locales except Covent Garden.

Soho House ⊠ *British*

20	22	23	£43

Soho | private club | 40 Greek St., W1 (Leicester Sq./
Tottenham Court Rd.) | 020-7734-5188 | www.sohohouselondon.com
"Hearty" Modern British fare is "done well" at this members-only
club with three "cosy" dining rooms on Greek Street; however, "people come here for the crowd" of "trendy" media people, "theatre
folk" and other "celebs" plus the accompanying "excellent ambience" and "attentive service" more than the food.

Solly's *Mideastern*

▽ 18	11	9	£30

Golders Green | 150 Golders Green Rd., NW11 (Golders Green) |
020-8455-2121
This Golders Green Middle Eastern turns out a "good variety" of
"great" kosher munchies, which are plated in "large portions"; but
the setting "lacks atmosphere" and service is "a joke", so make like
a local and do takeaway.

Som Tam House ⊠ *Thai*

-	-	-	M

Shepherd's Bush | 131 Askew Rd., W12 (Shepherd's Bush) |
020-8749-9030 | www.somtamhouse.co.uk
Closing in on its 20th anniversary, this "small but prettily decorated", wood-rich Thai near Ravenscourt Park in Shepherd's Bush

prepares an "excellent" menu "based on good-quality, fresh ingredients" imported every week from Asia; however, its best feature may be that "you could pay three-times as much for the same standard elsewhere."

Song Que Café   *Vietnamese*

23 | 8 | 13 | £17

Shoreditch | 134 Kingsland Rd., E2 (Old St.) | 020-7613-3222
When they "want really authentic, tasty Vietnamese food", pho fans make a "pilgrimage" to this Shoreditch "standout"; the "neon-lit, light-green room is definitely not appealing", nor is the "indifferent service", but "cheap-as-chips" costs mean it's always "packed", so consider going "on off hours."

Sonny's   *European*

▽ 23 | 18 | 16 | £36

Barnes | 94 Church Rd., SW13 (Hammersmith) | 020-8748-0393 | www.sonnys.co.uk
Barnes diners claim they "always eat nicely" at this "unpretentious" Modern European offering "reasonably priced" prix fixes at both lunch and dinner; meanwhile, the adjacent deli is a "no brainer for excellent, quick, gourmet" takeaway – and a boon to those who want to minimise their dealings with slightly "surly" staff.

Sophie's

19 | 18 | 17 | £39

Steakhouse & Bar ◐ *American/Chophouse*
Covent Garden | 29-31 Wellington St., WC2 (Covent Garden) | 020-7836-8836
Chelsea | 311-313 Fulham Rd., SW10 (South Kensington) | 020-7352-0088
www.sophiessteakhouse.co.uk
With no reservations accepted at this "hip" pair of "noisy, crowded" American steakhouses, you'll want to "show up before 7 PM" or face a "lengthy wait" (not to worry, "fab cocktails" at the "lively" bar will help pass the time); once you're seated at one of the "bare-wood tables", generally "friendly" staff bring the "huge slabs of meat" and "simple, delicious sides", which are sold at "prices that are not too outrageous for London."

Soseki ⌧ *Japanese*

- | - | - | VE

City | 20 Bury St., EC3 (Aldgate) | 020-7621-9211 | www.soseki.co.uk
In a "beautiful", "authentic" room inspired by the teahouses of 1920s Japan, City folk indulge in "extraordinary" meals starring "sustainable" sushi; for those who find the kaiseki-style menu "unfathomable", "welcoming", "attentive" staff are on hand to explain – which leaves the "astronomical" prices as "the only drawback."

Sotheby's Cafe ⌧ *British*

▽ 24 | 19 | 24 | £41

Mayfair | Sotheby's Auction Hse. | 34-35 New Bond St., W1 (Bond St./Oxford Circus) | 020-7293-5077 | www.sothebys.com
If you're "wandering down Bond Street, doing the galleries", this "intimate" cafe in Sotheby's auction house is "a splendid place" for a "civilised" Modern British breakfast or lunch (weekdays only, until 4.45 PM); "pleasant" staff serve arty clients who amuse themselves by "speculating" about the other patrons: "buyer, seller or dealer?"

	FOOD	DECOR	SERVICE	COST

NEW **Spice Market** *Asian*   ▽ 22 | 24 | 21 | £52

Chinatown | W London Leicester Square Hotel | 10 Wardour St., W1
(Piccadilly Circus) | 020-7758-1080 | www.spicemarketlondon.co.uk

Über-chef Jean-Georges Vongerichten returns to London with this
"trendy", "welcome" offshoot of the New York hot spot set in
Chinatown's plush new W Hotel; a ceiling of inverted woks, a wall of
spices, low-slung leather banquettes and a spiral staircase resem-
bling a gilded bird cage make a glossy backdrop for "remarkable",
"clever" all-day Southeast Asian fare, which, like the colourful cocktails, are "unsurprisingly pricey."

NEW **Spuntino** ● *American/Italian*   - | - | - | M

Soho | 61 Rupert St., W1 (Piccadilly Circus) | www.spuntino.co.uk

As tiny and cramped as it is nonchalant and earthy, this Polpo and
Polpetto offshoot in nearby Soho digs offers a pithy selection of
well-priced American small plates with Italian influences (the clue's
in the name, which means 'snack'), accompanied by a cocktail list
that harks back to U.S. Prohibition era; all the action takes place
around a horseshoe-shaped bar with low-hanging carbon-filament
lighting set against distressed Victorian glazed brick walls.

Ζ **Square, The** *French*   27 | 24 | 27 | £92

Mayfair | 6-10 Bruton St., W1 (Bond St./Green Park) | 020-7495-7100 |
www.squarerestaurant.com

"Magnificent from start to finish", this Mayfair "jewel" with "elegant, refined decor" stars chef Philip Howard's "creative, colourful,
divine" New French cuisine, which is "served with exacting preci-
sion" by "flawless" staffers who "anticipate your needs"; the food is
"seriously expensive", as is the "encyclopaedic wine list", but for a
"special occasion", it's "guaranteed sophisticated."

Sri Nam **Ⓢ** *Thai*   - | - | - | M

Canary Wharf | 10 Cabot Sq., E14 (Canary Wharf) | 020-7715-9515

This "dark", silk-swathed spot caters for both "business" and "pleasure" with "acceptable" versions of Thai classics plus "great" service;
a few feel it's "overpriced for what it offers", but others disagree, with
nonlocal fans saying they "trek out to Canary Wharf" just to dine here.

Star of India ● *Indian*   25 | 18 | 20 | £36

South Kensington | 154 Old Brompton Rd., SW5 (Gloucester Rd./
South Kensington) | 020-7373-2901 | www.starofindia.eu

"You don't get to be a 60-year-old Indian restaurant by being anything
less than a star", and this South Ken spot shines with "absolutely
amazing", "reliable" dishes whose prices are "good value"; service is
mostly "acceptable", but for a few respondents, some sparkle is lost
on the decor, which the glib dub "Pompeian spa, after the volcano."

Sticky Fingers *American*   15 | 19 | 16 | £27

Kensington | 1A Phillimore Gdns., W8 (High St. Kensington) |
020-7938-5338 | www.stickyfingers.co.uk

The "typical" ribs and burgers are "fine", but most folks who roll into
this "casual" Kensington American are there because they're

"Stones fans" and want to check out the "rock 'n' roll decor" (Bill Wyman is the founder); it's also "a lifeline" for "families" due to the "discounted" prices, so if you don't "like kids a lot", it might be best to "avoid" – the "good" cocktails only go so far.

St. James's Restaurant *British* | 23 | 24 | 23 | £46 |

St. James's | Fortnum & Mason | 181 Piccadilly, 4th fl., W1 (Piccadilly Circus) | 020-5602-5694 | www.fortnumandmason.com

"Sometimes shoppers just have to sit still", and those at Fortnum & Mason do so at this "quiet", "classy", champagne-hued eatery on the fourth floor whose "beautifully executed" Traditional British lunch and dinner "classics" "don't disappoint", just like the "impeccable" staff; however, the biggest draw is what may be "the most relaxing afternoon tea on the planet", "an eminently satisfying experience" (and an "expensive" one to boot).

⚡ St. John *British* | 26 | 19 | 22 | £55 |

Farringdon | 26 St. John St., EC1 (Barbican/Farringdon) | 020-7251-0848 | www.stjohnrestaurant.com

"Eating heart, lungs and kidney" in a "stark white" "operating-theatre setting" makes some "feel like Hannibal Lecter", but if you're not "squeamish", you'll most likely find chef Fergus Henderson's "snout-to-tail" Modern British cuisine "extraordinary" at his Farringdon flagship; indeed, it's a "unique" "must for foodies", accompanied by "efficient" (though "a bit cold") service and an "imaginative" wine list – just bear in mind "it does cost a lot."

St. John Bread & Wine *British* | 25 | 16 | 21 | £41 |

Shoreditch | 94-96 Commercial St., E1 (Liverpool St.) | 020-7251-0848 | www.stjohnbreadandwine.com

"Minimal" "mess-hall-chic" surroundings define this all-day Shoreditch outpost of chef Fergus Henderson's "nose-to-tail" mini-empire, where "helpful" staff deliver "inventive, soul-warming" Modern British fare that's often "not for the faint of heart" (e.g. "ox heart"); you can eat "tapas-style" at the bar or feast at the table whilst saving room for "exceptional baked goods" and desserts you'll "want to plant your face in" – either way, the prices are "lovely."

NEW St. John Hotel ● *British* | - | - | - | E |

Soho | St. John Hotel | 1 Leicester St., WC2 (Leicester Sq.) | 020-3301-8020 | www.stjohnhotellondon.com

Fans of nose-to-tail eating can indulge at this new Modern British offshoot from chef Fergus Henderson (St. John, St. John Bread & Wine), located on the ground floor of a skinny Soho building, where an open kitchen churns out the earthy, meat-centric, somewhat pricey dishes; the characteristically stark, whitewashed dining room is open from breakfast until 2 AM daily.

St. Pancras Grand Restaurant *British* | 17 | 24 | 17 | £39 |

King's Cross | St Pancras Int'l | Euston Rd., upper concourse, NW1 (King's Cross St. Pancras) | 020-7870-9900 | www.searcys.co.uk

"Above all the hubbub of St. Pancras", travellers killing time before travel find a "cosy refuge" in this "gorgeous", "art deco-inspired venue" where champagne is the drink of choice and service is usu-ally "smooth" (some feel it "needs some attention"); the consensus about the Modern British menu is that it's, whilst "nothing super special", "a cut above" what "one would expect" from a train-station snack stop – but then, so are the prices.

Strada *Italian* | 16 | 14 | 16 | £26 |

Holborn | 6 Great Queen St., WC2 (Holborn) | 020-7405-6293
Marylebone | 9-10 Market Pl., W1 (Oxford Circus) | 020-7580-4644
Mayfair | 15-16 New Burlington St., W1 (Oxford Circus) | 020-7287-5967
Clerkenwell | 8-10 Exmouth Mkt., EC1 (Farringdon) | 020-7278-0800
Islington | 105-106 Upper St., N1 (Angel/Highbury & Islington) | 020-7226-9742
Battersea | 11-13 Battersea Rise, SW11 (Clapham Junction Rail) | 020-7801-0794
Clapham | 102-104 Clapham High St., SW4 (Clapham N.) | 020-7627-4847
Earl's Court | 237 Earl's Court Rd., SW5 (Earl's Ct.) | 020-7835-1180
Fulham | 175 New King's Rd., SW6 (Parsons Green) | 020-7731-6404
Wimbledon | 91 Wimbledon High St., SW19 (Wimbledon) | 020-8946-4363
www.strada.co.uk
Additional locations throughout London
For "well-made pizza" and other "decent Italian" options at "cheap" prices, this chain is "never a letdown" – as long as you "don't go ex-pecting culinary creativity"; "many wines by the glass" and service that generally comes "with a smile" make it an altogether "lovely", "local" choice, either "with the kids or without"; P.S. a chain-wide refurb of the "stark" settings is underway and may not be reflected in the Decor score.

Sumosan ● *Japanese* | 25 | 21 | 17 | £60 |

Mayfair | 26 B Albemarle St., W1 (Green Park) | 020-7495-5999 | www.sumosan.com
"Fantastic", "innovative" sushi, a "great sake selection" and "high-end" pricing make this minimalist Mayfair Japanese "an excellent business meal location"; unfortunately, "service suffers" when it's "crowded", and since that's the norm here, come only "if you're not in a hurry."

Sushinho *Brazilian/Japanese* | ∇ 16 | 17 | 15 | £49 |

Chelsea | 312-314 King's Rd., SW3 (Sloane Sq./South Kensington) | 020-7349-7496 | www.sushinho.com
In "funky", "dark" digs on King's Road, "attentive" staff serve "Brazilian-accented Japanese" "fusion" fare that includes sushi; but even though the "excellent" Latin-laced cocktail list is "worth ex-ploring", for a contingent, the "pricey" cuisine amalgamation is just "a nice idea" that "doesn't really work."

Sweetings ⌧ *Seafood* | 23 | 17 | 19 | £51 |

City | 39 Queen Victoria St., EC4 (Bank/Mansion Hse.) | 020-7248-3062
City "businessmen" "celebrating a deal" revel in the "old-boy atmo-sphere" at this "informal" "throwback" that's been serving "wonder-

ful" fish 'n' chips and other "simple", "expensive" seafood in the same sawdust-floored setting since 1889; "professional" staff do their best to be "prompt", but be warned, it "gets very busy", and the no-reservations policy makes securing a spot at the communal tables "almost a scrum."

Ⓩ Tamarind *Indian*   25 | 22 | 23 | £57

Mayfair | 20 Queen St., W1 (Green Park) | 020-7629-3561 | www.tamarindrestaurant.com

"Incredible concoctions fit for a Raja" that are "beautifully presented" by "gracious" (if "too solicitous") staff make this "gilded" Mayfair basement "still the posh place to go" for "upscale Indian" cuisine in a "mix of traditional and modern" preparations; oh, "you pay through the nose", but you're also getting access to a "surprising wine list" and the possibility to "hobnob with celebrities."

Taqueria *Mèxican*   20 | 11 | 15 | £23

Notting Hill | 139-143 Westbourne Grove, W11 (Notting Hill Gate) | 020-7229-4734 | www.taqueria.co.uk

Since it's "already hard to get a table" at this "buzzy" Mexican, Notting Hillites "hate to tell you" just how "scrumptious" it is – but they can't resist anymore than they can help "ordering seconds" of the "big"-flavoured fare that, whilst portioned into "small plates", offer "reasonable" value; more of a "focus on service would help" the atmosphere, but order up a "great margarita" or two, and "all your cares will fade away."

Tas ⏺ *Turkish*   21 | 15 | 18 | £24

Bloomsbury | 22 Bloomsbury St., WC1 (Tottenham Court Rd.) | 020-7637-4555

Farringdon | 37 Farringdon Rd., EC1 (Farringdon) | 020-7430-9721

South Bank | 72 Borough High St., SE1 (London Bridge) | 020-7403-7200

Waterloo | 33 The Cut, SE1 (Southwark) | 020-7928-1444

Tas Pide ⏺ *Turkish*

South Bank | 20-22 New Globe Walk, SE1 (London Bridge) | 020-7928-3300 | www.tasrestaurant.com

"Some of the tastiest morsels this side of the Bosphorus" mean all outposts of this "impressive Turkish empire" are "usually crowded" with "groups" gobbling "efficiently served" grilled meats and "vegetarian choices" that "lend themselves to sharing" and are "reasonably priced"; for something different, head to the South Bank branch, which "specialises in pide", an "excellent" variation on pizza, and other "interesting Anatolian cuisine."

Tate Britain Restaurant *British*   19 | 20 | 18 | £35
(aka Rex Whistler at the Britain)

Westminster | Tate Britain | Millbank, SW1 (Pimlico) | 020-7887-8825 | www.tate.org.uk

"After perusing the exhibits" at Tate's Millbank museum, this on-site eatery is "a welcome respite" for "reasonably priced", "enjoyable" Modern British breakfasts and lunches served in digs dominated by

Rex Whistler's 'In Pursuit of Rare Meats' mural (it "makes the room"); indeed, it's "a very civilised way to spend an afternoon", especially with pours from the "brilliant wine list", rich with "terrific values."

Tate Modern *European*   18 | 20 | 16 | £27
South Bank | Tate Modern | Bankside, 7th fl., SE1 (Blackfriars/London Bridge) | 020-7887-8888 | www.tate.org.uk

"Spectacular views" "across the Thames" from the seventh-floor perch of this "handy", "informal" South Bank gallery canteen "outdo" the Modern European eats, but the fare is "tasty" enough, "reliable" and "reasonably priced"; "cheerful service" adds to an atmosphere that's so "inviting", "one can easily let the hours slip" from early to late afternoon, when the "nice tea" is served.

☑ Tayyabs ◐ *Pakistani*   26 | 12 | 16 | £20
Whitechapel | 83-89 Fieldgate St., E1 (Aldgate E./Whitechapel) | 020-7247-6400 | www.tayyabs.co.uk

"Even with a booking", expect to "wait" alongside the "queue of drooling punters snaking down the street", only to "sit elbow-to-elbow", get served by possibly "surly staff" and, when all is said and done, leave "smelling like a barbecue" at this BYOB Pakistani in Whitechapel; but any hassle is "worth it" for the "astonishing" fare "brimming with spices" (the "luscious" "lamb chops will haunt your dreams") and "amazing value for money."

NEW Tempo *Italian*   - | - | - | E
Mayfair | 54 Curzon St., W1 (Green Park) | 020-7629-2742 | www.tempomayfair.co.uk

On a "gilded stretch" of Mayfair, this somewhat pricey newcomer proffers a "modern" Italian menu highlighting "rich, well-made" small plates that "encourage sharing" and let you "explore new flavours"; "friendly" and "professional" describes the service, both in the "ice-blue and sea-green velvet" dining room and the wood-paneled upstairs bar.

Tendido Cero *Spanish*   23 | 18 | 20 | £45
South Kensington | 174 Old Brompton Rd., SW5 (Gloucester Rd./South Kensington) | 020-7370-3685 | www.cambiodetercio.co.uk

South Kensington snackers flock to this "cool" venue from the Cambio de Tercio crew for an "interesting variety" of "awesome", "beautiful" Spanish tapas; "classy" *camareros* convey "excellent" Iberian wines too, sips from which can help make the "adds-up-quickly" bill easier to swallow.

Tendido Cuatro *Spanish*   - | - | - | M
Fulham | 108-110 New King's Rd., SW6 (Parsons Green/Putney Bridge) | 020-7371-5147 | www.cambiodetercio.co.uk

If you like Cambio de Tercio and Tendido Cero, check out its "casual" Fulham *hermano* where the Spanish tapas and paella are similarly "superb", but the "prices are cheaper than on Old Brompton Road" though the digs are bigger, "it can get noisy", especially "if you're stuck in the back', but with the aid of the "great wine list", it "never fails to please."

	FOOD	DECOR	SERVICE	COST

Tentazioni ☒ *Italian* `24` `17` `22` `£49`

Tower Bridge | Lloyd's Wharf | 2 Mill St., SE1 (Bermondsey) | 020-7237-1100 | www.tentazioni.co.uk

"Upscale" and "friendly" is "a hard combination to pull off", but this Italian "off the beaten track" "near Tower Bridge" manages it with "to-die-for" "haute cuisine" that's "slightly unusual", complemented by "impeccable service"; the "intimate", burgundy-hued environs set the stage for a "truly lovely evening", abetted by "excellent" wines.

Ten Ten Tei ☒ *Japanese* `-` `-` `-` `I`

Soho | 56 Brewer St., W1 (Piccadilly Circus) | 020-7287-1738

It looks "just like a basic Tokyo restaurant", so it's no surprise that this Soho Japanese delivers "authenticity" in its "great" cooked dishes and sushi; it's a "good bargain" at lunchtime, and the "great prices" continue for pre-theatre and beyond.

Terroirs ☒ *Mediterranean* `23` `18` `20` `£39`

Covent Garden | 5 William IV St., WC2 (Charing Cross) | 020-7036-0660 | www.terroirswinebar.com

"Exceptionally rich, delicious cured meats and pâtés" are the "hits" of the "country-food"-centric Mediterranean menu at this "informal", "relentlessly busy", bi-level Covent Garden venue, whose plates are ideal for "grazing"; perhaps most "impressive", however, is the "extraordinary", "biodynamic"-heavy wine list, which oenophiles recommend you "read online before visiting"; as for the prices, considering the "quality" of everything offered, they're "miraculous."

Texas Embassy Cantina *Tex-Mex* `12` `15` `15` `£23`

St. James's | 1 Cockspur St., SW1 (Charing Cross/Piccadilly Circus) | 020-7925-0077 | www.texasembassy.com

"If you're young, American and drunk" (or want to get that way via "not-bad" margaritas), you'll probably find this "cavernous", "crowded" Trafalgar Square–area taqueria "decent" for a Tex-Mex "fix"; however, others leave "disappointed."

Texture ☒ⓂEuropean `25` `23` `26` `£70`

Marylebone | 34 Portman St., W1 (Marble Arch) | 020-7224-0028 | www.texture-restaurant.co.uk

"Layers and layers of surprises" are revealed in the "inventive", "intense", Icelandic-inclined Modern European fare that's plated to be "a feast for the eye" at this "spacious, elegant" Marylebone destination; the "knowledgeable" crew includes a "stellar" sommelier to oversee the "excellent champagne and wine list", and whilst prices are "expensive" at dinner, the "superb" set lunch is "truly a bargain."

Thai Square *Thai* `19` `15` `17` `£36`

Covent Garden | 148 The Strand, WC2 (Covent Garden) | 020-7497-0904 ●☒

Mayfair | 5 Princes St., W1 (Oxford Circus) | 020-7499-3333 ☒

(continued)

(continued)

Thai Square

Soho | 27-28 St. Anne's Ct., W1 (Tottenham Court Rd.) | 020-7287-2000 🛂

St. James's | 21-24 Cockspur St., SW1 (Charing Cross/Piccadilly Circus) | 020-7839-4000 ◗

City | 1 Great St. Thomas Apostle, EC4 (Mansion Hse.) | 020-7329-0001 🛂

City | 136-138 Minories, EC3 (Tower Hill) | 020-7680-1111 🛂

Islington | 347-349 Upper St., N1 (Angel) | 020-7704-2000

Putney | 2-4 Lower Richmond Rd., SW15 (Putney Bridge) | 020-8780-1811

Richmond | 29 Kew Rd., TW9 (Richmond) | 020-8940-5253

South Kensington | 19 Exhibition Rd., SW7 (South Kensington) | 020-7584-8359

www.thaisq.com

Additional locations throughout London

"Flavourful" renditions of "mainstream" Thai cuisine are what you'll find at this "consistent", "no-nonsense" chain; they lack decor appeal, but "efficient" staff and "reasonable prices" mean the experience "somehow always manages to be better than you expect."

Theo Randall at The InterContinental 🛂 *Italian*

23 | 19 | 21 | £67

Mayfair | InterContinental Park Ln. | 1 Hamilton Pl., W1 (Hyde Park Corner) | 020-7318-8747 | www.theorandall.com

"High-quality ingredients" are "cooked with zing" and ladled into "generous" portions of "delicious", "modern" Italian fare at this venture in Mayfair's InterContinental Park Lane; some think that the cream-and-brown "basement setting is somewhat off-putting", but at least the service is "friendly", and with lunch and pre-theatre set menus, it doesn't have to be "overly expensive."

Thomas Cubitt *British*

23 | 21 | 22 | £40

Belgravia | 44 Elizabeth St., SW1 (Victoria) | 020-7730-6060 | www.thethomascubitt.co.uk

"Posh bangers and mash, posh meat pies and posh cider" served in "beautiful" surrounds elevate this "stylish", "fabulous" Belgravia Traditional British option above the "average gastropub"; what's more, the "young, attractive" "locals" "jammed" into both the "buzzy" downstairs and "intimate" upstairs say that the fare coupled with "lovely" service justifies the "expensive" prices.

Timo 🛂 *Italian*

∇ 22 | 19 | 21 | £47

Kensington | 343 Kensington High St., W8 (High St. Kensington) | 020-7603-3888 | www.timorestaurant.net

It could be just another "cosy" "neighbourhood" Italian serving "well-prepared" staples and a "nice selection of decently priced wines", but what "really makes the difference" at this Kensington kitchen is an owner who "greets you at the entrance", setting the tone for a "high standard of service"; whilst some dig at the "dated decor", others say its "unpretentious" nature is perfectly "pleasant" for "a family lunch or a nice dinner."

	FOOD	DECOR	SERVICE	COST

NEW Tinello ⊠ *Italian* | 24 | 20 | 22 | £51 |

Pimlico | 87 Pimlico Rd., SW1 (Sloane Sq./Victoria Station) | 020-7730-3663 | www.tinello.co.uk

"*Fabuloso!*" enthuse those who "finally got a booking" at this new "something special" in Pimlico, where "generous" portions of "magnificent" Tuscan tucker come via the sort of "service you only expect in much more expensive restaurants"; other highlights include an "excellent wine list" and a "charming" ambience created by "dark, moody lighting" and brick walls.

Tokyo Diner ● *Japanese* | - | - | - | I |

Chinatown | 2 Newport Pl., WC2 (Leicester Sq.) | 020-7287-8777 | www.tokyodiner.com

"Budget diners" "love" this "beacon of goodness" on the outskirts of Chinatown, because not only is the Japanese sushi a "bargain", it's "delicious" to boot; no one feels the need to disparage the simple surroundings, maybe because staff won't accept tips.

Tom Aikens ⊠ *French* | 25 | 24 | 24 | £89 |

Chelsea | 43 Elystan St., SW3 (South Kensington) | 020-7584-2003 | www.tomaikens.co.uk

A "serene" stage is set for chef Tom Aikens' "beautifully prepared" Modern French fare at this Chelsea dining room with complementary "outstanding" wines and "knowledgeable, courteous" staff; that prices are "so expensive" shores up its reputation as "a place to impress", though lunch can be somewhat better value; P.S. it was set to close and reopen in late summer 2011 with a new menu, smarter look and less-formal service, possibly outdating all scores.

Tom Ilic Ⓜ *European* | ∇ 19 | 11 | 21 | £37 |

Battersea | 123 Queenstown Rd., SW8 (Queenstown Rd. Rail) | 020-7622-0555 | www.tomilic.com

"Pork heaven" is found at this "buzzy" Battersea joint where pig is the "speciality" of chef Tom Ilic's "robust" Modern European menu that "packs a punch of flavour and texture"; oenophiles feel the "wine list could do with an overhaul" and aesthetes say ditto the "tacky MDF chairs and awful table decorations", but there's no criticism of service or value – they're "charming" and "exceptional", respectively.

Tompkins *European* | - | - | - | E |

Canary Wharf | 4 Pan Peninsula Sq., E14 (South Quays DLR) | 020-8305-3080 | www.tompkins.uk.com

Situated at the base of the huge Pan Peninsula apartment complex on the edge of South Quays in the Canary Wharf area, this modern, glass-clad brasserie offers a business-oriented Modern European menu boosted by surf 'n' turf classics; in addition to the "cavernous" dining room, there's a capacious alfresco terrace and an informal, bi-level lounge crammed with comfy sofas, mix-and-match furniture and huge, evocative black-and-white prints of old London.

	FOOD	DECOR	SERVICE	COST

Tom's Deli *Eclectic* — | — | — | M

Notting Hill | 226 Westbourne Grove, W11 (Notting Hill Gate) | 020-7221-8818 | www.tomsdelilondon.co.uk

"Fantastic" breakfast and brunch options, including "great" eggs Benedict, are the main draws of this "loud", retro-looking Notting Hill Eclectic deli/diner; whilst some sniff they're "not as excited about" the place as they "used to be", others still "like the scene", not to mention the affordable prices – hence, there's "always a long queue."

Tom's Kitchen *British* — 22 | 19 | 18 | £40

Covent Garden | Somerset Hse. | The Strand, WC2 (Temple) | 020-7845-4646
Chelsea | 27 Cale St., SW3 (South Kensington) | 020-7349-0202
www.tomskitchen.co.uk

"Carefully selected" ingredients "elevate even the simplest of dishes to something special" at chef Tom Aikens' emporium of Modern British "comfort food" in Chelsea; the "casual" setting is a real "people-spotting hangout", especially at weekends when the "communal tables" get "loud and crowded" with "old Sloanie types" and their "kids" dropping in for "fantastic" if "expensive" brunch; P.S. the Somerset House offshoot caters for those "exploring Covent Garden."

Toto's *Italian* — 23 | 21 | 23 | £56

Chelsea | Walton Hse. | Walton St. at Lennox Garden Mews, SW3 (Knightsbridge) | 020-7589-2062

"Romantics" rave about this "quaint", "lovely" ristorante "hidden in a leafy mews" in Chelsea, reckoning it has all the essentials "for a date": "excellent" executions of "swish" Italian standards ("pricey but worth every penny"), "friendly", "attentive" staff, "well-spaced" tables and "inviting" lighting from a Milanese chandelier; when wooing in the summertime, the "delightful" garden is recommended.

Trinity *European* — 25 | 20 | 24 | £51

Clapham | 4 The Polygon, SW4 (Clapham Common) | 020-7622-1199 | www.trinityrestaurant.co.uk

Chef Adam Byatt's "inventive, big-flavoured", seasonal Modern European savouries and "desserts to die for" are sold for "suburban" prices at this "exquisite fine-dining" venue, which displays "cracking low markups" on the "good wine list" too; add in "service that truly cares", and no wonder Central Londoners say it's "worth the trip" to Clapham.

Trishna *Indian* — 26 | 19 | 20 | £53

Marylebone | 15-17 Blandford St., W1 (Baker St./Bond St.) | 020-7935-5624 | www.trishnalondon.com

Mumbai comes to Marylebone, literally, with this "relaxed, unstuffy" outpost of one of India's feted fooderies, where the focus is on "outstanding" fish and "modern, lighter" versions of familiar fare, all served by "kind" staff; it may be "on the edge of expensive", but the "fabulous set menu" with wine pairings is "a great deal", and 'educational' to boot.

Troubadour, The *Eclectic*

-	-	-	M

Earl's Court | 265 Old Brompton Rd., SW5 (Earl's Ct.) | 020-7370-1434 | www.troubadour.co.uk

A "trip back to the folk scene of '65", this bohemian Earl's Court cultural club where Hendrix and Dylan once played is "a must" for "blues, poetry and acoustic artists", who appear "throughout the week"; as for the Eclectic eats, they're more "good value" than gourmet, but they do what they're supposed to do: soak up "potent" cocktails.

Truc Vert *French*

19	15	16	£31

Mayfair | 42 N. Audley St., W1 (Bond St.) | 020-7491-9988 | www.trucvert.co.uk

A "frequently changing" menu of "great" cafe fare plus a "variety of tasty breads" bring Mayfair folk to this "rustic", "intimate" Frenchie; brunch is particularly popular, but it's also "nice" for lunch or an ultracasual dinner, especially if you snag a spot on the pavement in summer – and forgive the "inconsistent" service.

NEW Trullo *Italian*

▽ 19	15	20	£42

Islington | 300-302 St. Paul's Rd., N1 (Highbury & Islington) | 020-7226-2733 | www.trullorestaurant.com

Italophiles gather round paper-clad tables at this "small", "casual" newcomer at the Highbury end of Islington, whose "tempting" menu contains "some unusual ingredients" that result in "wonderful flavour combinations"; "friendly" service, "affordable prices" and a "good wine list" further make it "well worth" checking out.

Tsunami *Japanese*

25	19	19	£42

Bloomsbury | 93 Charlotte St., W1 (Goodge St.) | 020-7637-0050 ● ⌗

Clapham | 5-7 Voltaire Rd., SW4 (Clapham N.) | 020-7978-1610 | www.tsunamirestaurant.co.uk

You might be surprised to find such "lush, exotic surroundings" "nestled cosily in North Clapham", but they do exist at this "vibrant" Japanese serving what some believe is the "best sushi south of the river"; the "imaginative" eats are "sublime" on their own, but complemented by "delicious" cocktails, they're "heaven", here and at the "intimate, chic" Charlotte Street sib.

Tsuru ⌗ *Japanese*

-	-	-	M

NEW City | 10 Queen St., EC4 (Mansion House) | 020-7377-6367

City | 201 Bishopsgate, EC2 (Liverpool St.) | 020-7377-1166

South Bank | 4 Canvey St., SE1 (Southwark) | 020-7928-2228 | www.tsuru-sushi.co.uk

"Recommended for a quick takeaway sushi lunch", this bright, moderately priced, sustainably minded Bankside Japanese near the Tate Modern offers an expanded dinnertime menu featuring teriyaki and curries; newer branches in Mansion House and Bishopsgate serve similar stuff to the City crowd.

	FOOD	DECOR	SERVICE	COST

Tuttons Brasserie ● *British/French*   ▽ 16 | 15 | 16 | £36

Covent Garden | 11-12 Russell St., WC2 (Covent Garden) |
020-7836-4141 | www.tuttons.com

"Competent, quick, noisy" sums up this all-day Covent Gardener
proffering affordable classic British and French dishes to "tourists
and theatregoers" squeezed onto red banquettes; even long-timers
who find the fare "somewhat mediocre these days" concede that "if
you can find space" on the "great terrace" in summer, it's worth it, if
only to "watch the entertainment" of the piazza.

NEW **28-50 Wine**   22 | 21 | 25 | £40
Workshop & Kitchen 🅢 *French*

Holborn | 140 Fetter Ln., EC4 (Chancery Ln.) | 020-7242-8877 |
www.2850.co.uk

The "professional team" from Texture are behind this "brilliant addition" to Holborn, a "rustic", "softly lit" cellar boasting a "heavenly
wine list" (featuring "wonderful options" by the glass) and "excellent, unfussy" French bistro "classics"; "cheerful" service adds to
the appeal, and if the food prices are "more suited to those on expenses", "amazing value" can be found amongst the *vins*.

Two Brothers Fish 🅢🅜 *Seafood*   20 | 11 | 15 | £19

Finchley | 297-303 Regent's Park Rd., N3 (Finchley Central) |
020-8346-0469 | www.twobrothers.co.uk

"How lucky the locals" of Finchley are to have this "awesome" fish 'n'
chips shop where the "value" fillets are "fried in matzo meal" and
served in "great portions"; but given that they have to contend with
"tacky decor" and "not a lot of elbow room", many prefer takeaway.

202 *European*   18 | 20 | 18 | £28

Notting Hill | Nicole Farhi | 202 Westbourne Grove, W11
(Notting Hill Gate) | 020-7727-2722

The "trendy" "atmosphere is exactly what you would expect" at this
"fashionista outpost" inside Nicole Farhi's "vibrant" Notting Hill
store, where the "well-prepared" Modern European fare includes
"awesome" breakfast and brunch; "cramped quarters" mean there's
frequently a queue, but the wait is usually "short", plus you "often
see a celeb or two."

222 Veggie Vegan *Vegan*   ▽ 21 | 16 | 21 | £27

Fulham | 222 North End Rd., W14 (West Kensington) | 020-7381-2322 |
www.222veggievegan.com

Though there's little in the way of decor, this Fulham spot is still a "little
gem" for its "wonderful", "creative" vegan cooking; prices are always reasonable, but it's the £7.50 daily all-you-can-eat lunch buffet that has bargain-hunters coming back "time and time again."

2 Veneti 🅢 *Italian*   21 | 16 | 20 | £42

Marylebone | 8-10 Wigmore St., W1 (Bond St./Oxford Circus) |
020-7637-0789 | www.2veneti.com

A "focus on the Veneto region's wonderful, varied cuisine" makes
this "charming, casual" Italian eatery "unique" in Marylebone, and a

| | FOOD | DECOR | SERVICE | COST |

"real treat" at that; a "solid" wine list and affordable prices earn it its share of regulars, who appreciate that "the owner remembers" them and that staff pay "attention."

Uli 🗷 *Asian*   - | - | - | M

Notting Hill | 16 All Saints Rd., W11 (Ladbroke Grove) | 020-7727-7511 | www.uli-oriental.co.uk

"Japanese, Chinese, Thai – they have it all" at this "pleasant" Notting Hill neighbourhood Asian-fusion spot where frequenters recommend, "for a superb dinner, be brave, take the owner's advice, and don't ask what you're eating until you have swallowed"; "if the weather's nice" try grabbing a seat in the garden.

☑ Umu 🗷 *Japanese*   26 | 26 | 25 | £86

Mayfair | 14-16 Bruton Pl., W1 (Bond St./Green Park) | 020-7499-8881 | www.umurestaurant.com

"Bring a yen for exquisite Japanese food and plenty of yen to pay" at this "sexy", "intriguing" Mayfair purveyor of "masterfully prepared", "modern and traditional" Kyoto-influenced kaiseki and à la carte menus (including sushi), plus an "extraordinary wine and sake list", which "well-informed" staff deliver to a "hushed, reverential" crowd; meanwhile, the budget-minded note that the set lunches can be "good value."

Union Cafe *British/Mediterranean*   19 | 16 | 18 | £33

Marylebone | 96 Marylebone Ln., W1 (Bond St.) | 020-7486-4860 | www.brinkleys.com

"Like an old pair of slippers", this "bright" Marylebone "local" "never lets you down" thanks to "tasty", "reasonably priced" Modern British-Med "comfort food" that works as well for a "quick" bite "before a concert at the nearby Wigmore Hall" as it does for "excellent weekend brunch"; a wine list with "not-high markups" also pleases, but be aware that when it gets "busy", the atmosphere grows "noisy" and "friendly service" becomes "slow."

Vapiano *Italian*   17 | 17 | 11 | £19

Marylebone | 19-21 Great Portland St., W1 (Oxford Circus) | 020-7268-0080 | www.vapiano.co.uk

"Tasty" pizza, pasta and salads are "tweaked to your taste" and "made to order" while a chip card tallies your spend at this "novel" Italian chain link in Marylebone that's "lively, fun" and "great value for money"; at peak times "queues can be lengthy", but as a reward, you "might meet someone interesting at the communal tables."

Vasco & Piero's Pavilion *Italian*   ▽ 24 | 18 | 24 | £49

Soho | 15 Poland St., W1 (Oxford Circus) | 020-7437-8774 | www.vascosfood.com

For 40 years, this "lovely", "elegant" Soho Italian has been providing "pure pleasure" in its "old-fashioned", "immaculately cooked" Umbrian dishes; though it's "not cheap", the "prices are fair for London", plus you're also getting "friendly, efficient" service, a "relaxed" vibe and the promise of "never a bad meal."

	FOOD	DECOR	SERVICE	COST

Veeraswamy *Indian* | 24 | 23 | 22 | £50 |

Mayfair | Victory Hse. | 99-101 Regent St., W1 (Piccadilly Circus) | 020-7734-1401 | www.veeraswamy.com

An "enlightening menu" mixing "traditional" and "hip", "bursting with flavour and cooked to perfection" is delivered in "decadent" surrounds that juxtapose "modern" trappings with those of a Maharaja's palace at this 1926 Indian "a stone's throw from Piccadilly Circus"; "attentive" servers provide "explanations" for the "unfamiliar", and whilst some "question" relatively "small portions" for "expense-account prices", it's nevertheless "a treat" for "romantics" and "business" associates alike.

NEW Venosi Ⓢ *Italian* | - | - | - | E |

Chelsea | 87 Sloane Ave., SW3 (South Kensington) | 020-7998-5019 | www.venosi.co.uk

With four decades as a Soho restaurateur under his belt, Luigi Venosi and his chef son Gino have converted a former Chelsea Indian into this bright, minimalist Italian offering traditionally minded fare at upscale prices; the bare-brick and white-walled space is augmented with alfresco tables in the spacious rear courtyard.

NEW Verru *E European/Scandinavian* | - | - | - | E |

Marylebone | 69 Marylebone Ln., W1 (Bond St.) | 020-7935-0858 | www.verru.co.uk

An Estonian chef who earned his spurs at some big London names (Maze, Pied à Terre) makes his owner debut at this tiny Marylebone arrival that looks plush despite bare brick walls and simple, tightly packed tables; Scandinavia and the Baltic states are the inspiration for a pricey, daily changing menu, which is eased by a sub-£15 set lunch.

Viajante *Eclectic* | 25 | 19 | 23 | £80 |

Bethnal Green | Town Hall Hotel | Patriot Sq., E2 (Bethnal Green) | 020-7871-0461 | www.viajante.co.uk

"Innovative" but "approachable molecular gastronomy" is achieved via "superb" "technical ability" at this "adventurous", "exciting" Eclectic set in "understated, comfortable" digs in the erstwhile Bethnal Green Town Hall; "wonderful" staff serve the "delicious" fare only in tasting menus (up to 12 courses, with the option of "thoughtful drink pairings"), so if you can't spare "at least four hours" (and a "ridiculous" amount of money), hit the "über-hip" bar instead for "standout" snacks and "wonderfully creative cocktails". P.S. the first-floor Corner Room is more relaxed, quaint and affordable.

Viet Grill *Vietnamese* | ∇ 22 | 15 | 18 | £24 |

Shoreditch | 58 Kingsland Rd., E2 (Old St.) | 020-7739-6686 | www.vietnamesekitchen.co.uk

"A riot of colours, textures and tastes" from the streets of Saigon enlivens this "chic" Shoreditch Vietnamese offering serious "bang for your buck", particularly in its "big steaming bowls of pho"; whilst service seems sometimes "indifferent", it's "speedy", and with a "surprisingly good wine list" thrown into the mix, it's rare not to find the place "full."

Vote at ZAGAT.com

	FOOD	DECOR	SERVICE	COST

Viet Hoa ● _Vietnamese_
▽ 21 | 11 | 15 | £25

Shoreditch | 70-72 Kingsland Rd., E2 (Old St.) | 020-7729-8293 | www.viethoarestaurant.co.uk

A "cheap bowl of authentic pho" at this "spartan" spot is "great for hangovers" should you find yourself suffering in Shoreditch, but the "wonderful", "great-value" Vietnamese victuals "can't be beat" however you're feeling; "efficient service" and a basement bar mean there's nothing "not to like."

Villandry _French_
19 | 16 | 16 | £32

Bloomsbury | 170 Great Portland St., W1 (Great Portland St.) | 020-7631-3131 | www.villandry.com

This "bustling" Bloomsbury multitasker offers all-day options aplenty with a "casual", rustic cafe, a "more formal" (but "by no means grand") dining room and a "quality-takeaway" bar; throughout, you'll find "simple yet carefully prepared" Classic French fare that's a bit "expensive for what it is" but nevertheless "reliable" (the same can't be said of the service – it's somewhat "inattentive").

Vingt-Quatre ● _Eclectic_
▽ 14 | 11 | 14 | £25

Chelsea | 325 Fulham Rd., SW10 (South Kensington) | 020-7376-7224 | www.vingtquatre.co.uk

"Hungry at 3 AM after clubbing?" – hit this simply outfitted, "dependable little number on the Fulham Road", which serves a "value"-priced Eclectic menu 24/7; the "comfort food" may be "nothing special", but "when everywhere else has closed", it can seem "magnificent" (surveyors "wouldn't recommend it at 7 PM").

Vinoteca _European_
22 | 18 | 20 | £35

NEW Marylebone | 15 Seymour Pl., W1 (Marble Arch) | 020-7724-7288

Farringdon | 7 St. John St., EC1 (Farringdon) | 020-7253-8786 🗷 www.vinoteca.co.uk

"Go for the wines, stay for the food" say fans of this "crowded", informal Farringdon _bar à vin_ where the "fabulous, fairly priced", nearly 300-strong list, including around 25 by-the-glass options, is complemented by "well-executed", "tasty" Modern European eats; the place is "very small" and only accepts bookings at lunch, so get there early or have "a backup plan"; P.S. the new Marylebone offshoot offers similar sustenance, with the addition of Sunday lunch.

Vivat Bacchus 🗷 _European_
19 | 17 | 19 | £39

City | 47 Farringdon St., EC4 (Chancery Ln./Farringdon) | 020-7353-2648
Tower Bridge | 4 Hays Ln., SE1 (London Bridge) | 020-7234-0891 www.vivatbacchus.co.uk

The Modern European eats "deliver" at this "intimate", "candlelit" City and London Bridge duo, but the major "interest" lies in the "extensive wine list" ("check out the cellar") and "great" _fromage_ selection, from which you create your own board in separate cheese rooms; staff "treat you as friends" as they offer "excellent assistance", and while it "could do with some more sensibly priced" bottles, the lunch and dinner set meals are "great value."

	FOOD	DECOR	SERVICE	COST

Ζ Wagamama *Japanese*   19 | 13 | 17 | £19

Bloomsbury | 4 Streatham St., WC1 (Tottenham Court Rd.) |
020-7323-9223

Covent Garden | 1A Tavistock St., WC2 (Covent Garden) | 020-7836-3330

Knightsbridge | Harvey Nichols | 109-125 Knightsbridge,
lower ground fl., SW1 (Knightsbridge) | 020-7201-8000

Marylebone | 101A Wigmore St., W1 (Bond St.) | 020-7409-0111

Soho | 10A Lexington St., W1 (Oxford Circus/Piccadilly Circus) |
020-7292-0990

City | 1 Ropemaker St., EC2 (Moorgate) | 020-7588-2688 🛒

City | 109 Fleet St., EC4 (Blackfriars/St. Paul's) | 020-7583-7889 🛒

Camden Town | 11 Jamestown Rd., NW1 (Camden Town) |
020-7428-0800

Islington | N1 Ctr. | 40 Parkfield St., N1 (Angel) | 020-7226-2664

Kensington | 26A Kensington High St., W8 (High St. Kensington) |
020-7376-1717

www.wagamama.com
Additional locations throughout London

"Take the kids" to these "cavernous" Japanese "canteens" and
"tickle your taste buds" via "big", "addictive", "healthy" noodle
bowls delivered by "quick", "efficient youngsters" to "crowded,
noisy" communal tables; grousers gripe about settings that "lack atmosphere" and "individual orders" served at "different times", but
since everything's so "cheap", you really "can't fault" it.

Wahaca *Mexican*   20 | 16 | 17 | £25

Covent Garden | 66 Chandos Pl., WC2 (Charing Cross/Leicester Sq.) |
020-7240-1883

NEW **Soho** | 80 Wardour St., W1 (Piccadilly Circus) | 020-7734-0195

Canary Wharf | Park Pavilion, 40 Canada Sq., E14 (Canary Wharf) |
020-7516-9145

Shepherd's Bush | Westfield Shopping Ctr. | Ariel Way, ground fl., W12
(Shepherd's Bush) | 020-8749-4517

www.wahaca.co.uk

"*Muchas gracias a dios*" - or at least to Thomasina Miers for these
"brightly decorated", "convivial" "temples of Mexican street food",
where the dishes are "delicious", "designed for sharing", sold at "im-
plausibly affordable prices" and delivered by staff that "seem
cheery" even though their efforts are "hit-and-miss"; as ever, it's
"infuriatingly difficult to get a table" (no reservations), but "whiling
away" the wait with a "mean mojito" or margarita makes it a little
more bearable; P.S. a branch is slated for Westfield Stratford City,
the new shopping centre across from the Olympic Park.

Wallace, The *French*   17 | 21 | 14 | £33

Marylebone | Wallace Museum Collection | Hertford Hse.,
Manchester Sq., W1 (Baker St./Bond St.) | 020-7563-9505 |
www.thewallacerestaurant.co.uk

Even if you're not visiting the Wallace Museum, "one of the finest art
collections in the world", this Classic French lunch room is "worth a
trip" for its "beautiful", "glass-canopied" "courtyard" setting, as
"comfortable" "for a long catch up with an old friend" as it is for a
"romantic assignation"; if the fare "doesn't quite live up" to the setting

174

	FOOD	DECOR	SERVICE	COST

and service can be "à la *Fawlty Towers*", much is forgiven because the prices are moderate; P.S. dinner offered Fridays and Saturdays.

Wapping Food *European*

∇ 18	25	19	£40

Docklands | Wapping Hydraulic Power Station | Wapping Wall, E1 (Wapping) | 020-7680-2080 | www.thewappingproject.com

"Tables wedged between moribund machines" and an adjacent space exhibiting "compelling" art make this converted Victorian "hydraulic power station" one of the most "fascinating" venues in "all of London", and the "inventive, Aussie-influenced" Modern European menu is pretty "great" too; its Wapping location is "far out" for most, but "so worth it" – even though, some cheeky sorts say "you'll be wapping yourself upside the head once you see the bill."

Warrington, The *British*

16	20	16	£36

St. John's Wood | 93 Warrington Cres., W9 (Maida Vale/Warwick Ave.) | 020-7592-7960 | www.gordonramsay.com

Restored to its "traditional" Victorian splendour, this St. John's Wood British gastropub encompasses a "magnificent" ground-floor bar, a "bit-stiff" upstairs restaurant and a "superb" patio; but for its "Gordon Ramsay pedigree" (and prices), the "good-old-days" fare is "rather disappointing", and service is "patchy" too – though Sunday lunch is usually "good" in all respects.

Waterloo Bar & Grill ⊠ *British*

∇ 18	15	16	£32

Waterloo | 119 Waterloo Rd., SE1 (Waterloo) | 020-7960-0202 | www.waterloobarandgrill.com

With "a useful location" near the Old Vic, this moderately priced Modern British spot is "perfect for a casual night out" with "friends after work" or for a "pre-theatre" bite of "simple but effective", "hearty" grub; recently renovated, the decor is now lighter and brighter than it was before, with exposed brick, contemporary photography and yellow suede chairs.

⊠ Waterside Inn Ⓜ *French*

28	27	28	£113

Bray | Waterside Inn | Ferry Rd., Berkshire | 01628-620691 | www.waterside-inn.co.uk

"What perfection!" swoon admirers of this "exquisite" Roux family Classic French establishment perched amongst "willow trees" on a "tributary of the Thames" in Bray, where "painstaking" "attention to detail" is obvious in the "heavenly" fare and staff are so "gracious", "knowledgeable and helpful", they've earned the No. 1 Service rating; for the most "romantic", "magical experience", "book well in advance for a river view" – and be prepared to push the boat out, especially if indulging in "wonderful wines" from the "huge" list.

Waterway, The *European*

15	18	13	£33

St. John's Wood | 54 Formosa St., W9 (Warwick Ave.) | 020-7266-3557 | www.thewaterway.co.uk

A "lovely" location on the canal at Little Venice means this "crowded and loud" gastropub can be "wonderful" in "good weather" when "you can eat outside"; unfortunately, "consistency is a big problem" in regards to the Modern European menu, so for best results, "keep it simple" and pray that "stretched" staff aren't having one of their "rude and inattentive" days.

Wells, The *European*

23	21	22	£32

Hampstead | 30 Well Walk, NW3 (Hampstead) | 020-7794-3785 | www.thewellshampstead.co.uk

"Well-prepared, simple fare at reasonable prices" coupled with a "nice pub-wine selection" and "warm" staff pull in punters at this "deservedly popular" Modern European gastropub in Hampstead; reservations are "essential" both in the "boisterous pub" and "refined" upstairs dining rooms, especially "at weekends" when parents and their "noisy" children drop in for "lunch followed by a romp across the Heath."

Weng Wah House *Chinese*

-	-	-	M

Hampstead | 240 Haverstock Hill, NW3 (Belsize Park) | 020-7431-4502 | www.wengwah.co.uk

"A long-time favourite" for Hampstead locals, this unassuming Chinese (with an "upstairs karaoke room") produces "delicious", affordable dishes that suit "the British palate"; even though service is "good" and the setting is "pleasant", "takeaway seems to be the mainstay."

Westbourne, The *Eclectic*

▽ 15	18	16	£28

Notting Hill | 101 Westbourne Park Villas, W2 (Royal Oak/ Westbourne Park) | 020-7221-1332 | www.thewestbourne.com

"Brilliant for drinking!" bray the "noisy" clientele who keep this "hip" Notting Hill gastropub with an old-school setting "always packed", too bad then that it's just "not special enough" considering the "ropey" Eclectic food and "indifferent service"; though on the plus side, prices are moderate.

Wheeler's of St. James's 🗷 *Seafood*

21	17	20	£57

St. James's | 72-73 St. James's St., SW1 (Green Park) | 020-7408-1440 | www.wheelersrestaurant.org

Despite the modern photographs that adorn the dark-red walls, it's like "stepping back in time" at this St. James's seafood "institution" whose "succulent" dishes and "well-selected" wines are there but for the grace of Marco Pierre White, who "reworked" the place last year; "swift, quiet" staff circulate amongst the "business lunch"-heavy crowd, the type that can expense the pricey bill.

Whitechapel Gallery Dining Room Ⓜ *European*

▽ 18	18	19	£38

Whitechapel | Whitechapel Gallery | 77-82 Whitechapel High St., E1 (Aldgate E.) | 020-7522-7888 | www.whitechapelgallery.org

After a recent revamp by chef Angela Hartnett (Murano), this intimate, oak-panelled Modern European set in an East End gallery now boasts a more "innovative", "mouth-watering" menu that's also "well executed"; best of all, not only do diners depart "happy", they do so "not much poorer" to boot.

	FOOD	DECOR	SERVICE	COST

Whole Foods Market *Eclectic*
21 | 13 | 15 | £20

Kensington | Barkers Bldg. | 63-97 Kensington High St., W8 (High St. Kensington) | 020-7368-4500 | www.wholefoods.com

"If you're on Kensington High Street", this "functional", "self-service" Eclectic "food court" set above the "American yuppie phenomenon" is "convenient" for "whatever you fancy (sushi, burritos, waffles, soup, salad, mezze . . .)"; however, you should expect "confusing" "queues", "indifferent staff" and prices that are "expensive for dining in what's essentially a school lunchroom"; P.S. "busy"-bees hail takeaway as "a lifesaver."

Wild Honey *British*
23 | 20 | 22 | £56

Mayfair | 12 St. George St., W1 (Bond St./Oxford Circus) | 020-7758-9160 | www.wildhoneyrestaurant.co.uk

"Sophisticated palates" are sated by "delectable" Modern British dishes ("reasonably priced for the quality") at this "old townhouse" in Mayfair, where "unpretentious" staff are as "accommodating" as the "wonderful" wine programme, offering all selections by the 250-ml. carafe; though the ceilings are "high", "seating is so close it's almost communal", meaning there's a "lack of privacy", though chatty types appreciate that it "promotes conversation."

❷ Wilton's 🅱 *British/Seafood*
27 | 24 | 27 | £79

St. James's | 55 Jermyn St., SW1 (Green Park/Piccadilly Circus) | 020-7629-9955 | www.wiltons.co.uk

It's "not the cheapest or the hippest" – in fact, it's "wallet-busting" and "unapologetically old school" – but for "peerless" seafood, "perfect game" and additional "superior" Traditional British "treats", this "clubby" 1740s "national treasure" in St. James's is "not to be missed"; "waiters as old as the cobblestones outside" and "waitresses in nursery-room frocks" "coddle" their clientele, including "the Tory party at play" and other "gentlemen" who wouldn't dare "take their jackets off."

Wòdka *Polish*
21 | 17 | 20 | £42

Kensington | 12 St. Albans Grove, W8 (High St. Kensington) | 020-7937-6513 | www.wodka.co.uk

"Tucked away in a quiet" Kensington back street, this "warm", "relaxed" venue vends "simply delicious" Polish cuisine at "reasonable prices"; however, it's perhaps best known for its "fabulous" house-infused vodkas (the flights are "a must") and "beautiful waitresses" (they're "helpful" too).

❷ Wolseley, The ◑ *European*
22 | 26 | 22 | £52

Piccadilly | 160 Piccadilly, W1 (Green Park) | 020-7499-6996 | www.thewolseley.com

"You don't have to be famous to be treated famously" at London's Most Popular restaurant, a "gorgeous" Piccadilly "grand cafe" where "enthusiastic", "choreographed service" shuttles "varied" Modern Euro fare that's "sensational" "for breakfast, lunch, dinner or whenever" to "boisterous", "attractive clientele" ("hedgies, celebs, ladies who lunch", "tourists"); "it's not cheap", but "you do get what you pay for", and though reservations are "vital at virtually any time", "there are a few tables saved for walk-ins" – how "refreshing!"

Wong Kei ●⇄ *Chinese*

| 15 | 6 | 7 | £15 |

Chinatown | 41-43 Wardour St., W1 (Leicester Sq./Piccadilly Circus) | 020-7437-8408

"Don't expect swish decor or remotely good service", as this "functional", multilevel Chinatown "institution" "thrives on its reputation for being rude"; still, for a "good laugh", go "with a crowd", settle into a "noisy" "shared table", have "a few drinks" and dig into the "large plates" of "no-frills" Cantonese eats – it's "cheap" fun that "everyone should experience at least once."

Wright Brothers Oyster & Porter House *Seafood*

| 26 | 21 | 23 | £38 |

Borough | Borough Mkt. | 11 Stoney St., SE1 (London Bridge) | 020-7403-9554

Wright Brothers Soho Oyster House ● *Seafood*

NEW **Soho** | 12-13 Kingly St., W1 (Oxford Circus/Piccadilly Circus) | 020-7434-3611
www.wrightbros.eu.com

You'll be "squeezed in tighter than a mollusc in her shell", but it's worth the crush at (and "the wait" for) one of the "worn-wood counters" at this "bustling" Borough Market seafooder specialising in "oysters of many shapes and sizes" plus "fantastic" "simply cooked" fish dishes, all available with "a well-focused selection of beers and carefully chosen wines"; in Soho, a new offshoot offers a "rest for shoppers."

XO *Asian*

| 20 | 19 | 19 | £45 |

Hampstead | 29 Belsize Ln., NW3 (Belsize Park) | 020-7433-0888 | www.rickerrestaurants.com

This "relaxed, romantic" Pan-Asian hued in black and citron "feels like a trendy West End restaurant", but has "the convenience of being local" for those near Belsize Park in Hampstead; the "solid" small and large plates are "just what you expect" from the Will Ricker stable (E&O, Great Eastern Dining Room, etc.), and though a "price tag to match" disappoints pence-pinchers, "welcoming" staff and "good cocktails" keep the "fun" vibe alive.

Yalla Yalla *Lebanese*

| 21 | 12 | 16 | £21 |

Soho | 1 Greens Ct., W1 (Piccadilly Circus) | 020-7287-7663 ●
NEW **Soho** | 12 Winsley St., W1 (Oxford Circus) | 020-7637-4748 🗷
www.yalla-yalla.co.uk

The mezze and mains are as "packed with flavour" as the "tiny" digs are "packed with people" at this "lively" Soho Lebanese cafe; indeed, "getting a table" (there are only "a few") is "tricky", but those who persevere are rewarded with a "quick", "cheap" experience that "charms", despite staff that are "not always welcoming"; P.S. a bigger, more modern offshoot opened post-Survey in Winsley Street.

	FOOD	DECOR	SERVICE	COST

NEW Yashin Sushi *Japanese* ▽ 23 | 20 | 18 | £58

Kensington | 1A Argyll Rd., W8 (High St. Kensington) | 020-7938-1536 |
www.yashinsushi.com

From the lack of soy sauce to miso soup served in teacups to "cosy"
Victorian butcher-shop decor, this "lively" Kensington Japanese is
"nontraditional" to the nth degree, and its similarly "creative", "skil-
ful" take on sushi features "unique toppings" (garlic sauce, ponzu
jelly) that often work "spectacularly"; with mostly "competent
staff", the only real complaint is that it's "too expensive."

☑ Yauatcha ● *Chinese* 25 | 23 | 19 | £50

Soho | 15 Broadwick St., W1 (Piccadilly Circus) | 020-7494-8888 |
www.yauatcha.com

In this "dark", "stylish", "sexy" downstairs "scene", the "beautiful
people" of Soho dig into "meticulously made", "divine" dim sum
("don't miss the venison puffs") "under the watchful eye" of the
"goldfish and miniature carp" that live in the fish tank – but "keep
track of the number of dishes" you order, as the "cost spirals up-
wards quickly", especially when adding in the "stunning cocktails";
don't expect any sugar from sometimes "surly" staff, but count on a
high from the "tempting pastries", available in the "airier", "less
noisy" upstairs tearoom.

Ye Olde Cheshire Cheese *British* 13 | 22 | 15 | £24

City | 145 Fleet St., EC4 (Blackfriars) | 020-7353-6170

"First-time visitors to London" ramble through the "dark, narrow"
"rabbit warren of rooms" that comprise this "timeless" pub that's
been pulling pints in the City since 1667 ("you can still sit where
Dickens sat"); unfortunately, when it comes to the Traditional
English grub, critics contend that "tourism has trumped taste", with
"cheap", "mass-produced" eats that might be best eschewed in
favour of the "famous British beers."

Yming ●☒ *Chinese* ▽ 25 | 17 | 26 | £35

Soho | 35-36 Greek St., W1 (Leicester Sq.) | 020-7734-2721 |
www.yminglondon.com

"Fantastic" management and staff treat even newcomers "like old
friends" at this Soho "standby" serving "wonderful", "aromatic"
Chinese fare that's more "interesting" – if a touch more expensive –
than the usual "Chinatown standards"; the blue-heavy, colour-
splashed setting is as suited to "pre-theatre" snackers looking to eat
and run and "groups" who'd just as soon linger.

Yo! Sushi *Japanese* 16 | 13 | 15 | £25

Knightsbridge | Harrods 102 | 102-104 Brompton Rd., SW
(Knightsbridge) | 020-7841-0742

Knightsbridge | Harvey Nichols | 109-125 Knightsbridge, 5th fl., SW1
(Knightsbridge) | 020-7201-8641

Marylebone | Selfridges | 400 Oxford St., ground fl., W1 (Bond St.) |
020-7318-3944

Mayfair | Sedley Pl. | 15 Woodstock St., W1 (Bond St.) | 020-7629-0051

(continued)

(continued)

Yo! Sushi

Soho | 52 Poland St., W1 (Oxford Circus) | 020-7287-0443
Westminster | County Hall | 3 Belvedere Rd., SE1 (Westminster) |
020-7928-8871
Farringdon | 95 Farringdon Rd., EC1 (Farringdon) | 020-7841-0785
Fulham | Fulham Broadway Ctr. | 472 Fulham Rd., 1st fl., SW6
(Fulham Broadway) | 020-7385-6077
Bayswater | Whiteleys Shopping Ctr. | 151 Queensway, W2
(Bayswater) | 020-7727-9392
Paddington | The Lawn | Paddington Station, W2 (Paddington) |
020-7262-7408
www.yosushi.com
Additional locations throughout London

"Kids never tire" of this "hectic" "robo-sushi chain" where small
Japanese plates "twirl and whirl" around conveyor belts amidst decor "designed to draw your attention away from" how "mediocre"
the fare is and how "quickly" it all "adds up"; still, it's "yo-kay" for a
"lightning-fast" refuel; P.S. a branch is slated for Westfield Stratford
City, the new shopping centre across from the Olympic Park.

York & Albany *European*

`21` `21` `20` `£47`

Camden Town | 127-129 Pkwy., NW1 (Camden Town) |
020-7388-3344 | www.gordonramsay.com
The "muted-toned" but "bustling" street-level bar of this all-day
Modern European in Camden offers "carefully prepared" gastropub
grub, whilst the "less-noisy", ruby-hued downstairs restaurant does
"solid" bistro fare; as is par for the course with a Ramsay property,
there are grumblers who grouse that it's "unexciting for what it is,
and overpriced" to boot, though there are "good-value" set menus.

Yoshino ⓈJapanese

`22` `16` `22` `£31`

Piccadilly | 3 Piccadilly Pl., W1 (Piccadilly Circus) | 020-7287-6622 |
www.yoshino.net
Perhaps "the best value-to-quality ratio for sushi" in Piccadilly is found
at this "simple", "tiny" "treasure"; in fact, all of the Japanese dishes
are "delicious" and "affordable", and "friendly service" is a bonus.

ⓏZafferano *Italian*

`26` `22` `23` `£67`

Belgravia | 15 Lowndes St., SW1 (Knightsbridge) | 020-7235-5800 |
www.zafferanorestaurant.com
It's "always fun to be a part of the action" at this "busy", brick-walled,
"old-school" Italian where "well-heeled", "colourful" Belgravians go
for "a warm welcome" and "tempting", "terrific" tastes accompanied by "impressive" wines and "professional" service; it all comes
at "special-occasion" prices, but many are "willing to pay for the
quality", thus, it's "difficult to get a reservation."

Zaika *Indian*

`25` `22` `22` `£55`

Kensington | 1 Kensington High St., W8 (High St. Kensington) |
020-7795-6533 | www.zaika-restaurant.co.uk
"Wonderful spices" are "used to glorious effect" at this "contemporary" Kensington "temple to haute cuisine, Indian style", where

"knowledgeable, attentive" staff can recommend "fresh wine pairings"; set in a former bank, the space is rife with "massive marble columns", "high ceilings, rich tapestries and South Asian sculpture", and whilst some suppers say you need to "take out a loan for dinner", day-timers deem the set lunch menu "a great deal."

Zayna ● Indian/Pakistani
∇ 24 | 16 | 22 | £41

Marylebone | 25 New Quebec St., W1 (Marble Arch) | 020-7723-2229 | www.zaynarestaurant.co.uk

The "understated" carved-wood-filled setting belies the "quality" in both the "visually interesting", "delicious" dishes ("seasoned well" with spices ground in-house) and the "hospitable service" at this North Indian–Pakistani place "near Marble Arch"; it seems to have been recently "discovered", making it "harder to get a table as a walk-in", but however desperate you are, insiders recommend avoiding the "dungeon."

Ziani ● Italian
24 | 17 | 21 | £45

Chelsea | 45 Radnor Walk, SW3 (Sloane Sq.) | 020-7351-5297 | www.ziani.co.uk

Follow the "beautiful crowd" to this "hustling, bustling" Chelsea "standby" of "Sloane" "ladies who lunch" for "well-prepared" Venetian victuals that are "not cheap" but "consistent"; on the downside, with "the next table right on top of you", there's "not a lot of privacy", plus service seems to "rush you in and out", albeit in a "friendly" manner.

Zilli Fish ☒ Italian/Seafood
20 | 13 | 16 | £40

Soho | 36-40 Brewer St., W1 (Piccadilly Circus) | 020-7734-8649 | www.zillialdo.com

Aldo Zilli's Italian-influenced Soho "staple" suits a "pre- or post-theatre" dinner (lunch is served too) of "simple", "tasty", "fairly priced" seafood, which is ferried by largely "amiable" staff; but while the cream decor, complete with a giant fish tank, is "bright", it's definitely "time for an update."

Zilli Green Italian/Vegetarian
∇ 19 | 16 | 18 | £30

Soho | 41 Dean St., W1 (Tottenham Court Rd.) | 020-7734-3924 | www.zillirestaurants.co.uk

Even "meat lovers" approve of this "friendly", affordable Soho vegetarian where chef Aldo Zilli prepares an "interesting range" of dishes, including some "great vegan choices", with Italian flair; the eco-chic interior is garnished with "blond wood" that "makes the space feel larger than it is", although sensitive bods say the chairs are "great for green, but not for your butt."

Zizzi Pizza
15 | 15 | 15 | £24

Bloomsbury | 33-41 Charlotte St., W1 (Goodge St.) | 020-7436-9440
Covent Garden | 20 Bow St., WC2 (Covent Garden) | 020-7836-6101 ●
Covent Garden | 73-75 The Strand, WC2 (Charing Cross) | 020-7240-1717 ●
Marylebone | 110-116 Wigmore St., W1U (Bond St.) | 020-7935-2336
Marylebone | 35-38 Paddington St., W1U (Baker St.) | 020-7224-1450

(continued)

(continued)

Zizzi

Victoria | Cardinal Walk, Unit 15, SW1 (Victoria) | 020-7821-0402
Finchley | 202-208 Regents Park Rd., N3 (Finchley Central) |
020-8371-6777
Highgate | 1-3 Hampstead Ln., N6 (Highgate) | 020-8347-0090
Earl's Court | 194-196 Earl's Court Rd., SW5 (Earl's Ct.) | 020-7370-1999
Chiswick | 231 Chiswick High Rd., W4 (Chiswick Park) | 020-8747-9400
www.zizzi.co.uk
Additional locations throughout London

"Reasonably priced" "pizza and pasta basics" mean this "omnipres-ent" Italian chain "appeals to families" with "kids" and "groups of friends"; just "don't expect too much" – the fare is "ho-hum", the service "hit-and-miss" and the digs are "noisy" and "generic", making it ultimately "fine for refueling" but "not a place to linger."

Zucca Ⓜ *Italian*   25 | 20 | 21 | £41

Tower Bridge | 184 Bermondsey St., SE1 (London Bridge) |
020-7378-6809 | www.zuccalondon.com

"Delectable", "original" seasonal Italian cuisine from an "ex-River Café chef" is served in an "über-cool gallery"-like space of "white walls and bare concrete" at this "young" Bermondsey Street venue; "surprisingly", it's "reasonably priced", though the "smart wine list" is "more than capable of making up" the difference.

ⓩ Zuma *Japanese*   26 | 24 | 21 | £69

Knightsbridge | 5 Raphael St., SW7 (Knightsbridge) | 020-7584-1010 |
www.zumarestaurant.com

"Avant-garde sushi" is as much of a "knockout" as the rest of the "Japanese creations" at this "hip and happening, loud and lovely" Knightsbridge "zoo" that's invariably "cruelly overbooked", though walk-ins might try the robata grill or the "mosh pit" of "models, ac-tors, sports stars, rich Europeans and old men with pretty young girls" at the "glamourous" bar; wherever you "squash" in, you won't escape the sometimes "snooty" staff and their "manic table-turning", which can sting given the "high-end" prices; P.S. "if you can say 'fresh fish' three times fast, you haven't drunk enough from the excellent sake list."

INDEXES

LOCATION MAPS

Cuisines

Includes restaurant names, locations and Food ratings.

AMERICAN

All Star Lanes | **multi.**	12
Automat | **W1**	18
Big Easy | **SW3**	17
Byron | **multi.**	19
Christopher's | **WC2**	19
Eagle Bar Diner | **W1**	18
Ed's Easy Diner | **W1**	15
Hard Rock | **W1**	15
Hoxton Grill | **EC2**	18
Joe Allen | **WC2**	18
JW Steak | **W1**	21
Lucky 7 | **W2**	19
Palm | **SW1**	23
PJ's B&G | **multi.**	17
Planet Hollywood | **SW1**	12
Smollensky's | **multi.**	14
Sophie's Steak | **multi.**	19
NEW Spuntino | **W1**	-
Sticky Fingers | **W8**	15

ARGENTINEAN

Buen Ayre | **E8**	26
Constancia | **SE1**	-
El Gaucho | **multi.**	23
Z Gaucho | **multi.**	22
Santa Maria/Garufa | **multi.**	24

ASIAN

Asia de Cuba | **WC2**	21
Bam-Bou | **W1**	20
NEW Chesterfield | **W2**	-
Cocoon | **W1**	20
E&O | **W11**	22
Eight Over Eight | **SW3**	21
Gilgamesh | **NW1**	19
Great Eastern | **EC2**	20
Inamo | **multi.**	15
NEW Nopi | **W1**	-
Oxo Tower Brass. | **SE1**	19
Pacific Oriental | **EC2**	18
NEW Samarqand | **W1**	-
NEW Spice Mkt. | **W1**	22
Uli | **W11**	-
XO | **NW3**	20

BAKERIES

Baker & Spice | **multi.**	22
Ladurée | **multi.**	23

Le Pain Quot. | **multi.**	17
Ottolenghi | **multi.**	25
Princi London | **W1**	22

BARBECUE

NEW Barbecoa | **EC4**	20
Bodeans | **multi.**	19
Chicago Rib | **SW1**	15

BELGIAN

Belgo | **multi.**	19
Le Pain Quot. | **multi.**	17

BRAZILIAN

Rodizio Rico | **multi.**	15
Sushinho | **SW3**	16

BRITISH (MODERN)

Acorn Hse. | **WC1**	21
Admiral Codrington | **SW3**	19
Anchor & Hope | **SE1**	23
Anglesea Arms | **W6**	18
Annie's | **multi.**	21
Avenue | **SW1**	20
Axis | **WC2**	22
Balans | **multi.**	17
Bedford/Strand | **WC2**	18
Belvedere | **W8**	22
Bevis Marks | **EC3**	20
Bingham | **TW10**	25
Bluebird | **SW3**	16
Z Bob Bob Ricard | **W1**	20
Botanist | **SW1**	17
Bradley's | **NW3**	20
NEW Broadway B&G | **SW6**	-
Brompton B&G | **SW3**	22
Bumpkin | **multi.**	20
Cadogan Arms | **SW3**	15
Z Chez Bruce | **SW17**	27
Z Clarke's | **W8**	26
Corrigan's | **W1**	25
Cow Dining Room | **W2**	19
Dean St. | **W1**	21
Z NEW Dinner/Heston | **SW1**	27
Z Dorchester | **W1**	24
Duke of Cambridge | **N1**	-
Empress of India | **E9**	20
Engineer | **NW1**	21
Fifth Floor Cafe | **SW1**	18
Forman's Fish Island | **E3**	-

Vote at ZAGAT.com

NEW Fox/Grapes	SW19	—	Albion	N1	19
Frederick's	N1	20	Annabel's	W1	21
Gravetye Manor	RH19	—	Z Bentley's	W1	26
Great Queen St.	WC2	24	Bleeding Heart	EC1	22
Groucho Club	W1	18	Boisdale	multi.	20
Gun	E14	20	Boundary	E2	20
Z Harwood Arms	SW6	27	Browns	multi.	17
Hereford Rd.	W2	25	Builders Arms	SW3	17
Hix	W1	20	Bull & Last	NW5	23
Z Ivy	WC2	22	Butcher & Grill	multi.	17
Julie's	W11	19	Canteen	multi.	16
Just St. James's	SW1	18	Chelsea Kitchen	SW10	15
Kensington Pl.	W8	19	Cliveden Hse.	SL6	23
Kensington Sq.	W8	21	Ffiona's	W8	24
Launceston Pl.	W8	25	Fortnum's Fountain	W1	20
Z Le Caprice	SW1	23	Foxtrot Oscar	SW3	15
Luxe	E1	12	French Horn	RG4	25
Mews of Mayfair	W1	17	Frontline	W2	20
National Dining Rooms	WC2	17	NEW Gilbert Scott	NW1	—
1901	EC2	21	Goring	SW1	24
Northbank	EC4	—	Green's	multi.	22
Old Brewery	SE10	18	Grenadier	SW1	18
Paradise	W10	—	Grumbles	SW1	17
Paramount	WC1	16	NEW Henry Root	SW10	—
NEW Pollen St. Social	W1	—	Hinds Head	SL6	26
Portrait	WC2	21	Hix Oyster	EC1	23
Princess/Shoreditch	EC2	—	Hix Rest.	W1	23
Prism	EC3	18	Inn The Park	SW1	17
Quo Vadis	W1	21	Langan's Bistro	W1	21
Randall/Aubin	W1	19	Langan's Brass.	W1	19
Ransome's	SW11	19	Maggie Jones's	W8	19
NEW Restaurant/Arts	W1	—	Mall Tavern	W8	20
Roast	SE1	24	Z Mark's Club	W1	24
R.S.J.	SE1	20	Mercer	EC2	20
Seven Park	SW1	—	Milroy	W1	—
Smiths/Dining Rm.	EC1	23	Narrow	E14	21
Smiths/Top Fl.	EC1	21	Odin's	W1	21
Soho Hse.	W1	20	108 Marylebone	W1	19
Sotheby's Cafe	W1	24	Only Running	W1	19
Z St. John	EC1	26	NEW Penny Black	SW10	—
St. John Bread	E1	25	Pig's Ear	SW3	22
NEW St. John Hotel	WC2	—	Porters	WC2	15
St. Pancras	NW1	17	Princess Victoria	W12	—
Tate Britain	SW1	19	Rhodes 24	EC2	23
Tom's Kitchen	multi.	22	Richoux	multi.	17
Union Cafe	W1	19	Z Ritz	W1	25
Waterloo	SE1	18	Rivington Grill	multi.	18
Wild Honey	W1	23	Rotunda	N1	—
			Rowley's	SW1	18
BRITISH			Royal Oak	SL6	22
(TRADITIONAL)			Savoy Grill	WC2	23
Abbeville	SW4	17	Shepherd's	SW1	19
Albemarle	W1	23		

☑ Simpson's/Strand | **WC2**	22
☑ Sketch/Parlour | **W1**	23
St. James's | **W1**	23
Thomas Cubitt | **SW1**	23
Tuttons Brass. | **WC2**	16
Warrington | **W9**	16
☑ Wilton's | **SW1**	27
Ye Olde Cheshire | **EC4**	13

BURGERS

Automat | **W1**	18
Byron | **multi.**	19
Eagle Bar Diner | **W1**	18
Gourmet Burger | **multi.**	16
Haché | **multi.**	20
Hard Rock | **W1**	15
Lucky 7 | **W2**	19
Sticky Fingers | **W8**	15

CARIBBEAN

Cottons | **multi.**	-

CHINESE

(* dim sum specialist)

Barshu | **W1**	25
Ba Shan | **W1**	20
Cha Cha Moon | **W1**	16
China Tang* | **W1**	21
Chuen Cheng Ku* | **W1**	20
Dragon Castle | **SE17**	23
Empress of Sichuan | **WC2**	-
Four Seasons | **multi.**	22
Golden Dragon* | **W1**	20
Goldmine | **W2**	24
Good Earth | **multi.**	21
Green Cottage | **NW3**	22
☑ Hakkasan* | **W1**	26
Haozhan | **W1**	25
Harbour City* | **W1**	23
☑ Hunan | **SW1**	28
Imperial China* | **WC2**	18
Jenny Lo's Tea | **SW1**	19
Joy King Lau* | **WC2**	18
Kai Mayfair | **W1**	26
Mandarin Kitchen | **W2**	25
Mao Tai* | **SW6**	20
Memories/China | **multi.**	23
Min Jiang* | **W8**	23
Mr. Chow | **SW1**	22
Mr. Kong | **WC2**	22
New Culture Rev. | **multi.**	16
New World* | **W1**	18
Pearl Liang* | **W2**	23

Phoenix Palace* | **NW1**	25
Ping Pong* | **multi.**	16
Plum Valley | **W1**	21
Princess Garden* | **W1**	25
Red 'n' Hot | **WC2**	-
Royal China* | **multi.**	23
Royal China Club* | **W1**	25
Shanghai Blues* | **WC1**	22
Weng Wah House | **NW3**	-
Wong Kei | **W1**	15
☑ Yauatcha* | **W1**	25
Yming | **W1**	25

CHOPHOUSES

Black & Blue | **multi.**	19
Bountiful Cow | **WC1**	19
Butlers Wharf | **SE1**	22
Christopher's | **WC2**	19
Constancia | **SE1**	-
El Gaucho | **multi.**	23
☑ Gaucho | **multi.**	22
☑ Goodman | **multi.**	26
Green Door | **SW7**	25
Greig's | **W1**	22
Guinea Grill | **W1**	23
Hawksmoor | **multi.**	26
Hix Oyster | **EC1**	23
JW Steak | **W1**	21
Le Relais | **multi.**	23
Marco Pierre White | **E1**	19
Maze Grill | **W1**	22
Palm | **SW1**	23
Paternoster Chop | **EC4**	15
NEW Picasso | **SW3**	-
Rib Room | **SW1**	22
☑ Rules | **WC2**	23
Smollensky's | **multi.**	14
Sophie's Steak | **multi.**	19

CUBAN

Asia de Cuba | **WC2**	21

DELIS

Harry Morgan's | **multi.**	16
Reubens | **W1**	19

EASTERN EUROPEAN

NEW Verru | **W1**	-

ECLECTIC

Archipelago | **W1**	21
Blakes | **SW7**	22
NEW Bond/Brook | **W1**	-

Vote at ZAGAT.com

Roux/Parliament | **SW1**	24
NEW Roux/Landau | **W1**	–
Royal Exchange | **EC3**	15
Sam's Brass. | **W4**	20
Z Sketch/Gallery | **W1**	21
Z Sketch/Lecture | **W1**	24
Skylon | **SE1**	19
Sonny's | **SW13**	23
Tate Modern | **SE1**	18
Texture | **W1**	25
Tom Ilic | **SW8**	19
Tompkins | **E14**	–
Trinity | **SW4**	25
202 | **W11**	18
Vinoteca | **EC1**	22
Vivat Bacchus | **multi.**	19
Wapping Food | **E1**	18
Waterway | **W9**	15
Wells | **NW3**	23
Whitechapel | **E1**	18
Z Wolseley | **W1**	22
York & Albany | **NW1**	21

FISH 'N' CHIPS

Geales | **multi.**	21
Golden Hind | **W1**	25
Nautilus Fish | **NW6**	25
North Sea | **WC1**	24
Rock & Sole | **WC2**	24
Sweetings | **EC4**	23
Two Brothers Fish | **N3**	20

FRENCH

Z Alain Ducasse | **W1**	27
Almeida | **N1**	20
Annabel's | **W1**	21
NEW Antidote | **W1**	–
Auberge du Lac | **AL8**	24
Aubergine | **SL7**	24
Bellamy's | **W1**	23
Belvedere | **W8**	22
Z Bibendum | **SW3**	23
Bleeding Heart | **EC1**	22
Bonds | **EC2**	21
Boundary | **E2**	20
Bradley's | **NW3**	20
NEW Brawn | **E2**	23
Brula | **TW1**	–
Café des Amis | **WC2**	18
Z Capital Restaurant | **SW3**	26
NEW Cassis Bistro | **SW3**	25
Cellar Gascon | **EC1**	24
NEW Cigalon | **WC2**	–

Cliveden Hse. | **SL6**	23
Z Clos Maggiore | **WC2**	24
Z Club Gascon | **EC1**	26
Coq d'Argent | **EC2**	20
Elena's L'Etoile | **W1**	19
Z Espelette | **W1**	24
French Horn | **RG4**	25
French Table | **KT6**	–
Galvin at Windows | **W1**	24
Galvin La Chapelle | **E1**	25
Gauthier | **W1**	24
Z Gordon Ramsay/68 | **SW3**	28
Greenhouse | **W1**	26
Z Hélène Darroze | **W1**	24
Hibiscus | **W1**	26
Incognico | **WC2**	19
Z NEW Koffmann's | **SW1**	26
Ladurée | **multi.**	23
Langan's Bistro | **W1**	21
Z L'Atelier/Robuchon | **WC2**	27
Z La Trompette | **W4**	26
L'Aventure | **NW8**	26
Le Cercle | **SW1**	25
Z Ledbury | **W11**	29
Z Le Gavroche | **W1**	28
Z Le Manoir/Quat | **OX4**	28
Le Mercury | **N1**	19
Le Pont/Tour | **SE1**	21
Le Relais | **multi.**	23
L'Escargot | **W1**	22
NEW Les Deux | **WC2**	19
Les Trois Garçons | **E1**	20
Le Suquet | **SW3**	23
L'Etranger | **SW7**	24
Z L'Oranger | **SW1**	27
Lutyens | **EC4**	23
Z Marcus Wareing | **SW1**	27
Z Mark's Club | **W1**	24
Maze | **W1**	24
Morgan M | **N7**	26
My Dining Room | **SW6**	–
NEW Nottingdale | **W11**	–
Odin's | **W1**	21
1 Lombard | **EC3**	22
One-O-One | **SW1**	22
Orrery | **W1**	25
Z Oslo Court | **NW8**	26
Pearl | **WC1**	26
Petrus | **SW1**	25
Z Pied à Terre | **W1**	28
Plateau | **E14**	19
Poissonnerie | **SW3**	22

Vote at ZAGAT.com

Rhodes W1 | **W1** 24
🎦 Ritz | **W1** 25
🎦 Roussillon | **SW1** 26
Sauterelle | **EC3** 18
Savoy Grill | **WC2** 23
Savoy River | **WC2** 21
Seven Park | **SW1** -
🎦 Square | **W1** 27
Tom Aikens | **SW3** 25
Villandry | **W1** 19
Wallace | **W1** 17
🎦 Waterside Inn | **SL6** 28

FRENCH (BISTRO)

Aubaine | **multi.** 17
🎦 Bar Boulud | **SW1** 25
Bedford/Strand | **WC2** 18
Bibendum Oyster | **SW3** 24
Bistrot Bruno Loubet | **EC1** 23
Bistrotheque | **E2** 23
Café Boheme | **W1** 18
Café Rouge | **multi.** 15
🎞 Chabrot | **SW1** -
Comptoir Gascon | **EC1** 22
Ebury Wine | **SW1** 18
Galvin Bistrot | **W1** 24
Grumbles | **SW1** 17
La Bouchée | **SW7** 19
'Absinthe | **NW1** 21
La Poule au Pot | **SW1** 21
Le Boudin Blanc | **W1** 24
Le Café/Marché | **EC1** 24
Le Colombier | **SW3** 24
Le Vacherin | **W4** 23
Mon Plaisir | **WC2** 18
Patisserie Valerie | **multi.** 16
Truc Vert | **W1** 19
🎞 28-50 Wine | **EC4** 22

FRENCH (BRASSERIE)

Angelus | **W2** 23
Brasserie Blanc | **EC2** 20
🎞 Brasserie Joël | **SE1** -
Brasserie Roux | **SW1** 22
Brass. St. Jacques | **SW1** 21
Cheyne Walk | **SW3** 21
Chez Gérard | **multi.** 17
Côte | **multi.** 17
Kettner's | **W1** 16
La Brasserie | **SW3** 19
Langan's Brass. | **W1** 19
Le Bouchon | **E1** 16

Le Café Anglais | **W2** 22
Luc's Brasserie | **EC3** -
Pig's Ear | **SW3** 22
Racine | **SW3** 23
Tuttons Brass. | **WC2** 16

GASTROPUB

Abbeville | British/Euro. | **SW4** 17
Abingdon | Euro. | **W8** 20
Admiral Codrington | British/Euro. | **SW3** 19
Albion | British | **N1** 19
Anchor & Hope | British | **SE1** 23
Anglesea Arms | British | **W6** 18
🎞 Broadway B&G | British | **SW6** -
Builders Arms | British | **SW3** 17
Bull & Last | British | **NW5** 23
Cadogan Arms | British | **SW3** 15
Cow Dining Room | British | **W2** 19
Cross Keys | Euro. | **SW3** 17
Duke of Cambridge | British | **N1** -
Eagle | Med. | **EC1** 22
Empress of India | British | **E9** 20
Engineer | British | **NW1** 21
Enterprise | Eclectic | **SW3** 20
🎞 Fox/Grapes | British | **SW19** -
Great Queen St. | British | **WC2** 24
Gun | British | **E14** 20
🎦 Harwood Arms | British | **SW6** 27
Lansdowne | Euro. | **NW1** 21
Mall Tavern | British | **W8** 20
Narrow | British | **E14** 21
Only Running | British | **W1** 19
Orange | Euro. | **SW1** 22
Paradise | British | **W10** -
🎞 Phene | Euro. | **SW3** 13
Pig's Ear | British/French | **SW3** 22
🎞 Portman | Euro. | **W1** -
Princess/Shoreditch | British | **EC2** -
Princess Victoria | British | **W12** -
Royal Oak | British | **SL6** 22
Thomas Cubitt | British | **SW1** 23
Warrington | British | **W9** 16
Waterway | Euro. | **W9** 15
Wells | Euro. | **NW3** 23
Westbourne | Eclectic | **W2** 15
York & Albany | Euro. | **NW1** 21

GREEK

Carob Tree | **NW5** -
Halepi | **W2** 21
Lemonia | **NW1** 19
Real Greek | **multi.** 14

HUNGARIAN

Gay Hussar	**W1**	21

INDIAN

☑ Amaya	**SW1**	26
Benares	**W1**	23
Bengal Clipper	**SE1**	23
Bombay Bicycle	**multi.**	18
Bombay Brass.	**SW7**	23
Bombay Palace	**W2**	21
Café Spice	**E1**	25
Chor Bizarre	**W1**	23
Chowki	**W1**	20
Chutney Mary	**SW10**	23
☑ Cinnamon Club	**SW1**	25
Cinnamon Kitchen	**EC2**	23
Colony	**W1**	21
NEW Dishoom	**WC2**	23
Gopal's	**W1**	22
Haandi	**SW7**	-
Hot Stuff	**SW8**	24
Imli	**W1F**	17
NEW Indian Zilla	**SW13**	-
Indian Zing	**W6**	24
Khan's	**W2**	18
Khan's/Kensington	**SW7**	19
La Porte/Indes	**W1**	22
Malabar	**W8**	20
Malabar Junction	**WC1**	19
Masala Zone	**multi.**	19
Mela	**WC2**	21
Mint Leaf	**SW1**	22
Moti Mahal	**WC2**	25
Noor Jahan	**multi.**	20
Painted Heron	**SW1**	24
Quilon	**SW1**	26
Rasa	**multi.**	24
☑ Rasoi Vineet Bhatia	**SW3**	26
Red Fort	**W1**	24
Star of India	**SW5**	25
☑ Tamarind	**W1**	25
Trishna	**W1**	26
Veeraswamy	**W1**	24
Zaika	**W8**	25
Zayna	**W1**	24

ITALIAN

A Cena	**TW1**	23
Aglio e Olio	**SW10**	21
Alberico at Aspinall's	**W1**	24
Al Duca	**SW1**	19
Alloro	**W1**	21
NEW Amaranto	**W1**	-

Antonio's Ristorante	**N1**	-
Apsleys	**SW1**	25
Ark	**W8**	21
Armani Caffé	**SW3**	19
Artigiano	**NW3**	21
Ask Pizza	**multi.**	15
Assaggi	**W2**	26
Babbo	**W1**	22
Bertorelli	**multi.**	17
Bocca/Gelupo	**W1**	24
Buona Sera	**multi.**	-
Caffe Caldesi	**W1**	21
Cantina/Ponte	**SE1**	20
NEW Cantinetta	**SW15**	-
Caraffini	**SW1**	21
Caravaggio	**EC3**	19
Carluccio's	**multi.**	17
NEW Casa Batavia	**W8**	-
Cecconi's	**W1**	23
Ciro's Pizza	**SW3**	13
Citrus	**W1**	-
C London	**W1**	21
Como Lario	**SW1**	21
Da Mario	**SW7**	20
Daphne's	**SW3**	21
NEW Da Polpo	**WC2**	-
Dehesa	**W1**	24
Delfino	**W1**	21
Dolada	**W1**	-
NEW Dragoncello	**W2**	-
Elena's L'Etoile	**W1**	19
NEW Eleven Park Walk	**SW10**	-
Elistano	**SW3**	17
Enoteca Turi	**SW15**	25
Fifteen	**N1**	21
NEW 5 Pollen St.	**W1**	-
Franco's	**SW1**	22
Frankie's	**multi.**	15
Getti	**multi.**	15
Giovanni's	**WC2**	23
Harry's Bar	**W1**	23
Il Baretto	**W1**	23
Il Bordello	**E1**	25
Il Convivio	**SW1**	24
NEW Ilia	**SW3**	-
Il Portico	**W8**	23
Incognico	**WC2**	19
Jamie's Italian	**multi.**	19
Kitchen Italia	**multi.**	14
La Famiglia	**SW10**	22
La Genova	**W1**	25
L'Anima	**EC2**	25

La Porchetta | **multi.** — 19
Latium | **W1** — 24
🛛 Locanda Locatelli | **W1** — 25
Locanda Ottoemezzo | **W8** — 25
Lucio | **SW3** — 24
Made in Italy | **SW3** — 20
Manicomio | **multi.** — 15
Mediterraneo | **W11** — 22
Mennula | **W1** — 26
Montpeliano | **SW7** — 16
Mulberry St. | **W2** — 16
NEW Nottingdale | **W11** — -
Oliveto | **SW1** — 24
Olivo | **SW1** — 23
Olivomare | **SW1** — 24
NEW Opera Tavern | **WC2** — -
Orso | **WC2** — 21
Osteria Basilico | **W11** — 25
Osteria Dell'Angolo | **SW1** — 22
Osteria dell'Arancio | **SW10** — 19
Pellicano | **SW3** — 19
Pescatori | **W1** — 22
Pizza Express | **multi.** — 16
NEW Polpetto | **W1** — 22
Polpo | **W1** — 23
Princi London | **W1** — 22
Quadrato | **E14** — 22
Quirinale | **SW1** — 23
Red Pepper | **W9** — 23
Refettorio | **EC4** — 21
Riccardo's | **SW3** — 16
🛛 River Café | **W6** — 27
Rocca | **multi.** — -
Sale e Pepe | **SW1** — 21
Salt Yard | **W1** — 23
San Lorenzo | **multi.** — 21
Santini | **SW1** — 26
Sardo | **W1** — 22
Sardo Canale | **NW1** — 19
Sartoria | **W1** — 22
Scalini | **SW3** — 23
Semplice Bar | **W1** — 21
Semplice Rist. | **W1** — 23
Signor Sassi | **SW1** — 21
NEW Spuntino | **W1** — -
Strada | **multi.** — 16
NEW Tempo | **W1** — -
Tentazioni | **SE1** — 24
Theo Randall | **W1** — 23
Timo | **W8** — 22
NEW Tinello | **SW1** — 24
Toto's | **SW3** — 23

NEW Trullo | **N1** — 19
2 Veneti | **W1** — 21
Vapiano | **W1** — 17
Vasco & Piero's | **W1** — 24
NEW Venosi | **SW3** — -
🛛 Zafferano | **SW1** — 26
Ziani | **SW3** — 24
Zilli Fish | **W1** — 20
Zilli Green | **W1** — 19
Zizzi | **multi.** — 15
Zucca | **SE1** — 25

JAPANESE
(* sushi specialist)
Abeno | **multi.** — 22
Aqua Kyoto* | **W1** — 20
Benihana | **multi.** — 17
Bincho Yakitori | **W1** — 22
🛛 Café Japan* | **NW11** — 27
Chisou* | **W1** — 22
🛛 Defune* | **W1** — 26
🛛 Dinings* | **W1** — 28
Feng Sushi* | **multi.** — 17
Ikeda* | **W1** — 28
Inaho* | **W2** — 25
Itsu* | **multi.** — 16
Jin Kichi* | **NW3** — 26
🛛 Kiku* | **W1** — 27
Koi* | **W8** — 25
NEW Koya | **W1** — 23
Kulu Kulu* | **multi.** — 22
L'Etranger | **SW7** — 24
Matsuri* | **SW1** — 24
🛛 Miyama* | **multi.** — 26
🛛 Nobu Berkeley* | **W1** — 25
🛛 Nobu London* | **W1** — 27
Nozomi* | **SW3** — 21
🛛 Roka* | **multi.** — 26
Sake No Hana* | **SW1** — 23
Sakura* | **W1** — 19
Soseki* | **EC3** — -
Sumosan* | **W1** — 25
Sushinho* | **SW3** — 16
Ten Ten Tei* | **W1** — -
Tokyo Diner* | **WC2** — -
Tsunami* | **multi.** — 25
Tsuru* | **multi.** — -
🛛 Umu* | **W1** — 26
🛛 Wagamama | **multi.** — 19
NEW Yashin Sushi* | **W8** — 23
Yo! Sushi* | **multi.** — 16
Yoshino* | **W1** — 22
🛛 Zuma* | **SW7** — 26

CUISINES

JEWISH

Bevis Marks | **EC3**	20
Gaby's | **WC2**	22
Harry Morgan's | **multi.**	16
Reubens | **W1**	19
Solly's | **NW11**	18

KOREAN

Asadal | **WC1**	22

KOSHER/ KOSHER-STYLE

Bevis Marks | **EC3**	20
Reubens | **W1**	19
Solly's | **NW11**	18

LEBANESE

Al Hamra | **W1**	23
Al Sultan | **W1**	23
Al Waha | **W2**	24
Comptoir Libanais | **multi.**	17
Fairuz | **W1**	22
Fakhreldine | **W1**	20
Ishbilia | **SW1**	25
Maroush | **multi.**	22
Noura | **multi.**	21
Yalla Yalla | **W1**	21

MALAYSIAN

Awana | **SW3**	19
Champor | **SE1**	22
Singapore Gdn. | **multi.**	19

MEDITERRANEAN

Baker & Spice | **multi.**	22
Cafe Med | **NW8**	17
Cantina Vino. | **SE1**	18
Carob Tree | **NW5**	-
Del'Aziz | **multi.**	16
Eagle | **EC1**	22
Fifth Floor Cafe | **SW1**	18
Franco's | **SW1**	22
French Table | **KT6**	-
Jak's | **SW3**	22
Z La Petite Maison | **W1**	27
Leon | **multi.**	17
NEW Massimo | **SW1**	-
Morton's | **W1**	23
Ottolenghi | **multi.**	25
Oxo Tower Brass. | **SE1**	19
NEW Quince | **W1**	-
Raoul's | **multi.**	18
Rocket | **multi.**	20

Terroirs | **WC2**	23
Union Cafe | **W1**	19

MEXICAN

Benito's Hat | **W1**	19
Cafe Pacifico | **WC2**	19
NEW Cantina Laredo | **WC2**	-
Z Chilango | **multi.**	22
Crazy Homies | **W2**	18
El Camion | **multi.**	-
Mestizo | **NW1**	22
Taqueria | **W11**	20
Wahaca | **multi.**	20

MIDDLE EASTERN

Gaby's | **WC2**	22
NEW Nopi | **W1**	-
Solly's | **NW11**	18

MOROCCAN

Momo | **W1**	21
Original Tagines | **W1**	-
Pasha | **SW7**	18

NOODLE SHOPS

NEW Koya | **W1**	23
New Culture Rev. | **multi.**	16
Z Wagamama | **multi.**	19

NORTH AFRICAN

Del'Aziz | **multi.**	16
NEW Morito | **EC1**	26
Moro | **EC1**	26

PAKISTANI

Original Lahore | **multi.**	25
Salloos | **SW1**	24
Z Tayyabs | **E1**	26
Zayna | **W1**	24

PAN-LATIN

Floridita | **W1**	13

PERSIAN

Alounak | **multi.**	21

PERUVIAN

Z Nobu Berkeley | **W1**	25
Z Nobu London | **W1**	27

PIZZA

Ask Pizza | **multi.**	15
Buona Sera | **multi.**	-

Vote at ZAGAT.com

Ciro's Pizza | **SW3** 13
Delfino | **W1** 21
Franco Manca | **multi.** 24
La Porchetta | **multi.** 19
Made in Italy | **multi.** 20
Mulberry St. | **W2** 16
Oliveto | **SW1** 24
Osteria Basilico | **W11** 25
Pizza East | **multi.** 20
Pizza Express | **multi.** 16
Red Pepper | **W9** 23
Rocket | **multi.** 20
Strada | **multi.** 16
Zizzi | **multi.** 15

POLISH

Baltic | **SE1** 23
Gessler/Daquise | **SW7** -
Wòdka | **W8** 21

PORTUGUESE

Eyre Brothers | **EC2** 24
Nando's | **multi.** 16

SANDWICHES

Napket | **multi.** 14

SCANDINAVIAN

Madsen | **SW7** 16
NEW Verru | **W1** -

SCOTTISH

Albannach | **WC2** 16
Boisdale | **multi.** 20

SEAFOOD

🔒 Bentley's | **W1** 26
Bibendum Oyster | **SW3** 24
Christopher's | **WC2** 19
Fish | **SE1** 19
FishWorks | **multi.** 18
Geales | **multi.** 21
Golden Hind | **W1** 25
Green's | **multi.** 22
Hix Oyster | **EC1** 23
🔒 J. Sheekey | **WC2** 26
🔒 J. Sheekey Oyster | **WC2** 26
Le Pont/Tour | **SE1** 21
Le Suquet | **SW3** 23
Livebait | **multi.** 17
Loch Fyne | **multi.** 19
Mandarin Kitchen | **W2** 25

Nautilus Fish | **NW6** 25
North Sea | **WC1** 24
Olivomare | **SW1** 24
One-O-One | **SW1** 22
Pescatori | **W1** 22
Poissonnerie | **SW3** 22
Randall/Aubin | **W1** 19
Rock & Sole | **WC2** 24
🔒 Scott's | **W1** 27
Sweetings | **EC4** 23
Two Brothers Fish | **N3** 20
Wheeler's | **SW1** 21
🔒 Wilton's | **SW1** 27
Wright Brothers | **multi.** 26
Zilli Fish | **W1** 20

SINGAPOREAN

Singapore Gdn. | **multi.** 19

SMALL PLATES

(See also Spanish tapas specialist)
🔒 Amaya | Indian | **SW1** 26
NEW Bar Battu | Euro. | **EC2** -
Bocca/Gelupo | Italian | **W1** 24
NEW Bond/Brook | Eclectic | **W1** -
NEW Brawn | British | **E2** 23
Caravan | Euro. | **EC1** 22
Cellar Gascon | French | **EC1** 24
🔒 Club Gascon | French | **EC1** 26
NEW Da Polpo | Italian | **WC2** -
🔒 Dinings | Japanese | **W1** 28
NEW Henry Root | British/Euro. | -
  SW10
🔒 Hunan | Chinese | **SW1** 28
Imli | Indian | **W1F** 17
Kensington Wine | Euro. | **W8** 19
🔒 L'Atelier/Robuchon | French | 27
  WC2
Le Cercle | French | **SW1** 25
Maze | French | **W1** 24
NEW Polpetto | Italian | **W1** 22
Polpo | Italian | **W1** 23
Providores | Eclectic | **W1** 25
Real Greek | Greek | **multi.** 14
NEW Spuntino | Amer./Italian | -
  W1
Terroirs | Med. | **WC2** 23

SOUTH AFRICAN

NEW Shaka Zulu | **NW1** -

SOUTH AMERICAN

Sabor | **N1** -

SPANISH

(* tapas specialist)

Angels & Gypsies* | **SE5**	-
Aqua Nueva* | **W1**	19
Barrafina* | **W1**	26
Barrica* | **W1**	-
Brindisa* | **multi.**	23
Cambio de Tercio | **SW5**	23
Camino* | **multi.**	19
Cigala* | **WC1**	20
Dehesa* | **W1**	24
El Parador | **NW1**	-
El Pirata* | **multi.**	20
Eyre Brothers | **EC2**	24
Fino* | **W1**	24
Galicia* | **W10**	20
Iberica* | **W1**	-
NEW José* | **SE1**	-
Meson Don Felipe* | **SE1**	21
NEW Morito* | **EC1**	26
Moro* | **EC1**	26
NEW Opera Tavern* | **WC2**	-
Pinchito Tapas* | **multi.**	-
Pix Pintxos* | **multi.**	16
Salt Yard* | **W1**	23
Tendido Cero* | **SW5**	23
Tendido Cuatro* | **SW6**	-

TAIWANESE

Leong's Legend | **multi.**	23

TEAROOM

☒ Sketch/Parlour | **W1**	23

TEX-MEX

Texas Embassy | **SW1**	12

THAI

Bangkok | **SW7**	21
Blue Elephant | **SW6**	21
☒ Busaba Eathai | **multi.**	23
Churchill Arms | **W8**	21
Crazy Bear | **multi.**	19
Esarn Kheaw | **W12**	-
Mango Tree | **SW1**	21
Nahm | **SW1**	25
Patara | **multi.**	24
Pepper Tree | **SW4**	-
Som Tam House | **W12**	-
Sri Nam | **E14**	-
Thai Sq. | **multi.**	19

TURKISH

Efes | **W1**	20
Gallipoli | **N1**	21
Haz | **multi.**	19
Ishtar | **W1**	20
Kazan | **SW1**	20
Özer | **W1**	20
Pasha | **N1**	20
Sofra | **multi.**	19
Tas | **multi.**	21

UZBEKI

NEW Samarqand | **W1**	-

VEGETARIAN

(* vegan)

Food for Thought | **WC2**	22
☒ Gate | **W6**	26
Morgan M | **N7**	26
Rasa | **multi.**	24
☒ Roussillon | **SW1**	26
Saf* | **multi.**	20
222 Veggie Vegan* | **W14**	21
Zilli Green | **W1**	19

VIETNAMESE

Cây Tre | **multi.**	22
Mien Tay | **multi.**	19
Pho | **multi.**	20
Song Que | **E2**	23
Viet Grill | **E2**	22
Viet Hoa | **E2**	21

Locations

Includes names, cuisines, Food ratings and, for locations that are mapped, top list with map coordinates.

Central London

BELGRAVIA

(See map on page 210)

TOP FOOD

Marcus Wareing	French	**A9**	27
Koffmann's	French	**A9**	26
Zafferano	Italian	**B9**	26
Amaya	Indian	**B9**	26
Apsleys	Italian	**A10**	25

LISTING

☑ Amaya	Indian	26
Apsleys	Italian	25
Baker & Spice	Bakery/Med.	22
Boisdale	British/Scottish	20
Ebury Wine	Euro./French	18
Grenadier	British	18
Il Convivio	Italian	24
Ishbilia	Lebanese	25
Jenny Lo's Tea	Chinese	19
☑ NEW Koffmann's	French	26
☑ Marcus Wareing	French	27
Memories/China	Chinese	23
☑ Mosimann's	Eclectic	23
Motcombs	Eclectic	21
Nahm	Thai	25
Noura	Lebanese	21
Oliveto	Italian	24
Olivomare	Italian/Seafood	24
Ottolenghi	Bakery/Med.	25
Palm	Amer./Chops	23
Pantechnicon Rooms	Euro.	20
Patisserie Valerie	French	16
Petrus	French	25
Rib Room	Chops	22
Salloos	Pakistani	24
Santini	Italian	26
Thomas Cubitt	British	23
☑ Zafferano	Italian	26

BLOOMSBURY

Abeno	Japanese	22
All Star Lanes	Amer.	12
Archipelago	Eclectic	21
Ask Pizza	Italian	15
Bam-Bou	Asian	20
Barrica	Spanish	-
Benito's Hat	Mex.	19

Black & Blue	Chops	19
☑ Busaba Eathai	Thai	23
Carluccio's	Italian	17
Chez Gérard	French	17
Cigala	Spanish	20
Crazy Bear	Thai	19
Eagle Bar Diner	Amer.	18
Efes	Turkish	20
Elena's L'Etoile	French/Italian	19
Fino	Spanish	24
☑ Hakkasan	Chinese	26
Latium	Italian	24
Malabar Junction	Indian	19
Mennula	Italian	26
Nando's	Portug.	16
North Sea	Seafood	24
Pescatori	Italian/Seafood	22
Pho	Viet.	20
☑ Pied à Terre	French	28
Pinchito Tapas	Spanish	-
Ping Pong	Chinese	16
Rasa	Indian	24
NEW Riding Hse. Café	Euro.	-
☑ Roka	Japanese	26
Salt Yard	Italian/Spanish	23
Sardo	Italian	22
Tas	Turkish	21
Tsunami	Japanese	25
Villandry	French	19
☑ Wagamama	Japanese	19
Zizzi	Pizza	15

CHINATOWN

(See map on page 209)

TOP FOOD

Haozhan	Chinese	**C7**	25
Leong's Legend	Taiwanese	**C7**	23
Four Seasons	Chinese	**C7**	22

LISTING

Chuen Cheng Ku	Chinese	20
Empress of Sichuan	Chinese	-
Four Seasons	Chinese	22
Golden Dragon	Chinese	20
Haozhan	Chinese	25
Harbour City	Chinese	23
Imperial China	Chinese	18
Joy King Lau	Chinese	18

L O C A T I O N S

Leong's Legend	*Taiwanese*	23
Mr. Kong	*Chinese*	22
New World	*Chinese*	18
Plum Valley	*Chinese*	21
Red 'n' Hot	*Chinese*	-
NEW Spice Mkt.	*Asian*	22
Tokyo Diner	*Japanese*	-
Wong Kei	*Chinese*	15

COVENT GARDEN

(See map on page 209)

TOP FOOD

L'Atelier/Robuchon	*French*	**B8**	27
Hawksmoor	*Chops*	**B9**	26
J. Sheekey Oyster	*Seafood*	**C8**	26
J. Sheekey	*Seafood*	**C8**	26
Moti Mahal	*Indian*	**B10**	25

LISTING

Abeno	*Japanese*	22
Asia de Cuba	*Asian/Cuban*	21
Axis	*British*	22
Bedford/Strand	*British/French*	18
Belgo	*Belgian*	19
Bertorelli	*Italian*	17
NEW Bill's Produce	*British*	20
Browns	*British*	17
Byron	*Burgers*	19
Café des Amis	*French*	18
Cafe Pacifico	*Mex.*	19
Café Rouge	*French*	15
NEW Cantina Laredo	*Mex.*	-
Carluccio's	*Italian*	17
Chez Gérard	*French*	17
Christopher's	*Amer./Chops*	19
Z Clos Maggiore	*French*	24
Côte	*French*	17
Crazy Bear	*Thai*	19
NEW Da Polpo	*Italian*	-
NEW Dishoom	*Indian*	23
Food for Thought	*Veg.*	22
Forge	*Euro.*	23
Gaby's	*Jewish/Mideast.*	22
Giovanni's	*Italian*	23
Gourmet Burger	*Burgers*	16
Great Queen St.	*British*	24
Hawksmoor	*Chops*	26
Indigo	*Euro.*	22
Z Ivy	*British/Euro.*	22
Jamie's Italian	*Italian*	19
Joe Allen	*Amer.*	18
Z J. Sheekey	*Seafood*	26

Z J. Sheekey Oyster	*Seafood*	26
Kitchen Italia	*Italian*	14
NEW Kopapa	*Eclectic*	17
Kulu Kulu	*Japanese*	22
Ladurée	*French*	23
Z L'Atelier/Robuchon	*French*	27
Le Deuxième	*Euro.*	22
Leon	*Med.*	17
NEW Les Deux	*French*	19
Livebait	*Seafood*	17
Loch Fyne	*Seafood*	19
Masala Zone	*Indian*	19
Mela	*Indian*	21
Mon Plaisir	*French*	18
Moti Mahal	*Indian*	25
Nando's	*Portug.*	16
NEW Opera Tavern	*Italian/Spanish*	-
Orso	*Italian*	21
Patisserie Valerie	*French*	16
Pix Pintxos	*Spanish*	16
Pizza Express	*Pizza*	16
PJ's B&G	*Amer.*	17
Porters	*British*	15
Real Greek	*Greek*	14
Rock & Sole	*Seafood*	24
Z Rules	*Chops*	23
Savoy Grill	*British/French*	23
Savoy River	*French*	21
Z Simpson's/Strand	*British*	22
Smollensky's	*Amer./Chops*	14
Sofra	*Turkish*	19
Sophie's Steak	*Amer./Chops*	19
Terroirs	*Med.*	23
Thai Sq.	*Thai*	19
Tom's Kitchen	*British*	22
Tuttons Brass.	*British/French*	16
Z Wagamama	*Japanese*	19
Wahaca	*Mex.*	20
Zizzi	*Pizza*	15

HOLBORN

Asadal	*Korean*	22
Bleeding Heart	*British/French*	22
Bountiful Cow	*Chops*	19
Chez Gérard	*French*	17
Z Chilango	*Mex.*	22
NEW Cigalon	*French*	-
Z Gaucho	*Argent./Chops*	22
La Porchetta	*Pizza*	19
Le Pain Quot.	*Bakery/Belgian*	17
Pearl	*French*	26
Shanghai Blues	*Chinese*	22

Strada	*Italian*	16	

LOCATIONS

Vapiano	*Italian*	17
NEW Verru	*E Euro./Scan.*	-
Vinoteca	*Euro.*	22
Z Wagamama	*Japanese*	19
Wallace	*French*	17
Yo! Sushi	*Japanese*	16
Zayna	*Indian/Pakistani*	24
Zizzi	*Pizza*	15

MAYFAIR

(See map on page 209)

TOP FOOD

Le Gavroche	*French*	**B1**	28
Square	*French*	**B4**	27
Nobu London	*Japanese*	**E2**	27
Scott's	*Seafood*	**C2**	27
Murano	*Euro.*	**D3**	27

LISTING

Z Alain Ducasse	*French*	27
Albemarle	*British*	23
Alberico at Aspinall's	*Italian*	24
Al Hamra	*Lebanese*	23
Alloro	*Italian*	21
Al Sultan	*Lebanese*	23
NEW Amaranto	*Italian*	-
Annabel's	*British/French*	21
Ask Pizza	*Italian*	15
Automat	*Amer.*	18
Babbo	*Italian*	22
Bellamy's	*French*	23
Benares	*Indian*	23
NEW Bond/Brook	*Eclectic*	-
Browns	*British*	17
Carluccio's	*Italian*	17
Cecconi's	*Italian*	23
Chez Gérard	*French*	17
China Tang	*Chinese*	21
Chisou	*Japanese*	22
Chor Bizarre	*Indian*	23
C London	*Italian*	21
Corrigan's	*British*	25
Delfino	*Italian*	21
Dolada	*Italian*	-
Z Dorchester	*British*	24
El Pirata	*Spanish*	20
Z Espelette	*French*	24
NEW 5 Pollen St.	*Italian*	-
Flemings Grill	*Euro.*	-
Galvin at Windows	*French*	24
George	*Euro.*	22
Z Goodman	*Chops*	26
Z Gordon Ramsay/Clar.	*Euro.*	25

Greenhouse	*French*	26
Greig's	*Chops*	22
Guinea Grill	*Chops*	23
Z Hakkasan	*Chinese*	26
Harry's Bar	*Italian*	23
Z Hélène Darroze	*French*	24
Hibiscus	*French*	26
Hush	*Euro.*	19
Ikeda	*Japanese*	28
JW Steak	*Amer./Chops*	21
Kai Mayfair	*Chinese*	26
Z Kiku	*Japanese*	27
La Genova	*Italian*	25
Langan's Brass.	*British/French*	19
Z La Petite Maison	*Med.*	27
Le Boudin Blanc	*French*	24
Z Le Gavroche	*French*	28
Z Mark's Club	*British/French*	24
Maze	*French*	24
Maze Grill	*Chops*	22
Mews of Mayfair	*British*	17
Milroy	*British/Euro.*	-
Z Miyama	*Japanese*	26
Morton's	*Med.*	23
Z Murano	*Euro.*	27
Napket	*Eclectic/Sandwiches*	14
Z Nobu Berkeley	*Japanese*	25
Z Nobu London	*Japanese*	27
Noura	*Lebanese*	21
Only Running	*British*	19
Patara	*Thai*	24
Patterson's	*Euro.*	24
Pescatori	*Italian/Seafood*	22
NEW Pollen St. Social	*British*	-
Princess Garden	*Chinese*	25
NEW Quince	*Med.*	-
Rasa	*Indian*	24
Richoux	*British*	17
Rocket	*Med.*	20
Sakura	*Japanese*	19
Sartoria	*Italian*	22
Z Scott's	*Seafood*	27
Semplice Bar	*Italian*	21
Semplice Rist.	*Italian*	23
Z Sketch/Gallery	*Euro.*	21
Z Sketch/Lecture	*Euro.*	24
Z Sketch/Parlour	*British*	23
Sofra	*Turkish*	19
Sotheby's Cafe	*British*	24
Z Square	*French*	27
Strada	*Italian*	16
Sumosan	*Japanese*	25

☑ Tamarind	*Indian*	25
NEW Tempo	*Italian*	-
Thai Sq.	*Thai*	19
Theo Randall	*Italian*	23
Truc Vert	*French*	19
☑ Umu	*Japanese*	26
Veeraswamy	*Indian*	24
Wild Honey	*British*	23
Yo! Sushi	*Japanese*	16

PICCADILLY

(See map on page 209)

TOP FOOD

Bentley's	*British/Seafood*	**C5**	26
Ladurée	*French*	**D5**	23
Gaucho	*Argent./Chops*	**C5**	22
Wolseley	*Euro.*	**D4**	22
Yoshino	*Japanese*	**D6**	22

LISTING

Aubaine	*French*	17
Benihana	*Japanese*	17
☑ Bentley's	*British/Seafood*	26
Chowki	*Indian*	20
Citrus	*Italian*	-
Cocoon	*Asian*	20
Criterion	*Euro.*	18
Ed's Easy Diner	*Amer.*	15
Fakhreldine	*Lebanese*	20
FishWorks	*Seafood*	18
Fortnum's Fountain	*British*	20
☑ Gaucho	*Argent./Chops*	22
Hard Rock	*Amer.*	15
Ladurée	*French*	23
Living Room	*Euro.*	-
Momo	*Moroccan*	21
Napket	*Eclectic/Sandwiches*	14
Noura	*Lebanese*	21
Patisserie Valerie	*French*	16
Planet Hollywood	*Amer.*	12
NEW Restaurant/Arts	*British*	-
☑ Wolseley	*Euro.*	22
Yoshino	*Japanese*	22

SOHO

(See map on page 209)

TOP FOOD

Barrafina	*Spanish*	**B7**	26
Wright Brothers	*Seafood*	**B5**	26
Barshu	*Chinese*	**B7**	25
Yauatcha	*Chinese*	**B6**	25
Arbutus	*Euro.*	**A7**	25

LISTING

Albannach	*Scottish*	16
Andrew Edmunds	*Euro.*	23
NEW Antidote	*French*	-
Aqua Kyoto	*Japanese*	20
Aqua Nueva	*Spanish*	19
☑ Arbutus	*Euro.*	25
Aurora	*Euro.*	-
Balans	*British*	17
Barrafina	*Spanish*	26
Barshu	*Chinese*	25
Ba Shan	*Chinese*	20
Bincho Yakitori	*Japanese*	22
☑ Bob Bob Ricard	*British*	20
Bocca/Gelupo	*Italian*	24
Bodeans	*BBQ*	19
Brindisa	*Spanish*	23
☑ Busaba Eathai	*Thai*	23
Byron	*Burgers*	19
Café Boheme	*French*	18
Cây Tre	*Viet.*	22
Cha Cha Moon	*Chinese*	16
Côte	*French*	17
Dean St.	*British*	21
Dehesa	*Italian/Spanish*	24
Ed's Easy Diner	*Amer.*	15
El Camion	*Mex.*	-
Floridita	*Pan-Latin*	13
Gauthier	*French*	24
Gay Hussar	*Hungarian*	21
Giaconda Dining Room	*Euro.*	23
Giraffe	*Eclectic*	15
Gopal's	*Indian*	22
Groucho Club	*British*	18
Hix	*British*	20
Imli	*Indian*	17
Inamo	*Asian*	15
Incognico	*French/Italian*	19
Kettner's	*French*	16
NEW Koya	*Japanese*	23
Kulu Kulu	*Japanese*	22
Leon	*Med.*	17
Le Pain Quot.	*Bakery/Belgian*	17
L'Escargot	*French*	22
Made in Italy	*Italian*	20
Masala Zone	*Indian*	19
National Dining Rooms	*British*	17
NEW Nopi	*Asian/Mideast*	-
Paramount	*British*	16
Patara	*Thai*	24
Patisserie Valerie	*French*	16
Pho	*Viet.*	20
Ping Pong	*Chinese*	16

LOCATIONS

Pizza Express	*Pizza*	16
NEW Polpetto	*Italian*	22
Polpo	*Italian*	23
Portrait	*British*	21
Princi London	*Bakery/Italian*	22
Quo Vadis	*British*	21
Randall/Aubin	*British/Seafood*	19
Red Fort	*Indian*	24
Refuel	*Euro.*	20
Soho Hse.	*British*	20
NEW Spuntino	*Amer./Italian*	-
NEW St. John Hotel	*British*	-
Ten Ten Tei	*Japanese*	-
Thai Sq.	*Thai*	19
Vasco & Piero's	*Italian*	24
Z Wagamama	*Japanese*	19
Wahaca	*Mex.*	20
Wright Brothers	*Seafood*	26
Yalla Yalla	*Lebanese*	21
Z Yauatcha	*Chinese*	25
Yming	*Chinese*	25
Yo! Sushi	*Japanese*	16
Zilli Fish	*Italian/Seafood*	20
Zilli Green	*Italian/Veg.*	19

ST. JAMES'S

(See map on page 209)

TOP FOOD

L'Oranger	*French*	**E5**	27
Wilton's	*British/Seafood*	**D5**	27
Ritz	*British/French*	**D4**	25
Matsuri	*Japanese*	**D5**	24
Le Caprice	*British/Euro.*	**D4**	23

LISTING

Al Duca	*Italian*	19
Avenue	*British*	20
Brasserie Roux	*French*	22
Brass. St. Jacques	*French*	21
Franco's	*Italian/Med.*	22
Getti	*Italian*	15
Green's	*British/Seafood*	22
Inamo	*Asian*	15
Inn The Park	*British*	17
Just St. James's	*British*	18
Z Le Caprice	*British/Euro.*	23
Z L'Oranger	*French*	27
Matsuri	*Japanese*	24
Mint Leaf	*Indian*	22
Quaglino's	*Euro.*	18
Richoux	*British*	17
Z Ritz	*British/French*	25

Rowley's	*British*	18
Sake No Hana	*Japanese*	23
Seven Park	*British/French*	-
St. James's	*British*	23
Texas Embassy	*Tex-Mex*	12
Thai Sq.	*Thai*	19
Wheeler's	*Seafood*	21
Z Wilton's	*British/Seafood*	27

VICTORIA

Ask Pizza	*Italian*	15
Goring	*British*	24
Mango Tree	*Thai*	21
Noura	*Lebanese*	21
Olivo	*Italian*	23
Quilon	*Indian*	26
Zizzi	*Pizza*	15

WESTMINSTER

Bank Westminster	*Euro.*	20
Z Cinnamon Club	*Indian*	25
NEW Massimo	*Med.*	-
Osteria Dell'Angolo	*Italian*	22
Quirinale	*Italian*	23
Roux/Parliament	*Euro.*	24
Shepherd's	*British*	19
Tate Britain	*British*	19
Yo! Sushi	*Japanese*	16

East/South East London

CANARY WHARF/ DOCKLANDS

Boisdale	*British/Scottish*	20
Browns	*British*	17
Byron	*Burgers*	19
Café Rouge	*French*	15
Camino	*Spanish*	19
Canteen	*British*	16
Carluccio's	*Italian*	17
Z Gaucho	*Argent./Chops*	22
Gun	*British*	20
Haz	*Turkish*	19
Itsu	*Japanese*	16
Jamie's Italian	*Italian*	19
Leon	*Med.*	17
Plateau	*French*	19
Quadrato	*Italian*	22
Rocket	*Med.*	20
Z Roka	*Japanese*	26
Royal China	*Chinese*	23
Smollensky's	*Amer./Chops*	14
Sri Nam	*Thai*	-

LOCATIONS

Tas	*Turkish*	21
Vinoteca	*Euro.*	22
Yo! Sushi	*Japanese*	16

GREENWICH/ BLACKHEATH

Chapters All Day	*Euro.*	-
Nando's	*Portug.*	16
Old Brewery	*British*	18
Rivington Grill	*British*	18
Rodizio Rico	*Brazilian*	15

MILE END/ HACKNEY/ BETHNAL GREEN

Bistrotheque	*French*	23
Buen Ayre	*Argent.*	26
Empress of India	*British*	20
Forman's Fish Island	*British*	-
Nando's	*Portug.*	16
Viajante	*Eclectic*	25

SHOREDITCH/ HOXTON/ WHITECHAPEL

All Star Lanes	*Amer.*	12
Boundary	*British/French*	20
NEW Brawn	*British/French*	23
Z Busaba Eathai	*Thai*	23
Canteen	*British*	16
Cây Tre	*Viet.*	22
Eyre Brothers	*Portug./Spanish*	24
Fifteen	*Italian*	21
Giraffe	*Eclectic*	15
Great Eastern	*Asian*	20
Hawksmoor	*Chops*	26
Hoxton Grill	*Amer.*	18
Le Bouchon	*French*	16
Leon	*Med.*	17
Les Trois Garçons	*French*	20
Mien Tay	*Viet.*	19
Original Lahore	*Pakistani*	25
Pizza East	*Pizza*	20
Princess/Shoreditch	*British*	-
Real Greek	*Greek*	14
Rivington Grill	*British*	18
Saf	*Eclectic/Vegan*	20
Song Que	*Viet.*	23
St. John Bread	*British*	25
Z Tayyabs	*Pakistani*	26
Viet Grill	*Viet.*	22
Viet Hoa	*Viet.*	21
Whitechapel	*Euro.*	18

SOUTH BANK/ BOROUGH

Black & Blue	*Chops*	19
Brindisa	*Spanish*	23
Canteen	*British*	16
Cantina Vino.	*Eclectic/Med.*	18
Côte	*French*	17
Del'Aziz	*African/Med.*	16
Feng Sushi	*Japanese*	17
Fish	*Seafood*	19
Giraffe	*Eclectic*	15
Le Pain Quot.	*Bakery/Belgian*	17
Magdalen	*Euro.*	24
Oxo Tower	*Euro.*	21
Oxo Tower Brass.	*Asian/Med.*	19
Ping Pong	*Chinese*	16
Real Greek	*Greek*	14
Roast	*British*	24
Skylon	*Euro.*	19
Tas	*Turkish*	21
Tate Modern	*Euro.*	18
Tsuru	*Japanese*	-
Wright Brothers	*Seafood*	26

TOWER BRIDGE/ WAPPING

Ask Pizza	*Italian*	15
Bengal Clipper	*Indian*	23
Blueprint	*Euro.*	18
Browns	*British*	17
Butlers Wharf	*Chops*	22
Cantina/Ponte	*Italian*	20
Champor	*Malaysian*	22
Constancia	*Argent./Chops*	-
Z Gaucho	*Argent./Chops*	22
Il Bordello	*Italian*	25
NEW José	*Spanish*	-
Le Pont/Tour	*French/Seafood*	21
Narrow	*British*	21
Ping Pong	*Chinese*	16
Tentazioni	*Italian*	24
Vivat Bacchus	*Euro.*	19
Zucca	*Italian*	25

WATERLOO/ SOUTHWARK/ KENNINGTON

Anchor & Hope	*British*	23
Baltic	*Polish*	23
NEW Brasserie Joël	*French*	-
Byron	*Burgers*	19
Chez Gérard	*French*	17
Del'Aziz	*African/Med.*	16

Dragon Castle | *Chinese*	23
Hot Stuff | *Indian*	24
Leon | *Med.*	17
Livebait | *Seafood*	17
Meson Don Felipe | *Spanish*	21
R.S.J. | *British*	20
Tas | *Turkish*	21
Waterloo | *British*	18

North/
North West London

BELSIZE PARK/
HAMPSTEAD/
KILBURN/
SWISS COTTAGE

Artigiano | *Italian*	21
Ask Pizza | *Italian*	15
Bradley's | *British/French*	20
Café Rouge | *French*	15
Z Gaucho | *Argent./Chops*	22
Giraffe | *Eclectic*	15
Gourmet Burger | *Burgers*	16
Jin Kichi | *Japanese*	26
Little Bay | *Euro.*	19
Nando's | *Portug.*	16
Nautilus Fish | *Seafood*	25
Old Bull & Bush | *Euro.*	14
Paradise | *British*	-
Ping Pong | *Chinese*	16
Singapore Gdn. |	19
Malaysian/Singapor.	
Wells | *Euro.*	23
Weng Wah House | *Chinese*	-
XO | *Asian*	20

CAMDEN TOWN/
CHALK FARM/
KENTISH TOWN/
PRIMROSE HILL

Belgo | *Belgian*	19
Bull & Last | *British*	23
Camden Brass. | *Euro.*	19
Cottons | *Carib.*	-
Del'Aziz | *African/Med.*	16
El Parador | *Spanish*	-
Engineer | *British*	21
Feng Sushi | *Japanese*	17
Gilgamesh | *Asian*	19
Haché | *Burgers*	20
L'Absinthe | *French*	21
Lansdowne | *Euro.*	21
La Porchetta | *Pizza*	19

Lemonia | *Greek*	19
NEW Made in Camden | *Euro.*	-
Masala Zone | *Indian*	19
Mestizo | *Mex.*	22
Nando's | *Portug.*	16
Odette's | *Euro.*	18
Sardo Canale | *Italian*	19
NEW Shaka Zulu | *S African*	-
Z Wagamama | *Japanese*	19
York & Albany | *Euro.*	21

GOLDERS GREEN/
FINCHLEY/HENDON

Z Café Japan | *Japanese*	27
Good Earth | *Chinese*	21
Green Cottage | *Chinese*	22
Original Lahore | *Pakistani*	25
Solly's | *Mideast.*	18
Two Brothers Fish | *Seafood*	20
Zizzi | *Pizza*	15

HIGHGATE/
MUSWELL HILL/
CROUCH END

Café Rouge | *French*	15
Carob Tree | *Greek/Med.*	-
Harry Morgan's | *Deli/Jewish*	16
La Porchetta | *Pizza*	19
Zizzi | *Pizza*	15

ISLINGTON

Albion | *British*	19
Almeida | *French*	20
Antonio's Ristorante | *Italian*	-
Browns | *British*	17
Byron | *Burgers*	19
Carluccio's | *Italian*	17
Z Chilango | *Mex.*	22
Cottons | *Carib.*	-
Duke of Cambridge | *British*	-
Elk in the Woods | *Eclectic*	16
Fig | *Euro.*	24
Frederick's | *British/Euro.*	20
Gallipoli | *Turkish*	21
Giraffe | *Eclectic*	15
La Fromagerie | *Euro.*	22
La Porchetta | *Pizza*	19
Le Mercury | *French*	19
Masala Zone | *Indian*	19
Morgan M | *French/Veg.*	26
Nando's | *Portug.*	16
New Culture Rev. | *Chinese*	16
Ottolenghi | *Bakery/Med.*	25

LOCATIONS

Pasha	*Turkish*	20
Rasa	*Indian*	24
Rodizio Rico	*Brazilian*	15
Sabor	*S Amer.*	-
Santa Maria/Garufa	*Argent.*	24
Strada	*Italian*	16
Thai Sq.	*Thai*	19
NEW Trullo	*Italian*	19
Z Wagamama	*Japanese*	19

KING'S CROSS

Acorn Hse.	*British*	21
Camino	*Spanish*	19
NEW Gilbert Scott	*British*	-
Le Pain Quot.	*Bakery/Belgian*	17
Rotunda	*British*	-
St. Pancras	*British*	17

ST. JOHN'S WOOD

Baker & Spice	*Bakery/Med.*	22
Cafe Med	*Med.*	17
Café Rouge	*French*	15
Harry Morgan's	*Deli/Jewish*	16
L'Aventure	*French*	26
Z Oslo Court	*French*	26
Raoul's	*Med.*	18
Red Pepper	*Italian*	23
Richoux	*British*	17
Sofra	*Turkish*	19
Warrington	*British*	16
Waterway	*Euro.*	15

STOKE NEWINGTON

| La Porchetta | *Pizza* | 19 |
| Rasa | *Indian* | 24 |

South/
South West London

BARNES

Annie's	*British*	21
NEW Indian Zilla	*Indian*	-
Sonny's	*Euro.*	23

BATTERSEA

Buona Sera	*Italian*	-
Butcher & Grill	*British*	17
Giraffe	*Eclectic*	15
Gourmet Burger	*Burgers*	16
Mien Tay	*Viet.*	19
Pizza Express	*Pizza*	16
Ransome's	*British/Eclectic*	19
Santa Maria/Garufa	*Argent.*	24

| Strada | *Italian* | 16 |
| Tom Ilic | *Euro.* | 19 |

BRIXTON/CLAPHAM

Abbeville	*British/Euro.*	17
Belgo	*Belgian*	19
Bodeans	*BBQ*	19
Bombay Bicycle	*Indian*	18
Café Rouge	*French*	15
Franco Manca	*Pizza*	24
Nando's	*Portug.*	16
Pepper Tree	*Thai*	-
Strada	*Italian*	16
Trinity	*Euro.*	25
Tsunami	*Japanese*	25

CAMBERWELL/
DULWICH

Angels & Gypsies	*Spanish*	-
Café Rouge	*French*	15
Rocca	*Italian*	-

CHELSEA

(See map on page 210)

TOP FOOD

Gordon Ramsay/68	*French*	**H7**	28
Rasoi Vineet Bhatia	*Indian*	**F8**	26
Le Cercle	*French*	**E8**	25
Tom Aikens	*French*	**F6**	25
Ziani	*Italian*	**G6**	24
Lucio	*Italian*	**G3**	24
Le Colombier	*French*	**F4**	24
Painted Heron	*Indian*	**J3**	24
Chutney Mary	*Indian*	**J1**	23
Scalini	*Italian*	**D7**	23

LISTING

Admiral Codrington	*British/Euro.*	19
Aglio e Olio	*Italian*	21
Awana	*Malaysian*	19
Baker & Spice	*Bakery/Med.*	22
Benihana	*Japanese*	17
Big Easy	*Amer.*	17
Bluebird	*British*	16
Botanist	*British*	17
Brinkley's	*Eclectic*	17
Builders Arms	*British*	17
Buona Sera	*Italian*	-
Byron	*Burgers*	19
Cadogan Arms	*British*	15
Caraffini	*Italian*	21
Chelsea Brass.	*Euro.*	18
Cheyne Walk	*French*	21

LOCATIONS

Z Gaucho	*Argent./Chops*	22
Giraffe	*Eclectic*	15
Z Glasshouse	*Euro.*	26
Gourmet Burger	*Burgers*	16
Jamie's Italian	*Italian*	19
Petersham	*Euro.*	-
Petersham Nurseries	*Euro.*	24
Thai Sq.	*Thai*	19

SOUTH KENSINGTON

(See map on page 210)

TOP FOOD

Star of India	*Indian*	**F2**	25
L'Etranger	*French/Japanese*	**B1**	24
Patara	*Thai*	**F4**	24
Bibendum Oyster	*French/Seafood*	**E5**	24
Tendido Cero	*Spanish*	**F1**	23

LISTING

Ask Pizza	*Italian*	15
Aubaine	*French*	17
Bangkok	*Thai*	21
Z Bibendum	*French*	23
Bibendum Oyster	*French/Seafood*	24
Bistro K	*Euro.*	-
Black & Blue	*Chops*	19
Blakes	*Eclectic*	22
Bombay Brass.	*Indian*	23
Brindisa	*Spanish*	23
Bumpkin	*British*	20
Byron	*Burgers*	19
Cambio de Tercio	*Spanish*	23
NEW Cassis Bistro	*French*	25
Da Mario	*Italian*	20
El Gaucho	*Argent./Chops*	23
Gessler/Daquise	*Polish*	-
Khan's/Kensington	*Indian*	19
Kulu Kulu	*Japanese*	22
La Bouchée	*French*	19
La Brasserie	*French*	19
Le Pain Quot.	*Bakery/Belgian*	17
L'Etranger	*French/Japanese*	24
Madsen	*Scan.*	16
Noor Jahan	*Indian*	20
Pasha	*Moroccan*	18
Patara	*Thai*	24
Rocca	*Italian*	-
Star of India	*Indian*	25
Tendido Cero	*Spanish*	23
Thai Sq.	*Thai*	19

WANDSWORTH/ BALHAM/ WIMBLEDON/ STREATHAM

Butcher & Grill	*British*	17
Z Chez Bruce	*British*	27
Côte	*French*	17
NEW Fox/Grapes	*British*	-
Gourmet Burger	*Burgers*	16
Le Pain Quot.	*Bakery/Belgian*	17
Light House	*Eclectic*	19
Original Lahore	*Pakistani*	25
San Lorenzo	*Italian*	21
Strada	*Italian*	16

West London

BAYSWATER

All Star Lanes	*Amer.*	12
Alounak	*Persian*	21
Al Waha	*Lebanese*	24
Angelus	*French*	23
Bombay Palace	*Indian*	21
Four Seasons	*Chinese*	22
Goldmine	*Chinese*	24
Gourmet Burger	*Burgers*	16
Halepi	*Greek*	21
Inaho	*Japanese*	25
Khan's	*Indian*	18
Le Café Anglais	*French*	22
Leong's Legend	*Taiwanese*	23
Mandarin Kitchen	*Chinese/Seafood*	25
Masala Zone	*Indian*	19
Nando's	*Portug.*	16
Rodizio Rico	*Brazilian*	15
Royal China	*Chinese*	23
Yo! Sushi	*Japanese*	16

CHISWICK

Annie's	*British*	21
Balans	*British*	17
Café Rouge	*French*	15
Côte	*French*	17
Franco Manca	*Pizza*	24
Frankie's	*Italian*	15
Giraffe	*Eclectic*	15
Gourmet Burger	*Burgers*	16
High Road Brass.	*Euro.*	18
Z La Trompette	*Euro./French*	26
Le Vacherin	*French*	23
Sam's Brass.	*Euro.*	20

Singapore Gdn. | *Malaysian/Singapor.* 19

Zizzi | *Pizza* 15

HAMMERSMITH

Carluccio's | *Italian* 17
E Gate | *Veg.* 26
Indian Zing | *Indian* 24
Raoul's | *Med.* 18
E River Café | *Italian* 27

HOLLAND PARK/ WESTBOURNE GROVE

Belvedere | *British/French* 22
Bombay Bicycle | *Indian* 18
Julie's | *British* 19

KENSINGTON

(See map on page 212)

TOP FOOD

Clarke's | *British* | **G7** 26
Kitchen W8 | *Euro.* | **K6** 25
Launceston Pl. | *British* | **K10** 25
Koi | *Japanese* | **I10** 25
Zaika | *Indian* | **I9** 25
Locanda Ottoemezzo | *Italian* | **J9** 25
Ffiona's | *British* | **H7** 24
E Portico | *Italian* | **K5** 23
Min Jiang | *Chinese* | **I9** 23
Memories/China | *Chinese* | **K4** 23

LISTING

Abingdon | *Euro.* 20
Ark | *Italian* 21
Aubaine | *French* 17
Babylon | *Euro.* 20
Balans | *British* 17
Black & Blue | *Chops* 19
Byron | *Burgers* 19
NEW Casa Batavia | *Italian* -
Churchill Arms | *Thai* 21
E Clarke's | *British* 26
Côte | *French* 17
Feng Sushi | *Japanese* 17
Ffiona's | *British* 24
Giraffe | *Eclectic* 15
Green Door | *Chops* 25
Il Portico | *Italian* 23
Kensington Pl. | *British* 19
Kensington Sq. | *British* 21
Kensington Wine | *Euro.* 19
Kitchen W8 | *Euro.* 25
Koi | *Japanese* 25

Launceston Pl. | *British* 25
Le Pain Quot. | *Bakery/Belgian* 17
Locanda Ottoemezzo | *Italian* 25
Maggie Jones's | *British* 19
Memories/China | *Chinese* 23
Min Jiang | *Chinese* 23
Patisserie Valerie | *French* 16
Pizza Express | *Pizza* 16
Saf | *Eclectic/Vegan* 20
Sticky Fingers | *Amer.* 15
Timo | *Italian* 22
Z Wagamama | *Japanese* 19
Whole Foods | *Eclectic* 21
Wòdka | *Polish* 21
NEW Yashin Sushi | *Japanese* 23
Zaika | *Indian* 25

LADBROKE GROVE

Dock Kitchen | *Euro.* 21

NOTTING HILL

(See map on page 212)

TOP FOOD

Ledbury | *French* | **B5** 29
Assaggi | *Italian* | **D7** 26
Hereford Rd. | *British* | **C7** 25
Osteria Basilico | *Italian* | **C3** 25
Ottolenghi | *Bakery/Med.* | **C5** 25
Books for Cooks | *Eclectic* | **C3** 23
E&O | *Asian* | **C3** 22
Mediterraneo | *Italian* | **C3** 22
Notting Hill Brass. | *Euro.* | **D4** 22
Geales | *Seafood* | **F6** 21

LISTING

Ask Pizza | *Italian* 15
Assaggi | *Italian* 26
Books for Cooks | *Eclectic* 23
Bumpkin | *British* 20
NEW Chesterfield | *Asian* -
Côte | *French* 17
Cow Dining Room | *British* 19
Crazy Homies | *Mex.* 18
Daylesford | *Eclectic* 18
NEW Dragoncello | *Italian* -
E&O | *Asian* 22
El Camion | *Mex.* -
Electric Brasserie | *Eclectic* 17
El Pirata | *Spanish* 20
Feng Sushi | *Japanese* 17
Galicia | *Spanish* 20
Geales | *Seafood* 21
Hereford Rd. | *British* 25

Itsu	Japanese	16
Z Ledbury	French	29
Le Pain Quot.	Bakery/Belgian	17
Lucky 7	Amer.	19
Malabar	Indian	20
Mall Tavern	British	20
Mediterraneo	Italian	22
Mulberry St.	Italian	16
New Culture Rev.	Chinese	16
Notting Hill Brass.	Euro.	22
Osteria Basilico	Italian	25
Ottolenghi	Bakery/Med.	25
Ping Pong	Chinese	16
Pix Pintxos	Spanish	16
Pizza East	Pizza	20
Pizza Express	Pizza	16
Raoul's	Med.	18
Taqueria	Mex.	20
Tom's Deli	Eclectic	-
202	Euro.	18
Uli	Asian	-
Westbourne	Eclectic	15

OLYMPIA

| Alounak | Persian | 21 |

PADDINGTON

Frontline	British	20
Noor Jahan	Indian	20
Pearl Liang	Chinese	23
Yo! Sushi	Japanese	16

SHEPHERD'S BUSH

Anglesea Arms	British	18
Balans	British	17
Z Busaba Eathai	Thai	23
Byron	Burgers	19
Café Rouge	French	15
Comptoir Libanais	Lebanese	17
Del'Aziz	African/Med.	16
Esarn Kheaw	Thai	-
Jamie's Italian	Italian	19
Kitchen Italia	Italian	14
NEW Nottingdale	French/Italian	-
Pho	Viet.	20
Princess Victoria	British	-
Real Greek	Greek	14
Som Tam House	Thai	-
Wahaca	Mex.	20

In the Country

Auberge du Lac	French	24
Aubergine	French	24
Cliveden Hse.	British/French	23
Z Fat Duck	Euro.	27
French Horn	British/French	25
Gravetye Manor	British	-
Hinds Head	British	26
Jamie's Italian	Italian	19
Z Le Manoir/Quat	French	28
Royal Oak	British	22
Z Waterside Inn	French	28

CENTRAL LONDON

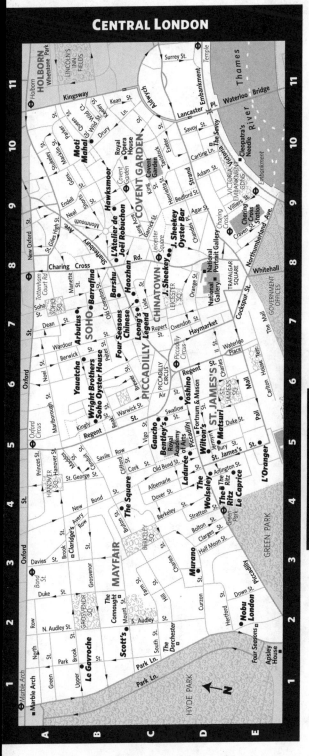

BUCKINGHAM
PALACE GDNS.

Grosvenor Pl.

Constitution Hill

Wellington
Arch

Apsley
House

Apsleys

Hyde Park
Corner

Eccleston St.

Wilton St.

Upper Belgrave St.

Chapel St.

Chester St.

Headfort Pl.

Halkin St.

Grosvenor Cres.

Koffmann's

Marcus Wareing
at The Berkeley

Knightsbridge

BELGRAVE
SQ.

Belgrave Pl.

EATON
SQ.

Eccleston Pl.

Ebury St.

Chester St.

Elizabeth St.

BELGRAVIA

Eaton Pl.

Lyall St.

Eaton St.

Kings Rd.

Eaton Terr.

Amaya

W. Halkin St.

Lowndes St.

Cadogan Ln.

Le Cercle

Lowndes Sq.

Zafferano

Cadogan Pl.

Ellis St.

SLOANE SQ.

Harvey
Nichols

Sloane St.

Dinner by
Heston Blumenthal

Bar
Boulud

Capital
Restaurant

Pavilion Rd.

Cadogan Gdns.

Knightsbridge

Hans Crescent

Port St.

Cadogan Sq.

Zuma

KNIGHTSBRIDGE

Ishbilia

Harrods

Hans Rd.

Lennox Gdns.

Moore St.

Hans St.

Trevor Pl.

Montpelier St.

Beauchamp Pl.

Scalini

Hasker St.

Milner St.

Rawlings St.

Cadogan St.

Draycott Ave.

Draycott Pl.

Sloane Ave.

HYDE PARK

Cheval Pl.

Brompton Rd.

Ennismore Gdns.

Brompton Rd.

Bibendum
Oyster Bar

South Terr.

Fulham Rd.

Kensington Rd.

Exhibition Rd.

Victoria
and Albert
Museum

Pelham St.

Onslow Sq.

Thurloe Pl.

Royal Albert Hall

Kensington Gore

Prince Consort Rd.

Imperial
College

Imperial College Rd.

Science
Museum

Natural
History
Museum

Cromwell Rd.

South
Kensington

Sumner Pl.

Onslow Gdns.

Queen's Gate

SOUTH
KENSINGTON

Brompton Rd.

Old Brompton Rd.

Queen's Gate Terr.

Elvaston Pl.

Queen's Gate

L'Etranger

Gloucester Rd.

Gloucester Rd.

Gloucester Pl.

Palace Gate

Queen's Gate

Gloucester Rd.

Kensington Rd.

Launceston Pl.

Victoria Rd.

Cornwall Gdns.

Grenville Pl.

Ashburn Pl.

Harrington Gdns.

Courtfield Gdns.

Wetherby

A B C D E

1 2 3 4 5 6 7 8 9 10 11

Vote at ZAGAT.com

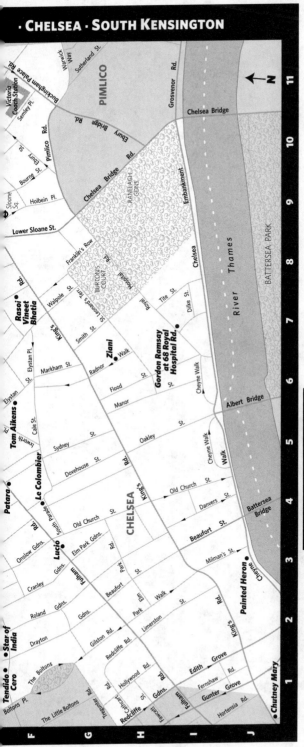

· CHELSEA · SOUTH KENSINGTON

PIMLICO

CHELSEA

MAPS

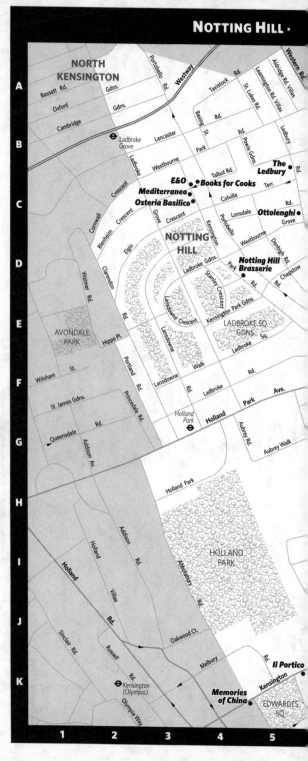

NORTH KENSINGTON

Bassett Rd.

Oxford

Cambridge

Ladbroke Grove

Westbourne

E&O • **Books for Cooks**

The Ledbury

Mediterraneo

Osteria Basilico

Colville

Lonsdale

Ottolenghi

NOTTING HILL

Notting Hill Brasserie

LADBROKE SQ. GDNS.

AVONDALE PARK

Hippo Pl.

Wilsham St.

St. James Gdns.

Queensdale

Holland Park

Holland

Aubrey Walk

HOLLAND PARK

Holland Rd.

Oakwood Ct.

Melbury

Il Portico

Kensington (Olympia)

Memories of China

EDWARDES SQ.

1   2   3   4   5

· KENSINGTON

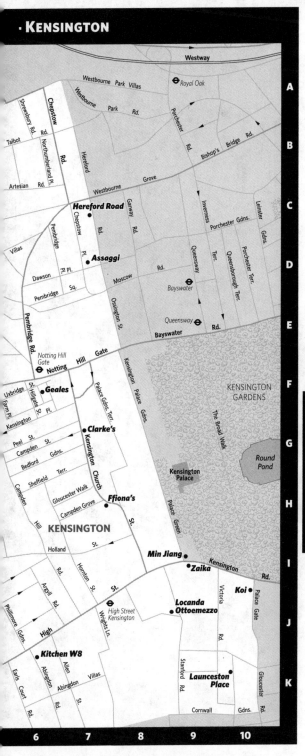

Westway

Westbourne Park Villas

Royal Oak **A**

Westbourne   Park   Rd.

Porchester   Rd. **B**

Bishop's   Bridge   Rd.

Shrewsbury Rd.

Chepstow   Rd.

Talbot   Rd.

Northumberland Pl.

Hereford   Rd.

Artesian   Rd.

Westbourne   Grove **C**

Hereford Road

Chepstow   Rd.

Garway   Rd.

Porchester   Gdns.

Leinster   Gdns.

Inverness   Terr.

Pembridge   Rd.

Villas

Assaggi **D**

Pl. Pl.

Moscow   Rd.

Queensway   Rd.

Queensborough Terr.

Porchester Terr.

Dawson   Pl.

Pembridge   Sq.

Ossington St.

Bayswater

Pembridge   Rd.

Queensway   Rd. **E**

Bayswater

Notting Hill Gate

Notting   Hill   Gate **F**

Uxbridge   St.

Geales

Kensington Palace Gdns.

KENSINGTON
GARDENS

The Broad Walk

Hillgate   St.

Farm Pl.

St. Pl.

Kensington

Peel   St.

Clarke's **G**

Camden   St.

Bedford   Gdns.

Round
Pond

Sheffield   Terr.

Kensington Church

Camden   Hill

Gloucester Walk

Kensington
Palace

Ffiona's **H**

Campden Grove

KENSINGTON

St.

Holland   St.

Palace   Green

Hornton   St.

Min Jiang

Kensington   Rd. **I**

Zaika

Argyll   Rd.

High Street Kensington

Koi

Palace   Gate

Phillimore   Gdns.

Wrights Ln.

Victoria   Rd.

Locanda
Ottoemezzo **J**

High   St.

Kitchen W8

Earls   Court

Abingdon   Rd.

Allen   St.

Abingdon   Villas

Stanford   Rd.

Launceston
Place **K**

Gloucester   Rd.

Cornwall   Gdns.

6   7   8   9   10

**M
A
P
S**

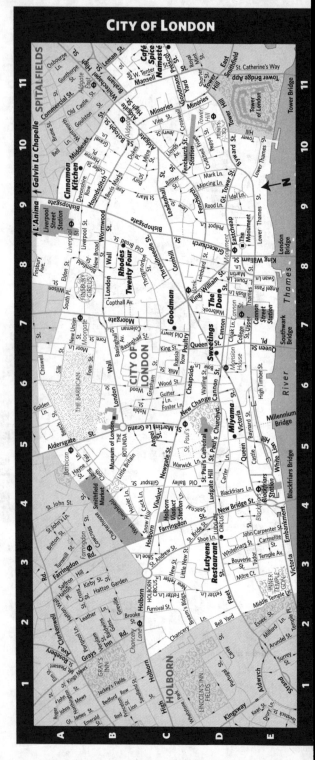

Special Features

Listings cover the best in each category and include names, locations and food ratings. Multi-location restaurants' features may vary by branch.

BREAKFAST

(See also Hotel Dining)

Ambassador | **EC1**	-
Aubaine | **multi.**	17
Automat | **W1**	18
Baker & Spice | **multi.**	22
Balans | **multi.**	17
Butlers Wharf | **SE1**	22
Café Boheme | **W1**	18
Café Rouge | **multi.**	15
Carluccio's | **multi.**	17
Cecconi's | **W1**	23
⁊ Cinnamon Club | **SW1**	25
Coq d'Argent | **EC2**	20
Electric Brasserie | **W11**	17
Empress of India | **E9**	20
Engineer | **NW1**	21
Fifteen | **N1**	21
Fifth Floor Cafe | **SW1**	18
Fortnum's Fountain | **W1**	20
Franco's | **SW1**	22
Giraffe | **multi.**	15
In The Park | **SW1**	17
Julie's | **W11**	19
La Brasserie | **SW3**	19
Ladurée | **SW1**	23
La Fromagerie | **W1**	22
Lucky 7 | **W2**	19
Lutyens | **EC4**	23
1 Lombard Brass. | **EC3**	21
Ottolenghi | **multi.**	25
Patisserie Valerie | **multi.**	16
Portrait | **WC2**	21
Providores | **W1**	25
Raoul's | **W9**	18
Richoux | **multi.**	17
Rivington Grill | **EC2**	18
Roast | **SE1**	24
Royal Exchange | **EC3**	15
1 Simpson's/Strand | **WC2**	22
Sotheby's Cafe | **W1**	24
St. John Bread | **E1**	25
Tate Britain | **SW1**	19
Tom's Deli | **W11**	-
Tom's Kitchen | **SW3**	22
Troubadour | **SW5**	-
202 | **W11**	18
Vingt-Quatre | **SW10**	14

⁊ Wolseley | **W1**	22
York & Albany | **NW1**	21

BRUNCH

Ambassador | **EC1**	-
Angelus | **W2**	23
Annie's | **multi.**	21
Aubaine | **multi.**	17
Automat | **W1**	18
Caravan | **EC1**	22
Cecconi's | **W1**	23
Christopher's | **WC2**	19
Fifth Floor Cafe | **SW1**	18
Giraffe | **multi.**	15
⁊ Hélène Darroze | **W1**	24
Joe Allen | **WC2**	18
L'Etranger | **SW7**	24
Lucky 7 | **W2**	19
Modern Pantry | **EC1**	22
Motcombs | **SW1**	21
PJ's B&G | **multi.**	17
Portrait | **WC2**	21
Providores | **W1**	25
Quadrato | **E14**	22
Sam's Brass. | **W4**	20
Sophie's Steak | **SW10**	19
Tom's Deli | **W11**	-
Tom's Kitchen | **SW3**	22
202 | **W11**	18
Villandry | **W1**	19
Vingt-Quatre | **SW10**	14
Wapping Food | **E1**	18

BUSINESS DINING

⁊ Alain Ducasse | **W1**	27
Albemarle | **W1**	23
Al Duca | **SW1**	19
Alloro | **W1**	21
Almeida | **N1**	20
NEW Amaranto | **W1**	-
⁊ Amaya | **SW1**	26
Angelus | **W2**	23
Apsleys | **SW1**	25
⁊ Arbutus | **W1**	25
Avenue | **SW1**	20
Awana | **SW3**	19
Axis | **WC2**	22
Babbo | **W1**	22
Bank Westminster | **SW1**	20

SPECIAL FEATURES

Restaurant	Area	Rating
NEW Bar Battu	EC2	-
NEW Barbecoa	EC4	20
Z Bar Boulud	SW1	25
Bellamy's	W1	23
Belvedere	W8	22
Benares	W1	23
Z Bentley's	W1	26
Z Bibendum	SW3	23
Bistro K	SW7	-
Bistrot Bruno Loubet	EC1	23
Blakes	SW7	22
Bleeding Heart	EC1	22
Bluebird	SW3	16
Blueprint	SE1	18
NEW Bond/Brook	W1	-
Bonds	EC2	21
Boundary	E2	20
Brasserie Blanc	EC2	20
Brass. St. Jacques	SW1	21
NEW Cafe Luc	W1	-
Caffe Caldesi	W1	21
NEW Cantinetta	SW15	-
Z Capital Restaurant	SW3	26
NEW Casa Batavia	W8	-
NEW Cassis Bistro	SW3	25
Cecconi's	W1	23
NEW Chabrot	SW1	-
Chez Gérard	multi.	17
China Tang	W1	21
Christopher's	WC2	19
NEW Cigalon	WC2	-
Z Cinnamon Club	SW1	25
Cinnamon Kitchen	EC2	23
Z Clarke's	W8	26
C London	W1	21
Z Club Gascon	EC1	26
Constancia	SE1	-
Corrigan's	W1	25
Criterion	W1	18
NEW Da Polpo	WC2	-
Dean St.	W1	21
Z NEW Dinner/Heston	SW1	27
Dock Kitchen	W10	21
Dolada	W1	-
Z Dorchester	W1	24
NEW Dragoncello	W2	-
Elena's L'Etoile	W1	19
Empress of Sichuan	WC2	-
Z Espelette	W1	24
Fakhreldine	W1	20
Fifth Floor	SW1	20
Fino	W1	24
NEW 5 Pollen St.	W1	-
NEW Folly	EC3	-
French Table	KT6	-
Galvin at Windows	W1	24
Galvin Bistrot	W1	24
Galvin La Chapelle	E1	25
Gauthier	W1	24
NEW Gilbert Scott	NW1	-
Gilgamesh	NW1	19
Z Glasshouse	TW9	26
Z Goodman	multi.	26
Z Gordon Ramsay/Clar.	W1	25
Z Gordon Ramsay/68	SW3	28
Goring	SW1	24
Green Door	SW7	25
Greenhouse	W1	26
Green's	multi.	22
Z Hakkasan	W1	26
Z Hélène Darroze	W1	24
Hereford Rd.	W2	25
Hibiscus	W1	26
High Road Brass.	W4	18
High Timber	EC4	21
Hix	W1	20
Hix Oyster	EC1	23
Hix Rest.	W1	23
Il Convivio	SW1	24
NEW Ilia	SW3	-
Incognico	WC2	19
NEW Indian Zilla	SW13	-
Indigo	WC2	22
Z Ivy	WC2	22
Z J. Sheekey	WC2	26
Z J. Sheekey Oyster	WC2	26
Just St. James's	SW1	18
JW Steak	W1	23
Kai Mayfair	W1	26
Kazan	SW1	20
Kitchen Italia	multi.	14
Kitchen W8	W8	25
Z NEW Koffmann's	SW1	26
La Genova	W1	25
Langan's Bistro	W1	23
Langan's Brass.	W1	19
L'Anima	EC2	25
Z La Petite Maison	W1	27
Z L'Atelier/Robuchon	WC2	27
Z La Trompette	W4	26
Launceston Pl.	W8	25
L'Autre Pied	W1	24
Le Café Anglais	W2	22
Le Café/Marché	EC1	24

SPECIAL FEATURES

Tom's Kitchen	SW3	22
Trinity	SW4	25
NEW 28-50 Wine	EC4	22
Z Umu	W1	26
NEW Venosi	SW3	-
Viajante	E2	25
Wallace	W1	17
Waterloo	SE1	18
Z Waterside Inn	SL6	28
Wheeler's	SW1	21
Whitechapel	E1	18
Wild Honey	W1	23
Z Wilton's	SW1	27
York & Albany	NW1	21
Z Zafferano	SW1	26
Zaika	W8	25
Z Zuma	SW7	26

CELEBRITY CHEFS

Tom Aikens
| Tom Aikens | SW3 | 25 |
| Tom's Kitchen | multi. | 22 |

Jason Atherton
| Pollen St. Social | W1 | - |

Pascal Aussignac
Cellar Gascon	EC1	24
Club Gascon	EC1	26
Comptoir Gascon	EC1	22
Le Cercle	SW1	25

Ed Baines
| Randall/Aubin | W1 | 19 |

Rainer Becker
| Roka | multi. | 26 |
| Zuma | SW7 | 26 |

Vineet Bhatia
| Rasoi Vineet Bhatia | SW3 | 26 |

Raymond Blanc
| Brasserie Blanc | EC2 | 20 |
| Le Manoir/Quat | OX4 | 28 |

Heston Blumenthal
Dinner/Heston	SW1	27
Fat Duck	SL6	27
Hinds Head	SL6	26

Claude Bosi
| Fox/Grapes | SW19 | - |
| Hibiscus | W1 | 26 |

Daniel Boulud
| Bar Boulud | SW1 | 25 |

Adam Byatt
| Trinity | SW4 | 25 |

Sally Clarke
| Clarke's | W8 | 26 |

Sam & Sam Clark
| Morito | EC1 | 26 |
| Moro | EC1 | 26 |

Richard Corrigan
| Bentley's | W1 | 26 |
| Corrigan's | W1 | 25 |

Hélène Darroze
| Espelette | W1 | 24 |
| Hélène Darroze | W1 | 24 |

William Drabble
| Seven Park | SW1 | - |

Alain Ducasse
| Alain Ducasse | W1 | 27 |

Nobu Matsuhisa & Mark Edwards
| Nobu Berkeley | W1 | 25 |
| Nobu London | W1 | 27 |

Pierre Gagnaire
| Sketch/Lecture | W1 | 24 |

Chris & Jeff Galvin
Galvin at Windows	W1	24
Galvin Bistrot	W1	24
Galvin La Chapelle	E1	25

Alexis Gauthier
| Gauthier | W1 | 24 |

Peter Gordon
| Kopapa | WC2 | 17 |
| Providores | W1 | 25 |

Angela Hartnett
| Murano | W1 | 27 |

Fergus Henderson
St. John	EC1	26
St. John Bread	E1	25
St. John Hotel	WC2	-

Mark Hix
Hix	W1	20
Hix Oyster	EC1	23
Hix Rest.	W1	23

Philip Howard
| Kitchen W8 | W8 | 25 |
| Square | W1 | 27 |

Atul Kochhar
| Benares | W1 | 23 |

Rowley Leigh
| Le Café Anglais | W2 | 22 |

Giorgio Locatelli
| Locanda Locatelli | W1 | 25 |

Bruno Loubet
| Bistrot Bruno Loubet | EC1 | 23 |

Thomasina Miers
| Wahaca | multi. | 20 |

Jamie Oliver
Barbecoa	EC4	20
Fifteen	N1	21
Jamie's Italian	multi.	19

Restaurant	Rating
Fifteen	N1	21
Fifth Floor	SW1	20
NEW 5 Pollen St.	W1	-
NEW Folly	EC3	-
Forge	WC2	23
French Horn	RG4	25
Frontline	W2	20
Galvin at Windows	W1	24
Galvin La Chapelle	E1	25
Gauthier	W1	24
NEW Gilbert Scott	NW1	-
Z Glasshouse	TW9	26
Z Goodman	EC2	26
Z Gordon Ramsay/Clar.	W1	25
Z Gordon Ramsay/68	SW3	28
Goring	SW1	24
Greenhouse	W1	26
Green's	multi.	22
Greig's	W1	22
Z Hélène Darroze	W1	24
High Timber	EC4	21
Il Convivio	SW1	24
Indigo	WC2	22
Julie's	W11	19
Kitchen W8	W8	25
La Fromagerie	multi.	22
La Poule au Pot	SW1	21
Z La Trompette	W4	26
Launceston Pl.	W8	25
Le Bouchon	E1	16
Le Café/Marché	EC1	24
Le Cercle	SW1	25
Z Ledbury	W11	29
Z Le Gavroche	W1	28
Z Le Manoir/Quat	OX4	28
Le Pont/Tour	SE1	21
L'Escargot	W1	22
L'Etranger	SW7	24
Z Locanda Locatelli	W1	25
Z L'Oranger	SW1	27
Lucio	SW3	24
Luc's Brasserie	EC3	-
Magdalen	SE1	24
Manicomio	multi.	15
Manson	SW6	-
Z Marcus Wareing	SW1	27
Mediterraneo	W11	22
Mercer	EC2	20
Modern Pantry	EC1	22
Mon Plaisir	WC2	18
Morgan M	N7	26
National Dining Rooms	WC2	17
Odette's	NW1	18
Odin's	W1	21
Olivo	SW1	23
Olivomare	SW1	24
One-O-One	SW1	22
Orrery	W1	25
Orso	WC2	21
Z Oslo Court	NW8	26
Osteria Basilico	W11	25
Osteria dell'Arancio	SW10	19
Oxo Tower	SE1	21
Oxo Tower Brass.	SE1	19
Pantechnicon Rooms	SW1	20
Paradise	W10	-
Paramount	WC1	16
Paternoster Chop	EC4	15
Patterson's	W1	24
Pearl	WC1	26
Pellicano	SW3	19
Petersham	TW10	-
NEW Phene	SW3	13
Z Pied à Terre	W1	28
Pig's Ear	SW3	22
Pinchito Tapas	EC1	-
Polpo	W1	23
Princess/Shoreditch	EC2	-
Prism	EC3	18
Providores	W1	25
Quirinale	SW1	23
Racine	SW3	23
Refettorio	EC4	21
Refuel	W1	20
Rhodes 24	EC2	23
Rhodes W1	W1	24
Rib Room	SW1	22
Z Ritz	W1	25
Z River Café	W6	27
Roast	SE1	24
Z Roussillon	SW1	26
Roux/Parliament	SW1	24
Royal Exchange	EC3	15
Royal Oak	SL6	22
R.S.J.	SE1	20
Salt Yard	W1	23
San Lorenzo	SW19	21
Santa Maria/Garufa	SW8	24
Savoy Grill	WC2	23
Z Scott's	W1	27
Semplice Bar	W1	21
Semplice Rist.	W1	23
Seven Park	SW1	-
NEW Shaka Zulu	NW1	-

hepherd's | **SW1**	19	Assaggi | **W2**	26
⎦ Sketch/Gallery | **W1**	21	Aubaine | **multi.**	17
⎦ Sketch/Lecture | **W1**	24	Axis* | **WC2**	22
⎦ Sketch/Parlour | **W1**	23	Babylon* | **W8**	20
kylon | **SE1**	19	Baker & Spice | **multi.**	22
miths/Dining Rm. | **EC1**	23	Barrafina | **W1**	26
miths/Top Fl. | **EC1**	21	Belgo* | **multi.**	19
otheby's Cafe | **W1**	24	Benihana | **multi.**	17
⎦ Square | **W1**	27	◪ Bibendum | **SW3**	23
t. James's | **W1**	23	Bibendum Oyster | **SW3**	24
t. John Bread | **E1**	25	Big Easy* | **SW3**	17
ate Britain | **SW1**	19	Black & Blue | **SW7**	19
ate Modern | **SE1**	18	Bluebird* | **SW3**	16
entazioni | **SE1**	24	Blue Elephant | **SW6**	21
erroirs | **WC2**	23	Bodeans* | **multi.**	19
exture | **W1**	25	Books for Cooks | **W11**	23
heo Randall | **W1**	23	Brasserie Roux* | **SW1**	22
homas Cubitt | **SW1**	23	Browns* | **multi.**	17
imo | **W8**	22	Buona Sera | **multi.**	-
om Aikens | **SW3**	25	Byron* | **multi.**	19
om Ilic | **SW8**	19	Cafe Pacifico* | **WC2**	19
om's Kitchen | **multi.**	22	Café Rouge* | **multi.**	15
oto's | **SW3**	23	Café Spice | **E1**	25
rinity | **SW4**	25	Cantina/Ponte | **SE1**	20
ruc Vert | **W1**	19	Caraffini | **SW1**	21
NEW Trullo | **N1**	19	Caravaggio | **EC3**	19
asco & Piero's | **W1**	24	Carluccio's* | **multi.**	17
NEW Verru | **W1**	-	**NEW** Cassis Bistro | **SW3**	25
illandry | **W1**	19	Cecconi's | **W1**	23
inoteca | **multi.**	22	Cha Cha Moon | **W1**	16
ivat Bacchus | **multi.**	19	Cheyne Walk | **SW3**	21
Vallace | **W1**	17	◪ Chez Bruce | **SW17**	27
Vaterloo | **SE1**	18	Chez Gérard* | **multi.**	17
⎦ Waterside Inn | **SL6**	28	Chicago Rib* | **SW1**	15
Vaterway | **W9**	15	Christopher's* | **WC2**	19
Vells | **NW3**	23	Chuen Cheng Ku | **W1**	20
Vestbourne | **W2**	15	Churchill Arms | **W8**	21
Vild Honey | **W1**	23	Cigala | **WC1**	20
⎦ Wilton's | **SW1**	27	◪ Cinnamon Club | **SW1**	25
⎦ Wolseley | **W1**	22	Citrus* | **W1**	-
e Olde Cheshire | **EC4**	13	C London | **W1**	21
ork & Albany | **NW1**	21	Daphne's | **SW3**	21
⎦ Zafferano | **SW1**	26	Daylesford* | **multi.**	18
		Eagle | **EC1**	22

CHILD-FRIENDLY

(Besides the normal fast-food laces; * children's menu available)

		E&O | **W11**	22
bbeville | **SW4**	17	Ed's Easy Diner* | **W1**	15
bingdon | **W8**	20	Electric Brasserie | **W11**	17
l Duca | **SW1**	19	Elistano | **SW3**	17
lmeida | **N1**	20	Fifteen | **N1**	21
rchipelago | **W1**	21	Fifth Floor Cafe* | **SW1**	18
sk Pizza* | **multi.**	15	Fino | **W1**	24
		Fish* | **SE1**	19

SPECIAL FEATURES

Fortnum's Fountain | **W1**	20
Frankie's* | **multi.**	15
Frederick's* | **N1**	20
Z Gaucho | **multi.**	22
Gay Hussar | **W1**	21
Giraffe* | **multi.**	15
Z Glasshouse | **TW9**	26
Gourmet Burger* | **multi.**	16
Great Eastern | **EC2**	20
Z Hakkasan | **W1**	26
Hard Rock* | **W1**	15
Il Baretto | **W1**	23
Indigo* | **WC2**	22
Inn The Park* | **SW1**	17
Itsu | **multi.**	16
Jenny Lo's Tea | **SW1**	19
Joe Allen | **WC2**	18
Julie's* | **W11**	19
Kensington Pl. | **W8**	19
Kettner's* | **W1**	16
La Brasserie* | **SW3**	19
Ladurée | **multi.**	23
La Famiglia | **SW10**	22
La Fromagerie | **W1**	22
La Porchetta | **multi.**	19
Le Café Anglais | **W2**	22
Z Le Caprice | **SW1**	23
Z Le Manoir/Quat* | **OX4**	28
L'Etranger | **SW7**	24
Livebait* | **multi.**	17
Z Locanda Locatelli | **W1**	25
Locanda Ottoemezzo | **W8**	25
Lucio | **SW3**	24
Lucky 7* | **W2**	19
Made in Italy | **SW3**	20
Mango Tree | **SW1**	21
Manicomio | **SW3**	15
Maroush | **multi.**	22
Masala Zone* | **multi.**	19
Mediterraneo* | **W11**	22
Mela | **WC2**	21
Min Jiang | **W8**	23
Z Nobu Berkeley | **W1**	25
Z Nobu London | **W1**	27
Noura | **multi.**	21
Oliveto | **SW1**	24
Orso | **WC2**	21
Ottolenghi | **multi.**	25
Oxo Tower* | **SE1**	21
Oxo Tower Brass.* | **SE1**	19
Patara | **multi.**	24
Patisserie Valerie | **multi.**	16
Pellicano | **SW3**	19
Petersham* | **TW10**	-
Pizza Express* | **multi.**	16
PJ's B&G* | **multi.**	17
Plateau* | **E14**	19
Porters* | **WC2**	15
Princi London | **W1**	22
Quadrato* | **E14**	22
Quaglino's* | **SW1**	18
Quilon | **SW1**	26
Randall/Aubin | **W1**	19
Ransome's | **SW11**	19
Raoul's | **multi.**	18
Rasa | **multi.**	24
Real Greek* | **multi.**	14
Red Pepper | **W9**	23
Reubens* | **W1**	19
Riccardo's | **SW3**	16
Richoux* | **multi.**	17
Z Ritz* | **W1**	25
Z River Café | **W6**	27
Rocket | **W1**	20
Z Roussillon* | **SW1**	26
Royal China | **multi.**	23
Royal China Club | **W1**	25
Z Rules | **WC2**	23
Sabor* | **N1**	-
Sale e Pepe | **SW1**	21
San Lorenzo | **SW3**	21
Santini | **SW1**	26
Semplice Bar | **W1**	21
Shepherd's | **SW1**	19
Smollensky's* | **WC2**	14
Sofra | **multi.**	19
Sonny's* | **SW13**	23
Sophie's Steak* | **SW10**	19
Sticky Fingers* | **W8**	15
Strada* | **multi.**	16
Tas | **multi.**	21
Texas Embassy* | **SW1**	14
Tom's Deli | **W11**	-
Tom's Kitchen* | **multi.**	22
Truc Vert | **W1**	19
Two Brothers Fish* | **N3**	20
202 | **W11**	18
Uli | **W11**	-
Villandry* | **W1**	19
Vingt-Quatre | **SW10**	14
Z Wagamama* | **multi.**	19
Wahaca | **multi.**	20
Z Wolseley | **W1**	22
Z Yauatcha | **W1**	25

Yo! Sushi* | **multi.**	16
Yoshino | **W1**	22
Z Zafferano | **SW1**	26
Zizzi* | **multi.**	15
Z Zuma | **SW7**	26

DELIVERY/ TAKEAWAY

(D=delivery, T=takeaway)

Alounak | D, T | **multi.**	21
Al Waha | D | **W2**	24
Ask Pizza | T | **multi.**	15
Baker & Spice | T | **multi.**	22
Big Easy | T | **SW3**	17
Blue Elephant | D, T | **SW6**	21
Bombay Bicycle | T | **multi.**	18
Café Spice | D, T | **E1**	25
NEW Cantina Laredo | T | **WC2**	–
Carluccio's | T | **multi.**	17
Chor Bizarre | T | **W1**	23
Chuen Cheng Ku | T | **W1**	20
Churchill Arms | T | **W8**	21
Crazy Homies | T | **W2**	18
Daylesford | T | **multi.**	18
Z Defune | T | **W1**	26
Ed's Easy Diner | T | **W1**	15
Esarn Kheaw | T | **W12**	–
Fairuz | D, T | **W1**	22
Fakhreldine | D, T | **W1**	20
Feng Sushi | D, T | **multi.**	17
Z Gaucho | T | **multi.**	22
Giraffe | T | **multi.**	15
Golden Dragon | T | **W1**	20
Gopal's | T | **W1**	22
Halepi | T | **W2**	21
Harbour City | T | **W1**	23
Ikeda | T | **W1**	28
Inn The Park | T | **SW1**	17
Ishbilia | D, T | **SW1**	25
Itsu | D, T | **multi.**	16
Jenny Lo's Tea | D, T | **SW1**	19
Jin Kichi | T | **NW3**	26
Khan's | T | **W2**	18
Khan's/Kensington | D, T | **SW7**	19
Z Kiku | T | **W1**	27
Koi | D, T | **W8**	25
Kulu Kulu | T | **multi.**	22
La Fromagerie | D, T | **W1**	22
La Porchetta | T | **multi.**	19
La Porte/Indes | T | **W1**	22
Leon | T | **multi.**	17
Lucky 7 | T | **W2**	19
Mango Tree | T | **SW1**	21

Manicomio | T | **multi.**	15
Mao Tai | T | **SW6**	20
Masala Zone | T | **multi.**	19
Matsuri | T | **SW1**	24
Mela | T | **WC2**	21
Memories/China | T | **multi.**	23
Mulberry St. | T | **W2**	16
Noor Jahan | T | **multi.**	20
North Sea | T | **WC1**	24
Noura | D, T | **multi.**	21
Original Lahore | T | **multi.**	25
Ottolenghi | T | **multi.**	25
Özer | T | **W1**	20
Patara | T | **multi.**	24
Pizza Express | T | **multi.**	16
Princi London | T | **W1**	22
Rasa | T | **multi.**	24
Red Pepper | T | **W9**	23
Reubens | T | **W1**	19
Riccardo's | T | **SW3**	16
Richoux | T | **multi.**	17
Rock & Sole | T | **WC2**	24
Royal China | T | **multi.**	23
Royal China Club | T | **W1**	25
Salloos | T | **SW1**	24
Singapore Gdn. | D, T | **NW6**	19
Solly's | T | **NW11**	18
Sonny's | T | **SW13**	23
Star of India | T | **SW5**	25
Sticky Fingers | T | **W8**	15
Strada | T | **multi.**	16
Z Tamarind | D, T | **W1**	25
Tas | D, T | **multi.**	21
Thai Sq. | T | **multi.**	19
Tom's Deli | T | **W11**	–
Truc Vert | D, T | **W1**	19
Two Brothers Fish | T | **N3**	20
Villandry | T | **W1**	19
Weng Wah House | T | **NW3**	–
Whole Foods | T | **W8**	21
Yo! Sushi | D, T | **multi.**	16
Yoshino | T | **W1**	22

DINING ALONE

(Other than hotels and places with counter service)

Z Amaya | **SW1**	26
Armani Caffé | **SW3**	19
Aubaine | **multi.**	17
Baker & Spice | **multi.**	22
Barrafina | **W1**	26
Bibendum Oyster | **SW3**	24
Books for Cooks | **W11**	23

Brindisa | multi.	23		Wolseley | W1	22
Brompton Quarter | SW3	19		Yauatcha | W1	25
Busaba Eathai | multi.	23		Yo! Sushi | multi.	16
Café Rouge | multi.	15			
Carluccio's | multi.	17			

ENTERTAINMENT

(Call for days and
times of performances)

Cha Cha Moon | W1	16	
Chowki | W1	20	
Chuen Cheng Ku | W1	20	Bengal Clipper | piano | SE1	23
Comptoir Gascon | EC1	22	Bentley's | piano | W1	26
Comptoir Libanais | multi.	17	Big Easy | live bands | SW3	17
Daylesford | multi.	18	Boisdale | jazz | SW1	20
Ed's Easy Diner | W1	15	Colony | jazz | W1	21
Fifth Floor Cafe | SW1	18	Coq d'Argent | jazz | EC2	20
Fino | W1	24	Efes | varies | W1	20
Fortnum's Fountain | W1	20	Floridita | Cuban/DJ | W1	13
Hakkasan | W1	26	Gilgamesh | DJ | NW1	19
Inaho | W2	25	Hakkasan | DJ | W1	26
Inn The Park | SW1	17	Ishtar | belly dancing | W1	20
Jenny Lo's Tea | SW1	19	Joe Allen | piano | WC2	18
Ladurée | multi.	23	Langan's Brass. | varies | W1	19
La Fromagerie | W1	22	Le Café/Marché | jazz/piano | EC1	24
Le Colombier | SW3	24	Le Caprice | piano | SW1	23
Leon | multi.	17	Le Pont/Tour | piano | SE1	21
Le Pain Quot. | multi.	17	Living Room | varies | W1	-
Manicomio | SW3	15	Maroush | belly dancing | multi.	22
Matsuri | SW1	24	Meson Don Felipe | guitarist | SE1	21
Mon Plaisir | WC2	18	Notting Hill Brass. | jazz | W11	22
New Culture Rev. | multi.	16	Oxo Tower Brass. | jazz | SE1	19
Noura | multi.	21	PJ's B&G | jazz | WC2	17
Ottolenghi | multi.	25	Quaglino's | jazz | SW1	18
Patisserie Valerie | multi.	16	Ritz | varies | W1	25
Ping Pong | multi.	16	NEW Shaka Zulu | varies | NW1	-
NEW Polpetto | W1	22	Simpson's/Strand | piano | WC2	22
Polpo | W1	23	Thai Sq. | DJ | SW1	19
Porters | WC2	15		

FIREPLACES

Portrait | WC2	21	
Princi London | W1	22	
Providores | W1	25	Abbeville | SW4	17
Randall/Aubin | W1	19	Admiral Codrington | SW3	19
NEW Restaurant/Arts | W1	-	Albemarle | W1	23
Richoux | multi.	17	Al Hamra | W1	23
Semplice Bar | W1	21	NEW Amaranto | W1	-
Sotheby's Cafe | W1	24	Anglesea Arms | W6	18
NEW Spuntino | W1	-	Aubergine | SL7	24
St. John Bread | E1	25	Babylon | W8	20
Taqueria | W11	20	Bam-Bou | W1	20
Tate Modern | SE1	18	Belgo | NW1	19
Tom's Deli | W11	-	Bleeding Heart | EC1	22
Tom's Kitchen | multi.	22	Boundary | E2	20
Truc Vert | W1	19	Builders Arms | SW3	17
Villandry | W1	19	Cafe Med | NW8	17
Wagamama | multi.	19	Cambio de Tercio | SW5	23
		Cheyne Walk | SW3	21

SPECIAL FEATURES

Don	**EC4**	23	Il Baretto	**W1**	23
☑ Dorchester	**W1**	24	Il Portico	**W8**	23
Duke of Cambridge	**N1**	-	Incognico	**WC2**	19
Eagle	**EC1**	22	☑ Ivy	**WC2**	22
Ebury Wine	**SW1**	18	Joe Allen	**WC2**	18
Electric Brasserie	**W11**	17	Julie's	**W11**	19
Elena's L'Etoile	**W1**	19	Just St. James's	**SW1**	18
Elistano	**SW3**	17	Kensington Pl.	**W8**	19
Elk in the Woods	**N1**	16	Kitchen W8	**W8**	25
El Pirata	**W2**	20	☑ NEW Koffmann's	**SW1**	26
Empress of India	**E9**	20	La Bouchée	**SW7**	19
Enoteca Turi	**SW15**	25	L'Absinthe	**NW1**	21
Enterprise	**SW3**	20	La Famiglia	**SW10**	22
Eyre Brothers	**EC2**	24	Langan's Bistro	**W1**	21
☑ Fat Duck	**SL6**	27	Langan's Brass.	**W1**	19
Ffiona's	**W8**	24	☑ La Petite Maison	**W1**	27
Fifteen	**N1**	21	La Poule au Pot	**SW1**	21
Fig	**N1**	24	☑ La Trompette	**W4**	26
Fino	**W1**	24	Launceston Pl.	**W8**	25
NEW 5 Pollen St.	**W1**	-	L'Autre Pied	**W1**	24
Forge	**WC2**	23	L'Aventure	**NW8**	26
Fortnum's Fountain	**W1**	20	Le Café Anglais	**W2**	22
Franco's	**SW1**	22	☑ Le Caprice	**SW1**	23
Frederick's	**N1**	20	Le Cercle	**SW1**	25
French Horn	**RG4**	25	Le Colombier	**SW3**	24
French Table	**KT6**	-	☑ Ledbury	**W11**	29
Frontline	**W2**	20	☑ Le Gavroche	**W1**	28
Galvin at Windows	**W1**	24	☑ Le Manoir/Quat	**OX4**	28
Galvin Bistrot	**W1**	24	Le Pont/Tour	**SE1**	21
Galvin La Chapelle	**E1**	25	L'Escargot	**W1**	22
Gauthier	**W1**	24	NEW Les Deux	**WC2**	19
NEW Gilbert Scott	**NW1**	-	Les Trois Garçons	**E1**	20
☑ Glasshouse	**TW9**	26	L'Etranger	**SW7**	24
☑ Gordon Ramsay/Clar.	**W1**	25	Le Vacherin	**W4**	23
☑ Gordon Ramsay/68	**SW3**	28	☑ Locanda Locatelli	**W1**	25
Goring	**SW1**	24	Lucio	**SW3**	24
Great Queen St.	**WC2**	24	Lutyens	**EC4**	23
Green Door	**SW7**	25	Luxe	**E1**	12
Greenhouse	**W1**	26	Manson	**SW6**	-
Green's	**multi.**	22	☑ Marcus Wareing	**SW1**	27
Grenadier	**SW1**	18	Modern Pantry	**EC1**	22
Grumbles	**SW1**	17	Mon Plaisir	**WC2**	18
☑ Harwood Arms	**SW6**	27	Montpeliano	**SW7**	16
Hereford Rd.	**W2**	25	Morgan M	**N7**	26
Hibiscus	**W1**	26	Moro	**EC1**	26
High Road Brass.	**W4**	18	Moti Mahal	**WC2**	25
High Timber	**EC4**	21	☑ Murano	**W1**	27
Hinds Head	**SL6**	26	My Dining Room	**SW6**	-
Hix	**W1**	20	Northbank	**EC4**	-
Hix Oyster	**EC1**	23	NEW North Rd.	**EC1**	-
Hix Rest.	**W1**	23	NEW Nottingdale	**W11**	-
Hush	**W1**	19	Notting Hill Brass.	**W11**	22

Odette's | **NW1**	18	Smiths/Dining Rm. | **EC1**	23
Odin's | **W1**	21	Smiths/Top Fl. | **EC1**	21
Olivo | **SW1**	23	Sonny's | **SW13**	23
1 Lombard | **EC3**	22	☑ Square | **W1**	27
Orange | **SW1**	22	St. James's | **W1**	23
Original Lahore | **multi.**	25	☑ St. John | **EC1**	26
Orrery | **W1**	25	St. John Bread | **E1**	25
☑ Oslo Court | **NW8**	26	NEW St. John Hotel | **WC2**	–
Osteria dell'Arancio | **SW10**	19	St. Pancras | **NW1**	17
Oxo Tower | **SE1**	21	Tate Britain | **SW1**	19
Paradise | **W10**	–	NEW Tempo | **W1**	–
Paramount | **WC1**	16	Tendido Cero | **SW5**	23
Patterson's | **W1**	24	Tentazioni | **SE1**	24
Pearl | **WC1**	26	Thomas Cubitt | **SW1**	23
Petersham | **TW10**	–	Timo | **W8**	22
Petersham Nurseries | **TW10**	24	NEW Tinello | **SW1**	24
Petrus | **SW1**	25	Tom Aikens | **SW3**	25
Pig's Ear | **SW3**	22	Tom Ilic | **SW8**	19
NEW Portman | **W1**	–	Tom's Kitchen | **multi.**	22
Prism | **EC3**	18	Trinity | **SW4**	25
Providores | **W1**	25	NEW Trullo | **N1**	19
Quadrato | **E14**	22	☑ Umu | **W1**	26
Quaglino's | **SW1**	18	NEW Venosi | **SW3**	–
Quirinale | **SW1**	23	NEW Verru | **W1**	–
Quo Vadis | **W1**	21	Villandry | **W1**	19
Racine | **SW3**	23	Vinoteca | **EC1**	22
NEW Restaurant/Arts | **W1**	–	Vivat Bacchus | **multi.**	19
Rhodes 24 | **EC2**	23	Wallace | **W1**	17
Rhodes W1 | **W1**	24	Wapping Food | **E1**	18
Rib Room | **SW1**	22	Warrington | **W9**	16
Riccardo's | **SW3**	16	☑ Waterside Inn | **SL6**	28
☑ Ritz | **W1**	25	Waterway | **W9**	15
☑ River Café | **W6**	27	☑ Wilton's | **SW1**	27
Rivington Grill | **multi.**	18	Wòdka | **W8**	21
Roast | **SE1**	24	☑ Wolseley | **W1**	22
Rodizio Rico | **multi.**	15	York & Albany | **NW1**	21
☑ Roussillon | **SW1**	26	☑ Zafferano | **SW1**	26
Roux/Parliament | **SW1**	24	Ziani | **SW3**	24
Royal Exchange | **EC3**	15	Zucca | **SE1**	25
Royal Oak | **SL6**	22		

HISTORIC PLACES

(Year opened; * building)

☑ Rules | **WC2**	23
San Lorenzo | **multi.**	21
Santini | **SW1**	26
Sardo | **W1**	22
Sartoria | **W1**	22
Sauterelle | **EC3**	18
Savoy Grill | **WC2**	23
Semplice Rist. | **W1**	23
Seven Park | **SW1**	–
NEW Shaka Zulu | **NW1**	–
☑ Simpson's/Strand | **WC2**	22
Skylon | **SE1**	19

1520 | Just St. James's* | **SW1**	18
1538 | Ye Olde Cheshire* | **EC4**	13
1550 | Aubergine* | **SL7**	24
1550 | Fat Duck* | **SL6**	27
1571 | Royal Exchange* | **EC3**	15
1598 | Gravetye Manor* | **RH19**	–
1662 | Bleeding Heart* | **EC1**	22
1680 | French Horn* | **RG4**	25
1690 | Giovanni's* | **WC2**	23
1690 | Hinds Head | **SL6**	26
1690 | Wells* | **NW3**	23

SPECIAL FEATURES

1700	Bellamy's*	**W1** 23
1700	Ransome's*	**SW11** 19
1700	Royal Oak*	**SL6** 22
1720	Grenadier*	**SW1** 18
1721	Old Bull & Bush	**NW3** 14
1725	Patisserie Valerie*	**WC2** 16
1740	Bingham*	**TW10** 25
1741	L'Escargot*	**W1** 22
1742	Princess/Shoreditch*	**EC2** –
1742	Wilton's	**SW1** 27
1750	Food for Thought*	**WC2** 22
1750	Gauthier*	**W1** 24
1750	Gun*	**E14** 20
1755	Randall/Aubin*	**W1** 19
1760	Auberge du Lac*	**AL8** 24
1760	Sotheby's Cafe*	**W1** 24
1776	Tom's Kitchen*	**WC2** 22
1779	Sketch/Gallery*	**W1** 21
1779	Sketch/Lecture*	**W1** 24
1780	Andrew Edmunds*	**W1** 23
1790	Carluccio's*	**EC1** 17
1790	Rowley's*	**SW1** 18
1798	Don*	**EC4** 23
1798	Rules*	**WC2** 23
1800	Anglesea Arms*	**W6** 18
1800	Axis*	**WC2** 22
1800	Belvedere*	**W8** 22
1800	Churchill Arms*	**W8** 21
1800	Rocket*	**multi.** 20
1800	Tokyo Diner*	**WC2** –
1810	Angelus*	**W2** 23
1810	Milroy's*	**W1** –
1810	Pig's Ear*	**SW3** 22
1820	Builders Arms*	**SW3** 17
1820	York & Albany*	**NW1** 21
1828	Simpson's/Strand*	**WC2** 22
1834	Albion*	**N1** 19
1837	Albemarle*	**W1** 23
1846	Les Trois Garçons*	**E1** 20
1851	Flemings Grill*	**W1** –
1851	Scott's	**W1** 27
1855	Baltic*	**SE1** 23
1855	Bonds*	**EC2** 21
1857	Warrington*	**W9** 16
1865	Petersham*	**TW10** –
1867	Kettner's*	**W1** 16
1867	Pantechnicon Rooms*	**SW1** 20
1868	St. Pancras*	**NW1** 17
1870	Pepper Tree*	**SW4** –
1873	Gilbert Scott*	**NW1** –
1874	Criterion	**W1** 18
1879	Opera Tavern*	**WC2** –
1880	Bombay Brass.*	**SW7** 23
1881	Duke of Cambridge*	**N1** –
1886	Tuttons Brass.*	**WC2** 16
1888	Da Mario*	**SW7** 20
1889	Savoy Grill	**WC2** 23
1889	Savoy River	**WC2** 21
1889	Sweetings	**EC4** 23
1890	Bradley's*	**NW3** 20
1890	La Fromagerie*	**W1** 22
1890	Maggie Jones's*	**W8** 19
1890	Notting Hill Brass.*	**W11** 22
1890	R.S.J.*	**SE1** 20
1890	Wapping Food*	**E1** 18
1896	Elena's L'Etoile*	**W1** 19
1896	J. Sheekey*	**WC2** 26
1897	Hélène Darroze*	**W1** 24
1900	Annie's*	**W4** 21
1900	Artigiano*	**NW3** 21
1900	Balans*	**SW5** 17
1900	Brinkley's*	**SW10** 17
1900	Frontline*	**W2** 20
1900	Goodman*	**W1** 26
1900	Julie's*	**W11** 19
1900	La Famiglia*	**SW10** 22
1900	Langan's Brass.*	**W1** 19
1900	St. John Bread*	**E1** 25
1905	Almeida*	**N1** 20
1906	Ritz*	**W1** 25
1910	Goring*	**SW1** 24
1910	Viajante*	**E2** 25
1911	Bibendum*	**SW3** 23
1911	Bibendum Oyster*	**SW3** 24
1914	Golden Hind	**W1** 25
1920	Orso*	**WC2** 21
1920	Prism*	**EC3** 18
1920	Tamarind*	**W1** 25
1921	Wolseley*	**W1** 22
1923	Bluebird*	**SW3** 16
1926	Patisserie Valerie	**W1** 16
1926	Quo Vadis	**W1** 21
1926	Veeraswamy	**W1** 24
1930	Sale e Pepe*	**SW1** ?
1930	Sonny's*	**SW13** 23
1931	Dorchester	**W1** 24
1933	Babylon*	**W8** 20
1935	Bistrotheque*	**E2** 23
1939	Geales	**W8** 21
1939	Lutyens*	**EC4** 23
1942	Mon Plaisir*	**WC2** 18
1946	Le Caprice	**SW1** 23
1947	Gessler/Daquise	**SW7** –
1948	Harry Morgan's*	**NW8** 16

SPECIAL FEATURES

Orange		
Orange	**SW1**	22

Park Lane Hotel		
Citrus	**W1**	-

Park Plaza Westminster Bridge Hotel		
NEW Brasserie Joël	**SE1**	-

Petersham Hotel		
Petersham	**TW10**	-

Renaissance Chancery Ct.		
Pearl	**WC1**	26

Ritz Hotel		
Z Ritz	**W1**	25

Royal Garden Hotel		
Min Jiang	**W8**	23

Savoy Hotel		
Savoy Grill	**WC2**	23
Savoy River	**WC2**	21

Sheraton Park Tower		
One-O-One	**SW1**	22

Sloane Sq.		
Chelsea Brass.	**SW1**	18

Sofitel St. James London		
Brasserie Roux	**SW1**	22

Soho Hotel		
Refuel	**W1**	20

St. James's Hotel		
Seven Park	**SW1**	-

St. John Hotel		
NEW St. John Hotel	**WC2**	-

St. Martins Lane Hotel		
Asia de Cuba	**WC2**	21

St. Pancras Renaissance Hotel		
NEW Gilbert Scott	**NW1**	-

Threadneedles Hotel		
Bonds	**EC2**	21

Town Hall Hotel		
Viajante	**E2**	25

Waterside Inn		
Z Waterside Inn	**SL6**	28

W London Leicester Sq.		
NEW Spice Mkt.	**W1**	22

Zetter		
Bistrot Bruno Loubet	**EC1**	23

LATE DINING

(Weekday closing hour)

Alounak	varies	**multi.**	21
Asia de Cuba	varies	**WC2**	21
Automat	1 AM	**W1**	18
Balans	varies	**multi.**	17
Belgo	11:30 PM	**SW4**	19
Bocca/Gelupo	12 AM	**W1**	24
Buona Sera	12 AM	**SW11**	-
Café Boheme	2:30 AM	**W1**	18
Cecconi's	1 AM	**W1**	23
Cinnamon Kitchen	12 AM	**EC2**	23
Ciro's Pizza	varies	**SW3**	13
Del'Aziz	12 AM	**W12**	16
Ed's Easy Diner	12 AM	**W1**	15
Efes	12 AM	**W1**	20
NEW Eleven Park Walk	12 AM	**SW10**	-
Floridita	1 AM	**W1**	13
Forge	12 AM	**WC2**	23
Four Seasons	varies	**W1**	22
Z Gaucho	11:30 PM	**W1**	22
Great Eastern	12 AM	**EC2**	20
Greig's	12 AM	**W1**	22
Z Hakkasan	varies	**W1**	26
Halepi	12 AM	**W2**	21
Hard Rock	12:30 AM	**W1**	15
Haz	12 AM	**E1**	19
Hoxton Grill	12 AM	**EC2**	18
Imperial China	12 AM	**WC2**	18
Inamo	12 AM	**SW1**	15
Ishbilia	12 AM	**SW1**	25
Ishtar	12 AM	**W1**	20
Z Ivy	12 AM	**WC2**	22
Joe Allen	12:45 AM	**WC2**	18
Z J. Sheekey	12 AM	**WC2**	26
Z J. Sheekey Oyster	12 AM	**WC2**	26
La Porchetta	12 AM	**N10**	19
Z Le Caprice	12 AM	**SW1**	23
Le Deuxième	12 AM	**WC2**	22
Le Mercury	1 AM	**N1**	19
Little Bay	12 AM	**multi.**	19
Maroush	varies	**multi.**	22
Montpeliano	12 AM	**SW7**	16
Mr. Chow	12 AM	**SW1**	22
Mr. Kong	2:45 AM	**WC2**	22
Mulberry St.	12 AM	**W2**	16
New World	12 AM	**W1**	18
Noura	varies	**SW1**	21
Original Lahore	12 AM	**multi.**	25
Original Tagines	12 AM	**W1**	-
Orso	12 AM	**WC2**	21
Özer	12 AM	**W1**	20
Pasha	12 AM	**SW7**	18
Ping Pong	varies	**multi.**	16
Pix Pintxos	12 AM	**W11**	16
Pizza East	12 AM, varies	**multi.**	20
Pizza Express	varies	**WC2**	16
Planet Hollywood	1 AM	**SW1**	12
Princi London	12 AM	**W1**	22

NEW Quince | 1 AM | W1	—	
Rocket | 12 AM | W1	20	
Rodizio Rico | 12 AM | multi.	15	
Sabor | varies | N1	—	
Santa Maria/Garufa | 12 AM | SW8	24	
Sophie's Steak | 12 AM | WC2	19	
NEW Spuntino | 12 AM | W1	—	
NEW St. John Hotel | 1:30 AM | WC2	—	
Sumosan | 12 AM | W1	25	
Tokyo Diner | 12 AM | WC2	—	
Vingt-Quatre | 24 hrs. | SW10	14	
Z Wolseley | 12 AM | W1	22	
Wright Brothers | 12 AM | W1	26	

NEWCOMERS

Amaranto | W1	—
Antidote | W1	—
Bar Battu | EC2	—
Barbecoa | EC4	20
Bill's Produce | WC2	20
Bistro du Vin | EC1	—
Bond/Brook | W1	—
Brasserie Joël | SE1	—
Brawn | E2	23
Broadway B&G | SW6	—
Cafe Luc | W1	—
Cantina Laredo | WC2	—
Cantinetta | SW15	—
Casa Batavia | W8	—
Cassis Bistro | SW3	25
Chabrot | SW1	—
Chesterfield | W2	—
Cigalon | WC2	—
Da Polpo | WC2	—
Z Dinner/Heston | SW1	27
Dishoom | WC2	23
Dragoncello | W2	—
5 Pollen St. | W1	—
Folly | EC3	—
Fox/Grapes | SW19	—
Gilbert Scott | NW1	—
Henry Root | SW10	—
Ilia | SW3	—
Indian Zilla | SW13	—
Z Koffmann's | SW1	26
Kopapa | WC2	17
Koya | W1	23
Les Deux | WC2	19
Made in Camden | NW1	—
Massimo | SW1	—
Morito | EC1	26
Nopi | W1	—
North Rd. | EC1	—
Nottingdale | W11	—
Opera Tavern | WC2	—
Penny Black | SW10	—
Phene | SW3	13
Picasso | SW3	—
Pollen St. Social | W1	—
Polpetto | W1	22
Portman | W1	—
Quince | W1	—
Restaurant/Arts | W1	—
Riding Hse. Café | W1	—
Roux/Landau | W1	—
Samarqand | W1	—
Shaka Zulu | NW1	—
Spice Mkt. | W1	22
Spuntino | W1	—
St. John Hotel | WC2	—
Tempo | W1	—
Tinello | SW1	24
Trullo | N1	19
28-50 Wine | EC4	22
Venosi | SW3	—
Verru | W1	—
Yashin Sushi | W8	23

OFFBEAT

Acorn Hse. | WC1	21
Albannach | WC2	16
All Star Lanes | multi.	12
Alounak | multi.	21
Annie's | multi.	21
Archipelago | W1	21
Asia de Cuba | WC2	21
Belgo | multi.	19
Benihana | multi.	17
NEW Bill's Produce | WC2	20
Blue Elephant | SW6	21
Boisdale | multi.	20
Books for Cooks | W11	23
NEW Brawn | E2	23
Brindisa | SE1	23
Cambio de Tercio | SW5	23
Cellar Gascon | EC1	24
Chor Bizarre | W1	23
Chowki | W1	20
Z Club Gascon | EC1	26
Cocoon | W1	20
Crazy Bear | W1	19
Crazy Homies | W2	18
Z Dinings | W1	28
Z NEW Dinner/Heston | SW1	27
Z Fat Duck | SL6	27

SPECIAL FEATURES

Ffiona's | **W8** — 24
Fifteen | **N1** — 21
Food for Thought | **WC2** — 22
Gessler/Daquise | **SW7** — –
Gilgamesh | **NW1** — 19
Inaho | **W2** — 25
Itsu | **multi.** — 16
Jenny Lo's Tea | **SW1** — 19
NEW Kopapa | **WC2** — 17
Kulu Kulu | **multi.** — 22
La Fromagerie | **multi.** — 22
La Porte/Indes | **W1** — 22
Le Cercle | **SW1** — 25
Les Trois Garçons | **E1** — 20
Lucky 7 | **W2** — 19
Maggie Jones's | **W8** — 19
Momo | **W1** — 21
Moro | **EC1** — 26
Nahm | **SW1** — 25
Nautilus Fish | **NW6** — 25
Ottolenghi | **multi.** — 25
Petersham Nurseries | **TW10** — 24
Pho | **EC1** — 20
NEW Polpetto | **W1** — 22
Polpo | **W1** — 23
Princi London | **W1** — 22
Providores | **W1** — 25
Randall/Aubin | **W1** — 19
Ransome's | **SW11** — 19
Z Rasoi Vineet Bhatia | **SW3** — 26
Rivington Grill | **multi.** — 18
Sabor | **N1** — –
Sale e Pepe | **SW1** — 21
Z Sketch/Gallery | **W1** — 21
Solly's | **NW11** — 18
NEW Spuntino | **W1** — –
Z St. John | **EC1** — 26
St. John Bread | **E1** — 25
Taqueria | **W11** — 20
Tate Britain | **SW1** — 19
Tom's Deli | **W11** — –
Troubadour | **SW5** — –
Truc Vert | **W1** — 19
Tsunami | **multi.** — 25
Z Wagamama | **multi.** — 19
Wapping Food | **E1** — 18
Yo! Sushi | **multi.** — 16

OUTDOOR DINING

(G=garden; P=patio; PV=pavement; T=terrace; W=waterside)

Abbeville | PV | **SW4** — 17
Abingdon | PV | **W8** — 20

Admiral Codrington | P | **SW3** — 19
Albion | G | **N1** — 19
Al Hamra | P | **W1** — 23
Almeida | T | **N1** — 20
NEW Amaranto | T | **W1** — –
Anglesea Arms | PV | **W6** — 18
Aqua Nueva | T | **W1** — 19
Archipelago | P | **W1** — 21
Ark | T | **W8** — 21
Artigiano | PV | **NW3** — 21
Aubaine | PV | **SW3** — 17
Babylon | T | **W8** — 20
Bam-Bou | T | **W1** — 20
Bank Westminster | T | **SW1** — 20
Barrafina | PV | **W1** — 26
Belvedere | T | **W8** — 22
Bistrot Bruno Loubet | P | **EC1** — 23
Blueprint | T, W | **SE1** — 18
Boundary | T | **E2** — 20
Builders Arms | PV | **SW3** — 17
Butlers Wharf | P, W | **SE1** — 22
Café Spice | G | **E1** — 25
Cantina/Ponte | P, W | **SE1** — 20
NEW Cantinetta | P | **SW15** — –
Caraffini | PV | **SW1** — 21
Cinnamon Kitchen | T | **EC2** — 23
Coq d'Argent | G, T | **EC2** — 20
Daylesford | PV | **multi.** — 18
Dean St. | PV | **W1** — 21
Eagle | PV | **EC1** — 22
E&O | PV | **W11** — 22
El Gaucho | T | **SW3** — 23
Elistano | PV | **SW3** — 17
Engineer | G | **NW1** — 21
Fifth Floor Cafe | T | **SW1** — 18
Fish | T | **SE1** — 19
Hard Rock | T | **W1** — 15
Hush | P | **W1** — 19
NEW Ilia | PV | **SW3** — –
Inn The Park | T | **SW1** — 17
Ishbilia | PV | **SW1** — 25
Julie's | P, PV | **W11** — 19
La Famiglia | G | **SW10** — 22
La Poule au Pot | P | **SW1** — 21
Z La Trompette | T | **W4** — 26
L'Aventure | T | **NW8** — 26
Le Colombier | T | **SW3** — 24
Z Ledbury | P | **W11** — 29
Le Pont/Tour | T, W | **SE1** — 21
Locanda Ottoemezzo | PV | **W8** — 25
Z L'Oranger | P | **SW1** — 27
Made in Italy | T | **SW3** — 20

Manicomio | P | **SW3**	15
Mediterraneo | PV | **W11**	22
Modern Pantry | PV | **EC1**	22
Momo | T | **W1**	21
Moro | PV | **EC1**	26
Motcombs | PV | **SW1**	21
Narrow | T, W | **E14**	21
Olivomare | PV | **SW1**	24
Orrery | T | **W1**	25
Osteria Basilico | PV | **W11**	25
Oxo Tower | T, W | **SE1**	21
Oxo Tower Brass. | T, W | **SE1**	19
Özer | PV | **W1**	20
Painted Heron | G | **SW1**	24
Paradise | T | **W10**	-
Pellicano | PV | **SW3**	19
Plateau | T | **E14**	19
Porters | PV | **WC2**	15
Quadrato | T, W | **E14**	22
Quo Vadis | T | **W1**	21
Ransome's | T, W | **SW11**	19
Riccardo's | T | **SW3**	16
☑ Ritz | T | **W1**	25
☑ River Café | P, W | **W6**	27
Rocket | PV | **W1**	20
☑ Roka | PV | **multi.**	26
Rotunda | T, W | **N1**	-
Santini | T | **SW1**	26
☑ Scott's | PV | **W1**	27
Semplice Bar | PV | **W1**	21
Smiths/Top Fl. | T | **EC1**	21
Texas Embassy | PV | **SW1**	12
Tom's Deli | G | **W11**	-
Toto's | G | **SW3**	23
202 | G, PV | **W11**	18
Uli | P | **W11**	-
Villandry | PV | **W1**	19
Wapping Food | G | **E1**	18
Westbourne | T | **W2**	15

PEOPLE-WATCHING

Abbeville | **SW4**	17
Admiral Codrington | **SW3**	19
Albemarle | **W1**	23
All Star Lanes | **WC1**	12
☑ Amaya | **SW1**	26
Anthologist | **EC2**	17
NEW Antidote | **W1**	-
Aqua Kyoto | **W1**	20
Asia de Cuba | **WC2**	21
Aubaine | **multi.**	17
Avenue | **SW1**	20
Bam-Bou | **W1**	20

Bangkok | **SW7**	21
NEW Bar Battu | **EC2**	-
☑ Bar Boulud | **SW1**	25
Barrafina | **W1**	26
Barshu | **W1**	25
Ba Shan | **W1**	20
Bellamy's | **W1**	23
☑ Bibendum | **SW3**	23
Bibendum Oyster | **SW3**	24
Blakes | **SW7**	22
Bluebird | **SW3**	16
☑ Bob Bob Ricard | **W1**	20
Bocca/Gelupo | **W1**	24
NEW Bond/Brook | **W1**	-
Boundary | **E2**	20
NEW Brawn | **E2**	23
Brindisa | **multi.**	23
Brinkley's | **SW10**	17
NEW Broadway B&G | **SW6**	-
Bumpkin | **multi.**	20
NEW Cafe Luc | **W1**	-
Caffe Caldesi | **W1**	21
Caraffini | **SW1**	21
NEW Cassis Bistro | **SW3**	25
Cecconi's | **W1**	23
NEW Chabrot | **SW1**	-
Cha Cha Moon | **W1**	16
Chelsea Brass. | **SW1**	18
NEW Chesterfield | **W2**	-
☑ Chilango | **multi.**	22
China Tang | **W1**	21
Christopher's | **WC2**	19
☑ Cinnamon Club | **SW1**	25
Cinnamon Kitchen | **EC2**	23
C London | **W1**	21
☑ Club Gascon | **EC1**	26
Corrigan's | **W1**	25
Daphne's | **SW3**	21
NEW Da Polpo | **WC2**	-
Daylesford | **multi.**	18
Dean St. | **W1**	21
Dehesa | **W1**	24
NEW Dishoom | **WC2**	23
Dock Kitchen | **W10**	21
E&O | **W11**	22
Eight Over Eight | **SW3**	21
Electric Brasserie | **W11**	17
Fifteen | **N1**	21
Fifth Floor | **SW1**	20
Fino | **W1**	24
Fish | **SE1**	19
NEW 5 Pollen St. | **W1**	-

NEW Folly | EC3	-	Olivomare | SW1	24
Franco Manca | multi.	24	NEW Opera Tavern | WC2	-
Galvin Bistrot | W1	24	Osteria Basilico | W11	25
Galvin La Chapelle | E1	25	Palm | SW1	23
Giaconda Dining Room | WC2	23	Pantechnicon Rooms | SW1	20
Gilgamesh | NW1	19	NEW Phene | SW3	13
Z Gordon Ramsay/Clar. | W1	25	NEW Picasso | SW3	-
Z Gordon Ramsay/68 | SW3	28	Pix Pintxos | W11	16
Great Queen St. | WC2	24	Pizza East | E1	20
Z Hakkasan | W1	26	Pizza Express | multi.	16
Hereford Rd. | W2	25	PJ's B&G | SW3	17
High Road Brass. | W4	18	NEW Pollen St. Social | W1	-
Hix | W1	20	NEW Polpetto | W1	22
Hix Oyster | EC1	23	Polpo | W1	23
Hix Rest. | W1	23	Princi London | W1	22
Hush | W1	19	Quaglino's | SW1	18
NEW Ilia | SW3	-	Quo Vadis | W1	21
Inamo | W1	15	Racine | SW3	23
Z Ivy | WC2	22	Riccardo's | SW3	16
Joe Allen | WC2	18	Z River Café | W6	27
Z J. Sheekey | WC2	26	Rocca | multi.	-
Z J. Sheekey Oyster | WC2	26	Z Roka | W1	26
Kensington Pl. | W8	19	Rotunda | N1	-
Kitchen Italia | multi.	14	Sake No Hana | SW1	23
La Famiglia | SW10	22	San Lorenzo | SW3	21
L'Anima | EC2	25	Santini | SW1	26
Z La Petite Maison | W1	27	Savoy Grill | WC2	23
Z L'Atelier/Robuchon | WC2	27	Z Scott's | W1	27
Z La Trompette | W4	26	Semplice Bar | W1	21
Le Café Anglais | W2	22	Semplice Rist. | W1	23
Z Le Caprice | SW1	23	NEW Shaka Zulu | NW1	-
Le Cercle | SW1	25	Z Sketch/Gallery | W1	21
Z Ledbury | W11	29	Z Sketch/Lecture | W1	24
NEW Les Deux | WC2	19	Sophie's Steak | SW10	19
Z Locanda Locatelli | W1	25	Sotheby's Cafe | W1	24
Lucio | SW3	24	NEW Spice Mkt. | W1	22
Lutyens | EC4	23	NEW Spuntino | W1	-
Luxe | E1	12	NEW St. John Hotel | WC2	-
Madsen | SW7	16	Sumosan | W1	25
Manicomio | SW3	15	Sushinho | SW3	16
Z Marcus Wareing | SW1	27	Tendido Cuatro | SW6	-
Maze | W1	24	Tom Aikens | SW3	25
Maze Grill | W1	22	Tom's Deli | W11	-
Mews of Mayfair | W1	17	Tom's Kitchen | SW3	22
Momo | W1	21	Tsuru | multi.	-
My Dining Room | SW6	-	202 | W11	18
Narrow | E14	21	Vingt-Quatre | SW10	14
Z Nobu Berkeley | W1	25	Wahaca | multi.	20
Z Nobu London | W1	27	Z Waterside Inn | SL6	28
NEW Nopi | W1	-	Whitechapel | E1	18
Old Brewery | SE10	18	Wild Honey | W1	23
Olivo | SW1	23	Z Wilton's | SW1	27

POWER SCENES

PRE-THEATRE MENUS

(Call for prices and times)

SPECIAL FEATURES

Forge | WC2	23
Frederick's | N1	20
Goring | SW1	24
Incognico | WC2	19
Indigo | WC2	22
Joe Allen | WC2	18
La Bouchée | SW7	19
Le Deuxième | WC2	22
L'Escargot | W1	22
Matsuri | SW1	24
Mela | WC2	21
Mint Leaf | SW1	22
Mon Plaisir | WC2	18
Orso | WC2	21
Oxo Tower Brass. | SE1	19
Porters | WC2	15
Quo Vadis | W1	21
Racine | SW3	23
Red Fort | W1	24
Ritz | W1	25
Savoy Grill | WC2	23
Theo Randall | W1	23
Veeraswamy | W1	24
Wild Honey | W1	23

PRIVATE ROOMS

(Call for capacity)

Admiral Codrington | SW3	19
Z Alain Ducasse | W1	27
Albannach | WC2	16
Alloro | W1	21
All Star Lanes | WC1	12
Almeida | N1	20
Z Amaya | SW1	26
Auberge du Lac | AL8	24
Babylon | W8	20
Baltic | SE1	23
Bam-Bou | W1	20
Belgo | WC2	19
Benares | W1	23
Benihana | multi.	17
Z Bentley's | W1	26
Z Bob Bob Ricard | W1	20
Bombay Bicycle | SW12	18
Boundary | E2	20
Cambio de Tercio | SW5	23
Z Capital Restaurant | SW3	26
Z Chez Bruce | SW17	27
China Tang | W1	21
Christopher's | WC2	19
Chuen Cheng Ku | W1	20
Chutney Mary | SW10	23
NEW Cigalon | WC2	-

Z Cinnamon Club | SW1	25
C London | W1	21
Cocoon | W1	20
Corrigan's | W1	25
Daphne's | SW3	21
Dehesa | W1	24
Z NEW Dinner/Heston | SW1	27
E&O | W11	22
Eight Over Eight | SW3	21
Fairuz | W1	22
Floridita | W1	13
Franco's | SW1	22
French Horn | RG4	25
Gilgamesh | NW1	19
Z Gordon Ramsay/Clar. | W1	25
Greenhouse | W1	26
Green's | multi.	22
Greig's | W1	22
Guinea Grill | W1	23
Z Hakkasan | W1	26
Hawksmoor | E1	26
Hibiscus | W1	26
Hush | W1	19
Il Convivio | SW1	24
Ishbilia | SW1	25
Z Ivy | WC2	22
Julie's | W11	19
Kai Mayfair | W1	26
Kensington Pl. | W8	19
Z NEW Koffmann's | SW1	26
L'Anima | EC2	25
La Porte/Indes | W1	22
La Poule au Pot | SW1	21
Z L'Atelier/Robuchon | WC2	27
Launceston Pl. | W8	25
Le Café Anglais | W2	22
Le Cercle | SW1	25
Le Colombier | SW3	24
Z Le Manoir/Quat | OX4	28
Le Pont/Tour | SE1	21
L'Escargot | W1	22
Les Trois Garçons | E1	20
Z L'Oranger | SW1	27
Luc's Brasserie | EC3	-
Manicomio | multi.	15
Mao Tai | SW6	20
Z Marcus Wareing | SW1	27
Masala Zone | multi.	19
NEW Massimo | SW1	-
Matsuri | SW1	24
Maze | W1	24
Memories/China | SW1	23

SPECIAL FEATURES

☑ Glasshouse | **TW9**	26
☑ Gordon Ramsay/Clar. | **W1**	25
☑ Gordon Ramsay/68 | **SW3**	28
Greenhouse | **W1**	26
☑ Hélène Darroze | **W1**	24
Hibiscus | **W1**	26
☑**NEW** Koffmann's | **SW1**	26
Ladurée | **multi.**	23
☑ L'Atelier/Robuchon | **WC2**	27
☑ La Trompette | **W4**	26
Launceston Pl. | **W8**	25
Le Café Anglais | **W2**	22
Le Cercle | **SW1**	25
☑ Ledbury | **W11**	29
☑ Le Gavroche | **W1**	28
☑ Le Manoir/Quat | **OX4**	28
☑ Locanda Locatelli | **W1**	25
☑ L'Oranger | **SW1**	27
☑ Marcus Wareing | **SW1**	27
NEW Massimo | **SW1**	-
Maze | **W1**	24
☑ Murano | **W1**	27
☑ Nobu Berkeley | **W1**	25
☑ Nobu London | **W1**	27
Orrery | **W1**	25
☑ Oslo Court | **NW8**	26
Ottolenghi | **multi.**	25
Palm | **SW1**	23
Patisserie Valerie | **multi.**	16
Petrus | **SW1**	25
☑ Pied à Terre | **W1**	28
Plateau | **E14**	19
NEW Pollen St. Social | **W1**	-
Princi London | **W1**	22
Providores | **W1**	25
☑ Rasoi Vineet Bhatia | **SW3**	26
Rhodes W1 | **W1**	24
Richoux | **multi.**	17
☑ Ritz | **W1**	25
☑ River Café | **W6**	27
Savoy Grill | **WC2**	23
Semplice Rist. | **W1**	23
☑ Sketch/Gallery | **W1**	21
☑ Sketch/Lecture | **W1**	24
☑ Sketch/Parlour | **W1**	23
☑ Square | **W1**	27
St. John Bread | **E1**	25
NEW St. John Hotel | **WC2**	-
Theo Randall | **W1**	23
Tom Aikens | **SW3**	25
Trinity | **SW4**	25
☑ Waterside Inn | **SL6**	28

☑ Wolseley | **W1**	22
☑ Yauatcha | **W1**	25
☑ Zafferano | **SW1**	26
☑ Zuma | **SW7**	26

QUIET CONVERSATION

☑ Alain Ducasse | **W1**	27
Al Sultan | **W1**	23
NEW Amaranto | **W1**	-
Apsleys | **SW1**	25
☑ Arbutus | **W1**	25
Axis | **WC2**	22
Babbo | **W1**	22
Bank Westminster | **SW1**	20
Bellamy's | **W1**	23
Benares | **W1**	23
Bengal Clipper | **SE1**	23
Bingham | **TW10**	25
Bistro K | **SW7**	-
Blakes | **SW7**	22
NEW Bond/Brook | **W1**	-
Brass. St. Jacques | **SW1**	21
☑ Capital Restaurant | **SW3**	26
NEW Casa Batavia | **W8**	-
NEW Chesterfield | **W2**	-
NEW Cigalon | **WC2**	-
☑ Clarke's | **W8**	26
☑ Clos Maggiore | **WC2**	24
Dolada | **W1**	-
☑ Espelette | **W1**	24
French Table | **KT6**	-
NEW Gilbert Scott | **NW1**	-
Goring | **SW1**	24
Green's | **multi.**	22
☑ Hélène Darroze | **W1**	24
Hibiscus | **W1**	26
High Timber | **EC4**	21
Il Convivio | **SW1**	24
NEW Indian Zilla | **SW13**	-
Indigo | **WC2**	22
JW Steak | **W1**	21
Kensington Sq. | **W8**	21
Kitchen W8 | **W8**	25
☑**NEW** Koffmann's | **SW1**	26
Koi | **W8**	25
La Genova | **W1**	25
Launceston Pl. | **W8**	25
L'Autre Pied | **W1**	24
☑ Le Gavroche | **W1**	28
☑ Le Manoir/Quat | **OX4**	28
☑ L'Oranger | **SW1**	27
Lutyens | **EC4**	23

SPECIAL FEATURES

Northbank	**EC4**	⁻
Odette's	**NW1**	18
Odin's	**W1**	21
Old Brewery	**SE10**	18
Orrery	**W1**	25
Paramount	**WC1**	16
Pasha	**SW7**	18
NEW Penny Black	**SW10**	⁻
Petrus	**SW1**	25
NEW Quince	**W1**	⁻
Z Rasoi Vineet Bhatia	**SW3**	26
Rhodes W1	**W1**	24
Z Ritz	**W1**	25
Z River Café	**W6**	27
Z Roussillon	**SW1**	26
San Lorenzo	**SW3**	21
Sardo Canale	**NW1**	19
Z Sketch/Lecture	**W1**	24
NEW Spice Mkt.	**W1**	22
Z Square	**W1**	27
NEW Tinello	**SW1**	24
Tom Aikens	**SW3**	25
Toto's	**SW3**	23
Veeraswamy	**W1**	24
Viajante	**E2**	25
Z Waterside Inn	**SL6**	28
Z Zafferano	**SW1**	26
Z Zuma	**SW7**	26

SENIOR APPEAL

Z Alain Ducasse	**W1**	27
Albemarle	**W1**	23
Al Duca	**SW1**	19
NEW Amaranto	**W1**	⁻
Z Amaya	**SW1**	26
Angelus	**W2**	23
Apsleys	**SW1**	25
Z Arbutus	**W1**	25
Aubaine	**multi.**	17
Aubergine	**SL7**	24
Babbo	**W1**	22
Z Bar Boulud	**SW1**	25
Bellamy's	**W1**	23
Belvedere	**W8**	22
Z Bentley's	**W1**	26
Z Bibendum	**SW3**	23
Bistro K	**SW7**	⁻
NEW Bond/Brook	**W1**	⁻
Bonds	**EC2**	21
Brasserie Roux	**SW1**	22
Brass. St. Jacques	**SW1**	21
Brompton B&G	**SW3**	22
Caffe Caldesi	**W1**	21

Z Capital Restaurant	**SW3**	26
NEW Casa Batavia	**W8**	⁻
Cecconi's	**W1**	23
Chelsea Brass.	**SW1**	18
Chelsea Kitchen	**SW10**	15
China Tang	**W1**	21
Citrus	**W1**	⁻
Cliveden Hse.	**SL6**	23
C London	**W1**	21
Corrigan's	**W1**	25
Côte	**multi.**	17
Dolada	**W1**	⁻
Z Dorchester	**W1**	24
Elena's L'Etoile	**W1**	19
Empress of Sichuan	**WC2**	⁻
Z Espelette	**W1**	24
Forge	**WC2**	23
Fortnum's Fountain	**W1**	20
Foxtrot Oscar	**SW3**	15
Franco's	**SW1**	22
French Table	**KT6**	⁻
Galvin at Windows	**W1**	24
Galvin Bistrot	**W1**	24
Galvin La Chapelle	**E1**	25
NEW Gilbert Scott	**NW1**	⁻
Z Glasshouse	**TW9**	26
Z Goodman	**multi.**	26
Z Gordon Ramsay/Clar.	**W1**	25
Z Gordon Ramsay/68	**SW3**	28
Goring	**SW1**	24
Green Door	**SW7**	25
Greenhouse	**W1**	26
Green's	**multi.**	22
Z Hélène Darroze	**W1**	24
Hibiscus	**W1**	26
High Timber	**EC4**	21
NEW Ilia	**SW3**	⁻
NEW Indian Zilla	**SW13**	⁻
Z Ivy	**WC2**	22
Z J. Sheekey	**WC2**	26
Z J. Sheekey Oyster	**WC2**	26
Kai Mayfair	**W1**	26
Kitchen W8	**W8**	25
Z **NEW** Koffmann's	**SW1**	26
Ladurée	**SW1**	23
La Genova	**W1**	25
Langan's Bistro	**W1**	21
La Poule au Pot	**SW1**	21
Z L'Atelier/Robuchon	**WC2**	27
Launceston Pl.	**W8**	25
L'Autre Pied	**W1**	24
Le Café Anglais	**W2**	22

Vote at ZAGAT.com

Le Caprice	SW1	23	
e Colombier	SW3	24	
Ledbury	W11	29	
Le Gavroche	W1	28	
Le Manoir/Quat	OX4	28	
NEW Les Deux	WC2	19	
e Suquet	SW3	23	
'Etranger	SW7	24	
Locanda Locatelli	W1	25	
L'Oranger	SW1	27	
utyens	EC4	23	
Magdalen	SE1	24	
Manson	SW6	-	
Marcus Wareing	SW1	27	
NEW Massimo	SW1	-	
Maze Grill	W1	22	
Min Jiang	W8	23	
Montpeliano	SW7	16	
Motcombs	SW1	21	
Murano	W1	27	
My Dining Room	SW6	-	
.901	EC2	21	
Noura	multi.	21	
Odin's	W1	21	
Olivomare	SW1	24	
One-O-One	SW1	22	
Orrery	W1	25	
Osteria Dell'Angolo	SW1	22	
Pantechnicon Rooms	SW1	20	
Paramount	WC1	16	
Patisserie Valerie	multi.	16	
etrus	SW1	25	
Poissonnerie	SW3	22	
Quadrato	E14	22	
Quirinale	SW1	23	
Quo Vadis	W1	21	
Racine	SW3	23	
ed Fort	W1	24	
eubens	W1	19	
hodes W1	W1	24	
Rib Room	SW1	22	
Richoux	multi.	17	
Ritz	W1	25	
Roast	SE1	24	
Roux/Parliament	SW1	24	
Rowley's	SW1	18	
Rules	WC2	23	
antini	SW1	26	
artoria	W1	22	
avoy Grill	WC2	23	
avoy River	WC2	21	
calini	SW3	23	

Ⓩ Scott's	W1	27	
Semplice Rist.	W1	23	
Seven Park	SW1	-	
Shepherd's	SW1	19	
Ⓩ Simpson's/Strand	WC2	22	
Ⓩ Sketch/Lecture	W1	24	
Sotheby's Cafe	W1	24	
Ⓩ Square	W1	27	
St. James's	W1	23	
St. Pancras	NW1	17	
Tate Britain	SW1	19	
NEW Tempo	W1	-	
Theo Randall	W1	23	
NEW Tinello	SW1	24	
Tom Aikens	SW3	25	
Toto's	SW3	23	
NEW Venosi	SW3	-	
Wallace	W1	17	
Ⓩ Waterside Inn	SL6	28	
Wild Honey	W1	23	
Ⓩ Wilton's	SW1	27	
Ⓩ Wolseley	W1	22	
Ⓩ Zafferano	SW1	26	

SET-PRICE MENUS

(Call for prices and times)

Abingdon	W8	20	
Ⓩ Alain Ducasse	W1	27	
Al Duca	SW1	19	
Alloro	W1	21	
Almeida	N1	20	
Ⓩ Amaya	SW1	26	
Angelus	W2	23	
Apsleys	SW1	25	
Ⓩ Arbutus	W1	25	
Axis	WC2	22	
Baltic	SE1	23	
Ⓩ Bar Boulud	SW1	25	
Bellamy's	W1	23	
Belvedere	W8	22	
Benares	W1	23	
Bengal Clipper	SE1	23	
Ⓩ Bibendum	SW3	23	
Blue Elephant	SW6	21	
Brasserie Roux	SW1	22	
Butlers Wharf	SE1	22	
Café des Amis	WC2	18	
Ⓩ Café Japan	NW11	27	
Café Spice	E1	25	
Ⓩ Capital Restaurant	SW3	26	
Caravaggio	EC3	19	
Ⓩ Chez Bruce	SW17	27	
Chor Bizarre	W1	23	

SPECIAL FEATURES

Christopher's | **WC2**	19
Chutney Mary | **SW10**	23
Cigala | **WC1**	20
☑ Cinnamon Club | **SW1**	25
☑ Clos Maggiore | **WC2**	24
☑ Club Gascon | **EC1**	26
Coq d'Argent | **EC2**	20
Crazy Bear | **W1**	19
Criterion | **W1**	18
☑ Defune | **W1**	26
El Pirata | **W1**	20
Enoteca Turi | **SW15**	25
☑ Fat Duck | **SL6**	27
Fifteen | **N1**	21
Forge | **WC2**	23
Galvin Bistrot | **W1**	24
Gauthier | **W1**	24
☑ Glasshouse | **TW9**	26
☑ Gordon Ramsay/Clar. | **W1**	25
☑ Gordon Ramsay/68 | **SW3**	28
Goring | **SW1**	24
Greenhouse | **W1**	26
☑ Hélène Darroze | **W1**	24
Hibiscus | **W1**	26
High Road Brass. | **W4**	18
☑ Hunan | **SW1**	28
Il Convivio | **SW1**	24
Indigo | **WC2**	22
☑ J. Sheekey | **WC2**	26
Kai Mayfair | **W1**	26
Kensington Pl. | **W8**	19
☑ Kiku | **W1**	27
Langan's Bistro | **W1**	21
La Poule au Pot | **SW1**	21
☑ L'Atelier/Robuchon | **WC2**	27
Latium | **W1**	24
☑ La Trompette | **W4**	26
Launceston Pl. | **W8**	25
L'Autre Pied | **W1**	24
L'Aventure | **NW8**	26
Le Café/Marché | **EC1**	24
Le Cercle | **SW1**	25
Le Colombier | **SW3**	24
☑ Ledbury | **W11**	29
☑ Le Gavroche | **W1**	28
☑ Le Manoir/Quat | **OX4**	28
L'Escargot | **W1**	22
Les Trois Garçons | **E1**	20
L'Etranger | **SW7**	24
Le Vacherin | **W4**	23
Locanda Ottoemezzo | **W8**	25
☑ L'Oranger | **SW1**	27
Lucio | **SW3**	24
☑ Marcus Wareing | **SW1**	27
Matsuri | **SW1**	24
Maze | **W1**	24
Maze Grill | **W1**	22
Mela | **WC2**	21
Memories/China | **W8**	23
Morgan M | **N7**	26
☑ Murano | **W1**	27
☑ Nobu Berkeley | **W1**	25
☑ Nobu London | **W1**	27
🆕 North Rd. | **EC1**	-
Noura | **multi.**	21
Olivo | **SW1**	23
One-O-One | **SW1**	22
Orrery | **W1**	25
☑ Oslo Court | **NW8**	26
Oxo Tower | **SE1**	21
Özer | **W1**	20
Patara | **multi.**	24
Patterson's | **W1**	24
Pellicano | **SW3**	19
☑ Pied à Terre | **W1**	28
Plateau | **E14**	19
Poissonnerie | **SW3**	22
Porters | **WC2**	15
Princess Garden | **W1**	25
Quilon | **SW1**	26
Racine | **SW3**	23
Rasa | **multi.**	24
☑ Rasoi Vineet Bhatia | **SW3**	26
Red Fort | **W1**	24
Rib Room | **SW1**	22
☑ Ritz | **W1**	25
☑ Roussillon | **SW1**	26
Roux/Parliament | **SW1**	24
Royal China | **W2**	23
Sartoria | **W1**	22
Savoy Grill | **WC2**	23
Semplice Rist. | **W1**	23
☑ Sketch/Lecture | **W1**	24
Sofra | **multi.**	19
Sonny's | **SW13**	23
Sophie's Steak | **multi.**	19
☑ Square | **W1**	27
☑ Tamarind | **W1**	25
Tentazioni | **SE1**	24
Theo Randall | **W1**	23
Tom Aikens | **SW3**	25
Toto's | **SW3**	23
Trishna | **W1**	26
☑ Umu | **W1**	26

Nautilus Fish | **NW6**	25
Osteria Dell'Angolo | **SW1**	22
Quadrato | **E14**	22
Quirinale | **SW1**	23
Red Pepper | **W9**	23
Roux/Parliament | **SW1**	24
Royal Oak | **SL6**	22
Santini | **SW1**	26
Sardo | **W1**	22
Sonny's | **SW13**	23
Sotheby's Cafe | **W1**	24
Timo | **W8**	22
Vasco & Piero's | **W1**	24
Viet Grill | **E2**	22
Yming | **W1**	25
Zayna | **W1**	24

SPECIAL OCCASIONS

Z Alain Ducasse | **W1**	27
Albemarle | **W1**	23
Almeida | **N1**	20
NEW Amaranto | **W1**	-
Z Amaya | **SW1**	26
Angelus | **W2**	23
Apsleys | **SW1**	25
Asia de Cuba | **WC2**	21
Auberge du Lac | **AL8**	24
Aubergine | **SL7**	24
Z Bar Boulud | **SW1**	25
Belvedere | **W8**	22
Z Bentley's | **W1**	26
Z Bibendum | **SW3**	23
Bistrot Bruno Loubet | **EC1**	23
Blakes | **SW7**	22
Bluebird | **SW3**	16
Blue Elephant | **SW6**	21
Bocca/Gelupo | **W1**	24
Z Capital Restaurant | **SW3**	26
NEW Cassis Bistro | **SW3**	25
Cecconi's | **W1**	23
Z Chez Bruce | **SW17**	27
China Tang | **W1**	21
Chutney Mary | **SW10**	23
NEW Cigalon | **WC2**	-
Z Cinnamon Club | **SW1**	25
Cinnamon Kitchen | **EC2**	23
Z Clarke's | **W8**	26
C London | **W1**	21
Z Club Gascon | **EC1**	26
Corrigan's | **W1**	25
Crazy Bear | **W1**	19
Criterion | **W1**	18
Daphne's | **SW3**	21

Dean St. | **W1**	21
Z **NEW** Dinner/Heston | **SW1**	27
Z Dorchester | **W1**	24
Z Fat Duck | **SL6**	27
Fifteen | **N1**	21
Fino | **W1**	24
NEW 5 Pollen St. | **W1**	-
Floridita | **W1**	13
French Horn | **RG4**	25
French Table | **KT6**	-
Galvin at Windows | **W1**	24
Galvin Bistrot | **W1**	24
Galvin La Chapelle | **E1**	25
Gauthier | **W1**	24
NEW Gilbert Scott | **NW1**	-
Z Glasshouse | **TW9**	26
Z Gordon Ramsay/Clar. | **W1**	25
Z Gordon Ramsay/68 | **SW3**	28
Goring | **SW1**	24
Green Door | **SW7**	25
Greenhouse | **W1**	26
Green's | **multi.**	22
Z Hakkasan | **W1**	26
Z Hélène Darroze | **W1**	24
Hibiscus | **W1**	26
NEW Ilia | **SW3**	-
Z Ivy | **WC2**	22
Z J. Sheekey | **WC2**	26
Z **NEW** Koffmann's | **SW1**	26
Z La Petite Maison | **W1**	27
Z L'Atelier/Robuchon | **WC2**	27
Z La Trompette | **W4**	26
Launceston Pl. | **W8**	25
Le Café Anglais | **W2**	22
Z Le Caprice | **SW1**	23
Le Cercle | **SW1**	25
Z Ledbury | **W11**	29
Z Le Gavroche | **W1**	28
Z Le Manoir/Quat | **OX4**	28
Le Pont/Tour | **SE1**	21
Z Locanda Locatelli | **W1**	25
Z L'Oranger | **SW1**	27
Lutyens | **EC4**	23
Luxe | **E1**	12
Z Marcus Wareing | **SW1**	27
NEW Massimo | **SW1**	-
Maze | **W1**	24
Maze Grill | **W1**	22
Min Jiang | **W8**	23
Momo | **W1**	21
Morgan M | **N7**	26
Z Murano | **W1**	27

Vote at ZAGAT.com

My Dining Room | **SW6**	–
Nahm | **SW1**	25
.901 | **EC2**	21
Nobu Berkeley | **W1**	25
Nobu London | **W1**	27
Orrery | **W1**	25
Palm | **SW1**	23
Paramount | **WC1**	16
Pearl | **WC1**	26
Petersham | **TW10**	–
Petrus | **SW1**	25
Pied à Terre | **W1**	28
Plateau | **E14**	19
NEW Pollen St. Social | **W1**	–
Providores | **W1**	25
Quaglino's | **SW1**	18
NEW Quince | **W1**	–
Quo Vadis | **W1**	21
Racine | **SW3**	23
Rasoi Vineet Bhatia | **SW3**	26
Rhodes W1 | **W1**	24
Ritz | **W1**	25
River Café | **W6**	27
Roast | **SE1**	24
Roux/Parliament | **SW1**	24
San Lorenzo | **SW3**	21
Santini | **SW1**	26
Savoy Grill | **WC2**	23
Savoy River | **WC2**	21
Scott's | **W1**	27
Semplice Rist. | **W1**	23
Seven Park | **SW1**	–
NEW Shaka Zulu | **NW1**	–
Sketch/Lecture | **W1**	24
Skylon | **SE1**	19
Smiths/Dining Rm. | **EC1**	23
Smiths/Top Fl. | **EC1**	21
NEW Spice Mkt. | **W1**	22
Square | **W1**	27
Texture | **W1**	25
Theo Randall | **W1**	23
NEW Tinello | **SW1**	24
Tom Aikens | **SW3**	25
Trinity | **SW4**	25
Umu | **W1**	26
Waterside Inn | **SL6**	28
Wilton's | **SW1**	27
Wolseley | **W1**	22
York & Albany | **NW1**	21
Zafferano | **SW1**	26
Zaika | **W8**	25
Zuma | **SW7**	26

TEA SERVICE

(See also Hotel Dining)

NEW Amaranto | **W1**	–
Anthologist | **EC2**	17
Bingham | **TW10**	25
Z Bob Bob Ricard | **W1**	20
Botanist | **SW1**	17
NEW Cafe Luc | **W1**	–
Chor Bizarre | **W1**	23
Cliveden Hse. | **SL6**	23
Criterion | **W1**	18
Daylesford | **multi.**	18
Dean St. | **W1**	21
Empress of India | **E9**	20
Z Espelette | **W1**	24
Fifth Floor | **SW1**	20
Fifth Floor Cafe | **SW1**	18
NEW 5 Pollen St. | **W1**	–
Flemings Grill | **W1**	–
NEW Folly | **EC3**	–
Food for Thought | **WC2**	22
Fortnum's Fountain | **W1**	20
Franco's | **SW1**	22
Goring | **SW1**	24
Gravetye Manor | **RH19**	–
Green Door | **SW7**	25
High Road Brass. | **W4**	18
Hix Rest. | **W1**	23
Indigo | **WC2**	22
Inn The Park | **SW1**	17
Julie's | **W11**	19
Just St. James's | **SW1**	18
Kensington Sq. | **W8**	21
Ladurée | **multi.**	23
La Fromagerie | **multi.**	22
Leon | **W1D**	17
NEW Les Deux | **WC2**	19
National Dining Rooms | **WC2**	17
1901 | **EC2**	21
Patisserie Valerie | **multi.**	16
Portrait | **WC2**	21
Quadrato | **E14**	22
NEW Quince | **W1**	–
Refuel | **W1**	20
NEW Restaurant/Arts | **W1**	–
Richoux | **multi.**	17
Z Sketch/Parlour | **W1**	23
Sotheby's Cafe | **W1**	24
St. James's | **W1**	23
St. Pancras | **NW1**	17
Tate Britain | **SW1**	19
Tate Modern | **SE1**	18

Tom's Kitchen	**WC2**	22
Truc Vert	**W1**	19
202	**W11**	18
Villandry	**W1**	19
Vingt-Quatre	**SW10**	14
Wallace	**W1**	17
Wild Honey	**W1**	23
Z Wolseley	**W1**	22
Z Yauatcha	**W1**	25

TRENDY

Admiral Codrington	**SW3**	19
All Star Lanes	**multi.**	12
Z Amaya	**SW1**	26
Anchor & Hope	**SE1**	23
Angels & Gypsies	**SE5**	-
Anthologist	**EC2**	17
NEW Antidote	**W1**	-
Aqua Kyoto	**W1**	20
Armani Caffé	**SW3**	19
Asia de Cuba	**WC2**	21
Assaggi	**W2**	26
Aubaine	**multi.**	17
Automat	**W1**	18
Avenue	**SW1**	20
Baker & Spice	**multi.**	22
Bam-Bou	**W1**	20
NEW Bar Battu	**EC2**	-
NEW Barbecoa	**EC4**	20
Z Bar Boulud	**SW1**	25
Barrafina	**W1**	26
Barrica	**W1**	-
Barshu	**W1**	25
Ba Shan	**W1**	20
Belgo	**multi.**	19
Belvedere	**W8**	22
Benito's Hat	**W1**	19
Bibendum Oyster	**SW3**	24
NEW Bill's Produce	**WC2**	20
Bincho Yakitori	**W1**	22
Bistrot Bruno Loubet	**EC1**	23
Blakes	**SW7**	22
Z Bob Bob Ricard	**W1**	20
Bocca/Gelupo	**W1**	24
NEW Bond/Brook	**W1**	-
Botanist	**SW1**	17
NEW Brawn	**E2**	23
Brindisa	**multi.**	23
NEW Broadway B&G	**SW6**	-
Bumpkin	**multi.**	20
Z Busaba Eathai	**multi.**	23
Cadogan Arms	**SW3**	15
NEW Cafe Luc	**W1**	-

Canteen	**multi.**	16
Caraffini	**SW1**	21
Carluccio's	**multi.**	17
NEW Cassis Bistro	**SW3**	25
Cecconi's	**W1**	23
Cellar Gascon	**EC1**	24
Cha Cha Moon	**W1**	16
Cheyne Walk	**SW3**	21
Z Chez Bruce	**SW17**	27
Z Chilango	**N1**	22
Christopher's	**WC2**	19
Z Cinnamon Club	**SW1**	25
Cinnamon Kitchen	**EC2**	23
Z Clarke's	**W8**	26
C London	**W1**	21
Z Club Gascon	**EC1**	26
Cocoon	**W1**	20
Comptoir Libanais	**multi.**	17
Constancia	**SE1**	-
Crazy Bear	**W1**	19
Crazy Homies	**W2**	18
Daphne's	**SW3**	21
NEW Da Polpo	**WC2**	-
Daylesford	**multi.**	18
Dean St.	**W1**	21
Dehesa	**W1**	24
Del'Aziz	**SE1**	16
NEW Dishoom	**WC2**	23
Dock Kitchen	**W10**	21
NEW Dragoncello	**W2**	-
E&O	**W11**	22
Eight Over Eight	**SW3**	21
Electric Brasserie	**W11**	17
Elistano	**SW3**	17
El Pirata	**W2**	20
Enterprise	**SW3**	20
Fifteen	**N1**	21
Fino	**W1**	24
Fish	**SE1**	19
NEW 5 Pollen St.	**W1**	-
NEW Folly	**EC3**	-
Forman's Fish Island	**E3**	-
Franco Manca	**multi.**	24
Galvin Bistrot	**W1**	24
Galvin La Chapelle	**E1**	25
Gilgamesh	**NW1**	19
Great Queen St.	**WC2**	24
Z Hakkasan	**W1**	26
Z Harwood Arms	**SW6**	27
Hawksmoor	**multi.**	26
Hereford Rd.	**W2**	25
High Road Brass.	**W4**	18

SPECIAL FEATURES

Restaurant	Rating
NEW Cafe Luc | W1	-
Caffe Caldesi | W1	21
Z Capital Restaurant | SW3	26
Caravaggio | EC3	19
NEW Casa Batavia | W8	-
NEW Cassis Bistro | SW3	25
Cecconi's | W1	23
Z Chez Bruce | SW17	27
China Tang | W1	21
Christopher's | WC2	19
Chutney Mary | SW10	23
NEW Cigalon | WC2	-
Z Cinnamon Club | SW1	25
Cinnamon Kitchen | EC2	23
Z Clarke's | W8	26
Cliveden Hse. | SL6	23
C London | W1	21
Z Club Gascon | EC1	26
Constancia | SE1	-
Coq d'Argent | EC2	20
Corrigan's | W1	25
Criterion | W1	18
Daphne's | SW3	21
Z NEW Dinner/Heston | SW1	27
Dock Kitchen | W10	21
Dolada | W1	-
Z Dorchester | W1	24
NEW Dragoncello | W2	-
Elena's L'Etoile | W1	19
Empress of Sichuan | WC2	-
Z Fat Duck | SL6	27
Fifteen | N1	21
Fifth Floor | SW1	20
Fino | W1	24
NEW 5 Pollen St. | W1	-
Forge | WC2	23
Galvin at Windows | W1	24
Galvin Bistrot | W1	24
Galvin La Chapelle | E1	25
NEW Gilbert Scott | NW1	-
Z Glasshouse | TW9	26
Z Goodman | multi.	26
Z Gordon Ramsay/Clar. | W1	25
Z Gordon Ramsay/68 | SW3	28
Green Door | SW7	25
Greenhouse | W1	26
Green's | multi.	22
Z Hakkasan | W1	26
Z Hélène Darroze | W1	24
Hibiscus | W1	26
High Timber | EC4	21
Hix | W1	20
Hix Rest. | W1	23
NEW Ilia | SW3	-
Z Ivy | WC2	22
Z J. Sheekey | WC2	26
Z J. Sheekey Oyster | WC2	26
JW Steak | W1	21
Kai Mayfair | W1	26
Kazan | SW1	20
Kitchen W8 | W8	25
Z NEW Koffmann's | SW1	26
Langan's Brass. | W1	19
L'Anima | EC2	25
Z La Petite Maison | W1	27
Z L'Atelier/Robuchon | WC2	27
Launceston Pl. | W8	25
L'Autre Pied | W1	24
Le Café Anglais | W2	22
Z Le Caprice | SW1	23
Z Ledbury | W11	29
Z Le Gavroche | W1	28
Z Le Manoir/Quat | OX4	28
Le Pont/Tour | SE1	21
NEW Les Deux | WC2	19
Z Locanda Locatelli | W1	25
Z L'Oranger | SW1	27
Lutyens | EC4	23
Luxe | E1	12
Marco Pierre White | E1	19
Z Marcus Wareing | SW1	27
NEW Massimo | SW1	-
Matsuri | SW1	24
Maze | W1	24
Maze Grill | W1	22
Min Jiang | W8	23
Z Murano | W1	27
My Dining Room | SW6	-
Nahm | SW1	25
1901 | EC2	21
Z Nobu Berkeley | W1	25
Z Nobu London | W1	27
NEW Nopi | W1	-
Northbank | EC4	-
Odin's | W1	21
One-O-One | SW1	22
Orrery | W1	25
Oxo Tower | SE1	21
Palm | SW1	23
Pantechnicon Rooms | SW1	20
Paramount | WC1	16
NEW Penny Black | SW10	-
Petrus | SW1	25
Z Pied à Terre | W1	28

SPECIAL FEATURES

Plateau | **E14**	19
Poissonnerie | **SW3**	22
NEW Pollen St. Social | **W1**	-
Providores | **W1**	25
NEW Quince | **W1**	-
Quirinale | **SW1**	23
Quo Vadis | **W1**	21
Z Rasoi Vineet Bhatia | **SW3**	26
Red Fort | **W1**	24
Rhodes 24 | **EC2**	23
Rhodes W1 | **W1**	24
Z Ritz | **W1**	25
Z River Café | **W6**	27
Roast | **SE1**	24
Z Roka | **W1**	26
Roux/Parliament | **SW1**	24
Sake No Hana | **SW1**	23
NEW Samarqand | **W1**	-
San Lorenzo | **SW3**	21
Santini | **SW1**	26
Sartoria | **W1**	22
Savoy Grill | **WC2**	23
Z Scott's | **W1**	27
Semplice Rist. | **W1**	23
Seven Park | **SW1**	-
NEW Shaka Zulu | **NW1**	-
Shanghai Blues | **WC1**	22
Z Sketch/Lecture | **W1**	24
Skylon | **SE1**	19
Smiths/Top Fl. | **EC1**	21
NEW Spice Mkt. | **W1**	22
Z Square | **W1**	27
St. Pancras | **NW1**	17
Sumosan | **W1**	25
Sushinho | **SW3**	16
Z Tamarind | **W1**	25
NEW Tempo | **W1**	-
Texture | **W1**	25
Theo Randall | **W1**	23
NEW Tinello | **SW1**	24
Tom Aikens | **SW3**	25
Tompkins | **E14**	-
Trinity | **SW4**	25
NEW 28-50 Wine | **EC4**	22
Z Umu | **W1**	26
Veeraswamy | **W1**	24
NEW Venosi | **SW3**	-
Viajante | **E2**	25
Z Waterside Inn | **SL6**	28
Wheeler's | **SW1**	21
Wild Honey | **W1**	23
Z Wilton's | **SW1**	27

York & Albany | **NW1**	21
Z Zafferano | **SW1**	26
Zaika | **W8**	25
Z Zuma | **SW7**	26

WINNING WINE LISTS

Z Alain Ducasse | **W1**	27
Albemarle | **W1**	23
Alloro | **W1**	21
NEW Amaranto | **W1**	-
Andrew Edmunds | **W1**	23
Angelus | **W2**	23
NEW Antidote | **W1**	-
Apsleys | **SW1**	25
Z Arbutus | **W1**	25
Auberge du Lac | **AL8**	24
Aubergine | **SL7**	24
NEW Bar Battu | **EC2**	-
Z Bar Boulud | **SW1**	25
Belvedere | **W8**	22
Z Bibendum | **SW3**	23
Bistrot Bruno Loubet | **EC1**	23
Bleeding Heart | **EC1**	22
Z Bob Bob Ricard | **W1**	20
Bocca/Gelupo | **W1**	24
Boisdale | **multi.**	20
NEW Brawn | **E2**	23
Cambio de Tercio | **SW5**	23
Cantina Vino. | **SE1**	18
Z Capital Restaurant | **SW3**	26
Caravaggio | **EC3**	19
NEW Cassis Bistro | **SW3**	25
Cellar Gascon | **EC1**	24
Z Chez Bruce | **SW17**	27
Christopher's | **WC2**	19
Chutney Mary | **SW10**	23
NEW Cigalon | **WC2**	-
Z Cinnamon Club | **SW1**	25
Z Clarke's | **W8**	26
Cliveden Hse. | **SL6**	23
C London | **W1**	21
Z Club Gascon | **EC1**	26
Coq d'Argent | **EC2**	20
Criterion | **W1**	18
Don | **EC4**	23
Z Dorchester | **W1**	24
Ebury Wine | **SW1**	18
Enoteca Turi | **SW15**	25
Z Fat Duck | **SL6**	27
Fifteen | **N1**	21
Fifth Floor | **SW1**	20
Fino | **W1**	24

Vote at ZAGAT.com

SPECIAL FEATURES

Wine Vintage Chart

This chart is based on our 0 to 30 scale. The ratings (by U. of South Carolina law professor **Howard Stravitz**) reflect vintage quality and the wine's readiness to drink. A dash means the wine is past its peak or too young to rate. Loire ratings are for dry whites.

Whites	95	96	97	98	99	00	01	02	03	04	05	06	07	08	09
France:															
Alsace	24	23	23	25	23	25	26	23	21	24	25	24	26	25	25
Burgundy	27	26	22	21	24	24	24	27	23	26	27	25	26	25	25
Loire Valley	-	-	-	-	-	-	-	26	21	23	27	23	24	24	26
Champagne	26	27	24	23	25	24	21	26	21	-	-	-	-	-	-
Sauternes	21	23	25	23	24	24	29	24	26	21	26	24	27	25	27
California:															
Chardonnay	-	-	-	-	22	21	25	26	22	26	29	24	27	25	-
Sauvignon Blanc	-	-	-	-	-	-	-	-	-	26	25	27	25	24	25
Austria:															
Grüner V./Riesl.	22	-	25	22	25	21	22	25	26	25	24	26	25	23	27
Germany:	21	26	21	22	24	20	29	25	26	27	28	25	27	25	25

Reds	95	96	97	98	99	00	01	02	03	04	05	06	07	08	09
France:															
Bordeaux	26	25	23	25	24	29	26	24	26	25	28	24	23	25	27
Burgundy	26	27	25	24	27	22	24	27	25	23	28	25	25	24	26
Rhône	26	22	23	27	26	27	26	-	26	25	27	25	26	23	26
Beaujolais	-	-	-	-	-	-	-	-	-	-	27	24	25	23	27
California:															
Cab./Merlot	27	25	28	23	25	-	27	26	25	24	26	23	26	23	25
Pinot Noir	-	-	-	-	-	-	25	26	25	26	24	23	27	25	24
Zinfandel	-	-	-	-	-	-	25	23	27	22	24	21	21	25	27
Oregon:															
Pinot Noir	-	-	-	-	-	-	-	26	24	26	25	24	23	27	25
Italy:															
Tuscany	25	24	29	24	27	24	27	-	25	27	26	26	25	24	-
Piedmont	21	27	26	25	26	28	27	-	24	27	26	25	26	26	-
Spain:															
Rioja	26	24	25	-	25	24	28	-	23	27	26	24	24	-	26
Ribera del Duero/ Priorat	26	27	25	24	25	24	27	-	24	27	26	24	26	-	-
Australia:															
Shiraz/Cab.	24	26	25	28	24	24	27	27	25	26	27	25	23	-	-
Chile:	-	-	-	-	25	23	26	24	25	24	27	25	24	26	-
Argentina:															
Malbec	-	-	-	-	-	-	-	-	25	26	27	25	24	-